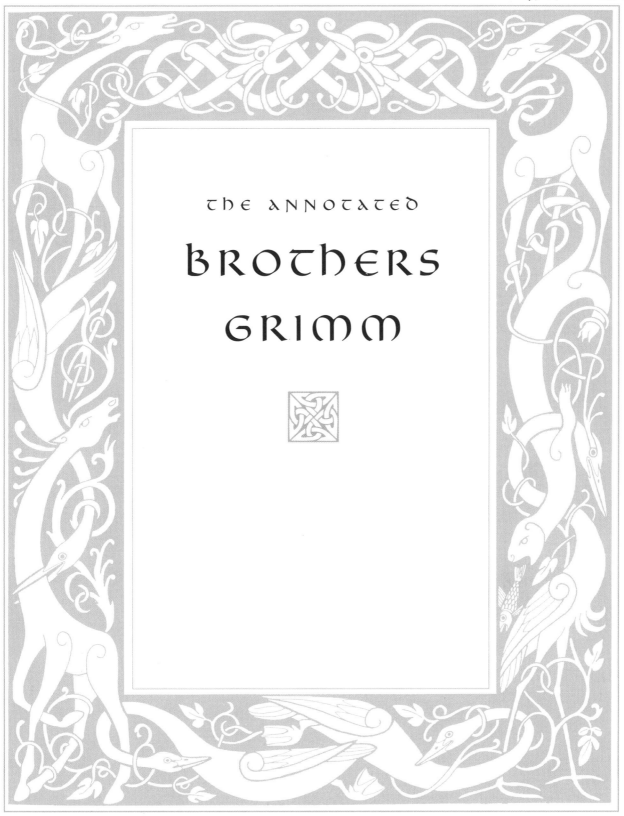

THE ANNOTATED

BROTHERS GRIMM

OTHER ANNOTATED BOOKS FROM W. W. NORTON & COMPANY

The Annotated Alice
by Lewis Carroll, edited with an
introduction and notes by Martin Gardner

The Annotated Wizard of Oz
by L. Frank Baum, edited with an
introduction and notes by Michael Patrick Hearn

The annotated Huckleberry Finn
by Mark Twain, edited with an
introduction and notes by Michael Patrick Hearn

The Annotated Christmas Carol
by Charles Dickens, edited with an
introduction and notes by Michael Patrick Hearn

The New Annotated Sherlock Holmes
Volumes I, II, and III
by Sir Arthur Conan Doyle, edited with an
introduction and notes by Leslie S. Klinger

The Annotated Classic Fairy Tales
Edited with an introduction
and notes by Maria Tatar

The Annotated Hunting of the Snark
by Lewis Carroll, with an introduction by Adam Gopnik,
edited with notes by Martin Gardner

The Annotated Hans Christian Anderson
Translated by Maria Tatar and Julie Allen,
with an introduction and notes by Maria Tatar

The Annotated Uncle Tom's Cabin
by Harriet Beecher Stowe, edited with an introduction
and notes by Henry Louis Gates Jr. and Hollis Robbins

The Annotated Secret Garden
by Francis Hodgson Burnett, edited with an introduction
and notes by Gretchen Holbrook Gerzina

The New Annotated Dracula
by Bram Stoker, edited with a foreword and notes
by Leslie S. Klinger, with an introduction by Neil Gaiman

The Annotated Wind in the Willows
by Kenneth Grahame, edited with a preface and notes
by Annie Gauger, with an introduction by Brian Jacques

The Annotated Peter Pan
by J. M. Barrie, edited with an introduction
and notes by Maria Tatar

ALSO BY MARIA TATAR

Secrets Beyond the Door: The Story of Bluebeard and His Wives

Lustmord: Sexual Murder in Weimar Germany

Off with Their Heads! Fairy Tales and the Culture of Childhood

The Hard Facts of the Grimms' Fairy Tales

Spellbound: Studies on Mesmerism and Literature

Enchanted Hunters: The Power of Stories in Childhood

The Grimm Reader: The Classic Tales of the Brothers Grimm

W. W. NORTON & COMPANY
New York London

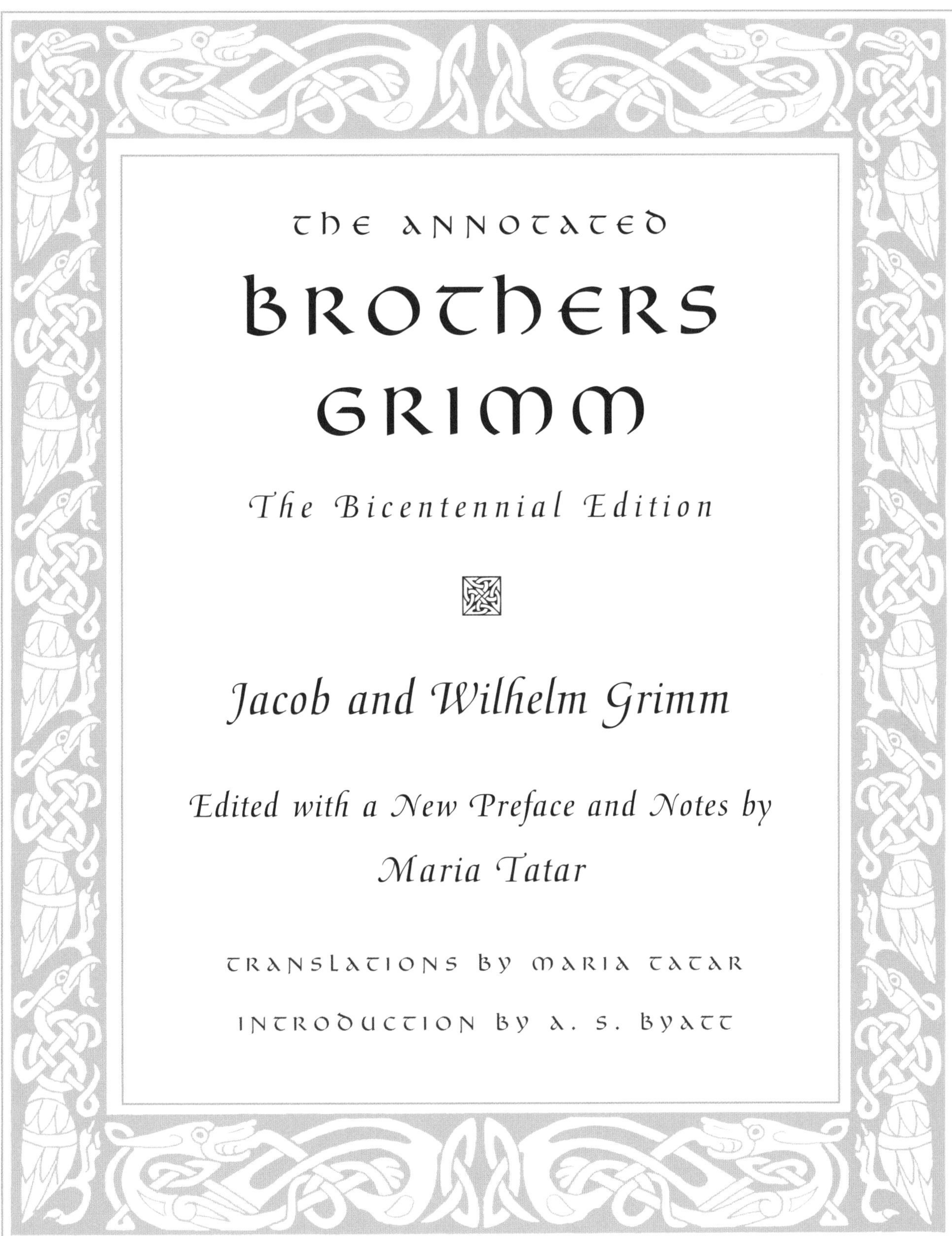

THE ANNOTATED

BROTHERS GRIMM

The Bicentennial Edition

Jacob and Wilhelm Grimm

Edited with a New Preface and Notes by

Maria Tatar

TRANSLATIONS BY MARIA TATAR

INTRODUCTION BY A. S. BYATT

Printed in the United States of America

Illustrations by Arthur Rackham, Gustave Doré, George Cruikshank, Kay Nielson, and Walter Crane courtesy of Department of Printing and Graphic Art, Houghton Library, Harvard College Library, and the Department of Rare Books, Houghton Library, Harvard College Library. Illustrations by Maxfield Parrish reproduced by permission of © Maxfield Parrish Family Trust, licensed by ASAP and VAGA, NYC, courtesy of American Illustrated Gallery, NYC. Illustrations by Wanda Gág reprinted with permission of the artist's estate. Portrait of Jacob and Wilhelm Grimm by Elisabeth Jerichau-Baumann.

Book design by JAM Design
Production managers: Andrew Marasia, Julia Druskin, and Devon Zahn

ISBN 978-1-62090-615-6

W. W. Norton & Company, Inc.
500 Fifth Avenue, New York, N.Y. 10110

W. W. Norton & Company Ltd.
Castle House, 75/76 Wells Street, London W1T 3QT

For my parents,

who introduced me

to the magic of

fairy tales

Acknowledgments

"Once upon a time"—this is the code term that opens the door to what the German philosopher Ernst Bloch called "a more colorful or easier elsewhere." For the last two decades, I have had the pleasure of spending a good deal of time in that elsewhere, first by reading fairy tales to my children, then by poring over them in libraries and at home. To the Harvard College Library I owe an immense debt of gratitude for creating a radiant elsewhere that gave me access to more stories and pictures than I could ever have imagined. But there were also many other sequestered nooks in libraries public and private, which offered the opportunity to browse and indulge in the pleasures of reading and discovery, among them the archive of the Brüder-Grimm Museum, the Cotsen Library at Princeton University, the Simmons College Library, and the Cambridge Public Library.

I have had the good fortune to work at W. W. Norton with Bob Weil, an editor whose sharp instincts, constructive imagination, and intellectual integrity guided this book to its completion. I am grateful to Brendan Curry for his helpful assistance in steering the manuscript through the production process and to Elizabeth C. Pierson for precision and tact in the copyediting process.

Stories bridge generations, and writing this book could never have been possible without the nurturing power of family connections. With heartfelt love, I dedicate this book to my mother and to the memory of my father, to my brothers and sister and their families, and to my children.

CONTENTS

EUGEN NEUREUTHER, *"Sleeping Beauty"*

PREFACE

Magical and Mythical—Two Hundred Years of the Brothers Grimm

Hardly a day goes by without a reminder from Hollywood and other sites of cultural production that fairy tales are here to stay, especially the stories collected two hundred years ago by Jacob and Wilhelm Grimm. "Little Red Riding Hood," "Cinderella," and "Snow White": these are the cultural myths we ritually repeat, reinvent, and remediate, today with undiminished narrative vigor. J. R. R. Tolkien once described "the cauldron of Story" as a constantly bubbling brew, with fresh, new ingredients added in every season to build up the flavors and zest. That cauldron, like Salman Rushdie's sea of stories or Angela Carter's potato soup (with its multiple recipes), is capacious and contains multitudes, both global master-narratives and colorful local variants that reveal just how up close and personal these stories remain.

It is something of an open secret that fairies rarely make an appearance in fairy tales. Those spritely creatures may be rarity in what the Brothers Grimm called *Märchen*, but magic remains in the form of gold and silver cascading down from trees, singing bones that indict murderers, tables that set themselves, cudgels that beat on command, or any number of other wonders, as well as horrors. Many folklorists prefer the term *wonder tale* to fairy tale, since it better captures the distinctive feature of the genre—magic in all its kaleidoscopic variation. Wonder tales are not only suffused with magic but also often structured by transformations—the leap from human to beast, the switch from scarcity to plenty, and the storied move from rags to riches.

For a good part of the last century, Disney Studios kept fairy tales alive and breathing. Many of those films began by nodding to the authority of the story as it was written down. They remained remarkably faithful to stories collected by Charles Perrault in France and the Brothers Grimm in Germany. In each case, a short sequence featuring storybook characters plunges us into the action, and, as pages turn, we are reminded of the written sources for the tale that will unfold. Even with the trademark additions of helpful mice in *Cinderella* or named dwarves in *Snow White*, the Grimm tale still shines through. But for several decades, the fairy-tale franchise came to be known by the name of Disney rather than Grimm, and the films became our portal to "tales as old as time," as Mrs. Potts puts it in *Beauty and the Beast.*

It took iconoclasts to remind us that the tales had a history. Beginning in the 1960s, writers with many different agendas rediscovered fairy tales, and they soon recognized that the stories were not written in granite. They were so elastic, malleable, and resilient that they could be stretched and molded into quirky new shapes without losing their narrative mass. Why not turn the wolf into a victim of porcine greed, the witch into a hospitable loner exploited by predatory children, and Rumpelstiltskin into an honest laborer, cheated of his contractual rights? Poets like Anne Sexton, writers like Roald Dahl, and films like *Shrek* demonstrated that you could radically change the terms and dramatically reconfigure fairy-tale plots, yet the story still shines through. Rewriting resurrected and revived the old story, calling attention to the original source material in the Grimms' *Children's Stories and Household Tales*, as much as it created playful new versions. It is, ironically, the fate of iconoclasts to keep alive the very myths they seek to demolish.

These days fairy tales are passed on to us through what the media gurus call multiple "delivery systems," and the stories have reclaimed their multigenerational appeal. Children can read versions of "Little Red Riding Hood" by the Brothers Grimm, but also by Jon Sczieska; adolescents can watch Catherine Hardwicke's *Red Riding Hood*, featuring Amanda Seyfried, or take in the camp version of her story in *Freeway*, with Reese Witherspoon; and adults can get their dose of that same story from Angela Carter's "Company of Wolves" or Anne Sexton's poem in *Transformations*. And now we have new versions like ABC's *Once Upon a Time* that aim not only to tell the story but also to draw viewers into the glow of a virtual reality constructed around fairy-tale narratives. Just tune in some day to the Magic Mirror on the Web site for the series.

Still, many of the most revered experts have insisted on a strict typological divide between fairy tales, banished to the culture of childhood, and myth, part of the childhood of culture. "Fairy tales are told for entertainment," Joseph Campbell declared in *The Power of Myth*. "You've got to distinguish between the myths that have to do with the serious matter of living life in terms of society and of nature, and stories with some of those same motifs that are told for entertainment." Campbell correctly recognized the shared repertoire of motifs in fairy tales and myth, just as he understood that both genres engaged with the nature/culture divide.

Just how robust is that shared repertoire and the commitment to working out cultural conflicts? If we turn to Greek mythology, we discover that one tale begins with a girl, a basket from mother, a meadow of flowers, and—a god disguised as a bull. Instead of the marauding wolf in fairy tales recorded by Charles Perrault and the Brothers Grimm, we find a bull, less ferocious than tame, playful, and seductive. The ancient tale about Zeus and Europa, which has, of course, been read by generations of *schoolchildren* raised on Bulfinch's *Mythology* and Edith Hamilton's *Mythology*, informs not only "Little Red Riding Hood" but also "Beauty and the Beast," two tales that circulate comfortably in adult popular culture. For the Greeks, as for us today, the story of Europa's abduction challenges us to think hard about the line dividing rape from seduction. Both myth and fairy tale about a girl, a wolf, and an encounter in the woods take up powerful questions about innocence and predatory behavior through the optic of the nature/culture divide.

That it is possible to miniaturize myths and dilute their "seriousness" and sacred energy becomes evident when we read Nathaniel Hawthorne's version of the Zeus/Europa encounter in his *Tanglewood Tales*. In that recasting, the girl (and I use that term advisedly) meets the god, who has disguised himself as a remarkably beautiful bull. Seduced by the scent of ambrosia and the sounds of sweet music, Europa climbs on the bull's back and is carried off to the sea. "Was there ever such a gentle, sweet, pretty, and amiable creature as this bull, and ever such a nice playmate for a little girl?" Hawthorne asks. By the same token, I would argue, fairy tales can be enlarged and made to rise to the "seriousness" that Campbell demands, as Anne Sexton, Angela Carter, Catherine Breillat, and others have vividly demonstrated.

In Anne Sexton's *Transformations*, the story of Hansel and Gretel becomes a rich opportunity for meditations on hunger, appetite, and feasting, as well as on fritters, goose liver, and chocolate chimneys. Sexton's Gretel, inspired by the tale told by the Brothers Grimm, famously becomes a trickster as well as something of a cultural hero. She "sees her moment in history" and "fast as Houdini," she shuts the oven and locks the door. The girl who once wept in the woods when she and her brother lost their way seems an unlikely candidate for a role that has been occupied by such mythical luminaries as the Greek Hermes, the African Anansi, the Native American Coyote and Hare, the African American Brer Rabbit, or the Scandinavian Loki, but in fact she fits right in—despite her gender—with those world-making tricksters by lying, cheating, stealing, and challenging property rights, as well as by speaking poetry and using enchantments to find a way back home.

Gretel serves as role model for a new female trickster in popular culture, a hunger artist who derives her creative intelligence from appetite, one that first emerges in children's literature through Astrid Lindgren's *Pippi Longstocking* and Suzanne Collins's *Hunger Games* and flourishes now in the adult entertainments of Stieg Larsson's Millennium Trilogy and the Hollywood construction of Lisbeth Salander, that skinny hacker in *The Girl with the Dragon Tattoo*.

Fairy tales, as the simple expression of complex thought, have a strange double aspect. As Arthur Frank, the author of *Letting Stories Breathe*, puts it about narratives in general: "First stories simplify complexity for humans . . . but then stories turn around and complicate reality." With a stunning economy of means, they manage to create thunderous effects, taking up matters primal and pertinent—the paradoxes and contradictions on which culture itself is based and with which we wrestle on a daily basis. In "Little Red Riding Hood," we saw that it was innocence and seduction; in "Beauty and the Beast," monstrosity and compassion; in "Hansel and Gretel," hostility and hospitality—or hostipitality as Jacques Derrida called it for philosophers and anthropologists. As cultural taboos and prohibitions are made or undone, our stories are refashioned. They remain relevant even as they preserve a whiff of the archaic.

It was Claude Lévi-Strauss who taught us that myths are made through a logic that resembles the workings of a kaleidoscope, "an instrument which also contains bits and pieces by means of which structural patterns are realized." His understanding of myth was far more capacious than Campbell's, and it was he who famously declared in "The Structural Analysis of Myth," "All versions belong to the myth." The mythmaker, or *bricoleur*, reassembles fragments—those bits and pieces of the old—to form models of intelligibility with new symbolic functions. Lévi-Strauss's kaleidoscope offers a telling metaphor—and one that is perhaps more accurate than the cauldron of story—for understanding the process of storytelling and reminds us of just how artificial the boundary is between myth and fairy tale.

In their preface to the *Children's Stories and Household Tales*, the Brothers Grimm recognized the strong connection between fairy tale and myth, and their missionary zeal was intensified by a deep faith in the transhistorical and transcultural importance of stories as well as their narrative vigor. Fairy tales address primal matters—survival, reproduction, and mortality—in ways that make direct hits. Eliminating inessential complications, they provide transparent models of cultural conflicts—stories that animate, energize, and enable us to talk about what otherwise might feel taboo. These are the stories that provide us with what James Baldwin called "the only light we've got in the darkness." He echoed words of the Brothers Grimm, who told us two hundred years ago that each of these stories "hits us like sunshine no matter where we are standing."

With so many different versions of the Grimms' tales available, why add another volume to make the process of selection even more daunting? This volume takes us back to the authoritative versions of the Grimms' stories, the versions that were published in 1857 for the seventh and final edition of the tales. It offers a selection of the tales, a sample of the 210 tales collected and put in print. Most readers who pick up hefty volumes containing the entire collection quickly lose interest in the tales, for the many anecdotes, legends, chronicles, and narratives feel dated and irrelevant to modern audiences. The tales collected here represent, for the most part, stories that contain magic—magic both as a device in the tale itself and as an effect on the reader. These are the tales that continue to enchant and entrance, the stories that invite us to engage with events that still matter to us today.

But this collection also goes beyond "Little Red Riding Hood," "Rapunzel," and "Snow White." It brings us a cast of characters that includes boys as well as girls, a multitude of heroes who are less dragon slayers and giant killers than sly simpletons and innocent tricksters who manage, against the odds, to win a princess and a kingdom. This collection attempts to redress the gender imbalance in most volumes that offer a sample of the Grimms' tales.

These days, parents searching for bedtime reading will come across such titles as *One-Minute Fairy Tales* or *Time for Bed, Oliver!* In our haste to use stories as devices for getting children to go to sleep, we forget that the tales are meant to provide opportunities for dialogue and discussion. They create a quiet space at the end of the day, one that frees us and our children from the rapid pace of a culture that relentlessly bombards us with new images and sensations. And they allow us, by proxy, to digest the events that have taken place in the course of the day. These are stories meant to slow us down, and the commentary and illustrations should invite readers to ponder different ways of reading what takes place in the tales.

When the Grimms launched their collecting efforts, they had other scholars in mind as their audience. Over the years, they discovered that children were taking possession of the book, and they made the collection more child-friendly. Still, many stories remained that are not appropriate for children's ears. For adults curious about those tales, I have included a section entitled "Tales for Adults" that will provide some sense of the cultural differences between the Grimms' era and our own.

Maria Tatar
Cambridge, Massachusetts
April 2012

INTRODUCTION

A. S. BYATT

This is the book I wanted as a child and didn't have, the book I'd have liked both to give to my children and keep for myself, the book I shall give my grandchildren. It took me some time to see that what I thought of as a "real" fairy tale was almost always one collected by the Grimms. But as a child—and even more as an adult—I had an instinct for the power and the—somewhat dangerous—delight of their collection.

I acquired a hunger for fairy tales in the dark days of blackout and blitz in the Second World War. I read early and voraciously and indiscriminately—Andrew Lang's colored Fairy Books, Hans Andersen, King Arthur, Robin Hood, and my very favorite book, *Asgard and the Gods*, a German scholarly text, with engravings, about Norse mythology, which my mother had used as a crib in her studies of Ancient Norse. I never really liked stories about children doing what children do—quarreling and cooking and camping. I liked magic, the unreal, the more than real. I learned from the Asgard book that even the gods can be defeated by evil. I knew nothing about the Wagnerian Nordic pageantry of the Third Reich. Nor did I have any inkling that the British occupying forces in Germany after the war were going to ban the Grimms because they fed a supposedly bloodthirsty German imagination. Indeed, I retreated into them from wartime anxieties.

I didn't have a book at that stage that was specifically the fairy tales of the Brothers Grimm. But I learned to distinguish between them and the authored tales of Hans Andersen (and de la Mare and Thackeray). My developing idea of the "real" (authentic) fairy tale centered on the Brothers Grimm. It included also some of the Nordic stories collected by Asbjørnsen, some Perrault, and some English tales—"Jack and the Beanstalk," for instance. These tales might be funny or horrible or weird or abrupt, but they were never *disturbing*, they never twisted your spirit with sick terror as Andersen so easily did. They had a discrete, salutary flatness.

It is interesting how impossible it is to remember a time when my head was not full of these unreal people, things, and events. When I ask friends and colleagues what is their first precise memory of a fairy tale, they almost all come up with some shock administered by that psychological terrorist, Andersen—the little mermaid walking on knives, Kai in the icy palace of the Snow Queen. But these shocks happen to people and children who already know and inhabit the other world which gets into our heads and becomes necessary—a world of suns and moons and forests, of princesses and goose girls, old men and women, benign and malign, talking birds and flying horses, magic roses and magic puddings, turnips and pigs, impenetrable castles and petrification, glass mountains and glass coffins, poisonous apples and blinding thorns, ogres and imps, spindles and spun gold, tasks and prohibitions, danger and comfort (for the good people) after it. The tales collected by the Grimms are older, simpler, and deeper than the individual imagination.

It is very odd—when you come to think of it—that human beings in all sorts of societies, ancient and modern, have needed these untrue stories. It is much odder than the need for religious stories (myths) or semihistorical stories (legends) or history, national or personal. Even as a little girl I perceived its oddity. These "flat" stories appear to be there because stories are a pervasive and perpetual human characteristic, like language, like play.

What are fairy stories for? Freud gave an answer—they were related to daydreams and wish-fulfillment fantasies, in which the questing self meets helpers and enemies, and in which the ending is always happy. He wondered if myths were the "secular dreams of youthful humanity" but distinguished myths from fairy tales by claiming that myth is "related to disaster." It can also be argued that myth is related to the human need to know what was before, and what will be after, the individual life, the living society. Myths are concerned with origins, the fear of death, and the hope for the overcoming of death in another world. The universe of Asgard and Valhalla, of Olympus and Hades, is not the fairy-tale unreal world with its visiting suns and moons, castles, and undifferentiated forests. We don't put it together in our imaginations in the same way. There is neither explanation nor teaching in the true wonder tale.

Other things which are not essentially part of true fairy tales are character, psychological causation, or real morality. Princesses are virtually interchangeable—they are either kind and modest and housewifely, or vain and stupid and inconsiderate. They are called "princesses," but peasants and merchants' daughters have the same limited and recognizable natures. Simpletons and gallant princes have the same chance of solving riddles, obtaining magic feathers, or keys, the same insect or fishy helpers. Lazy girls are caught out by boasts that they can spin flax into gold, and are helped by strange brownies or dwarves or other creatures. The best single description I know of the world of the fairy tale is that of Max Lüthi who describes it as an abstract world, full of discrete, interchangeable people, objects, and incidents, all of which are isolated and are nevertheless interconnected, in a kind of web or network of two-dimensional meaning. Everything in the tales appears to happen entirely by chance—and this has the strange effect of making it appear that nothing happens by chance, that everything is fated.

Lüthi even points out that folktales have certain colors—red, white, black, and the metallic colors of gold and silver and steel. The fairy tale world is called up for me by the half-abstract patternings of Paul Klee, or the mosaic definition of Kandinsky's early "Russian" paintings of horses and forests. Lüthi makes the point that green, the color of nature, is almost never specifically mentioned in folktales. It is interesting in that context that the Grimms' preface to volume II of the first edition of the *Children's Stories and Household Tales*, praising their "genuinely Hessian" Low German narrator, Viehmann, and the precision of her oral narrative, remarks that "The epic basis of folk poetry resembles the colour green as one finds it throughout nature in various shades: each satisfies and soothes without becoming too tiresome."

This is an image derived from Romantic nature poetry and is called up in support of the Grimms' claims for the German-ness of the tales. German perception of German folklore is bound up with the Germanic sense of the all-importance of the surrounding *Wald,* the forest. As a child, and now, I respond instinctively more powerfully to this mysterious wood than to the courtly manners and ladylike godmothers of French writers like Madame d'Aulnoy. But I think it can be argued that the Grimms, however they romanticized and fantasized the oral and Germanic purity of their sources, understood, as tellers, the peculiarly flat, unadorned nature of the true tale.

An all-important part of our response to the world of the tales is our instinctive sense that they have *rules.* There are things that can and can't happen, will and won't happen—a prohibition is there to be broken, two of three brothers or sisters are there to fail, the incestuous king will almost always dance at his daughter's wedding to the prince in whose court she has found refuge as a kitchen slave or a goose girl. Lüthi brilliantly compares the glittering mosaic of fairy tales to Hermann Hesse's Glass Bead Game. As a little girl I compared it in my mind to the pleasures of Ludo and Snakes and Ladders and Solitaire played with cards, in which certain moves only are possible and the restrictions are part of the pleasure. As an adult writer I think that my infant synapses grew like a maze of bramble shoots into a grammar of narrative, part of the form of my neuronal web as linguistic grammars are, and mathematical forms. Vladimir Propp's analysis of the structural forms of the folktale is exciting because it makes precise and complex something we had already intuited—that the people and events are both finite and infinitely variable. Another thing Lüthi finely says is that these are forms of *hope.* We fill our heads with improbable happy endings, and are able to live—in daydream—in a world in which they are not only possible but inevitable.

Italo Calvino, in "Cybernetics and Ghosts," makes the inevitable connection between storytelling and myth. He describes the storyteller of the tribe telling about the younger son getting lost in the forest—"he sees a light in the distance, he walks and walks; the fable unwinds from sentence to sentence, and where is it leading?" To a new apprehension which "suddenly appears and tears us to pieces, like the fangs of a man-eating witch. Through the forest of fairy-tale the vibrancy of myth passes like a shudder of wind."

Calvino himself knew a great deal about the workings of the stopped-off, rule-constructed tale, but he also knew that it is haunted by the unmanageable, the vast, and the dangerous. The Grimms too were interested in the borders between Germanic myths and folktales. They liked to draw connections between fairy-tale trees and the World-Ash, between Briar Rose in her thorn-surrounded sleep and Brunnhilde in her wall of fire. They included Christian legends at the edge of their world—the Virgin Mary finds strawberries in the snow of the forest.

The opposite experience, perhaps, from coming across the whiff of real danger, terror, or mystery that is myth, is the precise experience of meeting real individuated characters in a tale, people one begins to imagine in three dimensions. Looking back on my own experience, it seems to me that I inhabited stories with characters in a way I never inhabited the true fairy tales. I fell in love with Sir Lancelot and held long conversations with Robin Hood and his men. I went on new quests with them, rescued them and was rescued. I even ventured into the Asgard tales—I brought water secretly to the disguised Odin suspended between two fires, I fell in love with the ironic Loki. But I never loved or was loved in the context of a fairy tale. Dickens claimed that he wanted to marry Little Red Riding Hood, which to me is a category error. Either he had seen a pretty actress in a red hood in a pantomime, or his hugely animating imagination could even insinuate itself into the closed box of finite gestures. Character feels wrong in folktales.

In this context Lüthi gives a fine example of how the Grimms' narrative style moves from the impersonal oral to the "authored" story with psychology. In Wilhelm Grimm's "Rapunzel," he says, "The prince became overwhelmed with grief and in despair he jumped from the tower." Whereas in oral tellings derived from Grimm, a schoolchild from Danzig said "When the witch saw that it was a prince there, she threw him down," and a Swabian narrator said: "She gouged out his eyes and threw him down"—in both cases replacing psychological suffering by a physical blow.

The point is clear, but it is a long step from there to Andersen telling us the suffering of his mermaid, or Hoffmann frightening us with the Sandman. As Maria Tatar observes, the Grimms' revisions of "The Frog King" simply make the tale more flowing—they may take away the stark flatness of the oral "and then . . . and then . . . ," but they preserve more of the flat quality of the tales than the French courtly ladies, who exclaim and moralize in every paragraph. Most interesting of all in this context is "The Juniper Tree" which is an authored tale by Philipp Otto Runge, a work of art which entirely understands the arbitrary nature of the shape of the tale, and the repetitive form of its events, and yet inserts both psychological terror and pity, and as the Grimms feel able to suggest, is aware that the magic juniper tree is related to the Tree of Life. Narrators are free to vary or extemporize on the elements of the tales, which nevertheless constantly reassert themselves. Anyone who has looked at the 345 variants of the Cinderella stories collected by the redoubtable Marian Roalfe Cox in 1893 will know how the mosaic pieces slip, slide, and recombine.

What use do we make of fairy tales? The Grimms, as we see, thought, among other things, that they were recovering a German mythology and a German attitude to life. They saw themselves as asserting what was German against the French occupying forces of the Napoleonic Empire. The Allied occupying forces in Germany after the Second World War briefly tried to ban the Grimms because it was felt that their bloodthirstiness, gleeful violence, heartlessness, and brutality had helped to form the violent nature of the Third Reich. Some of the tales are unpleasant—very unpleasant—and it is good that Maria Tatar has collected one or two of the more heartless ones here, including one that is certainly anti-Semitic. There are places where a collection of folktales shades off into those other narrative forms, gossip and communal scapegoating anecdotes. But it is important to distinguish between the effects of tales of bludgeoned outsiders or gleefully tormented Jews and the folktale machinery of swallowed and regurgitated children, severed limbs miraculously restored, and even the dreadful punishments of the wicked stepmother or sisters, in barrels of nails or red-hot iron shoes. A modern child—or adult reader—needs both to remember the more brutal world of public hangings and public burnings of earlier times, and to understand that much of this suffering and restoration—not all—is the same as the endless hammering, drowning, flaying, flattening, stretching, snipping, and boiling of Tom by Jerry in the cartoons. There are moods in which—as child and woman—I could not bear to see these cartoons. And moods in which I laugh cheerfully. In a real fairy tale the eyes will usually be restored, the hands grow onto the stumps, the sleeper will awaken.

The most terrifying tale I have ever read in the Grimms is the one-paragraph tale about the obstinate child, in German *das eigensinnige Kind*, which means literally "the child with its own mind." In German a child is neuter in gender. All we are told about this one is that it would not do what its mother wanted, that God had therefore no goodwill toward it, and it died. When it was buried, it kept pushing its arm up through the earth—until its mother came and knocked its arm down with a stick. After that it was for the first time peaceful under the earth. The real terror of that is implicit in its bleak little form and the complete absence of character (we do not know if the child was boy or girl). It doesn't feel like a warning to naughty infants. It feels like a glimpse of the dreadful side of the nature of things.

I am not sure how much good is done by moralizing about fairy tales. This can be unsubtle—telling children that virtue will be rewarded, when in fact it is mostly simply the fact of being the central character that ensures a favorable outcome. Fairy tales are not—on the whole—parables. The king's three sons in "The Three Feathers" have nothing in common with Christ's succinct parable of the talents, where both psychology and morals are precise about what the three servants do with what they are given.

Psychoanalysts have revealed some of the ways in which the tales represent our secret fears and preoccupations—from being devoured to having a mother or stepmother who either starves you or stuffs you with food in order to eat you up. But all too easily psychoanalytic criticism can become overdetermined, constraining, and limiting. Bruno Bettelheim turns the tales into dream-imagery and paradigms of what he sees as essential sexual development. I remember being very excited by the idea that Sleeping Beauty represents the teenage laziness of the latency period, as also by the idea that the pricked finger represents either menstrual bleeding or a symbolic defloration. It is possible for a good modern writer to use those images in those contexts. But it somehow diminishes the compact, satisfactory nature of the tale itself to gloss it in this way. It takes away, not deepens, its mystery. In the same way many modern feminist defenses of the witch against the docile daughter (Snow White, for instance) take apart the form of the tale and leave us with not very much. It is interesting, as Maria Tatar suggests, how little attention has been paid to resourceful heroines, or suffering heroes, in revisionist criticism. We are overinfluenced by Disney—the great witch in *Snow White*, the saccharine heroine-doll. And I at least feel manipulated when modern films too obviously try to make contrary energetic heroines. Keats deprecated poetry that had a design on you. One of the true qualities of the real fairy tale is that it does not.

The forms of the fairy tales have provided a kind of narrative "grammar" for all sorts of other storytelling, both written and told, at least until very recently. Our sense of these forms informs our readings of novels, plays, and stories. The happy endings of fairy tales underpin the comedies of Shakespeare—we have the comfortable sense that tribulations will result in safety and reconciliation. The absence of those things is an intensifying part of the horror of *King Lear*, which could have ended differently. There is a layer of most nineteenth-century novels that is pulling with, or against, the fairy-tale paradigm. *Mansfield Park* is "Cinderella." *Middlemarch* contrasts the diligent and lazy daughters, the white and red of warmth and cold, and pulls against the paradigm with gritty moral realism. Witches and dwarves, ogres and wolves, lurk in Dickens and Hawthorne. Elizabeth Gaskell reunited the fairy-tale characters in a fantasy French chateau, in a tale of her own, and also played realist narrative games with stepmother and daughters in *Wives and Daughters*. Both Günter Grass and Virginia Woolf use the tale of "The Fisherman and His Wife." In Woolf's case, particularly, one of the novelist's purposes is to show that there is more than one way of telling the world, of imagining ambition and danger and safety.

In recent times Angela Carter and Salman Rushdie both claimed that there was more energy in the old tales than in the recent social realism. Carter made a glittering fantasy world of her own in which wolves and woodcutters, beauties and beasts, Bluebeard and his butchered wives, made new-old patterns. When she came to edit *The Virago Book of Fairy Tales* she had become suspicious of the popular culture and the social forms that underlay the old stories. She said that even in Perrault's day there was a sense that popular culture belonged to the past, "even perhaps, that it *ought* to belong to the past, where it posed no threat, and I am saddened to discover that I subscribe to this feeling too; but this time it might just be true."

Terry Pratchett too—a fantasist who both invents otherworlds and observes their limitations from outside them—writes the old stories into his plots in order to criticize their unthinking narrative constrictions. Godmothers and witches and princesses and frogs and woodcutters can and should be free to behave differently. We should beware of what stories can do to the way we put the world together. We live in a world very far from woods, castles, and gibbets. We live in a world of urban myths—alligators in sewers, grandmothers on car roofs, and as Diane Purkiss has suggested, a burgeoning virtual world of gossip and storytelling, real and fantastic, on the Web.

But we continue to love and need the Grimms' tales, and to be curious about where they came from, what they mean. Maria Tatar is the most exciting scholar I have read on this subject. Her Norton Critical Edition of *The Classic Fairy Tales*—variants old and new, authored and traditional, of six great tales—is full of wit, information, and unexpected revelations. Her book *The Hard Facts of the Grimms' Fairy Tales* is a profound and gripping exploration of the darker aspects of the Grimms' tales—sex and violence, eating and being eaten, ogres and monsters, victims and cruel stepmothers, husbands and enchanters. Her attitude to our taste for these things—as children and as adults—is wise and complex. She is a true scholar, who writes beautifully, not a theorist making use of the material for her own ends. Her new translation of the Grimms is clear, full of life, and enticing. This collection contains the essential favorites, from "Rapunzel" and "Hansel and Gretel" to "Snow White" and "Rumpelstiltskin" by way of "Cinderella" and "The Frog King." It also contains slightly less well-known stories which I found even more magical as a child because I hadn't been told them—"Mother Holle," "The Worn-Out Dancing Shoes," "Snow White and Rose Red." And tales many people may not know before they venture into the world of this book—"Godfather Death," "The Golden Key," and the unforgettable "A Fairy Tale about a Boy Who Left Home to Learn about Fear." The annotations and the delicious added quotations from entranced writer-readers will encourage the curiosity of both adults and children, who, like me, belong in a tale of "The Child Who Always Wanted to Know More." (That was why I loved the grown-up Asgard book so much.) Maria Tatar has a rare combination of steady good sense and an infinite taste for the uncanny and the marvelous. This book is a delight for the story-hungry and the curious and intelligent together.

Reading the Grimms'
Children's Stories and Household Tales

ORIGINS AND CULTURAL EFFECTS OF THE COLLECTION

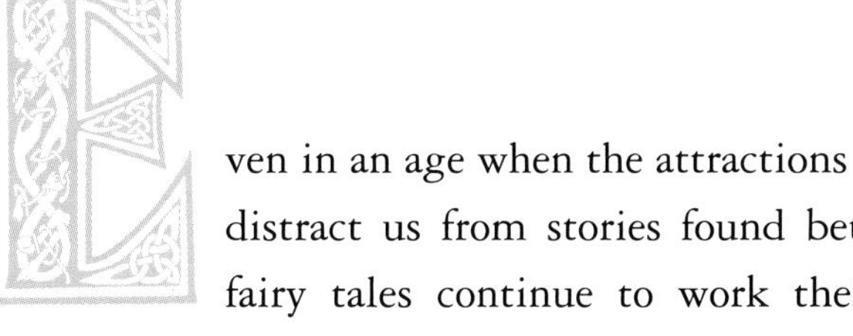

Even in an age when the attractions of high-tech entertainment distract us from stories found between the covers of books, fairy tales continue to work their magic. They ceaselessly migrate from one medium to another, shape-shifting to suit audiences both young and old and morphing into variants that crackle with renewed narrative energy. We may not all be familiar with Luke Skywalker's genealogy or understand how to navigate the complexities of Mortal Kombat, but we all know what happens when Little Red Riding Hood ventures into the woods and when Cinderella leaves for the ball.

Wanda Gág, an American illustrator of the Grimms' fairy tales, once recalled her first encounter with German fairy tales, or *Märchen,* and the nearly palpable sense of pleasure she felt while reading them: "The magic of *Märchen* is among my earliest recollections. The dictionary definitions—tale, fable, legend—are all inadequate when I think of my little German *Märchenbuch* and what it held for me. Often, usually at twilight, some grown-up would say 'Sit down, Wanda-chen, and I'll read you a *Märchen*.' Then, as I settled down in my rocker, ready to abandon myself with the utmost credulity to whatever I might hear, everything was changed, exalted.

A tingling, anything-might-happen feeling flowed over me, and I had the sensation of being about to bite into a juicy big pear."[1]

Gág's observations capture exactly what defines the fairy tale and distinguishes it from other forms ranging from fables and legends to fantasies and epics. It is the presence of magic—not the magic of Wonderland, Narnia, or Oz—but a form of magic that settles down comfortably in the world we inhabit. The fairy tale keeps us firmly rooted in reality: at home, in the village, on the road, or in the woods. We never stray into a world that requires us to navigate a new reality or to learn entirely new rules of behavior. But we do enter a world where good magic always triumphs over bad, where virtue is rewarded and vice is punished, where the small and meek get revenge over the large and powerful, and where children succeed in surviving the assaults of lions, tigers, and bears, oh my! and of ogres, witches, and giants.

J. R. R. Tolkien recognized how powerfully the magic of a happy end resonates with listeners and readers when he described the blissful relief that comes with the words "And they lived happily ever after": "The consolation of fairy-stories, the joy of the happy ending: or more correctly of the good catastrophe, the sudden joyous 'turn' (for there is no true end to any fairy-tale): this joy, which is one of the things which fairy-stories can produce supremely well, is not essentially 'escapist,' nor 'fugitive.' In its fairy-tale—or otherworld—setting, it is a sudden and miraculous grace: never to be counted on to recur." With that ending comes "a catch of the breath, a beat and lifting of the heart, near to (or indeed accompanied by) tears, as keen as that given by any form of literary art, and having a peculiar quality."[2]

Fantasy, escape, recovery, and consolation: these were for Tolkien the defining features of fairy tales, and they tell us something about how the fairy tale promises restitution for loss, injury, grief, damage, harm. For every girl who loses her mother and is persecuted by her stepmother, there will be a king who boils that stepmother in a vat of oil filled with snakes, toads, and lizards. For every boy who is about to become dinner for a cannibalistic witch, there will be a girl who shoves the witch into the oven. For every innocent blockhead who goes out into the world with nothing but beans or

1. Wanda Gág, *Tales from Grimm* (New York: Coward-McCann, 1936), p. vii.

2. J. R. R. Tolkien, "On Fairy-Stories," in *The Tolkien Reader* (New York: Ballantine, 1966), p. 132.

a few coppers, there will be a sack of gold waiting to be claimed. It was the great achievement of the Russian folklorist Vladimir Propp to discover that, among the thirty-one functions of every fairy-tale plot, there is always one that proclaims the presence of a lack and another that promises the liquidation of the lack.

Magic functions as the matrix of action in fairy tales, bringing good fortune to those with whom we sympathize and disaster to their adversaries. Despite our association of fairy tales with innocence, good fortune, and the satisfaction of desires, the conflicts between protagonist and persecutor mean that fairy-tale plots are fraught with merciless aggression, vicious brutality, and deadly hostility. Danger lurks in every corner of the world, and the encounter with it has a fierce inevitability that becomes a rule of the genre. *Villainy*: this was the name Propp gave to the function that fuels the plots of fairy tales.

If the violence that erupts from the friction between heroes and villains is common to fairy tales of every nation, German fairy tales—and the Grimms' collection in particular—have earned a reputation for carnage and cruelty of an excessive kind. In the wake of World War II, one historian found in the Grimms' tales "cruelty, violence, and atrocity, fear of and hatred for the outsider, and virulent anti-Semitism."[3] The Canadian novelist Margaret Atwood writes about her childhood encounters with an "unexpurgated" version of the tales: "Every bloodstained axe, wicked witch, and dead horse was right there where the Brothers Grimm had set them down, ready to be discovered by us."[4] And a landmark essay by historian Robert Darnton concludes that whereas "French tales tend to be realistic, earthy, bawdy, and comical, the German [tales] veer off toward the supernatural, the poetic, the exotic, and the violent."[5]

Yet a look at international versions of "Cinderella" reveals that the Grimms' punishment of the stepsisters at the end of their story—the girls'

3. L. L. Snyder, "Cultural Nationalism: The Grimm Brothers' Fairy Tales," in *Roots of German Nationalism* (Bloomington: Indiana Univ. Press, 1978), p. 51.

4. Margaret Atwood, "Grimms Remembered," in *The Reception of Grimms' Fairy Tales: Responses, Reactions, Revisions*, ed. Donald Haase (Detroit, Mich.: Wayne State Univ. Press, 1993), p. 291.

5. Robert Darnton, "Peasants Tell Tales: The Meaning of Mother Goose," in *The Great Cat Massacre and Other Episodes in French Cultural History* (New York: Basic Books, 1984), p. 50.

eyes are pecked out by doves—is not at all cruel and unusual by comparison with other variants, even if it seems astonishingly ghastly to us. An Indonesian Cinderella forces her stepsister into a cauldron of boiling water, then has the body cut up, pickled, and sent to the girl's mother as "salt meat" for her next meal. A Filipino "Cinderella" ends when the stepmother and her daughter are "pulled to pieces by wild horses." Other versions of the story conclude on a lighter note. A Tuscan "Cinderella" shows the stepsisters making fools of themselves by wearing so much makeup that they appear to be wearing masks. An Italian version reveals the jealous girls to be "furious as dogs" when they hear that Cinderella has married a prince. And then there are the kind and gentle versions, such as an Armenian "Cinderella," which ends with the heroine weeping copious tears and forgiving her sisters, or Charles Perrault's seventeenth-century French tale, in which Cinderella—"as good as she was beautiful"—forgives her sisters and marries them to two gentlemen of high rank.[6]

No matter how strong the bias against the Grimms' collection and no matter how often we worry about the witch being shoved into the oven in "Hansel and Gretel" or the wicked queen dancing to her death in red-hot iron shoes in "Snow White," it remains a fact that our culture has appropriated those stories for our children. Even in 1944, when the Allies were locked in combat with German troops, W. H. Auden decreed the Grimms' collection of tales to be "among the few indispensable, common-property books upon which Western culture can be founded." In collecting folktales from German-speaking regions, Jacob and Wilhelm Grimm had produced a work that Auden believed to rank "next to the Bible in importance."[7] Indeed, the numbers suggest that the Grimms' *Children's Stories and Household Tales* comes in at third, just after the Bible and Shakespeare, in lists of best-selling books. They are the narratives that seem here to stay, that have become part of the international canon of children's literature.

First published in two volumes in 1812 and 1815, the Grimms' collection, along with Charles Perrault's *Tales of Mother Goose* (1697), quickly

6. The international variations of "Cinderella" appear in *The Cinderella Story*, ed. Neil Philip (London: Penguin, 1989).

7. W. H. Auden, "In Praise of the Brothers Grimm," in *The New York Times Book Review*, 12 Nov. 1944, p. 1.

established itself as the authoritative source of tales now disseminated across many cultures. Joseph Jacobs, the British answer to Charles Perrault in France and to Jacob and Wilhelm Grimm in Germany, lamented the fact that—as a latecomer to the project of collecting tales from "the lips of the people," as the Grimms put it—he could not hope to have a powerful effect on shaping the Western canon of fairy tales. "What Perrault began," Jacobs lamented, "the Grimms completed. Tom Tit Tot gave way to Rumpelstiltskin, the three Sillies to Hansel and Gretel, and the English Fairy Tale became a *mélange confus* of Perrault and the Grimms."[8] For all of Jacobs's efforts to collect native lore and to move it into a dominant position in England, "Rumpelstiltskin" and "Hansel and Gretel" had taken root

GEORGE CRUIKSHANK, *German Popular Stories*

8. Joseph Jacobs, "Notes and References for English Fairy Tales," in *English Fairy Tales* (London: David Nutt, 1890), p. 289.

in the culture and tenaciously maintained their hold on British children and adults, along with the French tales. If the Grimms' "Little Red Cap" triumphed over the French version of the tale in which the wolf gobbles up the girl (no hunter comes to her rescue), Perrault's "Cinderella," with its fairy godmother who turns a pumpkin into a coach, conquered the Grimms' "Aschenputtel," with its lurid descriptions of the stepsisters cutting off their toes and heels to make a slipper fit.

Fairy tales had their origins in an adult oral storytelling culture, where tales were told to shorten the time devoted to mending, sewing, spinning, repairing tools—to the myriad repetitive household chores that required physical concentration but left the mind open to wander and daydream. They were the "life-lightening trash of a pre-literate era,"[9] John Updike tells us, and they were stories that made listeners sit up and pay attention with their violent twists and bawdy turns. Little Red Riding Hood was not always an innocent who strays from the path. In French peasant tales, she is a seductive young woman who performs a striptease before the wolf—complete with an inventory of each item of clothing she removes. Snow White's stepmother may ask for the heroine's heart in the Disney version of the tale, but in the Grimms' tale she plans to eat her lungs and liver. And if the "Sleeping Beauty" we know concludes with a kiss from the prince who has made his way through a hedge of thorns, in both Germany and France it has a sequel in which a vicious mother-in-law has an appetite for both her grandchildren and their mother.

When Jacob and Wilhelm Grimm first developed the plan to compile German folktales, they had in mind a scholarly project that would preserve storytelling traditions threatened by industrialization and urbanization. What they wanted was to capture the "pure" voice of the German people and to conserve their oracular *Naturpoesie* before it died away, and they talked freely in the preface to the collection about the sites where the tales were still told: "The places by the stove, the hearth in the kitchen, attic stairs, holidays still celebrated, meadows and forests in their solitude, and above all the untrammeled imagination have functioned as hedges preserv-

9. John Updike, "Fiabe Italiane," in *Hugging the Shore: Essays and Criticism* (New York: Knopf, 1983), p. 662.

ing [folk songs and household tales] and passing them on from one generation to the next."[10]

Fairy tales, as Walter Benjamin once remarked, offer "good counsel." "Where the need was greatest," he added, "its aid was nearest." For him, fairy tales were a response to the oppressive force of myth, offering wisdom about how to manage its numinous powers: "In the figure of the fool it shows us how mankind 'acts dumb' toward the myth; in the figure of the youngest brother it shows us how one's chances increase as the mythical primitive times are left behind; in the figure of the man who sets out to learn what fear is it shows us that the things we are afraid of can be seen through."[11] The Grimms would have agreed, and for them the residue of man-made myth shines through the more natural and protective undergrowth of fairy-tale lore: "The mythic element consists of small pieces from a shattered jewel which lie on ground that is overgrown by grass and flowers, only to be found by the most discerning eye."[12]

The Grimms did not have much to say about their actual sources until 1815, when the second volume of the collection appeared. In that second installment, they praised the storytelling prowess of "a peasant woman from the village of Zwehrn near Kassel" (a city in central Germany) and attributed to her many of the tales. Dorothea Viehmann, as it turns out, was neither a peasant nor a representative of the *Volk*. The wife of a tailor, she was of Huguenot descent and more than likely was as familiar with French *contes de feés* as with German *Märchen*. Still, she remained the star witness for the folkloric authenticity of the collection, and her portrait graced its second edition. Edgar Taylor, the first British translator of the *Children's Stories and Household Tales,* was so enamored by her image that he turned her—under the pseudonym Gammer Gretel—into the source for the entire collection. This "good-humored farmer's wife" (there is no indication that Dorothea Viehmann was the one or the other) knew "all the good stories that were

10. Jacob and Wilhelm Grimm, *Kinder- und Hausmärchen* (Berlin: Realschulbuchhandlung, 1812), p. vi.

11. Walter Benjamin, "The Storyteller: Reflections on the Work of Nicolai Leskov," in *Illuminations*, ed. Hannah Arendt, trans. Harry Zohn (New York: Schocken Books, 1968), p. 102.

12. Wilhelm Grimm, "Literatur," in *Kinder- und Hausmärchen gesammelt durch die Brüder Grimm* (Göttingen: Dieterich'sche Buchhandlung, 1856), vol. 3, p. 409.

told in the country. Every evening, about Christmas time, the boys and girls of the neighborhood gathered round her, to hear her tell some of her budget of strange stories."[13]

Old myths die hard, and the notion that the Grimms' informants were cheerful peasant women—expert raconteurs who told their tales to children to lift their spirits and stimulate their imaginations—has a powerful cultural tenacity. In reality, many of the storytellers from whom the Grimms transcribed tales were from their own social circle: members of the Wild family, the Hassenpflugs, and the Haxthausens. To be sure, there were other sources: Dorothea Viehmann, of course, and Johann Friedrich Krause, a retired soldier who told the Grimms stories in exchange for their old clothes. But the majority of the tales come not from peasants but from ordinary people who happened to be gifted with the power to recall, retell, or reconstruct traditional tales.

And yet, as Robert Darnton tells us, fairy tales existed long before anyone thought about collecting folklore, a term first coined in the nineteenth century by the popular antiquarian (as he called himself) William Thoms: "They belonged to a fund of popular culture, which peasants hoarded over the centuries with remarkably little loss."[14] Most of the tales of Mother Goose, Darnton further argues, were recounted "by peasants who had learned them as children long before literacy had spread throughout the countryside."[15] Each performance might introduce a certain degree of variation in details, but the main elements always remained intact and continued to remain so until they were recorded during the period 1870 to 1914, the so-called Golden Age of folklore in France.

The Grimms' tales may have come from middle-class sources, and they may have been "contaminated" more than they wished to admit by literary sources, non-native traditions, and idiosyncratic interventions on the part of their tellers, but they still reached back to an oral storytelling tradition that is fundamentally different from literary culture, that gives us what the

13. *German Fairy Tales and Popular Stories as Told by Gammer Gretel,* trans. Edgar Taylor (London: Joseph Cundall, 1846), p. xi.

14. Darnton, "Peasants Tell Tales," p. 17.

15. Darnton, "Peasants Tell Tales," p. 16.

Russian-American linguist Roman Jakobson has called "a socialized section of mental culture." Language and folklore, Jakobson asserts, are subject to "much stricter and more uniform laws than fields in which individual creation prevails."[16] Folklore operates as a system oriented toward conventions sanctioned by a cultural community. A folktale, unlike a literary text, must win the consensus of a collective body before it becomes part of a standard repertory of tales.

Who, then, told the stories in the centuries before the Grimms recorded the tales? Who created the cultural legacy that we still draw on today to frame our ideas about courtship, romance, and marriage, to reflect on our fantasies about wealth, power, and social mobility, or to work through our anxieties about loss, peril, and death? Was it Darnton's French peasants, the Grimms' middle-class informants, or Jakobson's collective cultural community? If we consult the authorities, we find dramatically different views on the subject.

The German philosopher Walter Benjamin, who was on familiar terms with the Grimms' collection, answers the question about the origins of tales with a global response. He tells us that the tales derive from "experience which is passed on from mouth to mouth."[17] To be more specific, he refers to two distinct groups: "the resident tiller of the soil" and the "trading seaman," men who create two "tribes," or storytelling regimes, the one rooted in local traditions, the other importing the exotic, fabulous, and alien. Peasants and seamen, like master craftsmen and traveling journeymen, combined the "lore of the past" with the "lore of faraway places" to produce robust hybrid forms that kept the culture of oral storytelling alive. What Benjamin does is call into question the matter of national purity, showing that native traditions are always enriched and deepened when they come into contact with other storytelling traditions. He reveals that the notion of a purely German tradition or purely French tradition is bogus—every culture relies on both native and non-native lore to construct the stories it tells. If the stories that we find in Homer and Herodotus, in the South Seas and in the Deep

16. Jakobson's analysis of the contrast between folklore and literature appeared in an essay coauthored with Petr Bogatyrev, "Die Folklore als eine besondere Form des Schaffens," in Jakobson's *Selected Writings* (The Hague: Mouton, 1966), vol. 5, pp. 1–15.

17. Benjamin, "The Storyteller," p. 84.

South, and in taverns and nurseries have much in common, it is not so much because they sprang up spontaneously in different locations but because they were constructed through a process of constant cross-fertilization.

Benjamin's tillers of the soil and trading seamen, his craftsmen and journeyman, make good candidates for folk raconteurs, but his proposal fails to take into account that oral storytelling is often affiliated with labor traditionally carried out by women: spinning, sewing, weaving, and cooking. That many of our metaphors for storytelling—spinning yarns, weaving tales, cooking up a plot, creating a text—derive from the domestic arts suggests that fairy tales were indeed related to "old wives' tales," stories told by midwives, nursemaids, female domestics, and others to transmit wisdom from one generation to the next. "Gossip and narrative are sisters," the British writer Marina Warner suggests, "both ways of keeping the mind alive when ordinary tasks call; the fictions of gossip—as well as the facts—act as compass roses, pointing to many possibilities."[18]

The folklore scholar Ruth B. Bottigheimer has recently suggested that a single individual, the Venetian "fairy godfather" Zoan Francesco Straparola, "invented" the modern fairy tale and "played a central role in the creation and transmission of many of these familiar tales."[19] Disputing the view that "peasants told tales," she asserts that "writers invented tales" and suggests that the Grimms' tales, like Perrault's, are rooted in literary traditions rather than in an oral storytelling culture. Bottigheimer is surely right to emphasize the importance of literary transmission, but it is impossible to deny the way in which the stories are rooted in a robust oral tradition, one that lives on today and that has created a form of communal property, one that seems to be in a state of perpetual construction.

Fairy tales can operate like powerful magnets, picking up bits and pieces of local culture and lore, drawing a turn of phrase from a song or another story, and fleshing out characters with features taken from the audience witnessing their performance. As Italo Calvino has noted in his writings on Italian folklore, the tale is beautiful only when something is added to it.

18. Marina Warner, *From the Beast to the Blonde: On Fairy Tales and Their Tellers* (New York: Farrar, Straus and Giroux, 1994), p. 49.

19. Ruth B. Bottigheimer, *Fairy Godfather: Straparola, Venice, and the Fairy Tale Tradition* (Philadelphia: Univ. of Pennsylvania Press, 2002).

GEORGE CRUIKSHANK, *German Popular Stories*

And so each fairy tale presents us with a multivoiced discourse, blending the high with the low, combining the coarse humor of peasants with the *bon mots* of aristocrats, the racy style of a raconteur with the poetic turn of phrase from an author, the adventuring spirit of the seaman with the focused domestic concentration of the spinner.

The polyphonic quality of every fairy tale adds a powerful dimension of complexity to tales that are often seen as simple stories, so transparent and accessible that they have become the matter of our childhood primers. Yet the Grimms' stories do not escape the interpretive challenges posed by narratives that blend multiple voices and discourses. To what degree, for example, do their tales reflect the local and the particular? To what extent do they have a global reach? Does the German girl who loses her slipper on the steps of a castle have anything in common with the small-footed Chinese girl who attends a festival in a cloak of kingfisher feathers? Is the disobedient German girl wearing a red cap as she wanders through the woods a close cousin of the Italian trickster on her way to her grandmother's house?

The Grimms themselves firmly believed that the stories in their collection, even if they shared features with other cultures, were distinctly German and both mirrored and shaped national identity. This narrow definition of fairy tales as narratives that captured the mentality of pagan ancestors, and that now offered a mirror of national character, was misguided in its failure to acknowledge the degree to which the tales weave together different cultural discourses, some that can be attached to a specific region, others not. A primer of 1899 celebrating the Grimms' tales as "mother's milk" for German children finds in "Snow White," "Briar Rose," and "Little Red Riding Hood" part of a "genuine German diet" for nourishing the "language and spirit" of children.[20] Enshrined as the authentic source of German folklore, the Grimms' collection was integrated into the educational curriculum of most German-speaking regions in the early twentieth century and came to figure as a monument to the virtues, values, ideals, and imaginative reach of the nation.

Although it is true that the Grimms had sought to consolidate national identity by identifying a common cultural heritage and wanted to mobilize the tales as part of an effort to mount intellectual resistance to the French occupation of their homeland, theirs was less a bid for chauvinistic grandeur than an appeal for national unity in the face of foreign domination. Furthermore, the brothers saw their own collection as a model, one that would inspire similar efforts to capture the lost poetry of other cultures. Both were committed to a folkloristic project carried out in the spirit of international collaboration and cooperation. Far from considering Germanic cultures superior to others, the Grimms, like the eighteenth-century philosopher Johann Gottfried Herder before them, endorsed a cosmopolitan outlook in which every culture was seen to merit scholarly engagement. Wilhelm Grimm's translations of Scottish ballads and of Irish folklore and Jacob Grimm's interest in Slavic folklore can be seen as part of a global folkloric enterprise launched by Herder and sustained by the brothers well into the nineteenth century.

20. Carl Franke, *Die Brüder Grimm: Ihr Leben und Wirken, in gemeinfasslicher Weise dargestellt* (Dresden: C. Reissner, 1899), p. 50.

Not surprisingly, the Third Reich intensified the cult of a pure German folklore, endorsing the Grimms' collection as a *Hausbuch*, or domestic manual, for instilling in children a sense of racial pride. For many Nazi commentators, the protagonists of the tales offered models of "folkish virtues," for these characters followed their racial instincts and demonstrated courage in the struggle to find a racially pure marriage partner. The *Arbeitsgemeinschaft für deutsche Volkskunde* (Central Committee for German Folklore) emphasized the importance of the Grimms' collection in building a sense of cultural kinship and forging a strong national identity. After World War II, the Allied occupation forces issued strong warnings about the sinister aspects of the stories in the collection—to little effect, for the collection never lost any of its popular appeal and was quickly reinstated (along with Heinrich Hoffmann's massively sadistic picture book *Struwwelpeter,* or *Shock-Headed Peter*) as obligatory bedtime reading.

Scholarly ambitions and patriotic zeal may have guided the Grimms in the early stages of collecting, but once their tales were in print they began to modify their vision for the collection. As reviewers weighed in, the brothers began to realize that what they had produced had a limited popular appeal in market terms. One early critic lamented the vast amounts of "pathetic" and "tasteless" material in the collection and urged parents to keep the volume out of the hands of children. Two literary worthies were disheartened by the raw tone of the folktales and recommended a bit of artifice to make the folktales more appealing and "natural." In other words, both matter and manner stood in the way of the book's popular success and its potential use as an *Erziehungsbuch*, or manual of manners, for German children. The Grimms began to realize that the collection's function as a cultural archive could be subordinated to its didactic role.[21]

Reviewers and friends repeatedly singled out "The Juniper Tree" and "The Fisherman and His Wife" as examples of a quintessential *Märchenstil*, or fairy-tale style, that captured the vitality of a poetry of the people even as it conformed to highbrow aesthetic standards. Those two tales, narrated in Low German dialect, became the gold standard by which other tales in the

21. On the rewriting of the tales, see John Ellis, *One Fairy Story Too Many: The Brothers Grimm and Their Tales* (Chicago: Univ. of Chicago Press, 1982), and Maria Tatar, *The Hard Facts of the Grimms' Fairy Tales*, rev. ed. (Princeton, N.J.: Princeton Univ. Press, 2003).

collection came to be measured. In successive editions of the *Children's Stories and Household Tales*, Wilhelm Grimm fleshed out the texts to the point where they were often double their original lengths. He polished the prose so carefully that no one could complain of its rough-hewn qualities. More importantly, the Grimms suddenly changed their view about the implied audience for the tales. What had originally been designed as documents for scholars gradually turned into bedtime reading for children. As early as 1815, Jacob wrote to his brother that the two of them would have to "confer extensively about the new edition of the first part of the children's tales,"[22] and he expressed high hopes for strong sales of the second, revised edition.

By 1819, the date of the second edition, the collection had received more than a face-lift. Eighteen tales had been so heavily revised, redacted, and rescripted that they were almost unrecognizable, and forty-five new tales were added. The expanded annotations were relegated to a separate volume, published three years later. Real popular success still eluded the Grimms, but it came at last, if in modest terms, with the Compact Edition of the *Children's Stories and Household Tales*, published in 1825.

Revisions to the opening paragraph of "The Frog King, or Iron Heinrich" provide a sense of what Wilhelm Grimm wrought with his stylistic interventions. The first edition of 1812 reads as follows:

> Once upon a time there lived a princess. One day she went into the forest and sat down by a cool well. A golden ball was her favorite toy. She loved to amuse herself by throwing it up into the air and catching it when it came back down.

In 1819, the first sentences read as follows:

> Once upon a time there lived a princess who was so bored that she didn't know what to do. She took a golden ball that she liked to play with and went out into the forest. In the middle of the woods there was a well with clear, cool water. She sat down next to it and threw the ball in the air, then caught it, and that's how she amused herself.

22. *Briefwechsel zwischen Jacob und Wilhem Grimm aus der Jugendzeit,* ed. Herman Grimm and Gustav Hinrichs, 2d ed., ed. Wilhelm Schoof (Weimar: Hermann Böhlaus Nachfolger, 1963), p. 438.

By 1857, the opening to the tale had lost its choppy quality and took a lyrical turn so that it produced, when read out loud, the effect of a narrative that flows naturally in a way that the unedited version did not.

> Once upon a time, when wishes still came true, there lived a king who had beautiful daughters. The youngest was so lovely that even the sun, which had seen so many things, was filled with wonder when it shone upon her face.
>
> There was a deep, dark forest near the king's castle, and in that forest, beneath an old linden tree, was a spring. Whenever the weather turned really hot, the king's daughter would go out into the woods and sit down at the edge of the cool spring. And if she was bored, she would take out her golden ball, throw it up in the air, and catch it. That was her favorite plaything.

In a book entitled *One Fairy Story Too Many*, the critic John Ellis has argued that the Grimms tampered with their sources in irresponsible ways: "The brothers never stopped recasting, rewriting, and rephrasing the tales over and over again; and this ever-present readiness on their part to tinker with the language of the tales is impossible to square with their professed reverence for the authentic folk quality of their material."[23] Ellis offers many examples of how the Grimms expanded, abbreviated, and reworded passages, yet he fails to note the challenges faced by the brothers in putting together the stories. A look at the original manuscript version of a tale called "Fledgling" reveals that fidelity to an oral source can result in a clumsy, wooden narrative. The passage below shows how an attempt to capture an oral account word for word comes at the expense of readability:

> Early the next morning the forester goes hunting at two o'clock, once he is gone Lehnchen says to Karl if you don't leave me all alone I won't leave you and Karl says never, then Lehnchen says I just want to tell you that our cook carried a lot of water into the house yesterday so I asked her why she was bringing so much water into the house and she told me if I wouldn't tell

23. Ellis, *One Fairy Story Too Many*, p. 92.

> anyone else, then she would tell me and so I told her I wouldn't tell a soul, and she told me after my father had gone hunting early the next morning she planned to boil a cauldron of hot water and throw you into it and cook you.

Had the Grimms produced 210 tales that read like the paragraph from "Fledgling," it is unlikely that their collecting efforts would have led to a landmark anthology of fairy tales.

The Grimms did not, however, limit their revisions to matters of style. Many critics had responded with shock to the content of some of the tales. "What proper mother or nanny could tell the fairy tale about Rapunzel to an innocent girl without blushing?" Friedrich Rühs, a contemporary of the brothers, gasped after reading the version of "Rapunzel" in the *Children's Stories and Household Tales*. Readers of modern variants of the story will not be aware that an early form of the tale, printed in the first edition of the collection, reveals that Rapunzel's daily romps up in the tower with the prince have weighty consequences.

> At first Rapunzel was frightened, but soon she came to like the young king so much that she agreed to let him visit every day and to pull him up. The two lived joyfully for a time, and the fairy did not catch on at all until Rapunzel told her one day: "Tell me, Godmother, why my clothes are so tight and why they don't fit me any longer."
>
> "Wicked child!" cried the fairy.

In the second edition of the collection, Wilhelm Grimm modified the tale to eliminate Rapunzel's naïve question about her weight gain and replaced it with another naïve question that represents a slip of the tongue rather than a moral lapse: "Tell me, Godmother," Rapunzel asks, "why is it that you are much harder to pull up than the young prince." To which the enchantress again replies: "Wicked child!"

In a letter to a friend, Jacob Grimm noted that the *Children's Stories and Household Tales* had never been "written for children" but that he was pleased to discover that the book appealed to them and to their parents. Wilhelm Grimm made sure that parents would not react as some of the critics had (with their disparaging remarks about gratuitous vulgarity) by deleting "every phrase unsuitable for children." In practice, this meant removing virtually every reference to premarital sex or pregnancy and anything that was slightly off-color. "Hans Dumm," for example, a story about a young man who has the power (and uses it) to impregnate women simply by wishing them to be with child, was eliminated from the first edition of the tales. "The Master Hunter," which recounts the fortunes of a young man who enters a tower, discovers a sleeping princess in a state of undress, and impregnates her, was soon modified so that the princess remained clothed and the young man became a model of decorum.

The rewriting of "The Frog King, or Iron Heinrich" reveals just how easy it was for Wilhelm Grimm to disguise the folkloric facts of a tale. In the manuscript version of the story, the princess dashes the frog against the wall, and he "falls down into her bed and lies there as a handsome young prince, and the king's daughter lies down next to him." No printed version of the *Children's Stories and Household Tales* contains that wording. In the first edition, the frog still falls on the princess's bed, and he becomes her "dear companion." "She cherished him as she had promised," we are told, and *immediately* thereafter the two fall "peacefully asleep." For the second edition, Wilhelm deprived the frog of his soft landing spot and simply observed that the transformation from frog to prince took place as soon as the frog hit the wall. In this version, the happy couple does not retire for the evening until vows have been exchanged, and those vows are exchanged only after the princess's father gives his approval. The king himself becomes a more prominent figure who advises his daughter on the importance of keeping promises. The Grimms' transformation of a tale replete with risqué humor into a morality tale is almost as striking as the metamorphosis of frog into prince.

It comes as no great surprise that the Grimms, recognizing that their collection was turning into reading for children, eliminated bawdy humor in the tales they had recorded. What is less predictable is that the brothers had no reservations whatsoever about preserving, and in some cases intensifying, the violence in the tales. Cinderella's stepsisters are spared their vision in the first recorded version of the story, but for the second edition of the fairy tales, doves peck out their eyes and a moral gloss is added to the story: "So both sisters were punished with blindness to the end of their days for being so wicked and false." Rumpelstiltskin beats a hasty retreat on a flying spoon at the end of some versions of his story, but the Grimms chose to show how he is so beside himself with rage that he tears himself in two. In successive editions of the fairy tales, the grisly particulars about the fate of Briar Rose's unsuccessful suitors become more vivid. When they fail to scale the hedge surrounding the castle, "the briar bushes clung together as though they had hands so that the young princes were caught in them and died a pitiful death."

A striking example of how the Grimms were not at all reluctant to expand descriptions of violence becomes evident from the changes they made in an episode from "The Magic Table, the Gold Donkey, and the Club in the Sack." The innkeeper is shown to get his deserved punishment for trying to steal the hero's magical cudgel:

> The turner placed the sack under his pillow. When the innkeeper came and pulled at it, he said: "Cudgel, come out of the sack!" The cudgel jumped out of the sack and attacked the innkeeper, danced with him, and beat him so mercilessly that he was glad to promise to return the magic table and the gold donkey.

The second edition turns the violence into a "dance," slowing it down and aestheticizing it to produce a carnivalesque moment of ritual violence:

> At bedtime the turner stretched out on the bench and used his sack as a pillow for his head. When the innkeeper was sure that his guest was fast asleep and that no one else was in the room, he went over and began to tug and pull very carefully at the sack, hoping to get it away and to put another in its place. But the turner had been waiting for him to do just that. The innkeeper was about to give a good hard tug, when the turner cried out: "Club, get out of that sack!" In a flash the little club jumped out, went at the innkeeper, and gave him a sound thrashing. The innkeeper began screaming pitifully, but the louder he screamed, the harder the club beat time on his back, until at last he fell down on the ground. Then the turner said: "Now hand over the magic table and the gold donkey, or the dance will start all over again." "Oh, no!" said the innkeeper. "I'll be glad

> to give you everything, if only you'll make that little devil crawl back into his sack." The journeyman answered: "This time I will, but watch out or there'll be more where that came from." Then he said: "Club, get back in the sack" and left him in peace.

The spectacle of punishment, in all its grotesque twists and violent turns, did not make the Grimms at all uncomfortable. In fact, it seemed to provide value-added for a volume designed to help parents teach children how to distinguish between virtue and vice. It is no secret that many children find cathartic pleasures in displays of physical violence, and for some of them too the volume gained in appeal when villains were subjected to burlesque violence. In the years following the publication of the first edition of the tales, Wilhelm Grimm charted a new course for the collection. Openly admitting that he was taking pains to eliminate "any phrase unsuitable for children," he was also no longer invested in the notion of literal fidelity to oral sources and aimed to turn the raw narrative energy of folktales into a tamer cooked version, one both safer for children and more attractive for the adults reading to them.

The Grimms' tales have had a powerful effect beyond the borders of German-speaking countries. Few cultural documents have played so key a role in constructing a national image. If the first association of many people in this country to the word "Germany" is to Hitler and the Holocaust, the second is more than likely to the Grimms' *Children's Stories and Household Tales*. This odd juxtaposition has resulted in a strange conflation of horror and fantasy, linking Germany with what the historian Saul Friedländer has described as a cult of death and kitsch in the popular imagination. The Grimms' *Children's Stories and Household Tales* has been denounced precisely for its narrative tolerance of these two extremes: "Typical of the German fairy tale is the juxtaposition of the commonplace and the intimate with the horrors of death and all the tortures of a calculated cruelty."[24]

As early as 1971, in the work of the American poet Anne Sexton, we find

24. Saul Friedländer, *Reflections of Nazism: An Essay on Kitsch and Death*, trans. Thomas Weyr (Bloomington: Indiana Univ. Press, 1993); the quotation is from V. Brun, "The German Fairy Tale," *Menorah Journal* 27 (1939): 153–54.

a rewriting of "Hansel and Gretel" that alludes to a "final solution" and turns the oven of the finale into a distinct reference to the concentration-camp crematoria.[25] Sexton, who was inspired by her daughter to rewrite the Grimms' tales, produced poetic versions intended for adults. The Italian author Roberto Innocenti cemented the link between fairy tales and the Holocaust by conflating one of the Grimms' fairy tales for children with a fictional account of a child's experience of the Holocaust in his *Rose Blanche*.[26] The title vignette of Innocenti's picture book alerts us to the presence of the subtext used to construct the story of the heroic Rose Blanche. Beneath the title, the reader sees the picture of a long, muddy road, at the end of which appears the heroine, running into the woods with a bag of provisions, a red ribbon adorning her head. The allusion to Little Red Riding Hood, on the road to Grandmother's house with her basket of bread and wine and her red adornment, is unmistakable.

From Jane Yolen's novel *Briar Rose* to Roberto Benigni's film *La Vita é bella*, we find the same haunting combination of fairy-tale text and Holocaust memoir to chart the harrowing journey of Holocaust victims and survivors.[27] What these narratives tell us has something to do with how the fairy tale is powerfully associated with the cultural notion of Germany. But they also remind us of how the stories capture human drama and emotion in their most extreme forms and conditions and thus provide the appropriate narrative vehicle for capturing historical events that defy intellectual comprehension.

Today fairy tales thrive in two very different cultural regimes. On the one hand, we have the literary tradition, a powerful folklore that has, for the most part, migrated into the nursery in the form of monumental national collections from earlier centuries, the many stories reissued, adapted, and retold, and the subtle appropriations of fairy-tale plots. There is another archive as well, one that is not written in granite or even on the pages of books, but that exists as a kind of collective cultural unconscious. Many

25. Anne Sexton, *Transformations* (Boston: Houghton Mifflin, 1971).

26. Roberto Innocenti and Christophe Gallaz, *Rose Blanche* (Mankato, Minn.: Creative Education, 1985).

27. Jane Yolen, *Briar Rose* (New York: Tor Books, 1992); Roberto Benigni, *La Vita é bella*, Buena Vista, 1997

of these are versions of the fairy tales in books but in a more elastic form, supple enough to be invoked as we try to understand daily experience and to work through events. With the help of those stories, we navigate daily experience, making sense of it, interpreting it, and digesting it. Just as proverbs offer help on how to size up a situation—telling us how to cope with perils and how to stand up to adversity—fairy tales can provide readers and listeners with counsel about how to manage anxieties that run particularly deep. How many times do we invoke "Cinderella" when it comes to thinking about courtship, marriage, and romance? How often do we think of "Little Red Riding Hood" when a vulnerable young innocent is pitted against a predator? And how frequently do we frame marriages as variations on "Beauty and the Beast"? That writers, filmmakers, and artists constantly recycle these stories reveals the degree to which they are perpetually in the back of our collective minds.

Like the Grimms, Italo Calvino is a firm believer in the deep connection between fairy tales and myths: "Through the forest of fairy-tale the vibrancy of myth passes like a shudder of wind."[28] The tales, up close and personal, create a sense of intimacy in the midst of mystery. For all their domestic familiarity and refusal to move beyond surfaces, fairy tales have a depth that keeps us talking about the characters in them without ever feeling that we have exhausted their richness. The tales not only reflect psychic realities and lived experience, they have also shaped lives through their construction of cultural anxieties and desires. "Where else could I have gotten the idea, so early in life," Margaret Atwood writes of the Grimms' collection, "that words can change you."[29] In Virginia Woolf's *To the Lighthouse*, Mrs. Ramsay reads the Grimms' "The Fisherman and His Wife" to her son, "reading and thinking, quite easily, both at the same time." For her, the fairy tale is "like the bass gently accompanying a tune, which now and then ran up unexpectedly into the melody." Her metaphor tells us, in trenchant terms, how fairy tales provide a subtle form of accompaniment to our lives, resonating gently with our thoughts and engaging us in dialogues about what matters in our lives.

28. Italo Calvino, "Cybernetics and Ghosts," in *The Literature Machine: Essays,* trans. Patrick Creagh (New York: Vintage, 2002), p. 18.

29. Atwood, "Grimms Remembered," p. 292.

PART I

THE TALES

The Frog King, or Iron Heinrich[1]

The Grimms led with this story because they considered it to be among the oldest in the collection. Yet it is an odd choice, especially since the hero of the title is disenchanted not by a kiss but by an act of violence. "The Frog King" endorses defiance and passion—rather than compassion as in "Beauty and the Beast"—as the means of release from the spell cast by an evil witch. Set in a time when "wishes still came true," it also upholds the value of action.

The story of an erotically ambitious frog offered many opportunities for bawdy humor, and the Grimms, once they became aware of the didactic possibilities of their collection, made certain that the princess and the disenchanted prince do not retire for the night together, as they had in the earliest recorded version of the tale, but that they go straight to the king to request permission to marry. In addition, the Grimms turned the tale into a miniature behavioral lesson by adding dialogue between father and daughter about the importance of honoring promises. This first tale in the collection offers a perfect illustration of how the Grimms toned down and removed the sexual humor that had once entertained adults and added maxims with the hope of teaching children lessons.

1. *Iron Heinrich.* The Grimms saw in Heinrich, both in his name and in his character, a quintessentially Germanic figure, combining fidelity with strength. That he receives equal billing in the tale's title reflects the degree to which they hoped to emphasize national virtues. Heinrich's loyalty stands in sharp contrast to the princess's betrayal of trust.

Competing versions of this story were recorded in the Grimms' annotations. One variant describes a bargain that has to do with the frog's ability to transform the murky waters of a spring into clear water. Two haughty sisters spurn the frog's offer, and the third, and youngest of the trio, accepts the offer of clear water in exchange for love and affection. When the frog arrives at the princess's doorstep, she reminds herself of her promise and lets him in. The creature sleeps under the princess's pillow, and this symbolic vow of devotion releases him from the spell. Another version adds a sequel to the story that charts the fortunes of the prince, who marries a false bride and is liberated from her when the true princess, disguised as a man, rides behind the coach of her beloved. Loud cracking noises catch the attention of the prince, who discovers his true bride when she tells him that the sounds are made when the bands around her heart begin to break.

The Scottish "Well of the World's End" was noted by the Grimms as a close folkloric cousin of "The Frog King." They quoted its refrain, which bears a resemblance to the verse in their tale:

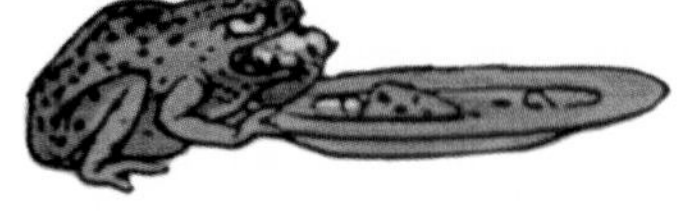

"Open the door, my hinny, my hart.
Open the door, mine ain wee thing;
And mind the words that you and I spak
Down in the meadow at the well-spring."

Once upon a time, when wishes still came true, there lived a king who had beautiful daughters. The youngest was so lovely that even the sun, which had seen so many things, was filled with wonder when it shone upon her face.

There was a deep, dark forest near the king's castle, and in that forest, beneath an old linden tree, was a spring. Whenever the weather turned really hot, the king's daughter would

Walter Crane, *The Frog Prince*

Deep in despair, the princess sits by the edge of a fountain while the frog comes crawling out of the water, ready to make her an offer. Crane's princess seems a bit mature for ball-tossing, but the trinkets and toys hanging from the chains at her waist suggest that she is still a child. Note how the flowers in the foreground repeat the floral patterns on the princess's dress, drawing nature to culture in a way that anticipates the union between frog and princess.

go out into the woods and sit down at the edge of the cool spring. And if she was bored, she would take out her golden ball, throw it up in the air, and catch it. That was her favorite plaything.[2]

One day it so happened that the golden ball didn't end up in the princess's hands when she reached up to catch it, but fell down on the ground and rolled right into the water. The princess followed the ball with her eyes, but it disappeared, and the spring was so deep that you couldn't even begin to see the bottom. The princess burst out crying, and she wept louder and louder, unable to stop herself. Suddenly a voice could be heard over her wailing: "What's going on, princess? Stones would be moved to tears if they could hear you."[3]

The princess turned around to try to figure out where the voice was coming from and caught sight of a frog,[4] which had stuck its big old ugly head out of the water.

"Oh, it's you, you old splish-splasher," she said. "I'm crying because my golden ball has fallen into the spring."

"Be quiet, and just stop that sniveling," said the frog. "I think I can help you, but what will you give me if I fetch your little plaything?"

"Whatever you want, dear frog," she said. "My dresses, my pearls and my jewels, even the golden crown I'm wearing."[5]

The frog said: "I haven't the least interest in your dresses, your pearls and jewels, or your golden crown. But if you promise to love me and let me be your companion and playmate, let me sit beside you at the table and eat from your little golden plate, let me drink from your little cup, and let me sleep in your little bed, if you promise me all that, I will dive right down into the spring and bring back your golden ball."

"Oh, thank you," she said. "I'll give you anything you want as long as you get that ball back for me." But all the while she was thinking: "What nonsense that stupid frog is talking! He's down there in the water croaking away with all the other frogs. How could anyone want to have him as a companion?"

2. *her favorite plaything.* Bruno Bettelheim has read "The Frog King" as a compressed version of the maturation process, with the princess navigating a path between the pleasure principle (represented by the ball) and the dictates of the superego (represented by her father's commands). Note also that the notion of the golden ball is introduced early on, in the description of the sun, which is filled with wonder at the beauty of the princess. The rounded perfection of the two shining objects introduces the notion of aesthetic brilliance.

3. *"Stones would be moved to tears if they could hear you."* In order to vouch for the folkloric authenticity of the tales, the Grimms repeatedly embedded colloquial language and folk sayings into the tales. This particular turn of phrase captures a German saying about something so deeply sad that even inanimate objects respond to it.

4. *caught sight of a frog.* Critics frequently call attention to the phallic nature of the frog. Julius Heuscher notes that "the innocent young girl's fear of and repugnance toward the male genitals and the transformation of this disgust into happiness and sanctioned matrimony can hardly be symbolized better than by this transformation of the frog into a prince." Bruno Bettelheim tells us that the child connects the "tacky, clammy sensations which frogs evoke . . . with similar feelings [attached] to the sex organs." Frogs are also animals that themselves undergo a metamorphosis, existing in one form when young, in another when mature. They are, therefore, the perfect creatures for a meditation on transformations.

5. *"My dresses, my pearls and my jewels, even the golden crown I'm wearing."* In "Rumpelstiltskin," the miller's daughter similarly tries to satisfy the demands of the helper with material possessions. This fairy tale, atypically, suggests that gold

Walter Crane, *The Frog Prince*

The princess appears horrified by the sight of the amphibian intruder, and the chambermaids in the background seem equally perturbed.

and goods cannot produce happiness. True brides also often attempt to make barters and exchanges with false brides, trading gold for the opportunity to be near the beloved.

6. *"Is there some kind of giant at the door coming after you?"* What the frog lacks in size, he makes up for with his "disgusting" appearance. Unlike the ogres and giants of fairy tales, he remains in a subordinate position, forced into the role of supplicant.

Once the frog had gotten her word, he put his head back in the water and dove down into the spring. After a while he came paddling back with the ball in his mouth, and he tossed it on the grass. When the princess saw her beautiful plaything in front of her, she was overjoyed. She picked it up and ran off with it.

"Wait for me," the frog cried out. "Take me with you. I can't run the way you can."

He croaked as loudly as he could, but it did him no good at all. The princess had lost interest in him, hurried home as fast as her legs would carry her, and quickly forgot about the poor frog, who had to crawl back down into the spring.

The next day the princess sat down to dinner with the king and with some courtiers and was eating dinner from her little golden plate when something came crawling up the marble staircase, splish, splash, splish, splash. When it reached the top of the stairs, it knocked at the door and called out: "Princess, youngest princess, let me in!"

The princess ran to the door to see who was there. When she opened it, she saw the frog standing in front of her. Terrified, she slammed the door as hard as she could and returned to the table. The king could see that her heart was pounding like mad, and he said: "My child, what are you afraid of? Is there some kind of giant at the door coming after you?"[6]

"Oh, no," she replied. "It wasn't a giant—it was just a disgusting frog."

"What in the world does a frog want with you?"

"Oh, Father dear, yesterday when I was playing by the spring, my little golden ball fell into the water. And because I was crying so hard, the frog got it for me, and because he insisted, I promised that he could become my companion. I never thought that he would be able to leave the water. Now he's outside, and he's demanding to come in to see me."

Just then there was another knock at the door, and a voice cried out:

"Princess, little princess,
Let me in.
Think back now
To yesterday's oath
Down by the cold, blue water.
Princess, little princess,
Let me in."

The king declared: "Once you make a promise to someone,[7] you have to keep it. Just go and let him in."

The princess went over and opened the door. The frog hopped right into the room and followed close on her heels until she reached her chair. Then he sat down and cried out: "Lift me up and put me next to you."

7. *"Once you make a promise to someone."* The Grimms added maxims like this one to strengthen the moral backbone of the tale.

Walter Crane, *The Frog Prince*

Reactions vary to the frog dining from the princess's little golden plate, but the father's raised finger makes it clear that he will not tolerate the idea of dismissing the frog, even if the princess is repelled and the servants find it difficult to contain themselves.

The princess hesitated, but the king ordered her to obey. Once the frog was up on the chair, he wanted to get on the table, and once he was there, he said: "Push your little golden plate closer to me so that we can eat together."

The princess did as he said, but it was plain to see that she was not happy about it. The frog had enjoyed his meal, but every bite she had stuck in her throat. Finally he said: "I've had enough to eat, and I'm really tired. Take me up to your room and turn down the silken covers on your little bed."

The princess began to weep, for she was terrified of the clammy frog. She didn't dare touch him, and now he was going to sleep in her beautiful, clean bed.[8] The king grew angry and said: "You shouldn't scorn someone who helped you when you were in trouble."

The princess picked up the frog with two fingers, carried him up to her room, and put him in a corner. While she was lying in bed, he came crawling over and said: "I'm tired and want to sleep as much as you do. Lift me up into your bed or I'll tell your father."

The princess became really annoyed, picked up the frog, and threw him with all her might against the wall.[9] "Now you'll get your rest, you disgusting frog!"

When the frog fell to the ground, he was no longer a frog but a prince with beautiful, bright eyes. At her father's bidding, he became her dear companion and husband. He told her that a wicked witch had cast a spell on him[10] and that only a princess could release him. The next day they planned to set out together for his kingdom.

The two fell asleep, and in the morning, after the sun had woken them, a coach drove up. It was drawn by eight white horses in golden harnesses,[11] with white ostrich feathers on their heads. At the back of the coach stood Faithful Heinrich,[12] the servant of the young king. Faithful Heinrich had been so saddened by the transformation of his master into a frog that three hoops had been placed around his chest to keep

8. *now he was going to sleep in her beautiful, clean bed.* In her version of the Grimms' story called "The Frog Prince," Anne Sexton describes the scene in the bedroom as follows: "Next came the bed. / The silky royal bed. / Ah! The penultimate hour! / There was the pillow / with the princess breathing / and there was the sinuous frog / riding up and down beside her." Sexton leaves no doubt about the frog's intentions. Note that the sharing, first of objects, then of the bed, alludes to the domestic intimacy of marriage rather than mere companionship. In that sense, the tale can be read as expressing a girl's anxiety about marriage.

9. *threw him with all her might against the wall.* Not all versions of the tale include the act of violence, which is very different from the premeditated brutality of fairy-tale villains. But Scottish and Gaelic versions of the tale require the princess to behead her suitor in order to release him from his enchanted state. A Polish variant replaces the frog with a snake and recounts in lavish detail how the princess tears it in two. A tamer Lithuanian text requires the burning of the snake's skin before the prince is freed from his reptilian state. Deeds of passion, as much as acts of compassion, have the power to disenchant. Although the princess of "The Frog King" is self-absorbed, ungrateful, and cruel, in the end she does as well for herself as the modest, obedient, and charitable Beauty of "Beauty and the Beast." Anglo-American versions have replaced the act of violence with a kiss, a symbolic gesture that has led to the widely disseminated maxim "You have to kiss a lot of frogs before you meet your handsome prince." Contemporary versions of the tale offer a range of possibilities, with one describing the princess's refusal to set up housekeeping with the frog (she subsequently dines on the frog's legs), another showing the princess turn-

Walter Crane, *The Frog Prince*

The princess throws the frog against the wall, and we witness his dismemberment and reconstitution into a fellow of regal bearing, who tips his hat to the princess. Crane's compositions may appear crowded with decorative effects, but they nonetheless have a compelling stylistic unity.

ing into a frog and joining the frog prince in a pond, and a third offering a cynical rescripting in which the frog has simply used the fairy tale about an enchanted prince as a strategy for getting into bed with the princess.

10. *a wicked witch had cast a spell on him.* The cause of the transformation is not elaborated in any variants of the tale. Imprisonment in an animal form in other tales is often the result of lack of compassion, but it is often a witch, female sorceress, or mother-in-law who is responsible for the enchantment.

11. *It was drawn by eight white horses in golden harnesses.* The coach with its golden harnesses has been read by some critics as connected to the sun—an echo of the tale's beginning, which refers to the sun, and a hint of the glory of the marriage. Those who probe for a deeper meaning and a mythic connection might end by associating the prince with Apollo, god of the sun, and read the tale as a miniature, domesticated myth.

12. *At the back of the coach stood Faithful Heinrich.* Note that Heinrich receives the attribute "faithful" here, in contrast to the treachery of the princess, who tries to back out of a promise. The cracking of the three iron bands around Heinrich's chest comes to symbolize the sense of liberation felt by all three characters. The roundness of the three bands can be associated with the sun and with the princess's golden ball, two other powerful symbols in the tale.

his heart from bursting with pain and sorrow. Now the coach had arrived to take the young king back to his kingdom, and Faithful Heinrich lifted the two of them into the carriage and took his place in the rear. He was elated by his master's transformation. When they had covered a good distance, the prince heard a cracking noise behind him, as if something had broken. He turned around and cried out:

"Heinrich, the coach is in danger!"
"No, my lord, it's not the coach,
But a hoop from round my heart,
Which was in deep pain,
While you were down in the spring,
Living as a frog."

Two more times the prince heard the cracking noise, and he was sure that the coach was falling apart. But it was only the sound of the hoops breaking from around Faithful Heinrich's chest, for his master had been set free and was happy at last.

Walter Crane, *The Frog Prince*

Heinrich, faithful servant to the prince, wears his heart on a tunic and is finally released from his martyrdom. The prince gazes at his servant in flirtatious gratitude as the princess peers out from the carriage and the servants on horseback turn around to observe the two.

A Fairy Tale About a Boy Who Left Home to Learn About Fear

lthough this story has the term "fairy tale" in its title, it deviates in important ways from the conventions of the genre. There may be supernatural events in the tale, but there is none of the fairy-tale magic that comes in the form of villains, donors, and helpers. This tale is closer to the saga or extended anecdote, with its series of self-contained episodes and its burlesque turns. It is the kind of tale told around campfires to send chills up the spine and to inspire the very affect that the hero lacks. Its hero possesses the kind of impractical nature and loopy innocence that is repeatedly associated with fairy-tale heroes. The boy achieves his goal and manages to accomplish tasks and perform feats that confound wiser, stronger, and braver men.

Through one hair-raising episode after another, the boy in this tale preserves his equanimity and coolly turns the tables on his would-be terrorizers. The inability to fear comes so close to courage here that the boy begins to take on heroic attributes. Unlike his humble and helpless kinsmen in classical fairy tales of three sons, he breezily accomplishes one task after another without recourse to aid from foreign agents. Providing comic entertainment and serving to reassure those who are

perceived as unpromising and incompetent, this tale has not traveled as well as stories about naïve and unknowing heroines.

If we take a look at German narrative traditions—both oral and literary—it becomes clear that the naïve hero is by no means a folkloristic aberration. He fits squarely into a long tradition that begins with Siegfried, the quintessential naïve boy who becomes a hero, and includes such figures as Wolfram von Eschenbach's Parzival, who comes to incarnate the highest chivalric ideals yet is described as der tumme *(the young and inexperienced one). No one was more surprised by the resemblances between the Grimms' fairy-tale character and Siegfried than Richard Wagner, whose operatic Siegfried learns fear when he sets eyes on the sleeping Brunhilde. "Haven't I ever told you this amusing story? It's the tale of the lad who ventures forth to learn what fear is and who is so dumb that he just can't do it. Imagine my amazement when I suddenly realized that that lad is no one else but—young Siegfried." The hero of this tale may lack a name, but his fame is well established in German-speaking lands.*

There once lived a man who had two sons. The older boy was bright and clever and knew just what to do and when. The younger was stupid and had trouble learning things, and he understood nothing. People would look at him and say: "His father's going to have his hands full with that one!" Whenever anything had to be done, it was always up to the older boy to do it.

If the father ever asked the older boy to go fetch something at dusk or, worse yet, at night, and if the path led through a graveyard or some other spooky place, then the boy would say: "Oh, no, Father, I can't possibly go there. That makes my flesh creep!" The boy was simply afraid. In the evening, when people sat around the fire and told stories that sent shivers down your spine, the listeners would sometimes say: "Oh, that really gives me the creeps!" But the younger of the two boys would just sit in the corner listening to what everyone said, and he could never figure out what they were talking about. "They're always saying: 'That gives me the creeps! That gives me the creeps!' That doesn't give *me* the creeps. That's just some kind of skill that I haven't been able to develop."[1]

One day the boy's father said to him: "Listen here, you over there in the corner. You're starting to get big and strong, and you will eventually have to learn a trade and make a living. Look at your brother and how hard he's working. As for you, talking to you just seems to be a lost cause."

"Oh, Father dear," he said. "I'm really anxious to learn a trade. If it were possible, I'd like to learn how to get the creeps. But I have no idea where to start."

When he heard that, the older son laughed out loud and thought: "Good God, my brother really is an idiot! He'll never amount to anything. As the twig is bent, so grows the tree."

The father sighed and said: "Getting the creeps, you'll learn that soon enough, but you're not going to be able to buy your bread with that."

Before long, the sexton dropped by for a visit,[2] and the boy's father started complaining to him about the problems he was having with a son who didn't know anything and was incapable of learning anything. "Just imagine: I asked him how he was planning to earn his bread, and he actually wanted to learn how to get the creeps."

"If that's all that's wrong," the sexton replied, "I can help him out. Send him over to my house, and I'll shape him up."

The father liked the idea, for he thought: "Maybe this will smooth his rough edges."

The sexton took the boy in and gave him the job of ringing the church bells. After a few days he woke him up at midnight, told him to get up and climb into the belfry to

1. *"some kind of skill that I haven't been able to develop."* The hero's inability to know how to be afraid, to shudder, or to get the creeps (as it has been variably described in English) can be traced in part to his youth, and in part to his artlessness and simplicity.

2. *the sexton dropped by for a visit.* With its undercurrent of anti-clerical sentiment, this tale lacks the innocence and piety that the Grimms found so reassuring in folktales. Tales about opportunistic priests, adulterous wives, and cuckolded husbands abounded in European and Slavic folklore, but, for obvious reasons, they did not make the cut when it came to assembling collections of representative native lore.

ring the bell. "You'll learn what it's like to have the creeps soon enough," he thought, and he secretly went on ahead of him. When the boy was at the top of the stairs and just turning around to grab the bell rope, he saw a white shape on the staircase, right across from the louvers.

"Who's there?" he cried out, but the shape refused to answer and didn't budge from where it was.

"Answer me," the boy said, "or get out! You've no business here in the middle of the night."

The sexton remained completely motionless so that the boy would think that he was a ghost.

A second time the boy shouted: "What are you doing here? Speak up if you're an honest man or I'll throw you down the stairs."

The sexton thought: "He doesn't really mean it." He didn't make a sound and just stood there, as if he were made of stone. The boy called out to him a third time, and when that did no good either, he took a running start and pushed the ghost down the stairs, sending him tumbling down ten steps so that he ended up lying in a corner of the staircase. Then he rang the bell, went home, got into bed without saying a word, and fell asleep.

The sexton's wife stayed up quite a while waiting for her husband, but he failed to return home. She started worrying about him, woke the boy up, and asked: "Do you have any idea where my husband is? Didn't he go up with you to the belfry?"

"No, no," the boy replied. "There was someone standing on the stairs across from the louvers, but he wouldn't answer when I talked to him and refused to go away. I'm sure he was up to no good, and so I pushed him down the stairs. Why don't you go over and then you'll see if it's your husband? If it is, I'm really sorry."

Off raced the sexton's wife, and she found her husband lying in the corner of the staircase. He was writhing in pain,

Ludwig Richter, *Ludwig Bechsteins Märchenbuch*

The boy calls out to the sexton, and when he gets no answer, he pushes the "ghost" haunting the belfry, sending him tumbling down the stairs.

and it turned out that he had broken a leg. She took her husband downstairs and then went running to the boy's father, hollering: "Your son has caused a really bad accident. He threw my husband down the stairs and now his leg is broken. Get that good-for-nothing out of our house."

The father was horror stricken and went running over to give the boy a piece of his mind. "What kinds of wicked things have you been doing? The devil must have put you up to it!"

"Father," he replied. "Just listen to me. I didn't do anything wrong. The sexton was standing there late at night like someone who was up to no good. I didn't know who it was and I warned him three times to say something or to go away."

The father said to him: "You're nothing but trouble. Just get out of my sight. I don't want to have you around any more."

"All right, Father," he said, "that's fine, but let's just wait until morning. Then I'll go out and learn about how to get the creeps. At least I'll have a way to make a living."

"Learn whatever you want," his father said. "It's all the same to me. Here are fifty talers. Go off and do whatever you want out in the world, but don't tell anyone where you're from or who your father is. I'm ashamed of you."

"Yes, Father, as you wish," he said. "If that's what you want, you can count on me."

Now at daybreak, the boy put the fifty talers in his pocket, went out to the main road, and kept mumbling to himself: "If only I could get the creeps! If only I could get the creeps!" A man joined him on the road and heard the words he kept repeating. When they had walked for a while, they came within sight of the gallows, and the man said to him: "If you look over at that tree, you'll see a place where seven men celebrated their wedding with the rope maker's daughter. Now they're learning how to fly. Sit down beneath the tree

3. *since he was a compassionate soul.* Fairy-tale heroes must often pass a test of compassion before rising to the challenges of tasks or facing trials. This episode, standing as the first in a series of adventures while the hero is on the road, offers a send-up of the test of compassion.

and wait until nightfall. Believe me, you'll learn how to get the creeps."

"If that's all there is to it," said the boy, "then I'll manage very well. If I learn how to get the creeps that quickly, you can come back tomorrow morning and have my fifty talers."

The boy walked over to the gallows, sat down beneath them, and waited for night to fall. Since it was cold, he decided to start a fire. But around midnight the wind was blowing so fiercely that he couldn't get warm, even though the fire was burning. When the wind started buffeting the hanged men so that they were hitting against each other, he thought: "If you are freezing down here by the fire, the guys hanging up there must be really cold." And since he was a compassionate soul,[3] he got a ladder, climbed up, untied them one after another, and brought all seven down. Then he blew on the embers, stoked the fire, and set the men all around so that they could get warm. But they all just sat there and didn't stir, even when flames started licking their clothes. The boy said: "Be careful or I'll string you up again." The dead men didn't pay attention, remained silent, and let their rags go on burning. Then the boy got really mad and said: "If you don't listen to me, then I can't help you at all. I'm not going to go up in flames with you." And he hung them back up, one by one. Then he sat down by the fire and fell asleep. The next day the traveler came for his fifty talers and said: "Well, then, did you learn how to get the creeps?"

"Not at all," he said. "How could I have learned it? The guys over there refused to open their mouths, and they were so stupid that they even let the old rags on their backs catch fire." And so the man realized that he wasn't going to get his fifty talers that day, and he left, saying to himself: "I've never met anyone like that in my whole life."

The boy too went his way, and he started talking to himself again: "Oh, if I could just learn how to get the creeps! If I could just learn how to get the creeps!" A wagoner walking along behind him heard what he was saying and asked: "Who are you?"

The boy answered: "I don't know."

The wagoner then asked: "Where are you from?"

"I don't know."

"Who is your father?"

"I'm not allowed to tell you."

"Why are you always mumbling to yourself?"

"Oh," the boy said, "I keep wishing that I could learn how to get the creeps, but no one seems to be able to teach me."

"Stop talking like a fool," the wagoner said. "Come along with me, and let me find you a place to stay." The boy went with the wagoner, and in the evening they arrived at an inn where they could spend the night. As they were stepping into the main room, the boy declared: "If I could just learn how to get the creeps! If I could just learn how to get the creeps!" The innkeeper heard what he was saying and started laughing. He said: "If that's really what you want, it can be arranged."

"Just stop it," the innkeeper's wife said. "Think of all the foolish young fellows who have already paid with their lives.[4] It would be a real shame if those pretty eyes never saw the light of day again."

The boy insisted: "I want to learn how to get the creeps no matter how hard it is. That's why I went out into the world." He refused to give the innkeeper a moment's peace until the man told him all about a haunted castle that was not very far away. He could learn how to get the creeps just by spending three nights there. The king of the land had promised his daughter's hand to anyone who dared stay there for three nights. She was the most beautiful maiden that the sun had ever shone down on.

In the castle were hidden great treasures guarded by evil spirits. These treasures could be set free, and they were enough to make a poor man richer than he could imagine.

4. *"Think of all the foolish young fellows who have already paid with their lives."* Like the suitors in "Sleeping Beauty," the boy in this tale is the last in a series of young men who have sought to satisfy the conditions for winning the hand of a princess. If the boy's adventures were limited to the village and the road up until this point, they now move into a fairy-tale setting, with a castle and a realm that must be "disenchanted" by the hero.

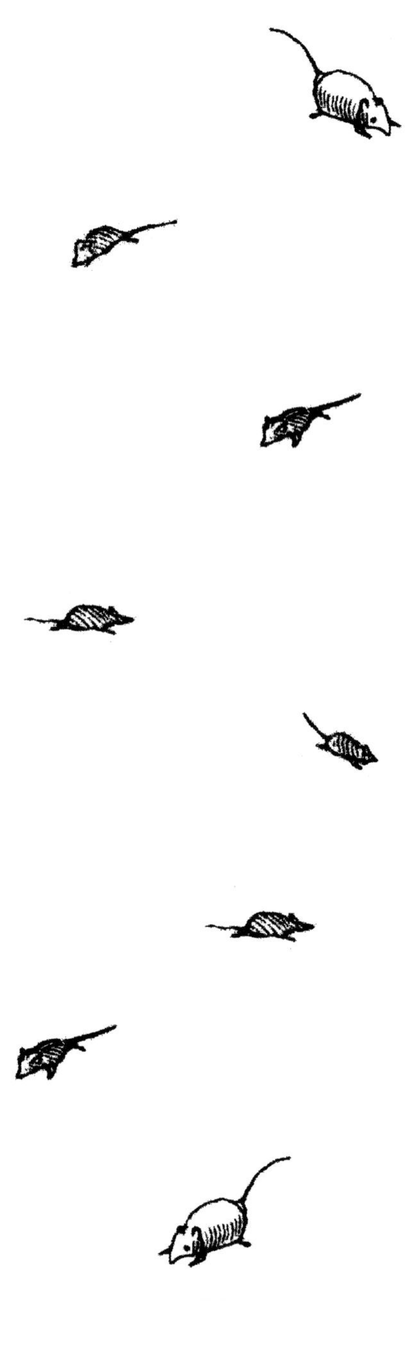

Many a man had gone in there, but no one had come back out again.

The next day, the boy appeared before the king and said: "If you are willing, I would like to spend three nights in the haunted castle." The king took a good look at him, and since he found him appealing, he said: "You can ask for three things to take with you into the castle, but they must all be objects without life."

Here was the boy's response: "I would like to have some fire, a lathe, and a woodcarver's bench with a knife."

The king let him take everything over to the castle during the day. When night fell, the boy made a bright fire in one of the rooms, set up the woodcarver's bench in the room, put the knife next to it, and sat on the lathe. "Oh, if only I could learn to get the creeps!" he said. "But I'm definitely not going to learn it here."

Toward midnight he decided to stir the fire again. While he was blowing at the embers, suddenly he heard a screeching noise in one corner. "Meow, meow, we're freezing to death!"

"You fools," he cried out. "Why are you screeching like that? If you're cold, come sit down by the fire and warm up here." Just as he was saying that, two great big black cats jumped over to him, sat down on each side of him, and glared fiercely at him with their wild, fiery eyes. After a while, when they had warmed themselves up, they said to him: "Well, old pal, how about a hand of cards?"

"Why not?" he replied. "But first show me your paws."

They put their paws out and stretched out their claws.

"Goodness," he said, "your nails are way too long! Hold on a minute, and I'll trim them for you." And he picked the cats up by the scruff of the neck, put them up on the carver's bench, and placed their paws in the vise.

"Now that I've seen your claws, I don't feel like playing cards any more." And he killed the two of them and threw them into the lake. No sooner had he gotten rid of those two than he sat down by the fire again, and suddenly, out of every nook and cranny of the castle, black cats and black dogs on red-hot chains started appearing, so many that he couldn't possibly get away. They were making a horrible racket, trampling on his fire, tearing it apart, and trying to put it out. He tolerated it for a while, then became so irritated that he grabbed his knife and lashed out at them, shouting "Get out of here, you rascals!" Some of them ran away, and the others he killed and threw into the pond. When he returned, he blew on the embers again and warmed himself up.

While he was sitting by the fire, he could hardly keep his eyes open and felt like going to sleep. When he looked around, he saw that there was a big bed in the corner. "Just what I need," he said as he crawled in. As his eyes closed, the bed started moving around on its own and was roaming all over the castle. "Perfect," he said, "just keep on going." The bed started rolling[5] as if six horses were harnessed to it, and it flew through doors and up and down stairs until, finally, crash, bang, boom, it turned upside down and lay on top of him like a mountain. He threw off the blankets and pillows, climbed out of the bed, and said: "Anyone else interested in a ride?" Then he lay down by the fire and slept until morning.

The next day the king came over, and when he saw the boy sleeping on the ground, he thought that spirits must have taken his life and that he was dead. Then he said: "It's really too bad about this handsome young man." The boy heard his words, sat up, and declared: "Not so fast. I'm still here." The king was astonished, but he was also pleased and asked how he had managed during the night. "Pretty well," the boy replied. "Now that one night's over, the other two will be behind me soon."

When he returned to the inn, the boy ran into the innkeeper, whose eyes nearly popped out of his head. "I didn't think I'd ever see you alive again. Have you finally learned how to get the creeps?"

5. *The bed started rolling.* The rolling bed is based on an episode in Wolfram von Eschenbach's medieval epic *Parzival.* The Grimms noted the parallel in their annotations and recognized the kinship between the folkloric hero and the legendary hero.

Ludwig Richter, *Ludwig Bechsteins Märchenbuch*

The bed into which the boy has climbed starts moving on its own as if six horses were harnessed to it. Stirring up dust, along with the mice in the castle, the bed goes flying from one room to the next.

"No," the boy said. "It's just hopeless. If only someone could teach me."

The second night, he went back again to the old castle, sat down by the fire, and started singing the same old tune: "If only I could learn how to get the creeps!" The midnight hour was fast approaching. There was a din and a clatter, at first soft, then louder and louder. It was quiet for a little bit, but suddenly, with a piercing scream, half a man came sliding down the chimney[6] and fell down right in front of him.

"Hey there," he called out to him. "You're missing your better half. Where's the rest of you?" The noise started up again, a howling and a screeching, and then the other half of the man came falling down.

"Hold on a minute," he said. "I'll stir up the fire for you."

He took care of the fire, and when he turned around he saw that the two halves had joined together again and that a ghastly looking person was sitting in his place.

"That wasn't part of the bargain," he said. "That's always been my seat." The man wanted to push him away, but the boy wouldn't let him. He shoved him with all his might and sat down at his place again. Suddenly more men started coming down the chimney, one after another. They brought nine dead men's bones with them, along with two skulls, and then started bowling. The boy wanted to bowl with them, and he asked: "Hey there, can I join you?"

"Sure, if you've got money."

"Plenty of money," he replied, "but your bowling balls aren't quite round."

He then took the skulls, sat down at the lathe, and worked on them until they were nice and round. "That's good. Now we should be able to bowl better," he said. "Hurrah! Let's go have a good time." He bowled with them and lost some of his money, but when the clock struck midnight, everything suddenly vanished. He decided to lie down and get some sleep.

The next morning the king returned to find out what had happened. "How did you fare last night?" he asked. "Did you get the creeps?"

"I played ninepins," he said, "and lost a few hellers."

"Did you get the creeps?"

"Are you kidding?" he said. "I had a terrific time. Now if I could just learn how to get the creeps."

6. *half a man came sliding down the chimney.* In some versions of the story, as the Grimms note, a man appears carrying his head under his arm. The hero orders him to put it back on his neck so that the two can play cards, and indeed, the man is able to put his head back on.

On the third night he sat down on his bench again and said in despair: "If only I could learn how to get the creeps!" Later on six big men walked in carrying a coffin. He said to them: "That must be the cousin of mine who died just a few days ago," and he signaled to the men and called out: "Come over here, cousin, right over here." They put the coffin down on the ground, and he went over and took off the lid: a dead man was lying in the box. The boy touched his face, but it was cold as ice.

"Hang on," he said, "I'm going to warm you up," and he went over to the fire, warmed his hand, and put it on the man's face. The dead man stayed cold. And so he took him out of the coffin, put him on his lap, sat down with him by the fire, and started rubbing his limbs so that the blood would start circulating again. When that didn't work, the boy recalled that when two people get under the covers, they can warm each other up. He brought the man over to the bed, tucked him in, and lay down next to him. After a while the dead man did warm up and began moving. The boy said: "See that, cousin! Imagine what would have happened if I hadn't warmed you up!" But the dead man just started shouting: "Now I'm going to strangle you!"

"What!" the boy said. "Is that the thanks I get? I'm going to put you right back in that coffin," and he lifted him up, shoved him back in, and put the lid back on. The six men returned and carried him away. "I just can't get the creeps," he said, "and if I stay here, I won't get them even if I live to be a hundred."

Suddenly a man walked in who was taller than all the others and even more terrifying, but he was older and had a long white beard. "You rascal," he cried out. "I'm going to teach you about getting the creeps, for now you are going to die."

"Not so fast," the boy replied. "If I'm going to die, I'll have to be there for it, won't I?"

"I'll catch you all right."

"Easy does it, and stop that bragging. I'm just as strong as you are, and probably even stronger."

"We'll see about that," the old man said. "If you're stronger than I am, I'll let you go. Come on, we'll give it a try."

The old man led him down some dark corridors to a smithy, and he picked up an ax and drove an anvil into the ground with one blow.

"I can do a better job," the boy said, and he walked over to the other anvil that was there. The old man stood next to him, with his white beard hanging down, and wanted to watch. The boy grabbed the ax, split the anvil in two with one stroke, and wedged the old man's beard into the crack.

"Now I've got you," the boy said. "It's your turn to die."

Then he took a crowbar and started beating the old man until he was whimpering in pain and begging him to stop. He promised to give him great riches. The boy took the ax out of the anvil and released him.

The old man took him over to the castle and showed him three chests of gold that were in the basement. "One of them is for the poor," he said, "another belongs to the king, and the third one is yours."

Just then the clock struck midnight and the ghost vanished, leaving the boy alone in the dark. "I won't have any trouble getting out of here," he said, and he groped around until he found his room, and then he fell asleep by the fire.

The next day the king returned and said: "Now I'm sure you've learned how to get the creeps."

"No," he replied, "what is that all about? My dead cousin was here, and a bearded man stopped by and he showed me where there was a lot of money. But no one has taught me how to get the creeps."

The king said: "You have broken the spell on the castle, and now my daughter is yours."

"That's all very well," the boy said, "but I still have no idea how to get the creeps."

Hermann Vogel, *Kinder- und Hausmärchen gesammelt durch die Brüder Grimm*

7. *his wife pulled back the covers.* Bettelheim declares that "it is the female partner who finally brings out the humanity in the male—because to feel fear is human; not being able to feel it is inhuman."

And so the gold was carried up from below, and the wedding was celebrated. The young king loved his wife dearly and was very happy, but he kept saying: "If I could just learn how to get the creeps! If I could just learn how to get the creeps!" The queen began to find that really annoying. Her chambermaid said: "I know how to fix that. He'll learn how to get the creeps soon enough." She went over to the brook that was running through the garden and fetched a bucket full of minnows. In the evening, when the young king was sleeping, his wife pulled back the covers[7] and poured the bucket of cold water with minnows on him. The little fish wriggled all over him. He woke up with a start and shouted: "Oh, I've got the creeps, I've got the creeps, dear wife! Finally I've learned how to get the creeps."

Ludwig Richter, *Ludwig Bechsteins Märchenbuch*

The Wolf and the Seven Little Goats

Like the story of "The Three Little Pigs," to which it bears a close resemblance, this tale is a cautionary fable, designed to convey a lesson to children. In the end, the kids are saved by the mother's intervention (in an episode similar to the alternate ending for the Grimms' "Little Red Riding Hood"), but not all versions end happily. The Grimms elected to use an ending that avoids tragedy and reunites the children with their mother, a figure who both nurtures and protects the children.

The utopian beginning to the story, with the cozy family at home, is marked by plenitude, despite the fact that one figure is notably absent—the father of the seven little goats. Harmony at home is disrupted by the threat of the wolf, a masculine presence who, with his desire to devour the children, stands in stark opposition to the mother. The wolf can be seen as representing cunning and deceit, powers that undermine domestic serenity. At the same time, he represents a threat that must be reckoned with as the little goats grow older and mature.

The wolf's gargantuan appetite turns him into a force of nature, a devouring magnus pater whose belly is filled with stones so heavy that he is pulled into the waters, where he is, in turn, engulfed by nature. Death and rebirth figure so powerfully in this story that its domestic plot begins to take a mythical turn, even if the cast of characters is derived from fables and fairy tales. Like Cronus or Saturn, the wolf can be seen as a paternal power posing a threat to his children. And if we recall that Zeus was spared because his mother gave Cronus a stone wrapped in swaddling clothes and that Cronus was tricked into taking a purgative which made him vomit up his children one by one, the links with "The Wolf and the Seven Little Goats" become even clearer.

Marina Warner has argued that the Greek myth casts Cronus as a "surrogate mother, giving birth from his mouth to the gods and goddesses as the issue of his body. Kronos' act of devouring his brood forms a prelude to birth; being eaten equals incorporation, and this in turn stands for a surrogate though unwitting pregnancy—of the male. In this way, his progeny re-enter the world, twice born of their father, begotten and brought forth." The wolf, by contrast with Cronus, is turned into pure predator, an unrelated creature of a different species who reconfigures the myth to translate the threat from within the family to a foreign source, with the result that the domestic sphere comes to be sanctified as the site of safety and tranquility.

Once upon a time there was an old goat who was living with her seven little kids, all of whom she loved as dearly as mothers love their children.[1] One day she decided to go into the woods to forage for food, and so she gathered the kids all around her and said: "Dear children, since I'm going off into the woods, you'll have to watch out for the wolf. If he manages to get into the house, he'll gobble you up, skin, hair, bones, and all. The old scoundrel often disguises himself, but

1. *as dearly as mothers love their children.* Maternal love, protection, and security are established from the start as a sharp contrast to the threat embodied in the wolf, who will be introduced as a predator whose gluttony knows no limits. The mother is nurturing and loving; the wolf is interested only in indulging his desires. The distinction between mother goat and wolf takes concrete form in the quality of voice and color of feet. The mother's voice is sweet, the wolf's is rough; the mother's paws are white, the wolf's are black.

Hermann Vogel,
Kinder- und Hausmärchen gesammelt durch die Brüder Grimm

The mother goat takes leave of her children, warning them to beware of the wolf.

you won't have any trouble recognizing him, because he has a gruff voice and black feet."

The little goats said: "Mother dearest, you can be sure that we'll be on our guard. You don't need to worry about us." The mother bleated and left for the woods, her mind at ease.

Before long there was a knock at the door: "Open the door, my dear children. Mother's back, and she's brought something for each one of you."

The little goats heard the gruff voice and knew that it was the wolf. "Don't think that we would be so stupid as to open the door for you," they cried out. "You're not our mother. She has a sweet, lovely voice, and your voice is rough and gruff. You must be the wolf."

The wolf went to the store and bought a big piece of chalk. He ate it up so that it would make his voice softer. Then he returned to the goats' house, knocked at the door, and cried out: "Open the door, dear children. Mother's back, and she's brought something for each of you." But the wolf had made the mistake of putting his black paw on the window ledge, and when the children saw it, they cried out: "Don't think that we would be so stupid as to open the door for you. Our mother doesn't have a black foot like that one. You must be the wolf."

The wolf ran off to the baker and said: "I've hurt my leg. Can you rub some dough on it?" After the baker had covered his paw with dough, he ran to the miller and said: "Sprinkle some white flour on my paw." The miller thought: "I'll bet that the wolf is planning to trick somebody," and he refused to do it. But the wolf said: "If you don't do it, I'll gobble you up!" The miller was terrified, and he made the paw white. Well, yes, that's just the way people are.

The old scoundrel went to the house a third time, knocked at the door, and said: "Open the door, dear children. Mother's back, and she's brought something from the woods for each of you."

The little kids shouted: "Show us your paw so that we will know for sure that you are our dear mother." The wolf put his paw on the window ledge, and when they saw that it was white, they believed they were hearing the truth and opened the door. But who should have come in the door but the wolf! They were horrified and tried to hide. One hid under the table, another in bed, a third in the oven, a fourth in the kitchen, a fifth in the cupboard, a sixth under the washbasin, and the seventh in the clock case.[2] The wolf had no trouble finding them and made short work of them. He sent one after another down his gullet, gobbling them all up. But he never did find the little goat that was hiding in the clock

2. *and the seventh in the clock case.* Cronus and *chronus*, the Greek word for time, merged with each other in the Middle Ages, thus turning Cronus into a god who represented Father Time, devouring everything in his path. It is interesting that the surviving kid takes refuge in an instrument that keeps time and that represents the technological incarnation of Father Time. The mythical Cronus is, of course, connected to time in his relentless effort to halt it, to do away with the next generation and thus preserve his position. This fact introduces an element of logic to the life-saving choice of the clock case as hiding place.

Hermann Vogel,
Kinder- und Hausmärchen gesammelt durch die Brüder Grimm

A bloodthirsty wolf wields a knife and a gun as he knocks on the door, hoping to fool the little goats.

case. When the wolf had satisfied his desires, he shuffled off into the woods, found a shady spot under a tree in the green meadow, and fell asleep.

Not much later the mother goat returned home from the woods. What a sight met her eyes! The front door was wide open: table, chairs, benches—everything had been turned upside down. The wash basin had been smashed into pieces. Blankets and pillows had been thrown off the bed. She searched for her children but couldn't find them anywhere.

3. *She sent the little kid home to fetch scissors, needle, and thread.* The mother uses domestic tools to perform a surgical operation that will liberate the children. Note that she sews the wolf back up, using stones only to deceive him rather than to murder him. Since the stories were often told in the context of sewing circles, the reference to scissors, needle, and thread (and later the kids jumping "up and down like a tailor at his wedding") reveals that tellers of tales drew on traditional plots even as they incorporated elements of the environment in which they were told.

One by one she called their names, but there was no answer at all. Finally, when she came to the name of the youngest, a faint voice called out: "Dear Mother, I'm in the clock case."

The mother got him out of there, and the littlest kid told her about how the wolf had managed to get in and gobble up the other children. You can imagine how hard the mother wept when she learned the news. Still sobbing and wailing with grief, she went out into the woods, and the youngest kid went with her. When they came to the meadow, they found the wolf lying under a tree and snoring so loudly that the branches were trembling. The mother looked at him carefully from all angles and could see that something was turning and squirming in his full belly.

"Good gracious," she thought, "is it possible that my children could still be alive, even though he ate them up for his supper!" She sent the little kid home to fetch scissors, needle, and thread.[3] Then she cut open the belly of the wolf, and as soon as she had made the first cut, one of the little goats stuck his head out. She kept cutting and all six jumped out, one after the other. They were all still alive and had not suffered any damage, because in his greed, the monster had swallowed them whole.

You can imagine how happy they all were! They kept hugging their dear mother and jumped up and down like a tailor at his wedding. The mother stopped them and said: "Let's go and find some stones. We have to fill the belly of this godless beast before he wakes up." The seven little kids hauled as many stones as they could, as fast as they could, and put them into the wolf's belly. Then their mother sewed him up so carefully that he didn't notice a thing and never even stirred in his sleep.

When the wolf had finished sleeping, he got back on his feet. The stones in his belly had made him really thirsty, and so he thought he would go over to the well to get a drink.

When he got up and started moving forward, the stones in his belly hit against each other and rattled. He called out:

"What's that rumbling down below?
Feels to me like vertigo.
It must be all those little bones,
But now they're heavy, just like stones."

When he got to the well, he leaned over to get a drink and the hefty stones made him lose his balance so that he fell into the well and drowned.[4] When the seven little kids saw what had happened, they went running over to the well and shouted: "The wolf is dead! The wolf is dead!"[5] They were so happy that they got their mother, and they all danced for joy around the well.

4. *he fell into the well and drowned.* The destroyer of life who devours children is returned to the waters, to the source of life. The tale, which tells of death and rebirth, has been read as an allegory of the perpetual renewal of life.

5. *"The wolf is dead! The wolf is dead!"* The wolf's wish to devour and destroy, Bruno Bettelheim argues in his interpretation of "The Three Little Pigs," is something that the small child recognizes within himself: "his wish to devour, and its consequence—the anxiety about possibly suffering such a fate himself." The wolf, Bettelheim adds, is "a projection of the child's badness—and the story tells how this can be dealt with constructively." Bettelheim's reading, in seeing the wolf's evil as nothing more than a projection of the child's desires, runs counter to the interpretation of the story as a domesticated version of the myth of Cronus/Saturn, which sees the parent, rather than the child, as the true villain.

Hermann Vogel, *Kinder- und Hausmärchen gesammelt durch die Brüder Grimm*

The seven goats dance with their mother around the well into which the wolf fell while trying to slake his thirst.

The Twelve Brothers

"The Twelve Brothers" gives us a heroine who is characterized by fortitude and industry. Bearing the responsibility for both the exile of her brothers and their enchantment, she vows to remain silent and to refrain from smiling for seven years. The girl's status as intruder in the family remains problematic. In the first edition of the Grimms' collection, the king is horrified at the idea of having a daughter for reasons that have nothing to do with inheritance customs: "There was once a king who had twelve children—all were boys. He did not want to have a daughter and told the queen: 'If the thirteenth child that you bear is a girl, I'll have the twelve others killed. But if it's a boy, they can all stay alive and live together.' The queen wanted to talk him out of it. But the king would hear nothing of it: 'If it is as I have said, then they must die. I would rather cut off all their heads than have a girl among them.'" The second edition reverses this situation, giving us a king who is so set on the idea of a daughter that he is prepared to sacrifice his sons for her financial welfare.

What is clear from both versions of the story is that the king's murderous feelings are directed at his sons. This is one of the few tales in which a father, rather than a mother, becomes the agent of homicidal energy directed at children. The mother, while distressed by the father's decision, can do little more than send the boys into exile. The French critic Jean Bellemin-Noël comments on the mythical and biblical dimensions of the paternal threat: "How can we fail to recognize there the jealous patriarch of the primitive band *of which Freud made so much? Or Laius attempting to oppose the oracle's threats by disposing of Oedipus?" In "The Twelve Brothers," the Grimms recorded a tale that shows fathers as the source of threats to children, as parents willing to undertake premeditated murders for the flimsiest reasons. The fairy tale—as opposed to the mythical or biblical story—tells us that hope comes in the form of sibling solidarity and the heroic behavior of a child.*

Jack Zipes tells us that this tale had a special appeal for the Grimms because it shows how "several brothers and one sister *overcome adversity after separation from their parents." He sees in the tale a reflection of the Grimms' own family situation and a celebration of "industry, cleanliness, and order," virtues the Grimms attempted to promote in their collection.*

nce upon a time a king and a queen lived peacefully with their twelve children, who were all boys. One day the king said to his wife: "If the thirteenth child you are about to bear turns out to be a girl, then the twelve boys will have to be put to death, so that her wealth can be great and so that she alone inherits the kingdom." Twelve coffins were prepared and filled with wood shavings, with a little pillow for each boy to rest his head. The king put them all into a locked room and gave the key to the queen. He told her not to tell anyone about it.

The mother of the boys was filled with sorrow, and she

grieved all day long. Finally, the youngest son, who was always around her and to whom she had given the name Benjamin (after the Bible)[1] asked her: "Mother dear, why are you so sad?"

"Dearest child," she replied, "I'm not allowed to tell you."

The boy was so persistent that she finally went to the room, unlocked the door, and showed him the twelve coffins with wood shavings in them. Then she said: "My dearest Benjamin, your father had these coffins made for you and for your eleven brothers. If the child I bear is a girl, you are all going to be killed and buried in these coffins."

She wept with each word she spoke, but her son comforted her and said: "Don't cry, Mother dear. We can take care of ourselves. We'll run away."

She replied: "Take your eleven brothers out into the woods. One of you can climb to the very top of the tallest tree in the woods. Keep an eye out there from the castle tower. If I give birth to a baby boy, I'll raise a white flag and you can come right back home again. If I give birth to a baby girl, I'll raise a red flag and then you must flee as fast as your legs can carry you. May the good Lord protect you. I'll get up every night and pray that in the winter you will have a fire to warm you and that in the summer you won't suffer from the heat."

She gave the sons her blessing, and they went out into the woods. They took turns keeping watch from the top of the tallest oak tree they could find and kept an eye out for the signal from the tower. When eleven days had gone by and it was Benjamin's turn, he saw that a flag had been raised. It was not a white flag but a flag red as blood, proclaiming that they were to die. When the brothers got the news, they grew angry and said: "Are we going to die just because of a girl! Let's take an oath to avenge ourselves. If we run into a girl, her red blood will flow."

Then they went deeper into the forest, right to its very

1. *to whom she had given the name Benjamin (after the Bible).* Benjamin was the last born of Jacob's twelve sons, the younger of the two children to whom Rachel gave birth (Genesis 35:24). He was the only one of Jacob's sons to be born in what is today Israel. Rachel died giving birth to him, and her last words were to name the infant Benoni, meaning "son of my sorrow," which was later changed by Jacob to Benjamin, meaning "son of my right hand." In this tale too, we have an all-powerful father and a mother who, although alive, is unable to intercede for her sons.

heart, where it was darkest, and there they found an enchanted hut that was completely empty. They said: "Let's live here. Benjamin, you are the youngest and weakest. You can stay home and keep house while we go out and look for food." They went into the woods and shot rabbits, deer, birds, and doves, whatever was good to eat. Then they brought the food back home for Benjamin, who had to prepare it in an appetizing way for them. They lived together in the little house for a stretch of ten years, and time was never heavy on their hands.

The little girl to whom the queen gave birth grew up to become a child who was kind of heart and fair of face. She had a golden star on her forehead.[2] Once, on a big washing day, she discovered twelve shirts and asked her mother: "These shirts are far too small for Father. Whose are they?"

The queen replied with a heavy heart: "They belong to your twelve brothers."

The girl said: "I've never heard anything about those brothers. Where are they?"

The queen replied: "God knows where they are. They are wandering about somewhere in the world." She took the girl by the hand and unlocked the room so that she could show her the twelve coffins with the wood shavings and pillows. "These coffins," she said, "were made for your brothers. But they managed to escape before you were born," and then she told her everything that had happened. The girl said to her: "Dearest Mother, don't cry. I'm going to go find my brothers."

She took the twelve shirts and headed straight for the forest, walking all day long until she reached the enchanted house at night. She walked right in and saw a young boy who asked her: "Where are you from and where are you going?" He was filled with wonder by her great beauty, by her majestic clothing, and by the star on her forehead.

The girl replied: "I'm a princess, and I'm searching for my twelve brothers. I'm willing to go as far as the sky is blue to find them."

2. *She had a golden star on her forehead.* The star (*Stern*) on the girl's forehead (*Stirn*), beyond its alliterative qualities, is a sign of the girl's cosmic connections, royal descent, and magical beauty.

She showed him the twelve shirts that belonged to them. Benjamin realized that it was his sister and said: "I'm Benjamin, your youngest brother." She began weeping for joy, and Benjamin did the same. They felt so much love for each other that they couldn't stop kissing and hugging.

"Dear sister," he said, "there's still a problem. We vowed some time ago that we would kill any girl who crossed our threshold, because it was a girl that forced us to leave our home."

"I would gladly give my life if I could save my twelve brothers," she said.

"No, no," he said, "you shall not die. Get down under this tub until our eleven brothers return. I'll manage to win them over."

And so she hid as he told her. When night fell, the brothers returned from hunting, and their dinner was on the table. While they were eating, they asked: "Any news?" Benjamin responded by asking: "Haven't you heard?"

"No, we haven't," they replied.

He continued: "You've been out in the woods, and I've stayed here at home, but I know more than you do."

"Well, tell us, tell us everything," they cried out.

He replied: "All right, as long as you promise not to kill the first girl who crosses our threshold."

"Yes, we promise," they shouted. "We will spare her life. Just tell us what's going on!"

"Our sister is here," and he lifted the tub, and out came the princess in her royal garments with the golden star on her forehead. She was unimaginably beautiful, delicate, and gracious. The boys were overjoyed, and they threw their arms around her, kissed her, and felt a deep love for her.

The princess stayed at home with Benjamin and helped him around the house. The eleven boys went into the woods, caught game, deer, birds, and doves, so that they would have enough to eat, and Benjamin and his sister made sure that everything was cooked in a tasty way. The princess gathered firewood, found herbs to cook the vegetables with, and stirred the pots on the fire so that there was always food on the table when the brothers returned home. She kept everything in the house in good order[3] and made the beds up with clean, white linens. The brothers were completely content, and they lived together in perfect harmony.

One day Benjamin and his sister had prepared a fine meal, and everyone was sitting at the table, eating, drinking, and overjoyed to be together. Now there was a little garden near the enchanted house, and in it were twelve lilies which are commonly known as "students." The princess wanted to do something nice for her brothers, and she picked the twelve flowers, hoping to give one to each of her brothers during dinner. But just as she was picking the flowers, the twelve brothers turned into twelve ravens and flew up over the trees, and the house vanished. The poor girl was left all alone in the wilderness. As she turned around, she caught sight of an old woman next to her who said: "Dear child, what have you done? Why didn't you leave those twelve white flowers alone? They were your brothers, and now they've been turned into ravens forever."[4]

The girl wept and said: "Isn't there any way to disenchant them?"

"Yes," the old woman said. "There is one way to save them, but it's so hard that you can't possibly hope to free them that way. You would not be able to say a word for seven years, and you wouldn't be able to smile at all. If you speak just one word, or if only a single hour is missing in the seven years, then everything will be in vain—in fact one word would kill your brothers."[5]

The girl vowed to herself: "I know that I will be able to free my brothers," and she went and found a hollow tree, seated herself in it, and began spinning. She neither spoke nor smiled.

3. *She kept everything in the house in good order.* Like Snow White, the heroine of this tale develops housekeeping skills that put her on display as a model of good behavior.

4. *now they've been turned into ravens forever.* The brothers' transformation turns their mother into a *Rabenmutter*, the German term for an abusive mother which means, literally, "mother of ravens."

5. *"in fact one word would kill your brothers."* The girl's vow of silence is what Ruth B. Bottigheimer calls a "redemptive silence," one that is always prolonged for female characters, whereas for male characters such vows of silence are "brief and attenuated."

One day a king was hunting in the forest, and the big greyhound that he had taken with him ran over to the tree in which the girl was sitting and started jumping up, yelping and barking. The noise brought the king over, and he set eyes on the beautiful princess with the golden star on her forehead. He was so enchanted with her beauty that he called up to her to ask if she would be his wife. She did not say a word, but she did nod her head. He then went up the tree himself, climbed down with her, got on his horse with her, and rode home. The marriage of the two was celebrated with great joy and splendor. But the wife still did not say a word, nor did she laugh.

The king and queen had been living happily for several years when the mother of the king, who was an evil woman, began to slander the young queen.[6] She said to the king: "The girl you brought back home is nothing but a common little beggar. Who knows what kinds of godless tricks she plays in secret. Even if she's mute and can't speak, she ought to be able to laugh. A person who can't laugh must have a bad conscience."

At first the king refused to believe her, but the old woman kept at him for so long and accused the queen of so many evil things that finally he was persuaded that she was evil. He had his wife sentenced to death.

In the courtyard a huge fire was lit, and the queen was going to be burned at the stake. The king was at his window and watched with tears in his eyes, for he still loved her. Just after she had been bound to the stake and at the moment when flames began to lick at her clothes with their red tongues, the seven years came to an end. Suddenly there was a whirring sound in the air and twelve ravens came flying through the air and swooped down. When they touched the ground, they turned into her twelve brothers, whom she had disenchanted. They stomped on the fire, put out the flames, and released their sister. They all hugged and kissed. Now

6. *began to slander the young queen.* If the father represents the villain at the beginning of the tale, the mother(-in-law) takes up the role of villain in the end. The father is responsible for the assault on the boys' safety; the mother-in-law seeks to get the heroine out of the way. The mother-in-law in Perrault's "Sleeping Beauty" plans to cook her grandchildren for supper. She is one of many evil, cannibalistic mothers-in-law in fairy tales.

that she could finally open her mouth and speak, she told the king why she had taken a vow to remain silent and never to laugh. The king was overjoyed when he discovered that she was innocent, and the two lived together in harmony until their death.

The wicked mother-in-law was brought before a judge and put into a barrel filled with boiling oil and poisonous snakes, and she died a painful death.

Arthur Rackham, *The Fairy Tales of the Brothers Grimm*

The wicked mother-in-law perishes in a barrel filled with boiling oil and poisonous snakes.

Little Brother and Little Sister

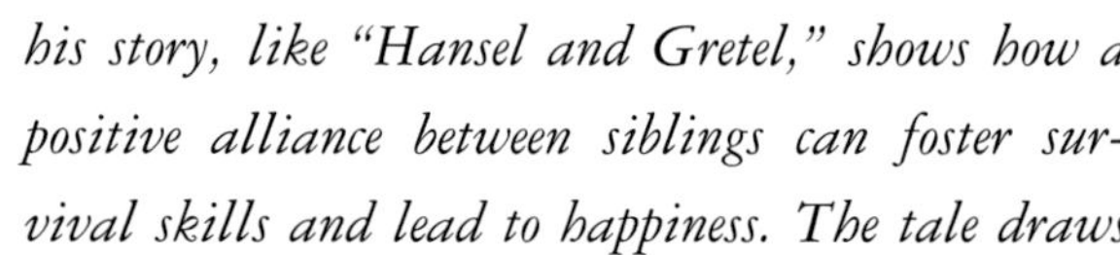

This story, like "Hansel and Gretel," shows how a positive alliance between siblings can foster survival skills and lead to happiness. The tale draws clear distinctions between the siblings along hunter-gatherer gender lines, with Little Brother unable to control his instincts (he drinks from the spring even though his sister warns him that it has been cursed, and he joins the hunt even when he puts his life at risk) and Little Sister as nurturer (she gathers roots and berries in the woods and returns from the dead to nurse her child). This division between hunters and gatherers is a reminder that the characters are situated in a culture of predators and prey, with the threat that Little Brother will turn on Little Sister once he transforms into a beast. It also underscores the vulnerability of the children, who could easily become the targets of ogres and other monsters in the woods.

Two episodes seem to be spliced together in the tale, with one depicting the flight from home and the struggle for survival in the woods, the other describing the queen's conflict with the wicked witch. The stepmother at the beginning of the tale is asserted to be identical to the "old woman" and "wicked witch" who emerges later in the tale to hound the heroine. A hybrid tale, "Little Brother and Little Sister"

combines stories about ogres and children with tales about false brides and true brides.

The writer Jane Yolen has pointed out that the tale seems "strangely conglomerate, as if two stories had been badly or inappropriately stitched together." This did not prevent her from becoming deeply attached to the story, which she saw as a celebration of profound "family loyalty."

Little Brother took Little Sister by the hand and said: "Since the day that our mother died, we haven't had a moment of peace. Our stepmother beats us every day,[1] and when we try to talk to her, she just gives us a swift kick and drives us off. All we get to eat are crusts of hard bread. Even the dog under the table is better off than we are. At least he gets an occasional tidbit. Our mother would be turning over in her grave if she knew what was happening. It's time for us to leave home and seek our fortune out in the world."

The two walked all day long across meadows and fields and over rocks. When it began to rain, Little Sister said: "God is weeping right along with our hearts!" When night fell, they reached the edge of a forest, and they were so worn down by their hunger, their misery, and by the long journey that they just managed to crawl into the hollow of a tree, where they fell fast asleep.

When they awoke the next morning, the sun was already high in the sky and shining directly into the hollow tree. Little Brother said: "Sister, I'm really thirsty.[2] If I could just find a brook around here, I'd go get a drink. I think that I heard one somewhere around here."

1. *"Our stepmother beats us every day."* The break with home is activated by the stepmother's abuse of the children. Rather than being abandoned in the woods like Hansel and Gretel, these two siblings take matters into their own hands and leave home.

2. *"Sister, I'm really thirsty."* Seeking immediate gratification for his desires, Brother is seen as the more "animalistic" of the two siblings.

Brother got up, took Sister's hand, and they started looking for a brook.

Now the evil stepmother, as it turns out, was really a witch and, when she saw that the children had decided to leave home, she followed them in secret, sneaking along behind them the way that witches do. And then she cast a spell on all the streams in the forest.

When the two children found a little brook, with water that sparkled as it leaped over the stones, Brother wanted to kneel down and get a drink. But Sister heard the words spoken by the brook: "He who drinks from me will turn into a tiger. He who drinks from me will turn into a tiger."[3]

Sister cried out: "Brother, I'm begging you, don't take a drink. If you do, you'll turn into a ferocious animal, and then you'll tear me to pieces."

Brother was really thirsty, but he didn't take a drink. He said to her: "All right, I'll wait until we get to the next brook."

When they came to the next stream, Sister could hear the words it was chanting: "He who drinks from me will turn into a wolf. He who drinks from me will turn into a wolf."

Sister cried out: "Brother, I'm begging you, don't take a drink, because if you do, you'll turn into a wolf and eat me up."

Little Brother promised not to take a drink and said: "I'll just wait until we get to the next brook. But then I'm going to have a drink no matter what you say. I'm really thirsty, and I just can't wait any longer."

When they got to the next brook, Sister heard the stream babbling as it flowed: "He who drinks from me will become a deer. He who drinks from me will become a deer."[4]

Sister said: "Oh, dear Brother, I'm begging you, don't drink or you'll turn into a deer and run away from me."

But Brother had already knelt down, bent over, and taken a drink from the stream. As soon as a few drops touched his lips, he was lying on the ground in the form of a fawn.

3. *"He who drinks from me will turn into a tiger."* A spell has been cast on the brook, but Sister, who is aligned as the closer of the two siblings to nature, is able to hear words of warning. Like the Goose Girl and Cinderella, she is linked to natural forces.

4. *"He who drinks from me will become a deer."* The gradual progression from tiger to wolf to deer reduces the ferocity of the animal into which Brother is transformed, suggesting that he has some control over his impulses, but not as much as his sister.

Arthur Rackham, *Little Brother and Little Sister and Other Tales by the Brothers Grimm*

After drinking from an enchanted stream, Little Brother is turned into a fawn. Little Sister fastens her garter around his neck, and the two discover a hut, where they set up housekeeping.

Sister started crying when she saw that poor Brother had been bewitched, and the fawn at her side wept as well. Finally the girl said: "Stop crying, dear fawn. Don't worry: I won't ever leave you." She undid her golden garter and tied it around the fawn's neck and then gathered reeds and braided them into a soft rope. The rope was fastened to the garter, and with it, she led the fawn deeper and deeper into the forest.

When they had traveled for a long, long time, they finally reached a little hut and the girl peered inside. Since it looked empty, she thought: "We can stop here and set up housekeeping." She gathered leaves and moss to make up a soft bed for the fawn. Every morning she got up and went into the woods to collect roots, berries, and nuts. For the fawn she found tender grass, which he ate right out of her hand. He was always in high spirits and frolicked merrily around.

In the evening, when Sister grew tired and after she had said her prayers,[5] she would rest her head on the fawn's back. That became her pillow, and she fell into a peaceful sleep. If Brother had only had his human shape, they would have had a glorious life out there.

The two had been living in the woods on their own for quite some time when it happened that the king in that land decided to hold a great hunt. The forest rang out with the sound of horns, the barking of dogs, and the hearty cries of the hunters. The fawn heard the sounds and longed to be part of the chase. He said to Sister: "Please, let me go out and join the hunt.[6] I just can't contain myself any longer." He pleaded with her until she finally gave in. "But you have to come back by nightfall," she said. "I must keep the door locked against those violent hunters. Knock on the door and say: 'Dear Little Sister, let me in.' That way I'll know who it is. I can't open up unless I hear those words."

The fawn darted out into the woods and was so glad to be out in the open that he leaped for joy. The king and his huntsmen saw the beautiful beast and gave chase, but they

5. *after she had said her prayers.* Despite pagan elements that include the casting of spells, the heroine is represented as a devout child, who needs no reminder to say her prayers.

6. *"Please, let me go out and join the hunt."* The tale relies on triple repetitions of events, with Brother stopping three times at streams and going on three hunts. The queen, in the conclusion to the tale, visits her child and the fawn many times, but only on three visits does she chant verse warning about her imminent departure.

couldn't catch him, and whenever they thought they were about to capture him, he bounded into a thicket and disappeared. When it started getting dark, he ran back to the little house, knocked at the door, and said: "Dear Little Sister, let me in." When the door opened, he raced inside and then slept soundly on his bed all night long.

The next morning the hunt began anew, and when the fawn heard the horns and the halloos of the hunters, he couldn't sit still and said: "Open the door, Sister, I just have to go out there."

Sister opened the door for him, but she reminded him: "You have to return by nightfall. And don't forget the words I told you to say."

When the king and his huntsmen caught sight of the fawn with the golden collar again, they chased after him, but he was far too nimble and speedy for them. He outran them all day long, but at last the huntsmen managed to surround him. One of them wounded him slightly on the foot so that he started limping and had to run more slowly. One of the hunters followed him back to the house and heard him saying: "Dear Little Sister, let me in." He watched as the door opened for him and then closed. The huntsman took note of everything that happened and went to the king to tell him what he had heard and seen. The king said: "We shall hunt again tomorrow."

Sister was deeply distressed when she saw that her fawn had been wounded. She washed the blood off, sprinkled the wound with soothing herbs, and said: "Go get some sleep, dear little fawn, so that your leg will heal."

The wound was so slight that the fawn was completely restored by morning. When he heard the sounds of the hunt outdoors once again, he said: "I can't contain myself. I have to get back out there. They'll never catch me." Sister began weeping and said: "This time they'll kill you, and then I'll be all by myself in the woods, alone and forsaken. No, I can't let you go."

7. *"Will you come to my palace and become my wife?"* Fairy tales are known for love at first sight—think of the prince who falls in love with Snow White while she is lying in the coffin—but this proposal comes faster than usual. Since beauty also stands for virtue, appearances count for everything.

"If I don't go, I'll die of grief," the fawn answered. "Whenever I hear the sound of the hunting horns, I feel as if I just have to take off." Sister had no choice but to let him go, and she opened the door with a heavy heart. The fawn, back to his old self, bounded out happily into the woods.

When the king set eyes on the fawn, he said to the huntsmen: "I want you to hunt him all day long, even into the night. But don't let him come to any harm." As soon as the sun began setting, the king said to the huntsman: "Show me the little house in the forest that you found." When the king got to the hut, he knocked on the door and said: "Dear Little Sister, let me in." The door opened, and the king walked in and discovered the most beautiful girl he had ever seen. She was frightened when she saw that it was not her fawn, but a man wearing a golden crown, who had entered. The king looked at her tenderly, took her hand, and said: "Will you come to my palace and become my wife?"[7]

"Oh, yes," she said, "but the fawn must come with me. I won't ever leave him." The king said: "He can stay with you as long as you live, and he will get whatever he needs." Just then the fawn leaped into the house, and Sister tied the rope to his collar, took the rope in her hand, and led him out of the house in the forest.

The king rode with the beautiful woman to his castle, where the wedding was celebrated with a magnificent feast. They ruled as king and queen and lived together happily for many years. The fawn received the best treatment and had plenty of room to frolic around in the gardens of the palace.

Now the wicked stepmother, the woman who had driven the children out of their home into the world, was sure that Sister had been torn to bits by ferocious beasts in the forest and that Brother, after turning into a fawn, had been shot by huntsmen. When she discovered that they were both living in peace and prospering, envy and jealousy began to stir in her heart and gave her no peace. She was constantly trying to figure out how to turn the tide on the two, bringing misfortune on them. Her own daughter, who was ugly as sin and who had only one eye, kept grumbling: "She has all the luck, when I'm really the one who deserves to be queen!"

"Never mind," the old woman said, calming her down. "When the right time comes, I'll figure out how to make things different."

The right time did come,[8] and it was when the queen gave birth to a beautiful little boy, and the king was still out hunting when it happened. The old witch disguised herself as a chambermaid and walked into the room where the queen was resting and said to her: "Your bath is ready. Come quickly before the water gets cold. It will do you a world of good and give you the strength you need."

The old witch's daughter was there too, and she and her mother carried the frail queen into the bathroom, put her in the tub, locked the door, and ran away. In the room where she was bathing, they had left a fire smoldering so that the beautiful young queen would suffocate before long.

When that was done, the old woman took the queen's nightcap and put it on her own daughter and had her take the queen's place in bed. She then gave the girl the face and appearance of the queen, but she couldn't do anything about the missing eye. She just had to lie on the side where the eye was missing so that the king wouldn't notice that anything was wrong.

In the evening, when the king returned home and learned that his wife had given birth to a son, he was overjoyed and was about to go to his dear wife's bedside to see how she was faring when the old woman cried out suddenly: "Watch out! Don't open the curtains! It's still way too early to let light in, and the queen needs her rest." The king withdrew, and he had no idea that a false queen was lying in the bed.

At midnight, everyone was asleep but the nurse, who was keeping watch beside the cradle in the nursery. Suddenly the

8. *The right time did come.* In earlier ages, the high mortality rate for women in childbirth meant that the queen would be particularly vulnerable after the birth of a son.

door opened, and the real queen walked in. She took the baby out of the cradle, put it to her breast, and gave it milk. Then she plumped up the pillow, put the baby back in the crib, and tucked the little quilt in the corners. She didn't forget the fawn and went right to the corner where he was sleeping and stroked its back. Then she tiptoed her way out through the door. The next morning the nurse asked the guards if anybody had come into the castle at night, but they said: "No, we haven't seen a soul."

Night after night the queen came, but she never said a word. The nurse saw her, but she didn't dare mention it to anyone.

After some time had passed, the queen started talking when she came to visit, saying:

"Where's my child? Where's my fawn?
Two more times, and then I'm gone."

The nurse didn't answer her, but after she had vanished, she went to the king and told him about what had happened. The king said: "Dear God! What can be happening? Tonight I'll stay by my child's side and keep watch."

In the evening he went to the nursery, and at midnight the queen appeared and said:

"Where's my child? Where's my fawn?
One more time, and then I'm gone."

The queen took care of the baby as before, and then she disappeared. The king did not dare to address her, but he kept watch again the following night. She spoke once again:

"Where's my child? Where's my fawn?
After this, I'm really gone."

The king could not restrain himself. He jumped to his feet and said: "You really are my dear wife." She replied: "It's true, I am your wife," and with one stroke, by the grace of God, she came back to life, flush with good health. She told the king about the terrible things that the wicked witch and her daughter had done to her. The king had the two brought to trial, and their sentences were read. The daughter was taken into the woods where she was torn to bits by wild animals.[9] The witch burned miserably at the stake. After she had burned to ashes, the spell was broken, and Brother returned to his human shape. Little Sister and Little Brother lived happily together until the end of their days.

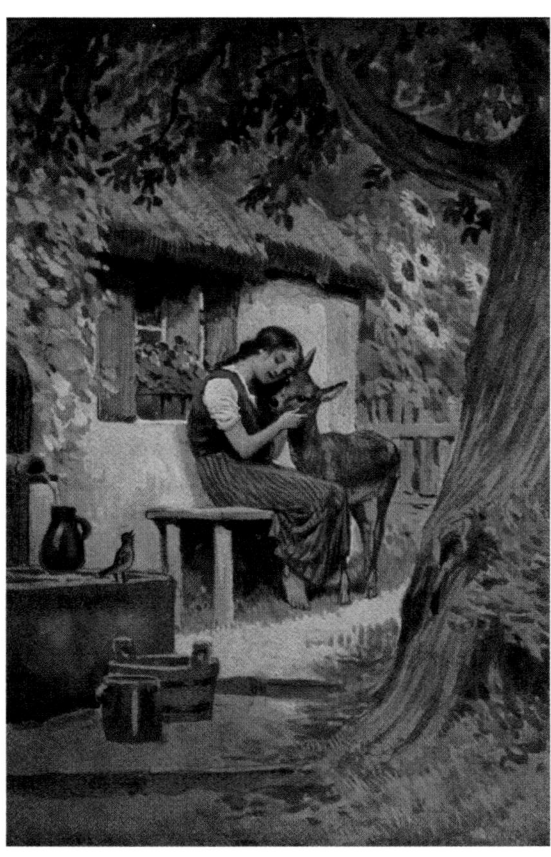

Paul Hey, *Die schönsten Kindermärchen der Brüder Grimm*

9. *The daughter was taken into the woods where she was torn to bits by wild animals.* Note that the daughter's punishment takes the form of one possible fate for the children, who end up in the woods and risk being attacked by wild animals. Brother's transformation also imperils Sister, for as a wolf or tiger, he would tear her to bits. The burning of the stepmother harks back to the plan to suffocate Sister with a fire smoldering in the room where she is bathing.

Rapunzel[1]

1. *Rapunzel.* Joyce Thomas points out that rapunzel, or rampion, is an autogamous plant, one that can fertilize itself. Furthermore, it has a column that splits in two if not fertilized, and "the halves will curl like braids or coils on a maiden's head, and this will bring the female stigmatic tissue into contact with the male pollen on the exterior surface of the column." Most versions of the story give the girl the name of a savory herb.

"Rachel Sommerville was captive. Not only was she practically imprisoned by her witch of an aunt in the Sommerville Towers, she was forced to sing for the San Franciscan hotel's guests." Linda Jones uses this line to entice readers to her romance novel Let Down Your Hair. *The story of a girl locked in a tower resonates powerfully in cultures that cloister young woman in convents, isolate them from society, segregate them from the male population, or police their behavior. It is a tale particularly rich in opportunities for bawdy humor, but its dominant form in our culture gives us the darker side to the plot, showing a young woman as the victim, first of parental thoughtlessness, then of her guardian's efforts to remove her from the social world.*

"The Maiden in the Tower," as "Rapunzel" is known to folklorists, has been thought to be based on the legend of Saint Barbara, who was locked by her father in a tower. In The Book of the City of Ladies *(1405), Christine de Pizan relates how Barbara's father shut her up in a tower for refusing marriage offers. But the story of Rapunzel seems rooted in a more general cultural tendency to "lock daughters up" and protect them from roving young men like the prince of the tale.*

"Rapunzel" unfolds in two acts, the first beginning with man, wife, and the desired rapunzel, which is forbidden and secured through a transgressive act (climbing over a wall). In the second phase of action, the child Rapunzel is kept in a tower forbidden to others. When the enchantress discovers the prince's transgression (scaling the wall of a tower), she punishes once again, this time with blindness. The conclusion reunites the separated partners, restores the prince's sight, and liquidates the forbidden desires that launched the narrative.

In "Rapunzel," as in "Rumpelstiltskin" and "Beauty and the Beast," an adult barters a child to secure personal welfare or security. This uneven exchange is presented in matter-of-fact terms, never interrogated or challenged in any way by the characters. It is, to be sure, a sign of desperation as well as a move that raises the stakes of the plot in a powerful way. Whereas the parents at the start of the story trade away the child in almost cavalier fashion, Mother Gothel figures as the consummate overprotective parent, isolating Rapunzel from human contact and keeping her prisoner in a tower that lacks both stairs and an exit. In the final tableau of the story, the power of love and compassion triumphs, and Rapunzel lives happily ever after with the prince and their twins. In some versions, as in the French "Godchild of the Fairy in the Tower," things end badly, with the fairy turning the Rapunzel figure into a frog and cursing the prince with a pig's snout. Much turns on the character of the maternal figure in the tale, who is presented as a wicked witch in some versions of the tale and as a benevolent guardian in other versions. Rapunzel's departure from the tower can be seen, depending on the character of the enchantress, as an act of clever resourcefulness or as an act of deep betrayal.

The first literary version of "The Maiden in the Tower" appeared in Giambattista Basile's Pentamerone *(1637). The name of Basile's heroine, Petrosinella, is derived from the word for parsley. Whereas the Grimms' "Rapunzel" moves in a dark register, with the heroine's exile and the blinding of the prince, Basile's version of the tale is sprightly, with humorous twists and bawdy turns. When*

the prince enters the tower, for example, he and Petrosinella at once become lovers: "Jumping in from the window into the room, he sated his desire, and ate of that sweet parsley sauce of love."

The Grimms based their "Rapunzel" on an eighteenth-century literary version by Friedrich Schulz, who in turn had borrowed from a French literary fairy tale published by Charlotte-Rose Caumant de La Force. Thus the Grimms' "Rapunzel" is a composite form, drawing elements from different cultures and social milieus.

Like many fairy-tale characters, Rapunzel has given her name to a syndrome, which Margaret Atwood defines in her analysis of the tale's characters: "Rapunzel, the main character; the wicked witch who has imprisoned her, usually her mother . . . ; the tower she's imprisoned in—the attitudes of the society, symbolized usually by her house and children . . . ; and the Rescuer, a handsome prince of little substantiality. . . . In the Rapunzel Syndrome the Rescuer is not much help." The best thing Rapunzel can do, according to Atwood, is to "learn how to cope." And cope she does, first in the wilderness with her twins, then when she encounters her beloved and restores his sight.

Rapunzel, Let Down Your Hair *is the title of a 1978 British film that begins with a reading of the Grimms' tale, then brings the story up to date with five different versions of the fairy tale.*

Once upon a time there lived a man and a woman[2] who, for many years, had been wishing for a child, but to no avail. One day the woman began to feel that God was going to grant their wish. In the back of the house where they lived, there was a little window that looked out onto a splendid garden, full of beautiful flowers and vegetables. A high wall surrounded the garden,[3] and no one dared enter it, because it

2. *Once upon a time there lived a man and a woman.* That the story will center on procreation becomes evident from its opening line. The story takes us, in a move that is unusual for fairy tales, from the birth of the heroine to the birth of her children, showing the risks attending pregnancy when the husband is present (as in the first birth) and when he is absent (as in the second birth).

3. *A high wall surrounded the garden.* Note that the garden, like the tower, is a forbidden site, and that both are enclosures for "rapunzel." Containment implies safety, but it also inhibits the satisfaction of desires.

belonged to a powerful enchantress,[4] who was feared by everyone around. One day the woman was looking out her window into the garden. Her eye lit on one patch in particular, which was planted with the finest rapunzel, a kind of lettuce. It looked so fresh and green that she was seized with a craving for it and just had to get some for her next meal. From day to day, her appetite grew, and she began to waste away because she was afraid she would never get any of it. When her husband saw how pale and wretched she had become, he asked: "What is the matter, dear wife?"

"If I don't get some of that rapunzel from the garden behind our house, I'm going to die," she replied.

Her husband loved her dearly and thought: "Rather than let my wife perish, I'll go get some of that rapunzel, no matter what the price."

As night was falling, he climbed over the wall into the garden of the enchantress,[5] hastily pulled up a handful of rapunzel, and brought it back to his wife. She made a salad out of it right away and devoured it with a ravenous appetite. The rapunzel tasted so good, so very good, that the next day her craving for it increased threefold. The only way the man could settle his wife down was to go back to the garden for more.

As night was falling, he returned, but after he climbed over the wall, he had an awful fright, for there was the enchantress, standing right in front of him. "How dare you sneak into my garden and take my rapunzel like a common thief?" she said with an angry look. "This is going to turn out badly for you."

"Oh, please," he replied, "show some mercy for my deed, for I did it only because I had to. My wife got a look at your rapunzel from our window. Her craving for it was so great that she said she would die if I did not get it for her."

The enchantress relented in her anger and said to the man: "If what you say is true, then I'm going to let you take as much rapunzel as you want back with you. But on one condition: You must hand over the child after your wife gives

4. *enchantress.* The Grimms initially described the proprietor of the garden as a "fairy," then changed her to an "enchantress." Some translations of the story into English change the enchantress into a "witch." In accordance with the ascendancy of the darker versions of the tale, the move from "fairy" to "witch" has a certain logic.

5. *he climbed over the wall into the garden of the enchantress.* The Grimms point out that some versions of "Rapunzel" begin with a different transgression, when the heroine, living with a witch, opens a door with a key forbidden to her. Behind the door, the girl catches a glimpse of the witch, with two huge horns on her head. As punishment, the girl is imprisoned in a tower.

birth.[6] I will take care of it like a mother, and it will not want for anything."

In his fright, the man agreed to everything. When it came time for the delivery, the enchantress appeared right away, gave the child the name Rapunzel, and whisked her away.

Rapunzel was the most beautiful child on earth. When she was twelve years old, the enchantress took her into the forest and locked her up in a tower that had neither stairs nor a door. At the very top of the tower was a tiny little window.[7] Whenever the enchantress wanted to get in, she stood at the foot of the tower and called out:

"Rapunzel, Rapunzel,
Let your hair down."

Rapunzel had long hair, as fine and as beautiful as spun gold.[8] Whenever she heard the voice of the enchantress, she would undo her braids, fasten them to a window latch, and let them fall twenty ells down, right to the ground. The enchantress would then climb up on them to get inside.

A few years later, it so happened that the son of a king was riding through the forest. He passed right by the tower and heard a voice so lovely that he stopped to listen. It was Rapunzel, who, all alone in the tower, was passing the time of day by singing sweet melodies to herself. The prince was hoping to go up to see her, and he searched around for a door to the tower, yet there was none. He rode home, but Rapunzel's voice had stirred his heart so powerfully that he went out into the forest every day to listen to her. Once when he was hiding behind a tree, he saw the enchantress come to the tower and heard her call up:

"Rapunzel, Rapunzel,
Let your hair down."

6. *"You must hand over the child after your wife gives birth."* Many cultures have legends about child-stealing witches or demons that hover around pregnant women, waiting for the opportunity to snatch an infant. The uneven exchange is not unusual in fairy tales, beginning with Jack's barter of a cow (the family's source of nourishment) for beans and on to the exchange exacted from Beauty's father, requiring him to relinquish his daughter for a rose.

7. *a tiny little window.* This window resembles the opening that looks down into the garden of the enchantress.

8. *as beautiful as spun gold.* Rapunzel's hair is a sign of her fairness in the double sense of the term. In fairy tales, golden hair is a marker of ethical goodness as well as aesthetic appeal.

Arthur Rackham, *Hansel and Gretel and Other Tales by the Brothers Grimm*

The enchantress climbs up the tower, using Rapunzel's golden tresses as a rope ladder. Although the enchantress's own hair is covered by a kerchief, her hands and feet remain bare. Note the pair of birds in the bottom foreground and how they make their nest near Rapunzel's window.

Rapunzel let down her braids, and the enchantress climbed up to her.

"If that is the ladder by which you climb up to the top of the tower, then I'd like to try my luck at it too," and the next day, when it was just starting to get dark, the prince went up to the tower and called out:

"Rapunzel, Rapunzel,
Let your hair down."

The braids fell right down, and the prince climbed up on them.

At first Rapunzel was terrified when she saw a man coming in through the window, especially since she had never seen one before. But the prince started talking with her in a kind way and told her that he had been so moved by her voice that he could not rest easy until he had set eyes on her. Soon, Rapunzel was no longer afraid, and when the prince, who was young and handsome, asked her if she wanted to marry him, she thought to herself: "He will be more loving than old Mother Gothel."[9] And so she said yes, put her hand in his, and said: "I want to get away from here with you, but I can't figure out how to get out of this tower. Every time you come to visit, bring a skein of silk with you, and I will braid a ladder from the silk. When it's finished, I'll climb down and you can take me with you on horseback."

The two agreed that he would visit her every evening,[10] for the old woman was there in the daytime. The enchantress didn't notice a thing until one day Rapunzel said to her: "Tell me, Mother Gothel, why are you so much harder to pull up than the young prince.[11] He gets up here in a twinkling."

"Wicked child!" shouted the enchantress. "What have you done? I thought I had shut you off from the rest of the world, but you betrayed me."

Flying into a rage, she seized Rapunzel's beautiful hair,

9. *Mother Gothel.* The term is a generic one in Germany, designating a woman who serves as godmother.

10. *The two agreed that he would visit her every evening.* Persinette, the French Rapunzel, invites the prince up to the tower so that she can make love to him. When a pet parrot threatens to divulge her secret to the fairy, she sews up his rear end so that all he can say is "Ass stitched, ass stitched." When the two escape, the fairy, in retaliation, changes Persinette's nose into the nose of an ass, but eventually she relents and restores her beauty.

11. *"Tell me, Mother Gothel, why are you so much harder to pull up than the young prince."* In the first version of the Grimms' *Children's Stories and Household Tales,* Rapunzel asks the enchantress why her clothes are getting so tight and don't fit any longer. The allusion to the fact that the daily meetings with the prince in the tower have led to pregnancy was considered inappropriate for children.

wound the braids around her left hand, and grabbed a pair of scissors with her right. Snip, snap went the scissors, and the beautiful tresses fell to the ground. The enchantress was so hard-hearted that she banished poor Rapunzel to a wilderness, where she had to live in a miserable, wretched state.

Kay Nielsen, *Hansel and Gretel and Other Stories by the Brothers Grimm*

With scissors in hand, the enchantress prepares to cut off Rapunzel's hair. Above Rapunzel's head is a caged bird which serves as a sign of her captive state.

On the very day she had sent Rapunzel away, the enchantress fastened the severed braids to the window latch, and when the prince came and called out

"Rapunzel, Rapunzel,
Let your hair down."

she let down the hair.

The prince climbed up, but instead of finding his precious Rapunzel, the enchantress was waiting for him with an angry, poisonous look in her eye. "Ha," she shouted triumphantly. "You want to come get your darling little wife,[12] but the beautiful bird is no longer sitting in the nest, singing her songs. The cat caught her, and before she's done, she's going to scratch out your eyes too. Rapunzel is lost to you forever. You will never see her again."

The prince was beside himself with grief, and in his despair he jumped from the top of the tower. He was still alive, but his eyes were scratched out by the bramble patch into which he had fallen. He wandered around in the forest, unable to see anything. Roots and berries were the only thing he could find to eat, and he spent his time weeping and wailing over the loss of his dear wife.

The prince wandered around in misery for many years[13] and finally reached the wilderness where Rapunzel was just barely managing to survive with the twins—a boy and a girl—to whom she had given birth. The prince heard a voice that sounded familiar to him, and so he followed it. When he came within sight of the person singing, Rapunzel recognized him. She threw her arms around him and wept. Two of those tears dropped into the prince's eyes,[14] and suddenly he could see as before, with clear eyes.

The prince went back to his kingdom with Rapunzel, and there was great rejoicing. They lived in happiness and good cheer for many, many years.

12. *wife.* Rapunzel becomes a "wife" because the Grimms did not want to suggest that Rapunzel's twins were born out of wedlock.

13. *The prince wandered around in misery for many years.* Neither Rapunzel nor the prince actively seeks out the other. Instead they seem ordained to meet again after a certain period of time has elapsed. Basile's "Petrosinella" ends quite differently, with the pair using magic to prevent the ogress of the tale from gaining on them. The heroine and the prince throw acorns behind them as they flee. The first acorn turns into a Corsican hound which is about to make a meal out of the ogress when she appeases him by tossing some bread behind her; the second acorn turns into a ferocious lion which is about to gobble up the ogress when she slips into an ass's skin and scares him; the third acorn turns into a wolf, which swallows up the ogress (who has not had the chance to shed her skin), "as if she were an ass."

14. *Two of those tears dropped into the prince's eyes.* Rapunzel's hair provided the means for building a connection to the outside world; now her tears produce a healing effect, showing the power of the body to effect transformation. In fairy tales, affect is always expressed in outer terms, and the tears are a visible sign of the wife's intensity of feeling for her husband.

The Three Little Men in the Woods

This tale, like "Mother Holle," tells of the rewards and punishments distributed to kind girls and unkind girls. But it also offers an excellent example of the way in which natural forces and the elements enter into the fairy-tale world, flowing with the events and moving them along or providing cross-currents and points of resistance. If wind and fire play a powerful role in some tales, water dominates "The Three Little Men in the Woods." The tale begins when water seemingly defies the laws of nature and fails to flow through a hole in a boot, and it ends when the villain is thrown into a barrel that rolls down a hill into a river. Snow, ice, streams, water for baths, and drinking water figure importantly in the remainder of the narrative. "The Three Little Men in the Woods" reveals how fairy tales, much as they engage with the nuclear family and with the question of how to find a way home, are rooted in a pagan world, one that is oriented toward fire, water, wind, the sun, the moon, and the stars. These cosmic forces are central to the fate of the hero, and they often shape the course of events in ways that escape our attention.

Ruth B. Bottigheimer has pointed out that "nature flourishes in the tales: birds flutter through the pages, prophesying, assisting,

1. *"you can bathe in milk every morning and drink wine."* This is the first in a series of motifs that draws on fluids, here water and wine, to construct the story. The fluids that bathe the body and that enter the body are seen as key to the formation of social identity.

guiding, and suffering; animals speak and are understood; winds respond and trees bend to incantations. The sun, moon, and stars sparkle above, fires crackle and waters of all kinds flow below on earth." "The Three Little Men in the Woods" shows the interaction between humans and nature, with the "little men," or gnomes, occupying a liminal position, mediating between man and nature.

nce there was a man whose wife had died, and there was a woman whose husband had died. The man had a daughter, and the woman also had a daughter. The girls knew each other, and one day they decided to take a walk and ended up at the woman's house. The woman said to the man's daughter: "Listen to me. If you tell your father that I'm interested in marrying him, I promise that you can bathe in milk every morning and drink wine[1] every day. My daughter will have to drink water and wash in water."

The girl went home and told her father what the woman had said. The man replied: "What should I do? Marriage can be a joy, but it can also be torture." Finally, when he couldn't make up his mind, he took one boot off and said: "Here, take this boot. There's a hole right in its sole. Take it up to the attic, hang it up on a big nail, and then pour some water into it. If it holds water, then I'll take a wife. If it runs out, I won't." The girl did as she was told, and it turned out that the water made the sides of the hole contract, and the boot filled up to the rim. The girl told her father what had happened. He went up the stairs to see for himself, and when he realized that it was all just as she described it, he went over to see the widow, courted her, and the wedding was celebrated.

The next morning, when the two girls woke up, the husband's daughter had milk to bathe in and wine to drink, but the wife's daughter had only water to bathe in and water to drink. The next morning there was water to bathe in and water to drink for both the husband's daughter and the wife's daughter. On the third morning there was water to bathe in and water to drink for the husband's daughter and milk to bathe in and wine to drink for the wife's daughter, and that's how things stayed. The woman grew hostile to her stepdaughter and racked her brains thinking of ways to make her life miserable. She was envious too, for her stepdaughter was beautiful and kind, while her own daughter was ugly and nasty.

Once on a winter day, when the ground was frozen solid, and hill and dale were blanketed with snow,[2] the woman made a dress out of paper, called the girl over, and said: "Here, put this dress on. I want you to go out into the woods and fetch me a little basket of strawberries. I've got a real craving for them."

"My goodness," the girl said. "There won't be any berries out there at this time of year. The ground is frozen, and there's a blanket of snow covering everything. And why should I put on this dress made of paper? It's so cold outside that your breath freezes in the air. The wind will blow right through me, and thorns will tear the dress into pieces."

"Why are you talking back to me?" the stepmother said. "Just get out of here and don't show your face until that basket is full of strawberries." She gave the girl a crust of hard bread and said: "You can chew on that for the rest of the day." She was thinking to herself: "Once she's out there, she'll be freezing and will end up starving to death. I'll never have to set eyes on her again!"

The girl was completely obedient, and after putting on the dress made of paper, she went out the door with her little basket. There was nothing but snow as far as the eye could see—not a blade of grass in sight. When she got to the forest, she found a tiny cottage, with three dwarfs peering out the

2. *the ground was frozen solid, and hill and dale were blanketed with snow.* The basket of strawberries stands in sharp contrast to the snow and ice outdoors. The stepmother proposes an impossible task, one that runs counter to the laws of nature operating during winter.

windows. She bade them good morning and knocked gently at their door. "Come in!" they called, and she walked into the parlor and sat down on a bench near the oven. She was hoping to warm herself up and to eat some breakfast. The dwarfs said to her: "Give us a piece of what you have."

"Gladly," she said, and she broke the crust of bread in two and gave them half of it. They asked her: "What are you doing wearing that thin little dress here in the woods at this time of year?"

"Oh," she replied, "I'm supposed to pick a little basket of strawberries, and I'm not allowed to go home until I've got it."

When she had eaten her bread, the dwarfs gave her a broom and said: "Sweep the snow away from the back door." While she was outside, the three little men conferred: "What should we give her for being so good and kind and sharing her bread with us?"

The first said: "My gift will be that she becomes more beautiful with each passing day."[3]

The second said: "My gift will be that gold pieces shall fall from her mouth whenever she says a word."

The third said: "My gift will be that a king will come and make her his wife."

The girl did exactly what the dwarfs told her to do, and she used the broom to sweep the snow from the back of the cottage. But what do you think she found while she was sweeping? Lots of ripe strawberries looking bright red in the snow. With great relief she picked a basketful, thanked the little men, and shook hands with each one of them. Then she ran straight home and was hoping to give her stepmother what she wanted.

When the girl walked into the house and said "Good evening," a piece of gold fell from her mouth. Then she told everyone what had happened in the woods, and as she spoke, pieces of gold continued to fall from her mouth so that before long the parlor was filled with them.

3. *"My gift will be that she becomes more beautiful with each passing day."* Like the Wise Women at Briar Rose's christening, these three little men have magical powers that allow them to endow the girl with beauty, wealth, and good fortune.

Arthur Rackham, *Little Brother and Little Sister and Other Tales by the Brothers Grimm*

Sweeping snow from the path, the heroine of a tale about kind and unkind girls discovers the ripe strawberries she needs to fulfill her stepmother's demand for fruit in the wintertime.

"How arrogant!" her stepsister cried. "Throwing money around like that!" Secretly she was, of course, envious and was hoping that she too could go out into the forest in search of strawberries. Her mother said: "No, my dear little daughter. It's much too cold. You'll freeze to death." But when the girl would not stop asking, she finally gave her consent and made a beautiful fur coat for her. She put it on, and her mother also gave her sandwiches and a cake to take with her.

The girl went into the woods and walked straight to the cottage. The three little dwarfs were looking out the window as before. But instead of saying good morning and without giving them so much as a glance or saying hello, she stumbled into the cottage, sat down at the oven, and began eating a sandwich and some cake.

"Will you share that with us?" the little men cried.

The girl responded: "It's really not enough for me. How can I possibly share this with anyone?"

When she finished eating, the men said: "Here's a broom for you. Sweep the snow away from the back door for us."

"Go sweep it yourself," she said. "I'm not your maid." When she realized that they were not going to give her anything, she went out the door. The little men conferred: "Why should we give her anything, when she behaves so badly and has a wicked, selfish heart, never giving anything away."

The first one said: "My gift is that she will become uglier with each passing day."

The second one said: "My gift is that a toad will jump out of her mouth whenever she speaks."

The third said: "My gift is that she will find an unhappy end."

The girl went searching outside for strawberries, but when she couldn't find any, she was irritated and returned home. When she opened her mouth to tell her mother what had happened out there in the woods, a toad jumped out of her mouth at every word. It didn't take long for everyone to learn to stay away from her.

The stepmother was more annoyed than ever, and all she could do was think about how to inflict pain on her husband's daughter, who was turning more beautiful every day. Finally she took a kettle, put it on the fire, and boiled yarn in it. When the yarn was boiled, she threw it over the girl's shoulder, gave her an ax, and told her to chop a hole in the frozen ice of the river and then to rinse the yarn. She was an obedient child, and she went over and cut a hole in the ice. While she was hacking away, a splendid carriage drove by, and a king was seated in it. The carriage came to a halt, and the king asked: "My child, what's your name and what are you doing over there?"

"I'm a poor girl, and I'm rinsing yarn."

The king took pity on her, and when he saw how beautiful she was, he said: "Do you want to ride in my carriage?"

"With all my heart," she replied, for she was happy to get away from her mother and her sister.

The girl got into the carriage and drove off with the king. When she arrived at his castle, their marriage was celebrated with great splendor, for the little men had given her that as a gift. A year later, the young queen gave birth to a boy, and when the stepmother learned of her great happiness, she went with her daughter to the castle and pretended that she was there to visit.

One day the king left the castle, and no one else was at home when the evil woman grabbed the queen by her head, and her daughter grabbed her by the feet. They lifted her out of her bed and threw her out the window into a river that flowed past the castle. Then the old woman put the ugly girl into the bed, and she tucked her in right up over her head. When the king returned home and wanted to go talk to his wife, the old woman said: "Hush, hush, you can't see her now. She's got a fever, and you'll have to let her rest today."

The king was not at all suspicious, and he returned the next day. When he started talking with his wife, a toad—instead of the usual gold piece—dropped out of her mouth whenever she said a word in reply. He asked what was wrong with her, and the old woman said it was just the high fever and that it would soon go away.

That night, the kitchen boy saw a duck swimming along in the drainage canal,[4] and the duck spoke these words:

"Your Royal Highness, what's the news?
Are you awake? Do you know of the ruse?"

When he didn't answer, the duck said:

"What are my guests doing today?"

The kitchen boy replied:

"They're sleeping soundly while you're away."

Then she asked:

"And my child, is he asleep?"

He answered:

"He's napping now, there's not a peep."

Then the duck turned into the queen, nursed the child, plumped up his bed, tucked him in, and swam back down the drainage canal, after turning back into a duck. She came two nights in a row, and on the third she said to the kitchen boy: "Go and tell the king that he must take his sword and swing it over me three times when I cross the threshold."

The kitchen boy ran to tell the king, who came with his

4. *the kitchen boy saw a duck swimming along in the drainage canal.* The girl's ability to transform herself into a creature of nature can be traced to the wishes of the three little men, who bestow good fortune on her. She possesses the ability to become a creature in nature, to be at home in the waters, but she also is able to give the instructions that lead to her transformation back to human form. The king's sword becomes the wand that reverses her metamorphosis.

sword and swung it three times over the ghost. The third time his wife stood before him: alive, healthy, and energetic, just as she had been before.

The king was elated, but he kept the queen hidden in the bedroom until that Sunday, when the child was to be christened.[5] And after the child had been christened, he asked: "What punishment should be given to a person who drags someone out of their bed and throws them into the water?"

The old woman replied: "The scoundrel should be put into a barrel studded with nails and rolled down a hill into the water."

The king said: "You have pronounced your own sentence," and he sent for a barrel like the one she had described and put the woman with her daughter into it. The lid was hammered tight, and the barrel went rolling down the hill and fell into the river.

Hermann Vogel, *Kinder- und Hausmärchen gesammelt durch die Brüder Grimm*

5. *when the child was to be christened.* The mention of the christening produces some friction with the pagan elements in the story. Although the story endorses kindness, hard work, and other virtues, it lacks a religious foundation and seems more invested in the power of nature than in the power of prayer.

Hansel and Gretel[1]

1. *Hansel and Gretel.* This tale was originally known as "Little Brother and Little Sister." The Grimms note similarities to Perrault's "Tom Thumb," in which a woodcutter and his wife abandon their seven sons in the woods.

"*ansel and Gretel" is a story that celebrates the triumph of children over hostile, predatory adults. Addressing anxieties about starvation, abandonment, and being devoured, it shows two young siblings joining forces to defeat monsters at home and in the woods. Folklorists refer to this and other stories pitting young, powerless protagonists against cruel brutes as "The Children and the Ogre." A child or a group of children innocently enter the abode of an ogre, wicked witch, giant, or other type of villain, succeed in turning the tables on a bloodthirsty antagonist, and flee, often with material goods in the form of jewels or gold.*

In their annotations to "Hansel and Gretel," the Grimms point out that it is not always a witch who inhabits the "house made of sugar." In a Swabian version of the tale, a wolf lures the children to his abode. The Grimms correctly point out that Hansel bears a close resemblance to Tom Thumb, who succeeds in rescuing his six siblings from an ogre. They also call attention to Madame d'Aulnoy's "Finette Cendron," in which a trio of girls with royal parentage is saved by the resourcefulness of the youngest.

Sibling solidarity is so rare in fairy tales (think of the sisters in

"Cinderella") that "Hansel and Gretel" provides a unique opportunity for displaying its advantages. Whereas Hansel takes the lead at the beginning of the tale, soothing Gretel's fears and using his wits to find the way back home, Gretel outsmarts the witch, tricking her into entering the oven. The siblings in the Grimms' version of "The Children and the Ogre" may be somewhat pious for modern sensibilities, but they were youthful insurgents by nineteenth-century standards, eavesdropping on their parents' nighttime conversations, deploying a ruse to get back home, greedily feasting on the house of the witch, and running off with the witch's jewels after Gretel pushes her into the oven. Determined to find a way back home, Hansel and Gretel survive what children fear more than anything else: abandonment by parents and exposure to predators.

In Engelbert Humperdinck's 1893 operatic version of the story, the children, who are sent into the woods to collect berries as a punishment for neglecting their chores, end up liberating themselves and also lifting the spell that transformed many other children into gingerbread. A happy ending reunites the children with both parents.

t the edge of a great forest, there once lived a poor woodcutter with his wife and two children.[2] The little boy was called Hansel, and the girl was named Gretel. There was never much to eat in their home, and once, during a time of famine,[3] the woodcutter could no longer put bread on the table. At night, he lay in bed worrying, tossing and turning in despair. With a deep sigh, he turned to his wife and said: "What is going to become of us? How can we possibly take care of our poor little children when the two of us don't have enough to eat?"

"Listen to me," his wife replied. "Tomorrow, at the crack

2. *a poor woodcutter with his wife and two children.* In early versions of the tale, the woodcutter and his wife are the biological parents of the children. By the fourth edition of the *Children's Stories and Household Tales* in 1840, the Grimms had turned the "wife" into a "stepmother" and made her the real villain of the piece. Although the father shares the blame for abandoning the children in the woods in early versions of the tales (as in Perrault's "Tom Thumb"), in later versions he protests the actions of his wife, even if without success. As P. L. Travers has pointed out, "the true mother, by her very nature, is bound to preserve, protect and comfort; this is why she is so often disposed of before the story begins. It is the stepmother, her cold heart unwittingly cooperating with the hero's need, who thrusts the child from the warm hearth, out from the sheltering walls of home to find his own true way."

3. *during a time of famine.* Historians tell us that fairy tales originated in an age marked by wars, plague, and famine. As Robert Darnton puts it, "great masses of people lived in a state of chronic malnutrition, subsisting mainly on porridge made of bread and water with some occasional, homegrown vegetables thrown in."

4. *"Wild beasts are sure to find them and tear them to pieces."* The fear of being torn to pieces by wild beasts haunts the minds of fairy-tale characters. It also occasionally serves as the punishment for villains who have exposed fairy-tale protagonists to woodland predators.

5. *glittering like silver coins.* The coinlike pebbles are reminiscent of the star-coins in the Grimms' tale of that title. The pebbles, like the star-coins, are heaven-sent and signal the possibility of salvation, even if only temporary.

6. *"God won't abandon us."* This reference, along with other religious allusions, was added to the second edition of the tales by the Grimms.

of dawn, let's take the children down into the deepest part of the forest. We'll make a fire for them out there and give them each a crust of bread. Then we'll go about our work, leaving them all by themselves. They'll never find their way back home, and we'll be rid of them."

"Oh, no," her husband said. "How could I ever do that! I don't have the heart to leave the children all alone in the woods. Wild beasts are sure to find them and tear them to pieces."[4]

"You fool," his wife replied. "Then all four of us can starve to death. You might as well start sanding the boards for our coffins."

The wife didn't give her husband a moment of peace until he finally agreed to her plan. "But still, I feel sorry for the poor children," he said.

The children had not slept a wink because they were so hungry, and they didn't miss a single word of what their stepmother had said to their father. Gretel wept bitter tears and said to her brother: "Well, now we've had it."

"Hush, Gretel," said Hansel, "and stop worrying. I'll figure something out."

When the old folks fell asleep, Hansel got up, put on his little jacket, opened the bottom half of the Dutch door, and slipped outside. The moon was shining brightly, and in front of the house there were some white pebbles, glittering like silver coins.[5] Hansel stooped down to pick them up and put as many as would fit into his jacket pocket. Then he returned to Gretel and said: "Don't worry, little sister. Just go to sleep. God won't abandon us."[6] And he went back to bed.

At daybreak, just as the sun was rising, the wife came in and woke the two children up. "Get up, you lazybones. We're going out to the forest to find some wood."

The wife gave each child a crust of bread and said: "Here's something for lunch. But don't eat it before then. That's all you'll be getting."

Wanda Gág, *Tales from Grimm*

The evil stepmother leads the way into the woods, while the siblings' woodcutter father follows. Hansel strews pebbles on the path, and Gretel trudges forward with provisions tucked in her arms.

Gretel put the bread in her apron pocket because Hansel already had the pebbles in his jacket pocket. Together they set out on the path into the forest. While they were walking, Hansel kept stopping and looking back at the house. Finally, his father said: "Hansel, why do you keep lagging behind and turning to look back home? Watch out for yourself, and don't forget what your legs were made for."

"Oh, Father," said Hansel. "I'm trying to get a last look at my little white kitten, which is perched up on the roof trying to bid me farewell."

The woman said: "You fool, that's not your kitten. Those are just the rays of the sun, shining on the chimney."

But Hansel had not been looking for his kitten. He had been taking the shiny pebbles from his pocket and dropping them on the ground.

When they reached the middle of the forest, the father said: "Go gather some wood, children. I'll build a fire so that you won't get cold."

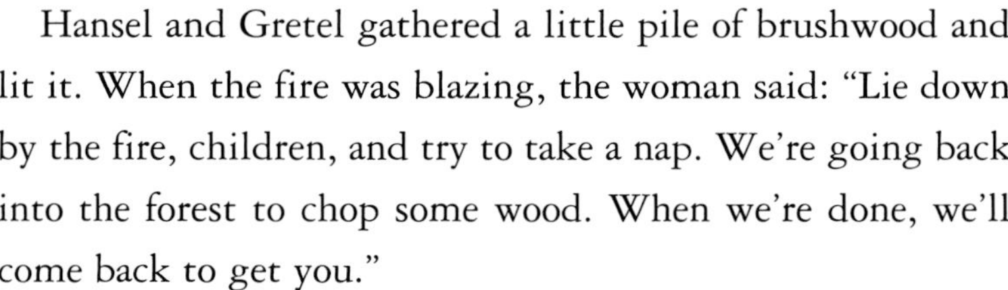

Hansel and Gretel gathered a little pile of brushwood and lit it. When the fire was blazing, the woman said: "Lie down by the fire, children, and try to take a nap. We're going back into the forest to chop some wood. When we're done, we'll come back to get you."

Hansel and Gretel sat down by the fire. At noontime they ate their crusts of bread. Since they could hear the sounds of an ax they were sure that their father was nearby. But it wasn't an ax that they heard, it was a branch that their father had fastened to a dead tree, and the wind was banging it back and forth. They had been sitting there for so long that finally their eyes closed from sheer exhaustion, and they fell fast asleep. When they awoke, it was pitch dark. Gretel began crying and said: "How will we ever get out of the woods!"

Hansel comforted her: "Just wait until the moon comes out. Then we'll find our way back."

When the moon came out, Hansel took his sister by the hand and followed the pebbles, which were shimmering like newly minted coins and pointing the way back home for them. They walked all night long and got to their father's house just as day was breaking. They knocked at the door, and when the woman opened and saw that it was Hansel and Gretel, she said: "You wicked children! Why were you sleeping so long in the woods? We thought you were never going to come back."

The father was overjoyed, for he had been very upset about abandoning the children in the forest.

Not long after that, every square inch of the country was stricken by famine, and one night the children could hear the mother[7] talking with their father after they had gone to bed: "We've eaten everything up again. All that's left is half a loaf of bread, and when that's gone, we're finished. The children have to go. This time we'll take them deeper into the forest so that they won't be able to find a way out. Otherwise there's no hope for us."

7. *the mother.* That the stepmother is twice referred to as a mother by the Grimms suggests that the stepmothers of fairy tales are proxies for biological mothers.

All this weighed heavily on the husband's heart, and he thought: "It would be better if we shared the last crust of bread with the children." But the woman would not listen to anything he said. She did nothing but nag and find fault. In for a penny, in for a pound, and since he had given in the first time, he also had to give in a second time.

The children were still awake and heard the entire conversation. When their parents had fallen asleep, Hansel got up and wanted to go out and pick up some pebbles as he had done before, but the woman had locked the door, and Hansel couldn't get out. Hansel comforted his sister and said: "Don't cry, Gretel. Just get some sleep. The good Lord will protect us."

Early the next morning the woman came and woke the children up. They each got a crust of bread, this time even smaller than last time. On the way into the woods, Hansel crushed the bread in his pocket and stopped from time to time to scatter crumbs on the ground.

"Hansel, why do you keep looking back and lagging behind?" asked the father. "Keep on walking."

"I'm looking at my little dove, the one sitting on the roof and trying to say good-bye to me," Hansel replied.

"You fool," said the woman. "That isn't your little dove. Those are the rays of the morning sun shining on the chimney."

Little by little, Hansel managed to scatter all the crumbs on the path.

The woman took the children deeper into the forest, to a place where they had never been before. Once again a large fire was built, and the mother said: "Don't move away from here, children. If you get tired, you can nap for a while. We're going to go into the forest to chop some wood. In the evening, when we're done, we'll come to get you."

It was noontime, and Gretel shared her bread with Hansel, who had used up his bread when he scattered crumbs on the

path. Then they fell asleep. The evening went by, but no one came to get the poor children. They awoke when it was pitch dark, and Hansel comforted his sister by saying: "Just wait until the moon comes out, Gretel. Then we'll be able to see the crumbs of bread I strewed on the path. They will point the way home for us."

When the moon came out, they left for home, but they couldn't find any of the crumbs because the many thousands of birds flying around in the forest and across the fields had eaten them. Hansel said to Gretel: "We'll find the way back," but they couldn't find it. They walked all night long and then on into the next day from early in the morning until late at night. But they couldn't find their way out of the woods, and they got hungrier and hungrier, for there was nothing to eat but a few berries that they found scattered on the ground. When their legs could no longer carry them and they were completely exhausted, they lay down under a tree and fell asleep.

Three days had passed since they had left their father's house. They started walking again but just got deeper and deeper into the woods. If help didn't arrive soon, they were sure to perish. At noontime they saw a beautiful bird, white as snow, perched on a branch. It was singing so sweetly that they stopped to listen to it. When it had finished its song, it flapped its wings and flew on ahead of them. They followed the bird, which led them to a little house, and the bird perched right up on the roof.[8] When they got closer to the house, they realized it was made of bread and that the roof was made of cake and the windows of sparkling sugar.[9]

"Let's have a taste," Hansel said. "May the Lord bless our meal. I'll try a piece of the roof, Gretel, and you can taste the window. That's sure to be sweet." Hansel reached up and broke off a small piece of the roof to see whether it was any good. Gretel went over to the windowpane and nibbled on it. Suddenly a gentle voice called from inside:

8. *They followed the bird which led them to a little house, and the bird perched right up on the roof.* The beautiful white bird that leads the children to danger at the witch's house stands in contrast to the white duck that carries the siblings across the lake to safety.

9. *sparkling sugar.* Bruno Bettelheim claims that "Hansel and Gretel" is a story about the oral greed of children. In his view, the tale enacts childhood feelings of hostility to the omnipotent mother, who, in her role as supreme provider, is always also the withholder of nourishment. By the end of the story, the children have mastered their "oral anxieties" and learned that "wishful thinking has to be replaced by intelligent action." By implying that the children in the story are "greedy," Bettelheim produces a one-sided interpretation that exonerates the adults and suggests that the real source of evil in the story is nothing more than an alter ego of the children.

Wanda Gág, *Tales from Grimm*

Hansel and Gretel make their way through woods that are adorned with a variety of decorative trees. Gretel nearly molds herself to her brother, who leads the way.

Wanda Gág, *Tales from Grimm*

In a clearing, the children discover the quaint and charming house of gingerbread, where a cat guards the front door. Only the arched back of the cat signals that there might be anything sinister behind the door.

"Nibble, nibble, where's the mouse?
Who's that nibbling at my house?"

The children replied:

"The wind so mild,
The heavenly child."

They continued eating, without being in the least distracted. Hansel, who liked the taste of the roof, tore off a big piece. Gretel knocked out an entire windowpane and sat down on the ground to savor it. Suddenly the door opened, and a woman as old as the hills,[10] leaning on a crutch, hobbled

10. *a woman as old as the hills.* The term "wicked witch" was not used in the first version of the story, nor was there much elaboration of the witch's physical appearance. Witches are not common in the Grimms' collection, but the witch from this particular story has taken on a representative importance.

out. Hansel and Gretel were so terrified that they dropped everything in their hands. The old woman wagged her head and said: "Well, dear little children. How in the world did you get here? Just come right in. You can stay with me, and no harm will come to you in my house."

She took them by the hand and led them into her little house. A fine meal of milk and pancakes, with sugar, apples, and nuts, was set before them. A little later, two beautiful little beds were made up for them with white sheets. Hansel and Gretel lay down in them and felt as if they were in heaven.

The old woman had only pretended to be kind. She was really a wicked witch, who waylaid little children and had built the house of bread just to get them inside. As soon as a child fell into her hands, she killed it, cooked it, and ate it. That meant a day of real feasting for her. Witches have red eyes and can't see very far, but like animals, they do have a keen sense of smell, and they can always tell when a human being is around. When Hansel and Gretel got near her, she laughed fiendishly and hissed: "They're mine! This time they won't get away!" Early in the morning, before the children were up, she got out of bed and gazed at the two of them sleeping so peacefully with their soft red cheeks. And she muttered quietly to herself: "They will make a tasty little morsel."

She grabbed Hansel with her scrawny arm, took him off to a little shed, and closed the barred door on him. Hansel could cry all he wanted, it didn't do him any good. Then she went back to Gretel, shook her until she was awake, and shouted: "Get up, lazybones. Go get some water and cook your brother something good to eat. He's staying out there in the shed until he's put on some weight. When he's nice and fat, I'll eat him up."

Gretel began crying as loud as she could, but it did no good at all. She had to do whatever the wicked witch told her. The finest food was cooked for poor Hansel, and Gretel got

Arthur Rackham, *Hansel and Gretel and Other Tales by the Brothers Grimm*

Hansel and Gretel cautiously approach a witch who, with her crutches, bent back, and bulbous nose, hovers over the children as a threatening presence. A barefoot Hansel takes the lead, while Gretel stands in her brother's shadow.

nothing but crab shells. Every morning the old woman would slink over to the little shed and shout: "Hansel, hold out your finger so that I can tell if you're plump enough."

Hansel would stick a little bone through the bars, and the old woman, who had poor eyesight, believed that it was Hansel's finger and couldn't figure out why he wasn't putting on weight. When a month had gone by and Hansel was still as scrawny as ever, she lost her patience and decided that she couldn't wait any longer. "Hey there, Gretel," she shouted at the girl. "Go get some water and be quick about it. I don't care whether Hansel's lean or plump. Tomorrow I'm going to butcher him, and then I'll cook him up for dinner."

The poor little sister sobbed with grief, and tears flowed down her cheeks. "Dear God, help us," she cried out. "If only the wild animals in the forest had eaten us up, at least then we would have died together."

"Spare me your blubbering!" the old woman said. "Nothing can help you now."

Early the next morning, Gretel had to go fill the kettle with water and light the fire. "First we'll do some baking," the old woman said. "I've already heated up the oven and kneaded the dough."

She pushed poor Gretel over to the oven, from which flames were leaping. "Crawl in," said the witch, "and see if it's hot enough to slide the bread in."

The witch was planning to shut the door as soon as Gretel got into the oven. Then she was going to bake her and eat her up too. But Gretel saw what was on her mind and said: "I don't know how to crawl in there! How in the world can I manage that?"

"Silly goose," the old woman said. "There's enough room. Just look, I can get in," and she scrambled over to the oven and stuck her head in it. Gretel gave her a big shove that sent her sprawling. Then she shut the iron door and bolted it.

Phew! The witch began screeching dreadfully. But Gretel ran off, and the godless witch burned to death in a horrible way.[11]

Gretel ran straight to Hansel, opened the door to the little shed, and shouted: "Hansel, we're saved! The old witch is dead."

Like a bird fleeing its cage,[12] Hansel flew out the door as soon as it opened. How thrilled they were: they hugged and kissed and jumped up and down for joy! Since there was nothing more to fear, they went right into the witch's house. In every corner there were chests filled with pearls and jewels. "These are even better than pebbles," said Hansel and put what he could into his pockets.[13]

Gretel said, "I'll take some home too," and she filled up her little apron.

"Let's get going right now," said Hansel. "We have to get out of this witch's forest."

After walking for several hours, they reached a lake. "We won't be able to get across," said Hansel. "There's not a bridge in sight."

"There aren't any boats around either," Gretel said, "but here comes a white duck. She will help us cross, if I ask." She shouted:

"Help us, help us, little duck,
Swim to us, then we're in luck.
Nary a bridge here, far or wide,
Help us, give us both a ride."

The duck came paddling over. Hansel got on its back and told his sister to sit down next to him. "No," said Gretel, "that would be too heavy a load for the little duck. She can take us over one at a time."

That's just what the good little creature did. When they were brought safely to the other side and had walked on for

11. *the godless witch burned to death in a horrible way.* The punishment of the witch has been read as a portent of the horrors of the Third Reich. That the witch is often represented as a figure with stereotypical Jewish traits, particularly in twentieth-century illustrations, makes this scene all the more ominous. In her rewriting of "Hansel and Gretel," the poet Anne Sexton refers to the abandonment of the children as a "final solution."

12. *Like a bird fleeing its cage.* Birds figure prominently in this story, first as the imaginary dove on the rooftop, next as creatures who devour the bread crumbs sprinkled on the path by Hansel, then as the beautiful bird that leads the children to the witch's house, and finally as the white duck carrying the siblings across the water. As representatives of nature, they ensure that the children remain in the woods, yet they also provide means for their escape.

13. *put what he could into his pockets.* Like Jack in "Jack and the Beanstalk," Hansel and Gretel feel no qualms about appropriating the riches of the witch and taking the jewels back home to their father. The "perfect happiness" of the ending is brought about in part by the acquisition of material wealth, which guarantees that the father and children will live happily ever after.

some time, the woods began to look more and more familiar. Finally they could see their father's house in the distance. They began running, and they raced right into the house, throwing their arms around their father. The man had not had a happy hour since the day that he had abandoned his children in the forest. His wife had died.[14] Gretel emptied her apron, and pearls and jewels rolled all over the floor. Hansel reached into his pockets and pulled out one handful of jewels after another. Their worries were over, and they lived together in perfect happiness.

My fairy tale is done.[15] See the mouse run. Whoever catches it gets to make a great big fur hat out of it.

Sing every one,
My story is done,
And look! round the house
There runs a little mouse,
He that can catch her before she scampers in,
May make himself a very very large fur-cap
out of her skin.

14. *His wife had died.* No explanation is offered for the death of the stepmother. That she is dead suggests some kind of inner identity between her and the wicked witch. Whereas the stepmother at home was intent on starving the children, providing neither food nor nurturing care, the witch in the forest initially appears to be a splendidly bountiful figure, offering the children a sumptuous repast and comfortable beds. Yet she represents an intensification of the maternal evil at home, for she feeds the children only in order to fatten them up for her next meal.

15. *My fairy tale is done.* Storytellers often ended their tales with whimsical touches, frequently in verse and with a request for monetary contributions embedded in the final lines. Bruno Bettelheim suggests that the lines at the end encapsulate a lesson: "Industry, making something good even out of unpromising material (such as by using the fur of a mouse intelligently for making a cap), is the virtue and real achievement of the school-age child who has fought through and mastered the oedipal difficulties." His view seems to ignore the pleasures of the narrative, emphasizing only its pragmatic qualities.

The White Snake

Tales about grateful animals abound in the Grimms' collection, and the hero of this tale is endowed with special powers that enable him to benefit from the help of grateful animals because he can hear them speak and understands their language. The tale begins with a servant's unrestrained curiosity about the food on which the king dines and shows that curiosity rewarded with adventures and a "happily ever after." Unlike Bluebeard's wife or Mary's child, in the tale of that title, the servant is not punished for failing to control his appetite, both intellectual and physiological.

There once lived a king who was renowned far and wide for his wisdom. Nothing could be kept hidden from him, and it seemed almost as if the winds must be carrying news to him about the most secret matters. He had one very strange custom. Every day at noon, when the table had been cleared and all the guests had left, a trusted servant would bring him one additional dish. It always had a cover on it, and the servant himself had no idea what was inside. No one knew, because the king always waited until he was all alone to lift the lid and eat from the dish.

This practice went on for some time until one day the servant, whose job it was to take the dish away, was overcome by curiosity so powerful that he could not resist it. He brought the dish into his own room. After making sure that the door was locked, he lifted the lid and discovered a white snake. One look at it and he was unable to resist the desire to have a taste of it. He cut off a small piece and put it in his mouth. As soon as his tongue touched it, he could hear the strange whispers of sweet voices outside his window. He went over to listen and discovered that some sparrows were talking to each other and sharing what they had seen in the fields and in the forest. Tasting the snake had given him the power to understand the language of animals.[1]

On that very same day the queen happened to lose her most precious ring. Suspicion fell on the trusted servant for the loss of the ring, for he was free to go wherever he wanted. The king ordered him to appear before him and used harsh words to threaten him, warning that if he did not name the thief by morning, then he would be declared guilty and beheaded. The servant protested his innocence but it did no good. The king dismissed him without further ado.

Agitated and worried, he went over to the courtyard and

1. *the power to understand the language of animals.* In Greek mythology, Melampus is endowed with the gift of understanding the language of animals. A soothsayer and healer, Melampus was said to have rescued orphaned snakes after servants killed the adult parents. He not only performed funeral rites for the snakes but also raised the young ones as pets. One day, while sleeping under a tree, the snakes licked his ears, and he woke up to discover that he could understand the speech of birds and other animals. Oddly, in "The White Snake," both king and servant are given the power to understand the language of animals by eating a piece of the snake rather than safeguarding its life. Harry Potter famously discovers, at age ten, that he has the power to understand the language of snakes, known as Parseltongue.

2. *three fish.* The servant has no reservations about slaughtering the duck that swallowed the ring, but, once on the road, he shows deep compassion for creatures of the water, land, and air—ducks, ants, and ravens.

tried to find a way out of the trouble he was in. Some ducks were sitting quietly by the edge of a babbling brook, preening themselves with their beaks and having a private chat. The servant stopped in his tracks and listened. They were talking about where they had been waddling about all morning as well as about the tasty things they had found. One of them said with a prickly voice: "There's something heavy lying in my stomach. I must have eaten too fast and swallowed a ring that was lying on the ground under the queen's window."

The servant grabbed the bird by the neck, carried her straight to the kitchen and said to the cook: "Here's a well-fed duck. Now is the time to slaughter it!"

"Yes, you are right," the cook replied, as he lifted the duck up in the air. "This one has been busy stuffing itself, and it's high time to roast it." He cut the duck's throat, and while he was cleaning it out, he discovered something in its stomach that turned out to be the queen's ring. At last the servant was able to prove his innocence to the king, who was eager to make amends for having wronged him. He offered to grant the servant a royal favor and told him he could have any post he wanted at court.

The servant declined everything offered. Instead he requested a horse and some money for a journey, since he was eager to see the world and to travel for a while. The wish was granted, and he went on his way. One day, while passing a pond, he noticed that three fish[2] were trapped in the reeds and gasping for lack of water. Even though people say that fish are mute, he could hear their distress about the miserable death they were facing. As a man with a kind heart, he got off his horse and put the three captives back into the pond. Wriggling for joy, they poked their heads out of the water and chanted: "We shall remember this and one day repay you for saving our lives."

The servant traveled on, and, after a while, he thought he could hear a voice in the sand at his feet. He listened carefully and heard an ant king complaining: "If only people would steer their clumsy beasts away from us! That stupid horse has no feelings at all and is trampling my people to death with its big heavy hooves!" The servant turned onto a side road, and the ant king called out: "We shall remember this and one day repay you."

The servant's path led him through a forest, and there he ran into a father raven and a mother raven next to their nest, tossing the chicks out. "Off with you, you freeloaders!" they cried. "We can't fill your bellies any longer. You're grown up now and can feed yourselves." The poor chicks flapped their

Arthur Rackham, *The Fairy Tales of the Brothers Grimm*

"The Fishes, in their joy, stretched up their heads above the water, and promised to reward him."

wings and struggled to lift themselves up from the ground: "We're only helpless children! How in the world can we feed ourselves when we can't fly? We'll end up starving to death!" When he heard that, the kind young man dismounted, slew his horse with his sword, and gave it to the young ravens as food. They hopped over, ate their fill, and cried out: "We shall remember this and one day repay you."

From then on he had to rely on his own legs, and after walking for a long stretch, he reached a big city. Noise filled the streets, and a man rode through the crowds on horseback to announce that the princess was looking for a husband. Anyone wishing to win her hand would have to carry out one difficult task, and, if he failed, he would be executed. Many young men had already attempted tasks, but in vain, for they had lost their lives. When the young man set eyes on the king's daughter, he was so dazzled by her great beauty that he paid no attention to the risk, went to see the king, and presented himself as a suitor.

The young man was taken straight out to sea, and, right before his eyes, a golden ring was tossed into the waters. The king ordered him to retrieve the ring from the bottom of the ocean, and he added, "If you come up without it, you will be pushed back in, again and again, until finally you will drown in the waves." Everyone felt pity for the handsome young man, but soon he was left all alone on the shores. As he stood there wondering what to do, he caught sight of three fish swimming toward him, and they were none other than the fish whose lives he had saved. The one in the middle had a shell in its mouth, and he put it down on the shore at the feet of the young man, who picked it up and found the golden ring inside.

Overjoyed, the young man took the ring to the king, expecting him to bestow the promised reward. But when the proud princess discovered that he was not her equal in birth, she felt nothing but disdain for him and demanded that he perform a second task. She went to the garden and strewed millet from ten sacks in the grass. "Before the sun comes up tomorrow, he must pick them all out," she declared, "and not a single grain can be missing."

The boy sat down in the garden and searched his mind for a way of completing the task, but nothing occurred to him, and he just sat there mournfully, waiting for the break of day, when he would be taken to his death. But when the sun's rays hit the garden, he found all ten sacks standing in a row, filled to the brim, and not even the tiniest bit of grain was missing. The ant king had appeared in the middle of the night with thousands upon thousands of ants, and the grateful animals had worked hard to gather the millet one grain at a time to fill the sacks.

The princess herself walked over to the garden and was astonished to see that the task had been completed. But she could not tame her proud heart, and instead said, "Even if he has completed the two tasks, he will not be my husband until he has brought me an apple from the tree of life."[3] The boy had no idea where he might find the tree of life, but he started off anyway and decided to keep walking as far as his legs would carry him, even though he had no hope of finding it.

He traveled across three kingdoms and reached a forest in the evening. Then he sat down under a tree to get some sleep. Suddenly he heard a noise in the branches, and a golden apple fell right into his hand. Just then three ravens flew down to him, perched on his knee, and said: "We are the three ravens you rescued from starvation. We grew up, and then we learned that you were seeking the golden apple, and so we flew across the ocean to the end of the world, where the tree of life grows, and we picked the apple for you."

Full of joy, the young man set off for home and brought the beautiful princess the golden apple. Now she had run out of excuses. They divided up the apple of life and shared it. Then her heart overflowed with love for him, and they lived to a ripe old age in peace and happiness.

3. *"tree of life."* In the book of Genesis, Adam and Eve eat from the tree of knowledge and are cast out of the Garden of Eden. In that garden, there is also a tree of life, guarded at the entrance to Eden by two cherubs with flaming swords.

The Fisherman and His Wife

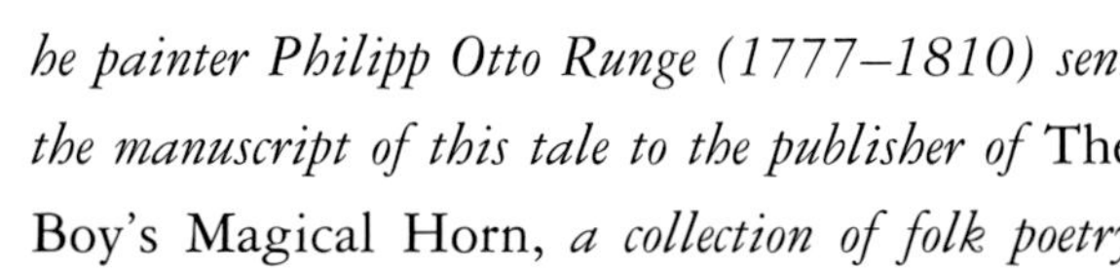

The painter Philipp Otto Runge (1777–1810) sent the manuscript of this tale to the publisher of The Boy's Magical Horn, *a collection of folk poetry edited by the German Romantic writers Achim von Arnim and Clemens Brentano. The Grimms read the manuscript in 1809 and decided to include it in their collection. Written in Low German* (plattdeutsch)*, the tale seemed to have a kind of folkloric authenticity that the Grimms were aiming to capture.*

The Thousand and One Nights *contains a story called "The Fisherman and the Genie," which tells of a poor fisherman who casts his net into the sea three times, each time catching worthless objects. On the fourth try, he brings up a copper jar containing a genie who threatens to kill him, despite the fisherman's pleas to spare his life. The fisherman manages to outwit the genie and get him back in the bottle. This story, like Runge's tale, gives us a series of repetitions leading up to a climactic event in which the supernatural manifests itself. "The Fisherman and His Wife" can be seen as a cumulative tale with the same basic structure—the fisherman's wife escalating her demands until finally the wrath of the heavens returns her to her original social and domestic misery.*

"The Fisherman and His Wife" lacks the fairy-tale magic usually associated with the Grimms' tales. It may begin with "Once upon a time," but it fails to end with the social elevation and rags-to-riches trajectory associated with the fairy tale. Instead, the tale offers a cautionary lesson about the importance of remaining satisfied with your station in life. The fisherman's wife, with her unbridled ambition, offers an example of the monstrosity of greed but also of feminine power. She stands in sharp contrast to her husband, the patient fisherman who is satisfied with a modest improvement to his life.

In Virginia Woolf's To the Lighthouse, *Mrs. Ramsey reads the story of the fisherman and his wife to her son James. She finishes the story when it is "growing quite dark" and watches her son: "She saw in his eyes, as the interest of the story died away in them, something else take its place; something wondering, pale, like the reflection of a light which at once made him gaze and marvel." Embedded in a narrative about marriage, intimacy, and ambition, the tale powerfully enriches the complexities of what is at stake in Woolf's novel.*

William J. Bennett included a "retold" version of "The Fisherman and His Wife" in his Book of Virtues. *He provides the following gloss on the tale: "We should know that too much of anything, even a good thing, may prove to be our undoing, as this old tale shows. We need to recognize when enough is enough." Bennett's message fails to take into account the interesting ways in which the tale inflects this message, reversing traditional gender roles, with the husband as patient fisherman, content with living in a pigsty, and the wife as a ruthlessly ambitious figure, willing to disturb the universe as she demands more and more power.*

Günter Grass's The Flounder, *based loosely on "The Fisherman and His Wife," takes place over the course of nine months, during which the narrator entertains his pregnant wife with tales about the various cooks the fisherman has met throughout his life. Grass uses the tale to draw contrasts between the contributions of men and women to culture and civilization.*

In their annotations, the Grimms pointed to the existence of versions in which both husband and wife indulge in excess. One variant, featuring a couple named Domine and Dinderlinde, ends when the husband makes a final wish to become God and the mother of God. Despite complaints from colleagues that this particular tale was not really a fairy tale for children, the Grimms felt strongly that "The Fisherman and His Wife" was a consummate example of folk poetry and deserved inclusion in their collection.

nce upon a time a fisherman lived with his wife in a pigsty[1] not far from the sea. Every single day, the fisherman went off to fish, and he fished and he fished.

One day he dropped his line into the water, stared out at the surface, and he sat and he sat.[2]

The line sank down to the bottom, way deep down, and when the fisherman pulled it back up, there was a huge flounder at the other end of it. The flounder said to him: "Listen to what I have to say, fisherman. I'm pleading with you. Why not let me live? I'm not really a flounder. I'm an enchanted prince.[3] What would be the point of killing me? I won't even taste very good. Put me back in the water and let me swim away."

"You can save your breath," the man replied. "Why in the world would I want a talking flounder?" And so he put him back into the peaceful waters, and the flounder swam back to the bottom, leaving a long trail of blood behind him.[4] The fisherman got up and went back home to his wife in the pigsty.

"Did you catch anything today, husband?" the wife said when her husband returned home.

"No," the fisherman replied. "I did catch a flounder who claimed he was an enchanted prince, but I let him get away."

1. *in a pigsty.* The couple's residence is called, in Runge's tale, a *Pisspott,* or "piss pot." Another printed collection of tales, assembled by August Wilhelm Büsching, used the term "P—pot." D. L. Ashliman points out that translators have resorted to a variety of strategies to avoid the vulgarities of "piss pot." Edgar Taylor, the first British translator, used the term "ditch"; Margaret Hunt described the home as a "miserable hovel"; Ralph Manheim called it a "pigsty"; Jack Zipes translated it as "dirty hovel"; Ashliman himself uses the term "filthy shack." "Pigsty" seems a reasonable compromise, avoiding the obscurities of "piss pot" while capturing its sense of squalor.

2. *he sat and he sat.* The repetition of verbs used to describe the fisherman intensifies the quality of patience in his character and introduces him as a powerful foil to his wife, who demands change and elevation rather than monotony.

3. *"I'm an enchanted prince."* The flounder bears a greater resemblance to the genies of the *Arabian Nights* than to the enchanted princes of western folklore. He is never liberated from his enchanted state and remains a figure with magical powers connected to the divine.

4. *leaving a long trail of blood behind him.* The trail of blood is the first hint of violence in the tale, and it suggests that there is already something sinister to the fisherman's catch.

"Did you make a wish?" his wife asked.[5]

"No," the fisherman replied. "What in the world would I wish for?"

"That's not hard to figure out," the wife said. "Living in a pigsty is pretty dreadful. The stench is really disgusting. You could have asked for a little cottage. Go back and talk to him. If you tell him we would like to have a little cottage, he's sure to give us one."

"How can I go back there again?" asked the fisherman.

"Didn't you catch him and then let him swim away? He's sure to help us. Go back there right now," the wife said to him.

The fisherman didn't really want to go back, but he also didn't want to irritate his wife, and so he made his way back to the shore.

When he got there, the sea was dark green with shades of yellow and not nearly as calm as before. He stood there and said:

"Flounder, flounder in the sea,[6]
Rise on up, swim here to me,
My wife whose name is Ilsebill
Has sent me here against my will."

The flounder swam up to him and asked: "Well, what does she want?"

"My wife tells me that since I managed to catch you, I should also have made a wish. She's tired of living in a pigsty, and she'd rather live in a little cottage."

"Just go on home," the flounder said. "She's already living in it."

The fisherman went home, and his wife was no longer stuck in the pigsty. Instead she was sitting on a bench by the door of a little cottage. She took him by the hand and said: "Come on in and take a look around. This is much better, isn't it?" They went indoors and found a little hallway and a

5. *"Did you make a wish?" his wife asked.* Although fairy tales are frequently seen as stories about wishes coming true, this is one of the few stories in the Grimms' collection in which wishes are articulated and then come true. And in this tale, the fulfillment of wishes does not have a utopian dimension and is seen more as curse than as blessing.

6. *"Flounder, flounder in the sea."* In the original German, the fisherman's oft-repeated call to the fish begins: "Mantje! Mantje! Timpe Te! / Buttje, Buttje in der See." *Mantje* is most likely a variant of *Männchen,* High German for "little man." Some critics have speculated that *Timpe Te* was once the name of the fisherman, who is called Domine in one version. It seems odd, however, that the fisherman begins by invoking his own name, then calling out to the flounder. The sea is presented here both as a force of nature and as a gauge of divine wrath.

lovely little parlor and a bedroom with a bed for each of them, and a kitchen with a pantry, and all the best furnishings and utensils, tin and brass, everything you could ever want. And behind the cottage there was a little farmyard with chickens and ducks, along with a garden full of vegetables and fruit. "Just look," said the wife, "isn't this wonderful?"

"Let's just hope it stays that way, and then we can live in peace."

"We'll see about that," said the wife. And they sat down to eat and went to bed.

Everything was fine for a week or two, then the woman said: "Listen to me, husband, this cottage is getting just a bit too crowded, and the barnyard and garden are really too small. That flounder could have given us a bigger house. I'd rather be living in a big stone castle. Go talk to the flounder and tell him to give us a castle."

"Dear wife," said the husband. "This cottage is really good enough for us.[7] Why would we want to live in a castle?"

"Nonsense," the wife replied. "Just go talk to the flounder. He'll take care of it."

"No, wife," said the man. "The flounder just gave us this cottage. I don't want to go back again. He might be offended."

"Get going now," said the wife. "He can do it, and he won't mind at all."

The man went with a heavy heart, and he wanted to turn back. He thought to himself: "This is just not right," but he left anyway.

When he arrived at the shore, he saw that the water was no longer green and yellow but purple and dark blue and gray and murky on top of that. But it was still calm. He stood there and said:

"Flounder, flounder in the sea,
Rise on up, swim here to me,

7. *"This cottage is really good enough for us."* The man's desire to stay put mirrors social realities having to do with upwardly mobile women and with men who are satisfied with what they have. In some ways the tale is as much about women with the desire for the ostentatious display of wealth as about power-hungry women.

My wife whose name is Ilsebill
Has sent me here against my will."

"Well, what does she want this time?" asked the flounder.

The fisherman was very upset and said: "Now she wants to live in a big stone castle."

"Just go home. She's already standing at the entrance," the flounder said.

The fisherman left and thought that he would go back home, but when he got there, he found a big stone castle, and his wife was standing at the top of the steps and was about to enter. She took him by the hand and said: "Come on inside."

He walked in with her. Inside the castle there was a great front hall with a marble floor. The many servants who were there flung open the doors for them. The walls were all bright and covered with beautiful tapestries, and in the rooms there were chairs and tables of pure gold. Crystal chandeliers hung from the ceilings. The rooms and bedchambers were all carpeted. The tables were weighed down with so much food and with so many bottles of the finest wine that they were on the verge of collapsing. Behind the castle there was a courtyard with barns and stables, and with the most elegant carriages, along with stalls for horses and cows. There was also a magnificent garden with the most beautiful flowers and fruit trees, and a park that was at least a half mile long, with stags and deer and hares in it, along with everything else you could possibly imagine.

"Well," said the woman, "now isn't this better?"

"Yes, it is," the fisherman said. "And may it stay that way. We can keep this beautiful castle and live in peace."

"We'll just see about that," his wife said. "Let's sleep on it." And with that they went to bed.

The next morning the wife woke up first. It was dawn, and she could see from her bed the magnificent countryside around the castle. Her husband was just beginning to stretch when she poked him in the side with her elbow and said:

8. *"tell him that we want to be king."* The wife's previous wishes had to do with property. Now she intends to expand her territorial reach and also to usurp the powers of potentates.

"Husband, get up and look out the window. Why can't we be the rulers of this land? Go talk to the flounder and tell him that we want to be king."[8]

"But my dear wife," said the man. "Why would we want to be king? I don't want to be king."

"Well," said the wife, "Maybe you don't want to be king, but I want to be king. Go talk to the flounder and tell him that I want to be king."

"But wife," said the fisherman. "Why would you want to be king? I can't tell him that."

"And why not?" asked the wife. "Just get going. I have to be king."

The fisherman was unhappy that his wife wanted to be king, but he went anyway. "That's just not right. It's not right at all," he thought. He didn't want to go, but he went anyway.

When he arrived at the shore, the sea was gray-black and the water was churning up from below and had a foul smell to it. He stood there and said:

> "Flounder, flounder in the sea,
> Rise on up, swim here to me,
> My wife whose name is Ilsebill
> Has sent me here against my will."

"What does she want now?" asked the flounder.

"Oh, my goodness," said the man, "now she wants to be king."

"Go on home. She is already," said the flounder.

The fisherman went back home, and when he got there, the castle had become much larger, with a tall tower and magnificent decorations. Sentries were keeping watch at the entrance, and there were many soldiers around, along with the sound of drums and trumpets. When the fisherman got inside, he saw

that everything was made of pure marble and gold, and the furniture was covered in velvet with large golden tassels. The doors of the great hall opened up, and the entire royal household was present. His wife was seated up high on a throne of gold and diamonds. She was wearing a big golden crown and holding a scepter made of pure gold and precious stones. To her left and right was a row of ladies-in-waiting, each one head shorter than the last.

The fisherman stood before her and said: "Goodness, wife! So now you really are king."

"That's right," she replied. "Now I'm king."

He stood there and looked at her, and after he had gotten a good look, he said: "Now that you're king, let's leave well enough alone. We don't have to wish for anything else."

"I'm afraid not, husband," said the woman, and she was beginning to look uneasy. "Time is already weighing heavily on my hands. I just can't stand it any longer. Go talk to the flounder. I may be king now, but I've got to become emperor as well."

"Wife, wife," said the man, "why would you want to become emperor?"

"Husband," she said, "go talk to the flounder. Tell him I want to be emperor."

"Oh, my dear wife," said the man, "he can't make you emperor. I can't tell the flounder to do that. There's only one emperor in the realm. The flounder can't make you emperor. He'll never be able to do that."

"What are you talking about?" the woman said. "I'm the king, and you are my husband. Just get going. Off with you! If the flounder can make me king, he can also make me emperor. I am going to become emperor no matter what. Now get out of here!"

And so he had to leave. But the fisherman was filled with dread when he went away. He thought to himself: "This is

not going to end well. Asking to be emperor is just going too far. The flounder is going to have had enough."

When he arrived at the shore, the sea was all black and murky. The waters were heaving up from the depths and throwing up bubbles. The wind was so strong that the waters were choppy and covered with foam. The fisherman was terrified. He stood there and said:

"Flounder, flounder in the sea,
Rise on up, swim here to me,
My wife whose name is Ilsebill
Has sent me here against my will."

"What does she want now?" asked the flounder.

"Oh, flounder," he replied, "my wife now wants to become emperor."

"Go on home," said the flounder. "She is already."

The fisherman returned home, and when he got there, he discovered a palace made of polished marble with alabaster statues and golden ornaments. Soldiers were marching around at the entrance, blowing trumpets and beating drums. Inside the building, barons and counts and dukes were going about discharging the duties of servants. They opened the doors for him, which were made of pure gold. He went inside and found his wife sitting on a throne made of a piece of solid gold a good two miles high. On her head was a golden crown three ells high and studded with diamonds and emeralds. In one hand she was holding a scepter and in the other the imperial orb. Bodyguards were standing in a row on both sides, each shorter than the one before him, beginning with an enormous giant, who was about two miles tall, to a tiny dwarf, no bigger than my little finger.[9] Princes and dukes were gathered in a crowd before her.

The fisherman went and stood among them and said: "Well, wife. It looks like you're finally emperor."

9. *beginning with an enormous giant, who was about two miles tall, to a tiny dwarf, no bigger than my little finger.* This particular tale is about domestic discord and marital asymmetries in the desire for worldly power more than anything else, but it draws, whenever possible, on fairy-tale elements, such as giants and dwarfs, to deepen its plot.

"Yes," she said, "I am the emperor."

He stood and took a good look at her, and after staring for a while, he said, "Wife, now that you're emperor, let's leave well enough alone."

"Husband," she said. "Why are you standing there? Now that I'm emperor, I want to become pope. Go talk to the flounder."

"Oh, wife!" the man said. "What will you be asking for next? You can't become pope. There's only one pope in all Christendom. The flounder can't make you pope."

"Husband," said the woman. "That's hogwash! If he can make me emperor, he can also make me pope. Do as you're told. I'm the emperor, and you're just my husband, so you had better get going."

The fisherman was filled with dread and felt faint, but he went back all the same. Shivering and shaking, his knees went weak and his legs wobbled. A strong wind was blowing, and clouds were racing across the skies. By evening it had turned dark and gloomy. Leaves were blowing from the trees, and the waters seemed to be boiling as they roared down below and foamed up above. In the distance, the fisherman could see ships sending out distress signals as they were tossed and turned about by the waves. There was still a patch of blue in the middle of the sky, but it was surrounded on all sides by red as in a terrible storm. Full of fear and despair, the fisherman stood there and said:

"Flounder, flounder in the sea,
Rise on up, swim here to me,
My wife whose name is Ilsebill
Has sent me here against my will."

"What does she want now?" asked the flounder.

"Dear me," said the man. "She now wants to become pope."

"Go home," said the flounder. "She already is."

And so he returned home, and when he got there, he found a large church surrounded by palaces. He forced his way through the crowds. Inside, the whole place was lit up by thousands and thousands of candles, and his wife was clothed in pure gold, sitting on a throne even higher than before. She was wearing three immense crowns of gold. Surrounded by papal splendor, she sat there with a line of candles on each side of her, the largest as thick and as tall as the biggest tower, down to the smallest kitchen candle. And all the emperors and kings were down on their knees before her, kissing her slipper.

"Wife," the man said, taking a good look at her, "so now you are pope?"

"Yes," she replied. "I am the pope."

He stood there looking at her, and he felt as if he were looking right into the bright light of the sun. After staring at her for a while, he said: "Well, wife, now that you are pope, maybe we can leave well enough alone!"

She stood there stiff as a board and neither stirred nor moved.

"Wife," he said to her. "You had better be satisfied now that you are pope. There is really nothing beyond that."

"We'll see about that," said the wife, and then they both went to bed. But she still wasn't satisfied. Her ambition would not allow her to go to sleep. She kept wondering what else there was.

The fisherman slept well and soundly, for he had covered a lot of ground that day. As for the wife, she could not even get to sleep. All night long she tossed and turned in her bed, thinking about what else she could become. But she was at a loss. Then the sun began to rise, and when she saw the light of dawn, she sat straight up in bed and looked out the window. She watched the sun rising and thought to herself:

Kay Nielsen, *Hansel and Gretel and Other Stories by the Brothers Grimm*

The fisherman's wife is seated on a throne that is bright as the sun. The seas become turbulent as the fisherman returns to the flounder to make one last request.

10. *Outside a storm was raging.* The landscape begins to take on an apocalyptic coloring once the wife demands divine powers.

"Ha, why couldn't I be the one to make the sun and moon rise?"

"Husband," she said, poking him in the ribs with her elbow. "Wake up and go talk to the flounder. I want to become like our dear God."

The fisherman was still half asleep, but her words gave him such a start that he fell right out of bed. He was sure that he had misunderstood her, and he rubbed his eyes. "Wife, what are you saying?"

"Husband," she replied, "If I can't make the sun and the moon rise, but have to watch them rise and set, I won't be able to stand it. I'll never have a moment's peace."

She gave him a look that sent shivers up and down his spine. "Get going now. I want to become like our dear God."

"Wife, wife," the fisherman said, falling on his knees before her, "the flounder can't do that. He may be able to make you emperor and pope, but that's it. I'm pleading with you to stay satisfied with being pope."

At that, she went into a rage and her hair flew wildly about her head. She tore her bodice open and gave him a swift kick, shouting: "Will you just get going! I'm not going to stand for this any longer. I've had it!"

The fisherman pulled his trousers on and ran off like a madman.

Outside a storm was raging,[10] and the wind was blowing so hard that the fisherman could hardly stay on his feet. Trees and houses were falling down, the mountains were trembling, great boulders went crashing into the sea, and the sky was pitch black. Thunder and lightning filled the air, and the sea was rising up in great black waves as tall as church towers and mountains and capped with crowns of white foam. The fisherman yelled at the top of his lungs but couldn't even hear his own words:

"Flounder, flounder in the sea,
Rise on up, swim here to me,
My wife whose name is Ilsebill
Has sent me here against my will."

"What does she want now?" asked the flounder.

"Dear me," he said. "Now she wants to become like our dear God."

"Go back home. She's sitting in her pigsty again."

And that's where they're still living today.[11]

11. *And that's where they're still living today.* The abrupt ending, with its return to the initial situation, turns the story into an anti–fairy tale, a narrative that, rather than tracing a rise in fortunes or a reversal, takes the protagonists back to the miserable condition in which they started.

Hermann Vogel, *Kinder- und Hausmärchen gesammelt durch die Brüder Grimm*

The fisherman returns home to find his wife back in their hovel, as the sun sets, with a smile on its face, and pigs dance.

The Brave Little Tailor

Folklorists use the term "trickster" to refer to a stock character in the lore of African, Native American, and Asian cultures. A master of craft and deception, he is modeled on the figure of Hermes from Greek mythology and has the same fleet-footed energy and transformative vitality. German folklore knows few classic tricksters. Instead the Grimms' collection is full of simpletons, nitwits, and fools—figures who are so witless that they turn out to be cunning and who are so fearless and naïve that they turn out to seem courageous.

The more hopelessly naïve and obtuse the hero of a tale in the Grimms' collection, the more likely it is that he will triumph over his adversaries and that his adventures will be crowned with success. The brave little tailor, who decorates himself for having dispatched seven flies at one blow, seems to stand as the very incarnation of vanity. Yet his bravado enables him to outwit powerful giants, to complete the impossible tasks given by his bride's hostile father, and to subdue a blue-blooded wife who is repelled at the thought of marriage to someone from a lower social station. In "The Brave Little Tailor," naïveté shades into shrewdness and bravado turns into courage. The blockhead, in other words, becomes a trickster.

*Still, Robert Darnton warns that, in French folklore at least, "trickster heroes stand out against a negative idea, the numbskull." French folktales, he argues, "show no sympathy for village idiots or for stupidity in any form," and they are filled with characters who are quick-witted and sharp-tongued. It is telling that the Grimms' numbskulls belong to the same species of underdog but differentiate themselves sharply from their French cousins by virtue of their innate good fortune rather than their talent for intrigue. If French heroes go by names that reveal their shrewdness (*Parlafine *or* Le Rusé Voleur*), German heroes remain steadfastly innocent, very much at ease as Hans Dumm or Dummling.*

The brave little tailor in the Grimms' tales turns the tables on the stupid and powerful (he has no trouble outwitting the giants), and in a second installment to his adventures, he captures a unicorn and a wild boar in order to win the hand of a princess. Even when he runs up against a third tyrant—class barriers that make a tailor an unsuitable husband for a princess—he manages to triumph. The story of the brave tailor is one of the few in the collection that articulates an emergent class consciousness and documents how reality can intrude on fairy-tale fantasies that turn tailors into monarchs.

One summer day a little tailor was sitting at a table[1] near a window. He was in high spirits, and sewing for all he was worth, when a peasant woman came walking down the street, crying out: "Sweet jams for sale! Sweet jams for sale!"

The words sounded tempting to the tailor's ears, and he poked his little head out the window and shouted down: "Up here, my good woman, there's a buyer waiting for you." The woman hauled her heavy basket up three flights of stairs to the tailor and then unpacked all her jars for him. He inspected

1. *a little tailor was sitting at a table.* Wilhelm Grimm sought to make the tale more child friendly by adding diminutive forms to some of the nouns. He turned the tailor (*Schneider*) of one version into a little tailor (*Schneiderlein*), who became more whimsical in revisions. The trade of the tailor, which requires manual dexterity and skill rather than brute strength, suits itself well to the plot. The Grimms saw in the figure of the little tailor a version of the classic heroes of German folklore—Dummy, who manages to outwit everyone through his naïveté, and Thumbling, the trickster fellow who outsmarts everyone through his agility and cleverness.

each one of them, raising the jars up to the light and giving them each a little sniff. Finally he declared: "This looks like good jam to me. Give me three ounces of it,[2] and if it comes to a quarter of a pound, my good woman, you won't hear me complaining."

The woman, who had been hoping for a big sale, gave him what he wanted but was annoyed and started grumbling to herself as she was leaving.

"May God bless this jam and let it give me strength and energy!" the tailor said while taking a loaf of bread from the cupboard, cutting a piece straight across, and spreading jam on the slice. "I'll bet this won't have a bitter taste," he said. "But before I take a bite,[3] I'm going to finish the work on this jacket." He set the piece of bread down next to him, continued sewing, and the stitches became bigger and bigger in his joyful anticipation.

Meanwhile, the smell of the sweet jam was wafting up to the ceiling, and the flies swarming on the walls were attracted by the smell and settled right down on the jam.

"Who in the world invited you to this party?" the tailor asked, and he shooed the unwelcome guests away. But the flies evidently did not understand English, and instead of getting discouraged, they came in even larger numbers. Finally the tailor was at his wit's end, as they say, and he snatched a rag from under his table: "Just you wait! I'll let you see who's boss!" and he began swatting the flies without mercy.

When he had finished, he counted up and found that no less than seven of the flies were dead, with their legs up in the air. "You're some fellow!" he said to himself, and he couldn't help but admire his own courage. "The whole town should know about this!" And in a flash he cut out a belt for himself, stitched it up, and embroidered large letters on it that read "Seven at one blow!"[4] And his heart started wagging with joy, just like the tail of a little lamb.

The tailor put the belt around his waist and decided to

2. *"Give me three ounces of it."* The tailor is presented as a frugal fellow who lives in a clearly defined sphere. That he limits his indulgences so carefully suggests that he is an unlikely giant killer.

3. *"But before I take a bite."* The work ethic triumphs here over the pleasure principle, making it clear that the tailor is a man who understands discipline.

4. *"Seven at one blow!"* The tailor proclaims a truth to the world that is nonetheless a misrepresentation. He clearly knows how to manipulate language and use it to his advantage, as becomes evident in the final scene of the story, when he boasts in his sleep about his feats in order to intimidate. Note that he never claims to have done anything beyond slaying seven at one blow.

go out into the world, for now the workshop was clearly too narrow for someone of his mettle. Before leaving, he looked around to see if there was anything he should take with him. The only thing he could find was a piece of old cheese, and he put it in his pocket. At the city gates, he noticed a bird that had gotten caught in some bushes, and the bird joined the cheese[5] in his pocket. Then he set out as brave as can be, with the road between his legs, and since he was light and nimble, he never got tired.

The road took him to a mountain, and once he had climbed up to its peak, he saw a powerful giant sitting there enjoying the view. The little tailor went right up to him, and feeling no fear, he said: "Greetings, comrade! Looking out at the great, wide world, are you? Well, that's where I'm headed to try my luck. Care to join me?"[6]

The giant looked at him with great contempt and said: "You little pipsqueak. You're nothing but a miserable wretch!"

"That's what you think!" the little tailor said, and he unbuttoned his jacket so that the giant could see his belt. "Now you can read for yourself what kind of man I am."

The giant read the letters: "Seven at one blow!" and he thought it meant that the tailor had slain seven men. He began to feel some respect for the little guy before him, but he decided that he would put that strength to the test. The giant picked up a rock and squeezed it until water began dripping from it. "If you're so strong," he said, "can you do that?"

"Is that all?" said the little tailor. "That's child's play[7] for someone like me." And he put his hand into his pocket, took out the soft cheese, and squeezed it until the whey ran out from it. "Well, what do you think? Not bad, eh?" the tailor said.

The giant was completely baffled and could hardly believe his eyes. He picked up a rock and threw it so high that it

5. *the bird joined the cheese.* Purely "by chance," the cheese and the bird will come in handy in an encounter with a giant. That the tailor is able to take advantage of the two objects he has in his pocket illustrates his resourcefulness but is also a reminder that the tailor is the beneficiary of sheer good fortune.

6. *"Care to join me?"* The affable tailor is perfectly willing to make friends and allies. He resorts to trickery only when challenged.

7. *"That's child's play."* Wilhelm Grimm added phrases like this one to make the story more appealing to younger audiences.

vanished into thin air. "All right, you little runt, let's see you do that."

"Not a bad throw," the tailor said, "but your rock must have landed somewhere. I'm going to throw a stone up so high that it will never come back down to earth." He reached into his pocket, took out the bird, and threw it in the air. Happy to be liberated at last, the bird flew up and away and never came back. "How'd you like that little trick, my friend?" asked the tailor.

"I have to admit that you're not bad at throwing," said the giant, "but let's see how good you are at carrying things." He walked on with the tailor until they reached a huge oak tree that had been felled, and he said: "If you're so strong, you can help me get this tree out of the woods."

"At your service," said the little fellow. "If you put the trunk on your shoulders, I'll take care of the harder part and lift the branches and leaves."

The giant lifted the trunk on his shoulders, and the tailor hopped up on a branch. Since the giant couldn't see behind him, he had to carry the whole tree, and the little tailor to boot, on his back. The tailor was so snug in his seat and felt so chipper that he started singing: "Three tailors went a-riding to town." He acted as if carrying huge trees was a lark. After lugging the heavy load for some distance, the giant had to take a break and he cried out: "Hold on, I have to stop and rest." The tailor quickly jumped off his perch, held on to the tree with both arms as if he'd been carrying it all along, and then he said to the giant: "I would have thought that a huge fellow like you wouldn't have had any trouble carrying this tree."

The two of them walked on for a while and came to a cherry tree. The giant grabbed the top of the tree, where the cherries ripen the soonest, bent it down, and handed it to the tailor so that he could eat some of the fruit. But when the giant let go of the tree, the treetop snapped back up and the tailor was catapulted into the air. He fell back down to the ground without hurting himself, and the giant said: "You mean you're not even strong enough to hold on to that measly little branch?"

"Don't fret about how strong I am," the tailor said. "Do you think that holding that branch down is hard for someone who's slain seven with one blow? I decided to jump over the tree because there are some hunters down there shooting in the bushes. Now let's see if you can jump over it." The giant tried with all his might, but he couldn't get over the tree and got stuck in the branches, so that, here too, the tailor had the upper hand.

The giant then declared: "If you're such a brave fellow, then come over to our cave and spend the night there." The tailor was perfectly willing and followed him. When they got to the cave, a number of giants were sitting around a fire. They had just roasted some sheep, and the giants were sinking their teeth into them. The tailor took a good look around him and thought: "It's much more spacious here than in my workshop." The giant showed him a bed and told him to lie down and get some sleep. The bed was way too large for the little tailor, and instead of lying down in it, he crawled into a corner. When midnight came around, the giant was sure that the tailor would be fast asleep, and so he got up, took a big iron club, and with one blow smashed the bed in two. He was pretty sure that he'd managed to get rid of that pesky critter at last.

At the crack of dawn, the giants decided to take a walk into the forest. They had managed to forget all about the tailor when all of a sudden there he was, marching along, sassier and friskier than you can imagine. The giants were terrified. They were afraid that he was going to kill them all with one blow, and they ran away as fast as their legs could carry them.

The tailor got back on the road,[8] using his nose to navigate the way. After he had gone some distance, he arrived at the

8. *The tailor got back on the road.* The first part of the tale recounts the pranks played by the tailor, showing how he outwits creatures of brute strength. His adventures have a serial quality—self-contained and leading to no particular goal. The second phase of his journey is marked by the performance of Herculean tasks: killing two giants, capturing a unicorn, and ridding the kingdom of a wild boar. By forming an alliance with the king and solving the problem of brutes and beasts laying waste to the land, the tailor wins the hand of his daughter and is entitled to enjoy a fairy-tale ending.

courtyard of a royal palace, and since he was beginning to get tired, he decided to lie down on the grass. Before long, he was fast asleep. He had been lying there for some time when a group of people came by, took a good look at him, and started reading the words on his belt: "Seven at one blow!"

"Why in the world would a great warrior come here where everything is as peaceful as it can be? He must be a really powerful ruler." They went to the king and told him that if war were to break out, this man would be a helpful ally of real importance, and he was worth recruiting at any price. The king was glad to have the advice, and he sent a deputy to the tailor and told him to offer the fellow a position in the royal military service just as soon as he woke up. The deputy found the sleeping tailor, and he stood there, waiting for him to stretch his limbs and open his eyes before making his offer.

"That's exactly why I came here!" the tailor replied. "Here I am, ready to serve the king." And so he was graciously received and given his own special living quarters.

The king's soldiers were up in arms about the tailor and wished him a thousand miles away. They began talking among themselves and wondered: "What will come of this? If we get into a quarrel with him and he decides to hit us, then seven of us will fall with each blow. None of us will be able to survive that." And so they all agreed to go to the king and ask him for a discharge from his service.

"We can't hold our own next to someone who can slay seven at one blow." The king was sorry to hear that he was going to lose all of his faithful servants just because of one man. He began to wish that he had never set eyes on the fellow, and he would not have minded at all getting rid of him. But he didn't dare dismiss him, for he was afraid the tailor might strike him dead along with everyone else and then seize the throne. He thought it over for a long time, and finally he hit upon an idea. He sent word to the tailor to let him know that, since he was such a great warrior, he wanted to strike a deal with him. Two giants were living in a forest that belonged to him, and they were wreaking havoc in the land with their acts of robbery, murder, and arson. If you got anywhere near them, you were taking a chance with your life. If the tailor could manage to defeat and kill these two giants, then he would give him his only daughter as wife, with half the kingdom as her dowry. In addition, the king would send a hundred knights to back him up.

"That's just the perfect job for someone like me," the tailor thought. "A beautiful princess and half a kingdom don't come along every day."

"Yes, indeed," he replied. "I'll tame those giants,[9] and I'll manage on my own without those hundred knights. A man who slays seven at a single blow has nothing to fear from a mere two."

The tailor started out, and the hundred knights were right behind him. When he got to the edge of the forest, he said to his companions: "You wait here. I think I can manage by myself with those giants." Then he sped into the woods and looked everywhere, first to the left, then to the right. After searching for some time, he found both of the giants. They were lying under a tree, sound asleep[10] and snoring so loudly that the branches on the trees were bobbing up and down. The tailor, who was anything but lazy, filled both his pockets with stones and climbed up a tree. When he got about halfway up to the top, he slid down a branch so that he was perched right above the sleepers. Then he picked out one of the giants and let one stone after another drop down on his chest. It took a while before the giant felt something, but finally he woke up, poked his companion, and said: "Why do you keep throwing things at me?"

"You must be dreaming," the other one replied. "I haven't been hitting you."

They both went back to sleep, and the tailor threw a rock at the other giant.

9. *"I'll tame those giants."* This episode builds a transition between the tailor's encounters with the giants and his decision to enter the service of the king and to perform feats (beginning with the defeat of two giants) that will save the kingdom.

10. *They were lying under a tree, sound asleep.* Sleep represents a state of supreme vulnerability, and it enters into the tale three times in connection with duplicity and intrigue. The tailor manages to cheat death when he sleeps in a corner of the giant's bed—had he curled up in the middle of the bed, the giant would have beaten him to death; the two giants in the second half of the tale are duped by the tailor because they are sleeping and unaware of his antics; and the princess tries to assassinate her husband while he is sleeping.

11. *But the king regretted his promise.* In this classic case of buyer's remorse, the king decides, once the deed has been accomplished, that the price is too high. In this particular folktale, class bias turns out to motivate his feelings of remorse.

"What's going on?" the giant yelled. "Why are you throwing things at me?"

"I haven't thrown anything," the other one said, and he started growling. They quarreled for a while, but since they were tired, they calmed down and closed their eyes again.

The tailor started his game up again. This time he found the biggest rock around and threw it with all his might at the chest of the first giant.

"I've had it!" the giant yelled, and he jumped up like a madman and slammed his companion so hard against a tree that the trunk started shaking. The other giant paid him back in kind, and the two of them flew into such a rage that they tore up trees and beat each other with them until, finally, they both ended up dead.

The tailor jumped down off the branch. "Lucky that they didn't pull up the tree that I was sitting in or I would have had to leap like a squirrel from one tree to the next. Thank goodness that we tailors are fleet-footed."

The tailor drew his sword and made a few hearty thrusts into the chests of the giants. Then he went over to the knights and said: "My work is done. I've finished those two off. But it was a real struggle, and those two giants became so desperate that they started uprooting trees. They tried to defend themselves, but what good is any of that when you're up against a man who can slay seven at one blow."

"You mean to tell us that you're not even wounded?" the knights asked.

"I should say not!" the tailor replied. "They never touched a hair on my head." The knights refused to believe a word he said. They decided to ride into the woods to investigate. There they found the giants lying in pools of their own blood, and all around them were the uprooted trees.

The tailor went to the king and demanded the reward he had been promised. But the king regretted his promise,[11] and he started planning a new way to get the hero off his back.

"Before you can have my daughter and half the kingdom," he told him, "you will have to perform one more heroic deed. There's a unicorn out in the forest,[12] and it's doing a lot of damage. I want you to capture it."

"If two giants don't scare me off, why would I worry about a unicorn! Seven at one blow—that's my game."

The tailor went out into the woods with a rope and an ax. Once again, he told the men who had been assigned to him to wait at the edge of the forest. He didn't have to wait long, for the unicorn appeared before long and rushed at the tailor, as if he were planning to just go ahead and gore him with his horn.

"Easy, easy," he said. "Things don't happen that fast." And the tailor stood still and waited until the animal got up close, then he jumped nimbly behind a tree. The unicorn charged the tree with all his might and rammed his horn into it so hard that he couldn't get it back out again. And so it was caught. "Now I've got my little birdie," the tailor said, and he came out from behind the tree and put a rope around the unicorn's neck. Then he took his ax and chopped the horn free of the tree. Once everything was all set, he led the animal off and took it to the king.

The king still didn't want to give him the promised reward, and he made a third demand. Before his wedding took place, the tailor was supposed to catch a wild boar that had been doing a lot of damage in the woods. The royal huntsmen were going to lend a hand.

"I'm game," said the tailor. "That will be child's play."

He didn't take the huntsmen with him into the woods, and they didn't mind at all, for the boar had already greeted them several times in a way that made them feel no desire to chase him down. When the boar set eyes on the tailor, his mouth started to foam, and gnashing his teeth, he charged the tailor and tried to throw him to the ground. The fleet-footed tailor ducked into a nearby chapel and then jumped right

12. *"There's a unicorn out in the forest."* The origins of the unicorn legend are not clear, but the unicorn is first mentioned in 400 b.c. in the writings of the Greek physician Ctesias, who tells of a wild ass in India with one horn. The unicorn appears in the Old Testament as well as in Greek and Roman writings. The unicorn here adds a touch of the exotic to a tale that is more firmly anchored in a realistic setting than most fairy tales.

Kay Nielsen, *Hansel and Gretel and Other Stories by the Brothers Grimm*

The tailor has nimbly stepped out of the path of a charging unicorn, and the unicorn, with his horn rammed into a tree, is caught by the tailor.

out the window. The beast had run after him, but the tailor had already hopped out and slammed the door behind him. The enraged animal was caught, for it was just too heavy and clumsy to jump out the window. The tailor called to the huntsmen, who were able to see the captive beast with their own eyes.

The hero went back to see the king, and now, whether he wanted to or not, the monarch had to keep his promise and give him his daughter and half the kingdom. If he had known that a little tailor rather than a heroic warrior was standing before him, it would have caused him even more grief. And so the wedding was celebrated with great splendor but with little joy, and a tailor became a king.

After some time had passed, the young queen heard her husband talking in his dreams at night. "Boy," he yelled, "finish up that jacket and get those breeches mended, or I'll whack you over the head with my measuring stick." That gave the queen a pretty good idea just where the young lord had come from. The next day she complained to her father and begged him to help her get rid of a husband who was nothing but a tailor.[13] The king reassured her and said: "Tonight you must keep your bedroom door open. My servants will be waiting outside, and once he's fallen asleep, they'll go in, tie him up, and carry him off on a ship that will take him out to sea." The woman was satisfied when she heard that. But in the meantime, the king's armor-bearer, who was well disposed to the tailor, overheard the whole conversation and disclosed the entire plot.

13. *husband who was nothing but a tailor.* The tale not only celebrates the wit, cunning, and ingenuity of tailors but also articulates its disdain for those who consider these honest tradesmen unworthy suitors.

"I'll put a quick end to that," the tailor said. That evening, he went to bed at the usual time with his wife. When she thought he had fallen asleep, she got up, opened the door, and went back to bed. The tailor, who was just pretending that he was asleep, began to shout loudly: "Boy, finish up that jacket and get those breeches mended, or I'll whack you over the head with a measuring stick! I've slain seven at one blow, killed two giants, captured a unicorn, and caught a wild boar. Why would I be afraid of anyone who is standing outside my bedroom!"

When the men heard what the tailor was saying, they were overcome with fear and started running as if an entire army were behind them. No one dared to lay a hand on him after that. And so the little tailor was and always remained a king.

Ludwig Richter, *Ludwig Bechsteins Märchenbuch*

The king's servants flee in terror when they overhear the brave little tailor talking in his sleep about his feats.

CINDERELLA[1]

The enduring appeal of "Cinderella" derives not only from the rags-to-riches trajectory of the tale's heroine but also from the way in which the story engages with classic family conflicts ranging from sibling rivalry to sexual jealousy. Cinderella's father may not have much of a part in versions of the tale told today, but the role of the (step)mother and (step)sisters, who dominate the tale as persecutors of the innocent heroine, is writ large. If Cinderella's biological mother is dead, her spirit reappears as the magic donor who provides the heroine with the gifts she needs to make a splendid appearance at the ball. With the good mother dead, the evil mother takes over—alive and active—undermining Cinderella in every possible fashion yet unable to hinder her ultimate triumph. In this splitting of the mother into two polar opposites, psychologists have seen a mechanism for helping a child work through the conflicts created in the process of maturing and separating from parents. The image of the good mother is preserved in all her nurturing glory, even as feelings of helplessness and resentment are given expression through the figure of the predatory wicked stepmother.

Fairy tales place a premium on surfaces, and Cinderella's beauty, along with her magnificent attire, singles her out as the fairest in

1. *Cinderella.* Aschenputtel is the name the Grimms used for their Cinderella. The term was originally used to designate a lowly kitchen maid, a servant who had to tend the ashes at the hearth. In German, the prefix "aschen-" can also be attached to "brother" or "sister" to designate a sibling who has been degraded or forced into a subordinate role. Cinderella is the quintessential innocent, persecuted heroine who moves from rags and a state of squalor to riches.

the land. Through labor and good looks, the heroine works her way up the social ladder of success. If the story in its older versions does not capture the dynamics of courtship and romance in today's world, it remains a source of fascination in its documentation of fantasies about love and marriage in an earlier time. Perrault's version of 1697 from Tales of Mother Goose *is among the first full literary elaborations of the story. It was followed by the more violent version recorded in 1812 by the Brothers Grimm. The Grimms delight in describing the blood in the shoes of the stepsisters, who try to slice off their heels and toes in order to get a perfect fit. The German version also gives us a far less compassionate Cinderella, one who does not forgive her stepsisters but invites them to her wedding, where doves peck out their eyes. Yet for all that, the Grimms' Cinderella is far more resourceful than Perrault's Cendrillon, on whom Disney modeled his cinematic heroine of 1950. In the German tale, Cinderella decides, on her own, to go to the ball, and she returns on foot, on her own schedule, without the need for a carriage. She eludes both the prince and her father when she leaves the ball, and she further demonstrates her agility and resourcefulness by using the dovecote and tree to fool her pursuers.*

The Grimms noted that some Cinderella tales include a postmarital episode. One such episode reveals that Cinderella opens a chamber forbidden to her, discovers a well filled with blood, and is thrown down it by her treacherous sister, who takes her place. When guards hear Cinderella's cries for help, they rescue her and punish her sister. Another tale tells how the stepmother and stepsister kidnap the queen's first two children and then send her into exile with her third child. The king succeeds in locating his lost wife and lives happily ever after with her after punishing the two women. These sequels bear a close resemblance to the second part of Perrault's "Sleeping Beauty," which relates the trials and tribulations of a new queen at the hands of her cannibalistic mother-in-law.

The first Cinderella we know was named Yeh-hsien, and her story was recorded in China around A.D. *850 by Tuan Ch'eng-shih. Yeh-hsien wears a dress made of kingfisher feathers and tiny shoes made of gold. She manages to survive the assaults of her stepmother and stepsister, who are killed by flying stones. Like Western Cinderellas, Yeh-hsien is a humble creature, who discharges the household chores and is subjected to humiliating treatment at the hands of her stepmother and stepsister. Her salvation appears in the form of a ten-foot-long fish that provides her with gold, pearls, dresses, and food. The Cinderellas who follow in Yeh-hsien's footsteps are all the beneficiaries of magical donors who provide food, garments, or whatever else it takes to escape an abusive situation at home. In the Grimms' "Aschenputtel," a tree showers Cinderella with gifts; in Perrault's "Cendrillon," a fairy godmother provides a coach, footmen, and beautiful garments; in the Scottish "Rashin Coatie," a little red calf produces a dress.*

Yeh-hsien, Cendrillon, Ashypet, Pepelluga, Mossy Coat, Katie Woodencloak, and Cenerentola: these are just a few of Cinderella's folkloric cousins. If Cinderella has been reinvented by nearly every known culture, her story is also perpetually rewritten within any given culture. Working Girl *with Melanie Griffith,* Pretty Woman *with Julia Roberts,* Ever After *with Drew Barrymore, and* Maid in Manhattan *with Jennifer Lopez: these films offer striking evidence that we continue to recycle the story to manage our cultural anxieties and conflicts about courtship and marriage. Few fairy tales have enjoyed the rich literary, cinematic, and musical afterlife of "Cinderella," and even when the story is not reinvented in imaginative ways, it provides opportunities for new dialogues about what is at stake in romance.*

he wife of a rich man fell ill one day. When she realized that the end was near, she called her only daughter to her bedside and said: "Dear child, if you are good and say your prayers faithfully, our dear Lord will always help you, and I shall look down

from heaven and always be with you." Then she closed her eyes and passed away.[2]

Every day the little girl went to her mother's grave and wept. She was always good and said her prayers. When winter came, snow covered the grave with a white blanket, and when the sun took it off again in the spring, the rich man remarried.

The man's new wife brought with her two daughters[3] with beautiful faces and fair skin, but with hearts that were foul and black. This marked the beginning of a hard time for the poor stepchild. "Why should this silly goose be allowed to sit in the parlor with us?" the girls asked. "If you want to eat bread, you'll have to earn it. Get back in the kitchen where you belong!"

The sisters took away the girl's beautiful clothes, dressed her in an old gray smock, and gave her some wooden shoes. "Just look at the proud princess in her finery!" they shouted and laughed, taking her out to the kitchen. From morning until night she had to work hard.[4] Every day, she got up before daybreak to carry water, get the fire going, cook, and wash. On top of that the two sisters did everything imaginable to make her life miserable. They made fun of her and threw peas and lentils into the ashes so that she would have to bend down over the ashes and pick them out. In the evening, when she was completely exhausted from work, she didn't even have a bed to lie down in[5] but had to sleep at the hearth in the ashes. She began looking so dusty and dirty that everyone called her Cinderella.

One day when the father was going to the fair,[6] he asked the two stepdaughters what he should bring back for them. "Beautiful dresses,"[7] one of them said. "Pearls and jewels," said the other.

"But you, Cinderella," he asked. "What do you want?"

"Father," she said, "break off the first branch that brushes against your hat on your way home and bring it to me."

2. *Then she closed her eyes and passed away.* In many fairy tales, the mother is split into two figures: the good dead mother who remains alive through nature and comes to the assistance of the protagonist, and a wicked, evil stepmother who is the opposite of a nurturing presence and instead represents artifice and calculation.

3. *two daughters.* In folktales, stepsisters and stepmothers are nearly always fair game for demonization, providing a safe cover for the animosity sometimes felt for biological parents and siblings. The Grimms, like Perrault, often equated fair skin with virtue and associated vice with blackness.

4. *From morning until night she had to work hard.* Cinderella is always the household drudge, a creature who not only has to discharge domestic chores but whose true beauty is concealed by soot, dust, and cinders. That she is always hardworking and kind points to the way in which character can create powerfully attractive figures.

5. *she didn't even have a bed to lie down in.* That Cinderella has to sleep in the ashes can be connected with the fact that she continues to mourn her lost mother.

6. *One day when the father was going to the fair.* The father in the Grimms' version of "Cinderella" remains a presence throughout the tale, bringing home gifts and using an ax to break down the dovecote and chop down the pear tree where the mysterious young woman at the ball is thought to be hiding. In Perrault's version, we simply learn that the father remarries and that he is dominated by his wife.

7. *"Beautiful dresses."* Vanity ranks high among the cardinal sins of fairy-tale figures, and the two sisters distinguish themselves from their downtrodden stepsister

Arthur Rackham, *Cinderella*

Cinderella, dressed in rags, looks out the window from her attic garret. The tattered dress creates a pleasing aesthetic effect, with the barefoot Cinderella as an appealing waif.

A. H. Watson, *Told Again: Traditional Tales Told by Walter de la Mare*

Cinderella is exiled to the hearth, where she keeps company with mice.

And so he bought beautiful dresses, pearls, and jewels for the two stepsisters. On the way home, while he was riding through a thicket of green bushes, a hazel branch brushed against him and knocked his hat off. When he arrived home, he gave his stepdaughters what they had asked for, and to Cinderella he gave the branch from the hazel bush. Cinderella thanked him, went to her mother's grave, and planted the hazel sprig on it. She wept so hard that her tears fell to the ground and watered it. It grew to become a beautiful tree.[8] Three times a day Cinderella went and sat under it and wept and prayed. Each time a little white bird would also fly to the tree, and whenever she made a wish, the little bird would toss down what she had wished for.[9]

It happened that one day the king announced a festival that was to last for three days. All the beautiful young ladies in the land were invited so that his son could choose a bride. When the two stepsisters discovered that they had been invited, they were in high spirits. They called Cinderella and said: "Comb our hair, brush our shoes, and fasten our buckles. We're going to the wedding at the king's palace."

Cinderella did as she was told, but she felt sad, for she too would have liked to go to the ball, and she begged her stepmother to let her go.

"Cinderella," the stepmother said. "How can you possibly go to a wedding when you're constantly covered with dust and dirt? How can you plan to go to a ball when you have neither a dress nor shoes?"

Cinderella kept pleading with her stepmother, and she finally relented: "Here, I've dumped a bowl of lentils into the ashes. If you can pick out the lentils in the next two hours, then you may go."[10]

Cinderella went into the garden through the back door and called out: "Oh tame little doves, little turtledoves, and all you little birds in the sky, come and help me put

by demanding finery and jewels. Cinderella, by contrast, makes the modest choice and thereby prepares the way for her accession to a throne.

8. *It grew to become a beautiful tree.* A good stretch of time passes between the father's remarriage and Cinderella's attendance at the ball. The girl must suffer for many years before she is liberated from the persecutions of her wicked stepmother and is elevated to a higher social rank. Unlike her stepsisters, who are invested in beautiful clothing and precious stones, Cinderella turns to the beauty of nature as she mourns, and, in the process, reaps rewards from her surroundings. The tears watering the tree on the grave become a source of glittering garments that transcend ordinary dresses and diamonds and enable her to use beauty to reestablish justice in the world.

9. *whenever she made a wish, the little bird would toss down what she had wished for.* In other versions of "Cinderella," nature comes to the rescue of the heroine. Sometimes it is a calf, a cow, a fish, a goat, or some other animal that is connected to the mother and becomes Cinderella's magic helper or donor. In the Scottish "Rashin Coatie," a calf supplies the heroine with beautiful clothes.

10. *"If you can pick out the lentils in the next two hours, then you may go."* Picking out lentils from the ashes is one of the many impossible tasks delegated to fairy-tale figures. In some versions of "Cinderella," the heroine is required to spin or to sift grain. Note that this particular task is not only impossible but also degrading. Yet it has an interesting moral dimension in that the birds are ordered to sort out the "good" lentils from the "bad" ones.

A. H. Watson, *Told Again: Traditional Tales Told by Walter de la Mare*

Cinderella's stepsisters wear wigs and dresses that exaggerate their grotesque features and figures.

> the good ones into the little pot,
> the bad ones into your little crop."

Two little white doves came flying in through the kitchen window,[11] followed by little turtledoves. And finally all the birds in the sky came swooping and fluttering and settled down in the ashes. The little doves nodded their heads and began to peck, peck, peck, peck, and then the others began to peck, peck, peck, peck and put all the good lentils into the bowl. Barely an hour had passed when they were done and flew back out the window.

Cinderella brought the bowl to her stepmother and was overjoyed because she was sure that she would now be allowed to go to the wedding. But the stepmother said: "No, Cinderella, you have nothing to wear, and you don't know how to dance. Everyone would just laugh at you."

When Cinderella began to cry, the stepmother said: "If you can pick out two bowls of lentils from the ashes in the next hour, then you can go."

But she thought to herself: "She'll never be able to do it."

After the stepmother had dumped the two bowls of lentils into the ashes, the girl went into the garden through the back door and called out: "Oh tame little doves, little turtledoves, and all you little birds in the sky, come and help me put

> the good ones into the little pot,
> the bad ones into your little crop."

Two little white doves came flying in through the kitchen window, followed by little turtledoves. And finally all the birds in the sky came swooping and fluttering and settled down in the ashes. The little doves nodded their heads and began to peck, peck, peck, peck, and then the others began to peck, peck, peck, peck and put all the good lentils into the

11. *Two little white doves came flying in through the kitchen window.* The color white connects these two doves with the bird in the tree that serves as the magical donor for Cinderella's dress.

bowl. Barely a half hour had passed when they were finished and flew back out the window.

The girl brought the bowls back to her stepmother and was overjoyed because she was sure that she would now be able to go to the wedding. But her stepmother said: "It's no use. You can't come along because you don't have anything to wear and you don't know how to dance. You would just embarrass us." Turning her back on Cinderella, she hurried off with her two proud daughters.

Now that no one else was left at home, Cinderella went to her mother's grave under the tree and cried:

"Shake your branches, little tree,
Toss gold and silver down on me."[12]

The bird threw down to her a dress of gold and silver, along with slippers embroidered with silk and silver. Cinderella quickly slipped on the dress and left for the wedding.[13] Her sisters and her stepmother had no idea who she was. She looked so beautiful in the dress of gold that they thought she must be the daughter of some foreign king. It never occurred to them that it could be Cinderella, for they were sure that she was still at home, sitting in the dirt and picking lentils out of the ashes.

The prince approached Cinderella, took her by the hand, and danced with her. He didn't intend to dance with anyone else there and never even let go of her hand. Whenever anyone else asked her to dance, he would just say: "She's my partner."

Cinderella danced well into the night, and then she wanted to go home. The prince said: "I will go with you as your escort," for he was hoping to find out something about the family of this beautiful young woman. But Cinderella managed to slip away from him, and she bounded into a dovecote.[14] The prince waited until Cinderella's father arrived and told him that the strange girl had disappeared into the

12. *"Shake your branches, little tree, / Toss gold and silver down on me."* If Cinderella finds help by turning to nature, she wears a dress that is associated with the realm of artifice. Gold and silver are spun into fine threads, and jewels often cover her garment. The dress contributes powerfully to the radiant appearance she makes at the ball. Note that the Grimms' Cinderella does not rely on a fairy godmother for help, as does Perrault's Cinderella, but on the tree that she has cultivated and that can be seen as representing the return of her mother from the dead. In modern versions of "Cinderella," say *Pretty Woman*, a credit card becomes the magical instrument for securing the dresses that will catch the "royal" eye.

13. *Cinderella quickly slipped on the dress and left for the wedding.* There is no coach driven by six horses attended by six footmen in the Grimms' version of the tale. Cinderella simply makes her own way to the ball.

14. *she bounded into a dovecote.* The dovecote is home to the birds that sorted the lentils and helped Cinderella perform the impossible task assigned to her.

A. H. Watson, *Told Again: Traditional Tales Told by Walter de la Mare*

Cinderella leaves the ball and races down the staircase, hoping to outrun the prince.

15. *Cinderella climbed up through the branches as nimbly as a squirrel.* The pear tree is a reminder of the hazel tree and offers Cinderella temporary refuge. Birds and trees, allied with nature, figure as the heroine's salvation.

dovecote. The old man thought: "Could it be Cinderella?" He sent for an ax and pick and broke into the dovecote, but no one was inside it. And when they returned home, there was Cinderella, lying in the ashes in her filthy clothes with a dim little oil lamp burning on the mantel. Cinderella had jumped down from the back of the dovecote and had run over to the little hazel tree, where she slipped out of her beautiful dress and then put it on the grave. The bird took the dress back, and Cinderella put on her gray smock and settled back into the ashes in the kitchen.

The next day, when the festivities started up again and the parents had left with the stepsisters, Cinderella went to the hazel tree and said:

"Shake your branches, little tree,
Toss gold and silver down on me."

The bird tossed down a dress that was even more splendid than the previous one. And when she appeared at the wedding in this dress, everyone was dazzled by her beauty. The prince, who had been waiting for her to arrive, took her by the hand and danced with her alone. Whenever anyone came and asked her to dance, he would say: "She is my partner."

As night fell, Cinderella wanted to leave, and the prince decided to follow her, hoping to see which house she would enter. But she bounded away and disappeared into the garden behind the house, where there was a beautiful, tall tree with magnificent pears hanging from its branches. Cinderella climbed up through the branches as nimbly as a squirrel,[15] and the prince had no idea where she was. He waited until her father got there and said to him: "The strange girl escaped, but I believe that she climbed up into the pear tree."

The father wondered: "Could it be Cinderella?" and he sent for an ax and chopped down the tree. But no one was in it. When he went to the kitchen with the prince, Cinderella was, as usual, lying in the ashes, for she had jumped down the other side of the tree, taken her beautiful dress to the bird on the hazel tree, and slipped on her little gray smock again.

On the third day, when the parents and sisters had left, Cinderella went to her mother's grave and said to the little tree:

> "Shake your branches, little tree,
> Toss gold and silver down on me."

The bird tossed down a dress that was more splendid and radiant than anything she had ever seen, and the slippers were covered in gold. When she got to the wedding in that dress, everyone who saw her was speechless with amazement. The prince danced with her alone, and if someone asked her to dance, he would say: "She is my partner."

When night fell, Cinderella was planning to return home, and the prince wanted to escort her, but she slipped away so quickly that he was unable to follow her. The prince had planned a trick. The entire staircase had been coated with pitch, and when Cinderella started running down the stairs, her left slipper got stuck in the tar. The prince lifted it up: it was a dainty little shoe covered with gold.

The next morning the prince went with the shoe to his father and said to him: "Only the woman whose foot fits this golden shoe will be my bride."[16] The two sisters were overjoyed to hear the news, for they both had beautiful feet. The elder went with her mother into a special room to try it on. But the shoe was too small for her, and she couldn't get her big toe into it. Her mother handed her a knife and said: "Cut your toe off. Once you're queen, you won't need to go on foot any more."

The girl sliced off her toe, forced her foot into the shoe, gritted her teeth, and went out to meet the prince. He lifted her up on his horse as his bride, and rode away with her. But

16. *"Only the woman whose foot fits this golden shoe will be my bride."* Like the shoe made of glass, the golden shoe cannot stretch to fit its wearer. In the Grimms' version of the story, the prince himself seeks out the owner of the shoe, and Cinderella takes it in her hand and tries it on. The glass slipper in Perrault's "Cendrillon" was thought by some scholars to be made of "vair" (an obsolete French term for "fur") rather than "verre" ("glass"). Folklorists have now discredited the view that the slipper was made of fur and endorse the notion that the slipper has a magical quality to it and is made of glass. Strabo's ancient fable about an eagle that steals the sandal of a beautiful courtesan named Rhodope, then drops it on the pharaoh, who searches all of Egypt for its owner, reminds us of how feet and footwear are connected to femininity and sexual attractiveness. In some Cinderella stories, a golden ring, rather than a shoe or a slipper, must fit the true bride.

they had to pass by the mother's grave, and two little doves were perched on the hazel tree, calling out:

"Roo coo coo, roo coo coo,
Blood is dripping from the shoe:[17]
The foot's too long and far too wide,
Go back and find the proper bride."

When the prince looked down at the girl's foot, he saw that blood was spurting from the shoe, and he turned his horse around. He brought the false bride back home, and said that since she was not the true bride, her sister should try the shoe on. The sister went into her room and succeeded in getting her toes into the shoe, but her heel was way too big. Her mother handed her a knife too and said: "Cut off part of your heel. Once you're queen, you won't need to go on foot anymore."

The girl sliced off a piece of her heel, forced her foot into the shoe, gritted her teeth, and went out to meet the prince. He lifted her up on his horse as his bride and rode away with her. When they passed by the little hazel tree, two little doves were perched on a branch, calling out:

"Roo coo coo, roo coo coo,
Blood is dripping from the shoe:
The foot's too long and far too wide,
Go back and find the proper bride."

When he looked down at her foot, he saw blood spurting from it and staining her white stockings completely red. Then he turned his horse around and brought the false bride back home. "She's not the true bride either," he said. "Don't you have another daughter?"

"No," said the man, "there's no one left but puny little Cinderella, the daughter of my first wife, but she can't possibly become your bride."

17. *"Roo coo coo, roo coo coo, / Blood is dripping from the shoe."* In "Rashin Coatie," a Scottish Cinderella tale, the stepmother also forces her daughter to cut off her heel and toes in order to get her foot in the slipper. On the way to church a bird sings: "Minched fit, and pinched fit / Beside the king she rides, / But braw fit, and bonny fit / In the kitchen neuk she hides." The stepsisters are positioned as false brides who are willing to engage in deception in order to win the prince. Their self-mutilation prefigures the pecking out of the eyes by doves at Cinderella's wedding.

The prince asked that she be sent for, but the mother said: "Oh no, she's much too dirty to show her face."

The prince insisted, and Cinderella was summoned. First she washed her hands and face until they were completely clean, then she went and curtsied before the prince, who handed her the golden shoe. She sat down on a stool, took her foot out of the heavy wooden shoe, and put it into the slipper. It fit perfectly. And when she stood up and the prince looked her straight in the face, he recognized the beautiful girl with whom he had danced, and he shouted: "She is the true bride."

The stepmother and her two daughters were horrified, and they turned pale with rage. But the prince lifted Cinderella up on his horse and rode away with her. When they passed by the little hazel tree, the two little white doves called out:

"Roo coo coo, roo coo coo,
No blood at all in that shoe,
The foot's not long and not too wide,
The true bride's riding at his side."

After they had chanted those words, the doves both came flying over and perched on Cinderella's shoulders, one on the right, the other on the left, and there they stayed.

On the day of the wedding to the prince, the two false sisters came and tried to curry favor with Cinderella and share in her good fortune. When the bridal couple entered the church, the elder sister was on the right, the younger on the left. The doves pecked one eye from each sister. Later, when they left the church, the elder sister was on the left, the younger on the right. The doves pecked the other eye from each sister. And so they were punished for their wickedness and malice[18] with blindness for the rest of their lives.

18. *they were punished for their wickedness and malice.* Perrault's Cinderella is, by contrast, a model of compassion. After her marriage to the prince, she invites the stepsisters to live with her, and then marries them to two great lords of the court.

MOTHER HOLLE

Folklorists refer to stories like the Grimms' "Mother Holle" as "tales of kind and unkind girls." The earliest recorded version of this tale type can be found in Giambattista Basile's seventeenth-century Pentamerone *under the title "The Three Fairies." In it, Cicella, the virtuous girl, receives a gold star for her forehead, while Grannizia, her ill-tempered stepsister, has to wade through a pile of manure, and when she raises her head to get her reward, "an ass's testicle fell on her forehead and stuck to her skin." In Charles Perrault's "The Fairies," pearls and diamonds drop from one sister's mouth whenever she speaks; snakes and toads emerge from the mouth of the unattractive girl every time she utters a word.*

Driven as much by the opposition "hard-working versus lazy" or "dutiful versus disobedient" as by the contrast "kind versus unkind" and "beautiful versus ugly," these stories show one girl unloading an oven, milking a cow, shaking a tree, or discharging other household chores, whereas the other turns up her nose at any tasks requested of her. Tales like these surely played a powerful role in training children to assist in discharging domestic duties, particularly since the punished sibling was so often put on display in ways that discouraged bad behavior. In one story, for example, the "unkind" girl is "torn into a thousand pieces and hung up in the trees."

Not all renditions of "The Kind and the Unkind Girls" are as explicitly didactic as the Grimms' "Mother Holle." In their commentary to the tales, the Grimms describe a version in which one girl is simply more beautiful and fleet-footed than her sister. It is easy to understand why the brothers, who openly acknowledged the didactic power of their collection, favored a story that commended the virtues of hard work over a tale that credited beauty with winning all the prizes.

There was once a widow who had two daughters. One of them was beautiful and hardworking, the other ugly and lazy. The woman was much fonder of the ugly, lazy girl, because she was her own daughter. The other one was forced to do all the work and became the Cinderella of the household. Every day that poor girl had to go sit down by a well near the roadside and spin for so long that her fingers would start bleeding.

One day it happened that her spindle was covered with blood, and so she went over to the well to rinse it off. The spindle slipped out of her hands and fell all the way down to the bottom of the well. The girl burst into tears and ran home to tell the stepmother about her misfortune. The woman scolded her mercilessly and was so nasty that, in the end, she told her: "If you let the spindle drop into the well, then go back and get it."

The girl went back to the well and tried to figure out what to do. She was so terrified about having lost the spindle that she finally just jumped into the well to retrieve it. She lost consciousness down at the bottom, and when she came to her senses and woke up, she found that she was lying in a beautiful meadow.[1] The sun was shining and there were thousands of lovely flowers around.

The girl wandered around on the meadow and discovered in the middle of it an oven that was full of bread.[2] The bread called out to her: "Take me out, take me out, otherwise I'll burn. I was done a long time ago." The girl went over to the oven, and took the loaves out, one at a time.

The girl continued on her way until she came to a tree whose branches were heavy with apples. The tree called out to her: "Shake me, shake me, all of my apples are ripe[3] and ready." She shook the tree until the apples all came down as if it were raining fruit. She put the apples into a pile and continued on her way.

Finally the girl arrived at a little house. At the window there was an old lady with teeth so huge that the girl got scared[4] and wanted to run away. But the woman called after her: "What are you afraid of, dear child? Stay with me, and if you're good about doing the household chores, you won't be sorry. But you have to be sure to make my bed right and to shake the eiderdown so that the feathers start to fly. That's how you get snow on earth.[5] I am called Mother Holle."

The woman had spoken so gently with her that the girl felt encouraged and agreed to work for her. It was settled. She carried out all her chores to Mother Holle's satisfaction, shaking the bed so vigorously that the feathers flew about like snowflakes. In return, her life was not unpleasant—there were no harsh words spoken, and every day there was meat on the table, boiled or roasted.

The girl had been living with Mother Holle for a while when she began to feel sad. She wasn't sure what the matter was, but she soon realized that she was feeling homesick. Even though she was a thousand times better off here than at home, still she longed to go back. Finally she said to Mother Holle: "I have a strange yearning to return home. I know that

1. *she was lying in a beautiful meadow.* The girl's move from home, the site of persecution, through the waters of the well into a utopian meadow suggests that she is undergoing a rite of passage, one that will lead her to a higher form of existence. Like Persephone, she goes underground for a period of time, though staying with a maternal figure rather than with a bridegroom from the underworld.

2. *an oven that was full of bread.* The first of the two tests of character is connected with domestic skill, but it also requires a degree of compassion. Here the girl must assist talking loaves and a loquacious tree, whereas in other tales the protagonists must come to the rescue of animals.

3. *"all of my apples are ripe."* The apples, like the bread, are in a state of transition, requiring assistance if they are to have a nutritional value rather than burn up or rot. By assisting the loaves and the apples, the girl qualifies for support from Mother Holle, who helps her make the transition to economic independence.

4. *with teeth so huge that the girl got scared.* Like Baba Yaga of Russian folklore, the woman appears morally ambiguous, frightening in her appearance but benevolent in her manner. Mother Holle is clearly more benign than Baba Yaga, who also takes in girls for apprenticeships but who has a reputation for cannibalistic desires.

5. *"That's how you get snow on earth."* There is a hint here too of a kinship with Persephone, who goes underground in the wintertime, although the girl's experience involves apprenticeship rather than marriage.

Walter Crane, *Household Stories from the Collection of the Brothers Grimm*

The kind girl beats the mattress, and the feathers turn into the snow that falls on Earth.

I'm better off here than back there, but I just can't stay any longer. I have to see my family again."

Mother Holle replied: "I'm not at all angry that you're asking to go back home. Since you served me so loyally, I'll take you back myself." She took the girl by the hand and guided her to a large gate. When the gate opened and the girl was passing through it, gold showered down on her, and it stuck to her so that she was covered with it from head to toe. "That's your reward for working so hard," said Mother Holle, and she gave her back the spindle that had fallen into the well. Then the gate closed, and suddenly the girl found herself back up on earth, not far from her mother's house. When she got to the yard, a rooster was perched at the well, crowing:[6]

> "Cock-a-doodle-doo, cock-a-doodle-doo,
> Golden-girl's here and she's well-to-do."

Then she went into the house, and since she was covered with gold, her mother and sister made a big fuss over her.

The girl told them everything that had happened to her, and when the mother learned how she had come by such

6. *a rooster was perched at the well, crowing.* That recognition comes in the form of a barnyard animal seems odd, although the symbolic overtones of a dominant male proclaiming the one girl's success and the other's later failure are important.

Hermann Vogel,
Kinder- und Hausmärchen gesammelt durch die Brüder Grimm

The unkind girl pricks her finger on some thorns and throws the spindle into the well before jumping in after it.

great wealth, she was anxious to bring the same good fortune to the ugly, lazy girl. She told her daughter to go over to the well and start spinning. To make the spindle bloody, the girl put her hand into a hedge of thorns and pricked her finger. Then she threw the spindle into the well and jumped in after it. Like her sister, she found herself on a beautiful meadow. But when she saw the oven with the bread crying: "Take me out, take me out, otherwise I'll burn. I was done long ago," the lazy girl replied: "Do you really think I want to get all dirty doing that?" And she kept going. Soon she came to the apple tree, which called out to her: "Shake me, shake me, all my apples are ripe and ready!" Here was her answer: "What are you thinking? Why would I want to get hit on the head?" And she kept on going. When she arrived at Mother Holle's house, she was not at all afraid, for she had already learned that she had big teeth, and so right away she agreed to work for her.

On the first day, she forced herself to work hard and did everything that Mother Holle told her to do, for she really wanted to get her hands on all that gold. On the second day, she began to take things a little easier. On the third, she took it even easier and decided to stay in bed. She even refused to make Mother Holle's bed as she had promised, forgetting that she was supposed to shake it until the feathers flew around. Before long Mother Holle was fed up and ended her service. The lazy girl didn't mind at all and was sure that gold would now rain down on her. Mother Holle took her to the gate, and when she passed through it, a cauldron of pitch—not gold—poured down over her head.

"That's the reward for your service," Mother Holle said as she closed the gate.

Hermann Vogel, *Kinder- und Hausmärchen gesammelt durch die Brüder Grimm*

A cauldron of pitch is the punishment for the unkind girl's behavior. Two monkeys hold the cauldron and chuckle with amusement.

The lazy girl got back home, but she was covered with pitch, and when the rooster at the well saw her, he cried out:

"Cock-a-doodle-doo, cock-a-doodle-doo,
Tar-girl's here and she needs shampoo."

But the pitch wouldn't come off, and it stayed on her for the rest of her life.

Walter Crane,
Household Stories from the Collection of the Brothers Grimm

A rooster proclaims the return of the lazy sister.

The Seven Ravens

The power of curses, as this tale reveals, is equal to the power of wishes. When a father mindlessly hopes that his sons will turn into ravens, he finds himself faced with the sight of seven black birds ascending into the heavens. In this tale, as in "The Twelve Brothers" and "The Six Swans," a sister is responsible for liberating the boys from their enchanted state. Although she is a character who has been baptized, she does not resort to prayer or wishes, but rather takes a journey to the sun, the moon, and the stars in search of the means to transform the ravens back into boys. Although she receives the gift of a wishbone from the stars, in the end she has to rely on her own resourcefulness and on her own body to enter the domain of her brothers. Like Snow White and Goldilocks, the heroine of this tale is something of an intruder, but a welcome one whose presence effects the transformation.

There once lived a man who had seven sons, and no matter how often he wished it, he still didn't have a little daughter. Finally his wife gave him hope for another child, and when it was born, it turned out to be a little girl. There was great rejoicing, but the baby was so small and weak that she had to be baptized at home. The father told one of the boys to hurry off to the well to get some baptismal water. The other six boys ran after him, and when they got there, there was such a scramble to be the first to get the water that the pitcher fell into the well.[1] They all stood there stunned, not knowing what to do and not daring to go back home.

When the boys failed to return home, their father became impatient and said: "Those wicked boys must have forgotten what they were supposed to do. They're probably playing games." He was afraid that the girl would die unbaptized, and in his frustration, he cried out: "I wish those boys would all turn into ravens!"[2] As soon as he finished the sentence, he heard a whirring sound over his head and looked up to see seven coal-black ravens flying off into the distance.

It was too late to undo the curse, and no matter how sad the parents felt about the loss of their seven sons, they consoled themselves somewhat with their precious little daughter, who gained strength quickly and became more beautiful with each passing day.

For a long time, the child was not aware that she had brothers, for the parents were careful not to mention them. But one day she happened to hear some people talking about her, saying that, as beautiful as she was, she was still the one responsible for the unfortunate fate of her seven brothers. Upon hearing this, she felt heartbroken and went to her father and mother to ask if she really did have some brothers and what had happened to them. Then the parents knew that they could no longer keep the secret from her, but they told her that the will of heaven had caused her brothers' misfortune and her birth really had nothing to do with it. But day after day the girl's conscience plagued her, and she believed that it was up to her to disenchant her brothers. She didn't have

1. *the pitcher fell into the well.* Dropping the pitcher is the fatal event that sets the plot in motion. That the boys are fetching baptismal water suggests a degree of irreverence in their carelessness and aligns them with pagan forces. Why does the father turn his sons into ravens? Some critics point out that Wotan keeps two ravens, Huginn and Muninn (Thought and Memory), who report back to the god on their travels around Earth. The innocent daughter becomes a savior figure, who releases her brothers from a curse and enables them to experience a return from nature to culture.

2. *"I wish those boys would all turn into ravens!"* In some versions of the story, it is the mother who curses her sons, in one case for playing cards in the churchyard. Fairy tales emphasize the importance of words, showing how thoughts and wishes have transformative energy.

Die sieben Raben.

a moment's peace until finally she secretly decided to leave home and go out into the world to find her brothers and rescue them, no matter what it cost. All that she took with her was a little ring to remind her of her parents, a loaf of bread in case she got hungry, a jug of water in case she got thirsty, and a little stool in case she got tired.

And so she started walking, and she traveled very far to the end of the world. She came to the sun, but it was way too hot and frightening, and besides it ate small children up. She ran away as fast as she could and went to the moon, but it was way too cold and also scary and evil, and when the moon saw the child, it said: "I smell something, and it's human flesh." The girl raced off as fast as she could and got to the stars, which were friendly and kind, and each one was sitting on its own little chair. The morning star stood up, handed her a wishbone,[3] and said: "Unless you have this wishbone, you won't be able to open up the glass mountain,[4] and that's the place where your brothers are living."

The girl took the wishbone, wrapped it up carefully in a cloth, and kept going until she reached the glass mountain. The gates were locked, and she was about to take out the wishbone, but when she took the cloth out, there was nothing in it, and she must have lost the gift given to her by the good star. What should she do now? She wanted desperately to save her brothers, but she no longer had the key to the glass mountain. The little sister took a knife, cut off her little finger, put it into the lock, and presto, it opened up. After she had walked in, a little dwarf came up to meet her and asked: "My dear child, what are you looking for?"

"I'm looking for my brothers, the seven ravens," she replied.

The dwarf said: "My masters, the ravens, aren't at home, but you can come in and wait for them until they return." Then the dwarf carried in the food for the ravens on seven little plates and in seven little glasses. The little sister took a

3. *The morning star stood up, handed her a wishbone.* In "The Twelve Brothers," the sister has a star on her forehead. Here aid comes from the stars rather than from the central heavenly bodies.

4. *"you won't be able to open up the glass mountain."* The glass mountain, with its slippery slope, becomes accessible only to those with special footwear or, as in this case, a special key.

Arthur Rackham, *The Fairy Tales of the Brothers Grimm*

The sister of the seven ravens cuts off her little finger, fits it into the lock of the gate that will open the glass mountain, and manages to enter.

tiny bite from each little plate, and she took a little sip from each little cup. Then she dropped the ring she had brought with her into the last cup.

All of a sudden she heard a whirring and fluttering of wings high up in the air, and the dwarf said: "My masters, the ravens, will be here in a minute." They arrived just as he said, and they were so hungry and thirsty that they started looking for their plates and cups. One after another of them said: "Who's been eating from my plate? Who's been drinking from my cup? It must have been a human mouth."

When the seventh raven reached the bottom of his glass, the little ring rolled out. He took a good look at it and recognized that it was a ring belonging to his father and mother and said: "May God grant that our little sister be here. Then we would be saved." Their sister was standing behind the door listening to every word, and when she heard what he said, she came out and all the ravens returned to their human form. They hugged and kissed each other and went happily home.

Little Red Riding Hood[1]

1. *Little Red Riding Hood.* The French and German titles for the story—"Le petit chaperon rouge" and "Rotkäppchen"—suggest caps rather than hoods. Psychoanalytic critics have made much of the color red, equating it with sin, passion, blood, sexuality and thereby suggesting a certain complicity on the part of Red Riding Hood in the symbolic seduction enacted in the tale. But these views have been rebutted by folklorists and historians, who point out that the color red was first introduced in Perrault's literary version of the tale and that it can have political as well as moral associations. These days, a girl wearing red produces a nearly automatic association to the story, and advertisers ceaselessly exploit that allusion as they turn Little Red Riding Hood from a childish innocent into a red-hot femme fatale.

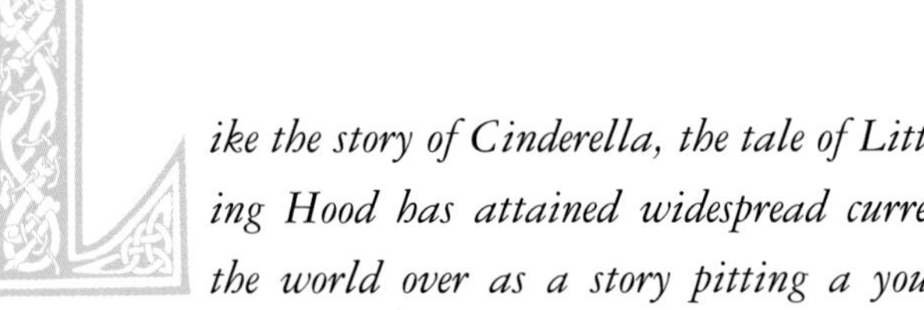

Like the story of Cinderella, the tale of Little Red Riding Hood has attained widespread currency, known the world over as a story pitting a young innocent against an evil predator. For Charles Dickens, the heroine of the tale first published in France by Charles Perrault was his "first love": "I felt that if I could have married Little Red Riding Hood, I should have known perfect bliss." Since then, her story has been recycled in many different media, attracting the attention of poets, filmmakers, musicians, advertisers, and novelists. Catherine Orenstein, whose Little Red Riding Hood Uncloaked *maps the dissemination and adaptation of the story, tells us that, despite its seeming simplicity, the story of the girl in the woods embodies "complex and fundamental human concerns." The tale "brings together archetypal opposites, through which it explores the boundaries of culture, class, and, especially what it means to be a man or a woman."*

Perrault published his literary adaptation of "Little Red Riding Hood" in 1697, but few parents choose to read that particular version of the tale to their children, for it ends with the "wicked wolf" throwing himself on Little Red Riding Hood and gobbling her up. In the Grimms' version, the young girl and her grandmother are rescued by a huntsman, who dispatches the wolf after performing a caesarian section with a pair of scissors. The Grimms discarded a version of the story in which a girl encounters a wolf and tries to appease him by offering him first her silk shirt, then her silver shoes, and finally a golden crown. He rejects the offers, and she escapes immediate danger by climbing up an oak tree. The wolf digs up the tree by its roots, and the girl's cries for help bring her beloved to the rescue, but—too late—for all he finds is a bloody arm.

"Little Red Riding Hood" has a revealing history. Early versions of her story, told around the fireside or in taverns, show a shrewd young heroine who does not need to rely on hunters to escape the wolf and to find her way back home. In "The Story of Grandmother," an oral version of the tale recorded in France at the end of the nineteenth century, Little Red Riding Hood performs a striptease before the wolf, and then ends the litany of questions about the wolf's body parts by asking if she can go outside to relieve herself. The wolf is outwitted by Little Red Riding Hood, who is more resourceful trickster than naïve young girl.

Both Perrault and the Grimms worked hard to excise the ribald grotesqueries of the original peasant tales (in some versions, Little Red Riding Hood eats the wolf's leftovers, tasting the "meat" and "wine" in her grandmother's pantry). They rescripted the events to produce a cautionary tale that accommodates a variety of messages about vanity and idleness. Perrault's Little Red Riding Hood has a "good time" gathering nuts, chasing butterflies, and picking flowers, and it is not by chance that she falls into the hands of a savage predator. The Grimms' "Little Red Riding Hood" (literally "Little Red Cap") also erased all traces of the erotic playfulness of oral versions and placed the action in the service of teaching lessons to the child inside and outside the book.

Critics of this story have played fast and loose with its elements, displaying boundless confidence in their interpretive pronouncements. To be sure, the tale itself, by depicting a conflict between a weak, vulnerable protagonist and a large, powerful antagonist, lends itself to a certain interpretive elasticity. But the multiplicity of interpretations does not inspire confidence, with some critics reading the story as an allegory of rape, others as a parable about man-hating, still others as a blueprint for the initiation of girls into sexuality and adulthood. Nazi ideologues were even able to turn the tale into an encounter between a trusting Aryan innocent and a predatory Jew.

"Little Red Riding Hood" taps into many childhood anxieties, but especially into one that psychoanalysts call the dread of being devoured. Although Perrault's story and even the Grimms' tale may take too violent a turn for some children, for others those same stories will end with a squeal of delight and a cry for more. And for those who are irritated by Little Red Riding Hood's failure to perceive that the creature lying in her grandmother's bed is a wolf, James Thurber's "The Little Girl and the Wolf" and Roald Dahl's "Little Red Riding Hood and the Wolf" are healthy antidotes to Perrault and the Grimms. In Thurber's version, we learn that a wolf does not look any more like your grandmother than the Metro-Goldwyn lion looks like Calvin Coolidge, and we watch the girl take an automatic out of her basket and shoot the wolf dead. "It is not so easy to fool little girls nowadays as it used to be," Thurber concludes in the moral appended to the tale. And Roald Dahl's Little Red Riding Hood "whips a pistol from her knickers," and in a matter of weeks, she sports a "lovely furry wolf skin coat."

Cinematic adaptations move in many different directions, from the sinister horror of Neil Jordan's In the Company of Wolves *(1985), based on a Little Red Riding Hood story by the British novelist Angela Carter, to the dark satire of Matthew Bright's* Freeway *(1996), but they unfailingly explore the erotic dimensions of the story.*

nce upon a time there lived a dear little girl. Everyone who met her liked her, but the person who loved her best of all was her grandmother, and she was always giving her gifts. Once she made her a little hood of red velvet. It was so becoming to her that the girl wanted to wear it all the time, and so she came to be called Little Red Riding Hood.

One day the girl's mother said to her: "Little Red Riding Hood, here are some cakes and a bottle of wine.[2] Take them to your grandmother. She's ill and feels weak, and they will make her strong. You'd better start off now, before it gets too hot, and when you're out in the woods, look straight ahead like a good little girl[3] and don't stray from the path. Otherwise you'll fall and break the bottle, and then there'll be nothing for Grandmother. And when you walk into her parlor, don't forget to say good morning, and don't go poking around in all the corners of the house."

"I'll do just as you say," Little Red Riding Hood promised.

Grandmother lived deep in the woods, about a half hour walk from the village. No sooner had Little Red Riding Hood set foot in the forest than she met the wolf.[4] Little Red Riding Hood had no idea what a wicked beast he was, and so she wasn't in the least bit afraid of him.

"Good morning, Little Red Riding Hood," the wolf said.

"Good morning to you too, Mr. Wolf," she replied.

"Where are you headed so early this morning, Little Red Riding Hood?"

"To Grandmother's house," she replied.

"What's that tucked under your apron?"

"Some cakes and wine. Yesterday we did some baking, and Grandmother needs something to make her better, for she is ill and feeling weak," she replied.

"Where is your grandmother's house, Little Red Riding Hood?"

"It's a good quarter of an hour's walk into the woods, right under the three big oak trees. You must know the place from all the hazel hedges around it," said Little Red Riding Hood.

The wolf thought to himself: "That tender young thing

2. *some cakes and a bottle of wine.* The cakes and wine have been seen as representing the Christian Communion and form a counterpart to the flesh and blood that the wolf leaves on the table at Grandmother's house for Little Red Riding Hood in some versions of the tale. In Perrault's French version, Little Red Riding Hood takes some cakes and a pot of butter to her grandmother. Trina Schart Hyman's illustrations for *Little Red Riding Hood* depict a red-nosed, alcoholic grandmother, perhaps triggering the banning of the story in two California school districts in 1990. Recent modern rescriptings, such as Lois Lowry's *Number the Stars* and Roberto Innocenti's *Rose Blanche*, use the girl's function as courier to construct a heroic figure who saves lives by making it through the woods with her basket of food.

3. *"when you're out in the woods, look straight ahead like a good little girl."* The Grimms added this warning, along with the behavioral imperatives that follow. Acutely aware that their collection would model behavior for children, they looked for opportunities to encode the stories with morals, messages, and lessons in etiquette. Note that Little Red Riding Hood's curiosity is discouraged, for she must not "stray from the path" or poke around "in all the corners of the house."

4. *the wolf.* The predator in this story is unusual, for he is a real beast rather than a cannibalistic ogre or witch. Folklorists have suggested that the story of Little Red Riding Hood may have originated relatively late (in the Middle Ages) as a cautionary tale warning children about the dangers of the forest. Wild animals, sinister men, and the hybrid figure of the werewolf were thought to menace the safety of children with powerful immediacy. In seventeenth-century Germany, shortly after the Thirty Years War, fear of wolves

Warwick Goble, *The Fairy Book*

Little Red Riding Hood is not sure what to make of the predator who eyes her as a tasty morsel. Ears perked and tongue hanging out, this wolf may not seem ferocious, but he is ready to pounce.

will make a nice dainty snack! She'll taste even better than the old woman. If you're really crafty, you'll get them both."

The wolf walked beside Little Red Riding Hood for a while. Then he said: "Little Red Riding Hood, have you noticed the beautiful flowers all around?[5] Why don't you stay and look at them for a while? I don't think you've even heard how sweetly the birds are singing. You act as if you were on the way to school, when it's really so much fun out here in the woods."

Little Red Riding Hood opened her eyes wide, looked around, and saw the sunbeams dancing in the trees. She caught sight of the beautiful flowers all around and thought: "If you bring Grandmother a fresh bouquet, she'll be delighted. It's still early enough that I'm sure to get there in plenty of time."

Little Red Riding Hood left the path and ran off into the woods looking for flowers. As soon as she picked one, she spotted an even more beautiful one somewhere else and went after it. And so she went even deeper into the woods.

The wolf ran straight to Grandmother's house and knocked at the door.

"Who's there?"

"Little Red Riding Hood. I've brought some cakes and wine. Open the door."

"Just raise the latch," Grandmother called out. "I'm too weak to get out of bed."

The wolf raised the latch, and the door swung wide open. Without saying a word, he went straight to Grandmother's bed and gobbled her right up. Then he put on her clothes and her nightcap,[6] lay down in her bed, and drew the curtains.

Meanwhile, Little Red Riding Hood was running around looking for flowers. When she had gathered so many that she couldn't hold any more in her arms, she suddenly remembered Grandmother and got back on the path leading to her house. She was surprised to find the door open, and when she

and hysteria about werewolves reached especially high levels. The wolf, with his predatory nature, is frequently seen as a metaphor for sexually seductive men, but he can also be read as a hybrid figure who crosses the boundary between wilderness and civilization, "the male counterpart of the female witch," as Marjorie Garber puts it in *Vested Interests.*

5. *"the beautiful flowers all around."* Little Red Riding Hood is described as a child with magnetic looks, and she herself is attracted to the beauty of nature: the colors and aromas of the flowers, the sweet sounds of the birds in the woods, and the sunbeams dancing in the trees. That she decides to pick flowers for her grandmother speaks less to a desire for pleasure than a desire to please others.

6. *he put on her clothes and her nightcap.* Anne Sexton referred to the Grimms' wolf as a "kind of transvestite" in her verse collection *Transformations.*

stepped into the house, she had such a strange feeling that she thought: "Oh, my goodness, I'm usually so glad to be at Grandmother's house, but something feels really strange."

Little Red Riding Hood called out a greeting, but there was no answer. Then she went over to the bed and drew back the curtain. Grandmother was lying there with her nightcap pulled down over her face. She looked very odd.

"Oh, Grandmother, what big ears you have!"[7]

"The better to hear you with."

"Oh, Grandmother, what big eyes you have!"

"The better to see you with."

"Oh, Grandmother, what big hands you have!"

"The better to grab you with!"

"Oh, Grandmother, what a big, scary mouth you have!"

"The better to eat you with!"

No sooner had the wolf said these words than he leaped out of bed and gobbled up poor Little Red Riding Hood.[8]

Once the wolf had eaten his fill, he lay back down in the bed, fell asleep, and began to snore very loudly. A huntsman[9] happened to be passing by the house just then and thought: "How loudly the old woman is snoring! I'd better check to see if anything's wrong." He walked into the house, and when he reached the bed, he realized that a wolf was lying in it.

"I've found you at last, you old sinner,"[10] he said. "I've been after you for a long time now."

He pulled out his musket and was about to take aim when he realized that the wolf might have eaten Grandmother and that he could still save her. Instead of firing, he took out a pair of scissors and began cutting open the belly of the sleeping wolf.[11] After making a few cuts, he caught sight of a red cap. He made a few more cuts, and a girl leaped out,[12] crying: "Oh, I was so terrified! It was so dark in the belly of the wolf."

Although she could barely breathe, the frail grandmother also found her way back out of the belly. Little Red Riding Hood quickly fetched some large stones and filled the wolf's

7. *"Oh, Grandmother, what big ears you have!"* In the classic dialogue between girl and wolf, Little Red Riding Hood invokes the senses of hearing, sight, feeling, and taste, leaving out the sense of smell. The invocation of different body parts was no doubt expanded by folk raconteurs, who took advantage of opportunities for ribald humor. A parallel dialogue in oral versions of the tale provides an inventory of Red Riding Hood's clothes, which she removes and discards one by one. Djuna Barnes understood the power of the scene for children when she wrote that "Children know something they can't tell; they like Red Riding Hood and the wolf in bed!"

8. *he leaped out of bed and gobbled up poor Little Red Riding Hood.* Many critics have viewed this scene as a symbolic death, followed by rebirth, once Little Red Riding Hood is released from the belly of the beast. The connection with biblical and mythical figures (most notably Jonah) is self-evident, though Little Red Riding Hood has also been interpreted as a figure that symbolizes the sun, engulfed by the night and reemerging at dawn. More recently, the swallowing whole of the grandmother and the girl has been seen as a symbolic double rape.

9. *a huntsman.* Note that the male figures in the story are either predators or rescuers, signifiers of male sexual desire or of male governance. The wolf is usually positioned as male seducer, out to stalk innocent young girls, whereas the huntsman has been seen as representing patriarchal protection for the two women who are unable to fend for themselves. In oral versions, the girl in the story does not need to rely on a huntsman passing by Grandmother's house.

10. *"you old sinner."* The wolf is aligned with satanic forces, and in keeping with

Arthur Rackham, *Hansel and Gretel and Other Tales by the Brothers Grimm*

Little Red Riding Hood's cloak builds a powerful contrast to the dark patterns of "Grandmother's" sheet, blanket, and curtain. The sharp teeth are in clear evidence when Little Red Riding Hood draws the floral curtain.

belly with them.[13] When the wolf awoke, he tried to race off, but the stones were so heavy that his legs collapsed, and he fell down dead.

Little Red Riding Hood, her grandmother, and the huntsman were elated. The huntsman skinned the wolf and took the pelt home with him. Grandmother ate the cakes and drank the wine that Little Red Riding Hood had brought her and recovered her health. Little Red Riding Hood said to herself: "Never again will you stray from the path and go into the woods, when your mother has forbidden it."

There is a story about another time that Little Red Riding Hood met a wolf on the way to Grandmother's house, while she was bringing her some cakes. The wolf tried to get her to stray from the path, but Little Red Riding Hood was on her guard and kept right on going. She told her grandmother that she had met a wolf and that he had greeted her. But he had looked at her in such an evil way that "if we hadn't been out in the open, he would have gobbled me right up."

"Well then," said Grandmother. "We'll just lock the door so he can't get in."

A little while later the wolf knocked at the door and called out: "Open the door, Grandmother. It's Little Red Riding Hood, and I'm bringing you some cakes."

The two kept completely quiet and refused to open the door. Then old Graybeard circled the house a few times and jumped up on the roof. He was planning on waiting until Little Red Riding Hood went home. Then he was going to creep up after her and gobble her up in the dark. But Grandmother figured out what was on his mind. There was a big stone trough in front of the house. Grandmother said to the child: "Here's a bucket, Little Red Riding Hood. Yesterday

the Christian allusions to flesh and blood and to cakes and wine, he becomes the disruptive figure of the sinner.

11. *began cutting open the belly of the sleeping wolf.* Freud and others read this scene as an allusion to the birth process, with the wolf subjected to an operation that ends in his death. As Anne Sexton wryly notes, he undergoes "a kind of caesarian section." One psychoanalytic critic views the wolf as suffering from pregnancy envy. Little Red Riding Hood's emergence from the belly of the wolf reprises Jonah's emergence from the belly of the whale.

12. *a girl leaped out.* Little Red Riding Hood's eagerness to emerge from the belly of the wolf seems to suggest that she has undergone a powerful transformation. Children reading the story, Bettelheim notes, will understand that "Little Red Cap really 'died' as the girl who permitted herself to be tempted by the wolf; and that when the story says 'the little girl sprang out' of the wolf's belly, she came to life a different person."

13. *fetched some large stones and filled the wolf's belly with them.* The stones have been read as a sign of sterility, but they are more likely an appropriate retaliation for the incorporation of Little Red Riding Hood and her grandmother.

I cooked some sausages in it. Take the water in which they were boiled and pour it into the trough."

Little Red Riding Hood kept taking water to the trough until it was completely full. The smell from those sausages reached the wolf's nostrils. His neck was stretched out so far from sniffing and looking around that he lost his balance and began to slide down the roof. He slid right down into the trough and drowned. Little Red Riding Hood walked home cheerfully, and no one ever did her any harm.[14]

14. *Little Red Riding Hood walked home cheerfully, and no one ever did her any harm.* Note the contrast between the two endings, with the first emphasizing the lesson that Little Red Riding Hood herself has learned and the second suggesting a confident heroine who has discovered how to outsmart those who attempt to prey on her. Of course the second installment also gives us a Little Red Riding Hood who has learned her lesson and who is "on her guard."

The Bremen[1] Town Musicians

1. *Bremen.* Although the town of Bremen prides itself on the four creatures that make it their destination, the geographical designation is probably an arbitrary one that changed according to the location of the teller. As a seaport, Bremen represents a blend of the domestic and the exotic, a liminal space that combines home and abroad and that figures as a point of departure for life's final journey.

Fairy tales depicting the antagonism between man and beast are unusual, yet the Grimms included several in their collection. Unlike the fable, with its allegorical turn suggesting that each figure represents a certain trait, tales like "The Bremen Town Musicians" have an underlying didactic thrust, but one that is not readily apparent. The beasts featured in the tale—donkey, dog, cat, and rooster—become allies because each has outlived his usefulness. Cast off by their cruel masters, who value them only for their labor, the four join ranks to harmonize with each other as musicians in the town of Bremen, which is less of a real geographical destination than a utopian dream.

Before reaching Bremen, the animals find a home in a place that was once a den of thieves. Both beasts and robbers are social renegades, but whereas the beasts exhibit egalitarian solidarity, the robbers remain locked in rigid hierarchies, with a captain heading the group who gives commands and jeopardizes the safety of individual members by sending them out on reconnaissance. The animals invade the house of the robbers, and they manage to occupy it, but they never shed a drop of blood. Using their wits to outsmart the thieves, they succeed in creating a comfortable retirement home for themselves, in a place where they are no longer required to wear themselves out by earning a living.

Once there lived a man who owned a donkey[2] that never grew ornery even though he had been hauling sacks of grain to a mill year in and year out. The animal's strength was beginning to fail, and he was becoming less and less suited for that type of work. The master was thinking about doing away with him, but when the donkey realized that there was trouble in the air, he ran off and started out on a journey to Bremen. He thought that he might be able to become one of the town musicians there.

After he had been on the road for a while, the donkey saw a hound[3] lying by the side of the road, panting like someone who had been walking to the point of exhaustion.

"Hey there, Packer," said the donkey, "why are you panting so hard?"

"Alas," the dog replied, "I'm beginning to get old, and every day I feel a little weaker. Now that I'm having trouble keeping up on hunts, my master is thinking of doing away with me. I've run away now, but I don't know how I'm going to earn my daily bread."

"Listen to me," the donkey said. "I'm on my way to Bremen to become a town musician. Why don't you join me and become a member of the band?[4] I'll play the lute and you can play the drums." The dog thought that was a mighty good idea, and they went back on the road together.

Before they had gotten very far, they ran into a cat making a face as long as three days of rain in a row.

"What's gotten into you, Mr. Tidypaws?" asked the donkey.

"How can you enjoy anything when your life is hanging by

2. *Once there lived a man who owned a donkey.* From the start, the tale sets up an opposition between master and slave, with the masters exploiting the labor of the good-natured domesticated beasts.

3. *saw a hound.* Note that the beasts do not signify any particular attributes, nor do they have clearly differentiated personalities. They each seem to carry out a household function and are defined by their use to their owners.

4. *"Why don't you join me and become a member of the band?"* Despite the fact that the animals are not particularly skilled musicians, they are able to make an art of their noise through their solidarity. The minstrels form a band that stands in sharp contrast to the other social configurations in the story.

5. *"Our Dear Lady is planning to wash the Christ Child's shirts."* The insertion of a reference to the Madonna anchors the tale in a culture where weather was described in religious terms.

a thread?" the cat replied. "Just because I'm getting old and my teeth aren't as sharp as they used to be, and just because I'd rather sleep near the oven and purr than chase mice, my mistress started thinking about drowning me. It's true that I managed to get away in time, but now I need some good advice. Where in the world should I go?"

"Come with us to Bremen. As an expert in nighttime serenades, you'll make a good town minstrel." The cat thought that was not a bad idea at all and decided to join up.

The three fugitives passed by a barnyard, where a rooster was perched up on the gate, crowing with all his might. "That crowing of yours could shatter glass," the donkey exclaimed. "What in the world are you trying to do?"

"I'm predicting good weather," said the rooster, "because today is the day that Our Dear Lady is planning to wash the Christ Child's shirts[5] and hang them up to dry. But my own mistress is heartless. Tomorrow we're having company, and I heard her tell the cook that she was going to put me in tomorrow's soup and eat me up. They're going to chop my head off tonight. And so I'm crowing as loud as I can while the crowing's good."

"Don't be a fool, Redcomb," said the donkey. "You can come with us instead. We're heading for Bremen, and you're sure to find something better than death if you join us. You have a fine voice! Why don't you come sing with us? We're sure to be a great success."

The rooster let them talk him into it, and the four of them continued on the journey together. It was already getting dark, and since it was impossible to get to Bremen that day, they decided to spend the night in the forest they had reached. The donkey and the dog found a spot to sleep under a tall tree. The cat and the rooster settled down for the night in the tree's branches, although the rooster—just to be on the safe side—flew up to the very top of the tree. Before going to sleep, he decided to take a good look in every direction, and he happened to notice a light burning in the distance.[6] He let his companions know that there must be a house nearby, for he had seen some sign of life.

The donkey said: "I'm all for leaving this place and trying our luck elsewhere. This place isn't really all that comfortable." The dog said he wouldn't mind having a bone or two, and if there was some meat on those bones, that would be all the better. And so they headed off in the direction of the light, which grew more and more vibrant until they reached a brightly lit house where some robbers were living.[7]

The donkey, who happened to be the tallest, went up to the window and peered into the house. "What do you see, Old Gray?" the rooster asked.

"What do I see?" the donkey replied. "I can see a table covered with good things to eat and drink. The robbers are sitting down at it, and they're having a good time."

"That sounds like just the thing for us," said the rooster.

"I'll say! If only we could get inside," the donkey said.

The animals went into a huddle to figure out how to chase the robbers out of there, and finally they hit on a plan. The donkey got up on his hind legs[8] and put his front legs down on the window ledge; the dog jumped up on the donkey's back; the cat climbed up on the dog; and finally the rooster flew up to the very top and perched on the cat's head.

When they were in formation, someone gave a signal, and they started making their music: the donkey brayed, the dog barked, the cat meowed, and the rooster crowed. Then they came crashing into the room through the window to the sound of shattering glass. The robbers, who were sure that a ghost had burst into the room, nearly jumped out of their skins in terror and fled into the woods.[9]

The four good fellows sat down at the table, happy to make do with leftovers, and they ate as if they were planning to go on a starvation diet the very next day. When the minstrels had finished eating, they put out the light and each one

6. *he happened to notice a light burning in the distance.* The light in the distance represents a form of hope for the animals. With darkness all around and without a home, they are not comfortable in the woods and are attracted to the notion of rediscovering civilization. These animals project onto an urban space (Bremen) the freedom that is usually associated with the wilderness.

7. *where some robbers were living.* In variants of the tale, the inhabitants of the cottage are often wild animals, and occasionally a witch or werewolves. The criminality of the human inhabitants makes them fair game for the animals.

8. *The donkey got up on his hind legs.* The acrobatic formation created by the animals signals their willingness to cooperate according to their strengths and turns them into the artists that they aspire to become in Bremen.

9. *fled into the woods.* The robbers are not only criminals; they are also cowards who are easily intimidated by the cunning beasts.

L. Leslie Brooke, *The House in the Wood and Other Old Fairy Stories*

The four musicians stand ready to perform for the evening.

looked for a place that would be just the right size,[10] and comfortable to boot. The donkey settled down on the dung heap, the dog behind the door, the cat over where the ashes were still warm, and the rooster perched on a roof beam. They had no trouble falling asleep right away, for they were exhausted by the long journey.

Shortly after midnight the robbers took a look at their house and saw that the lights were out. Everything seemed to be quiet. The captain of the band announced: "We shouldn't have abandoned ship so quickly," and he ordered one of the robbers to go over and investigate.[11] The scout noticed that there was no sound at all in the house, and so he went into

10. *a place that would be just the right size.* Breaking and entering is a familiar theme in fairy tales, and these intruders, like Goldilocks and Snow White, search for resting places that will be "just right."

11. *ordered one of the robbers to go over and investigate.* Note that the robber captain and his band replicate the hierarchical relationship of the masters and servants. The captain has no reservations about exposing a member of his band to danger.

George Cruikshank, *German Popular Stories*

Robbers flee in terror when the four aspiring musicians burst in through the window.

the kitchen to make some light. He saw the cat's glowing, fiery eyes and mistook them for live coals. When he held up a match to them, thinking he could get a light, the cat, who didn't have a sense of humor at all, flew into the robber's face, spitting and scratching. Scared out of his wits, the robber took off and was hoping to get out the back door when the dog, who happened to be lying right in his way, jumped up and bit him in the leg. The robber managed to cross the yard, but when he got to the dung heap, the donkey gave him a good swift kick with his hind legs. The rooster, who had been roused from his slumber and was now wide awake, crowed out from his perch: "Cock-a-doodle-doo!"

The robber fled back to his captain as fast as his legs would carry him and reported: "There's a hideous old witch back there in the house. She hissed at me and scratched my face with her long claws. And there's an old guy behind the door with a knife, and he stabbed me in the leg. In the yard I ran into a huge black monster that started beating me with a big, wooden club. Up on the roof there was a judge[12] who started shouting: 'Bring me that scoundrel!' And so I got out of there as fast as I could."

After that the robbers didn't dare return to their house, and the four Bremen musicians enjoyed it so much that they decided not to leave.

And the lips of the person who last told this story are still warm.[13]

12. *Up on the roof there was a judge.* The rooster's crowing is mistaken for the voice of a judicial authority, in part because the robber knows that he is an intruder, even if on his own domain, in part because the rooster is seen as a commanding presence in the barnyard.

13. *And the lips of the person who last told this story are still warm.* Storytellers often finished their tales with a flourish that embodied their presence in the narrative. Functioning like a signature on a painting, the final line reminds us that the story was crafted by a raconteur with his own personal style.

The Devil and His Three Golden Hairs

In the first British translation of the Grimms' collection, this particular tale, to avoid giving offense, was given the title "The Giant and the Three Golden Hairs." That change alerts us to the fact that the devil does in fact occupy a narrative function that could also be filled by a giant. In fact, the happy-go-lucky lad in this tale displays remarkable similarities to Jack, who is protected from a man-eating ogre by a tender-hearted maternal figure. The Grimms' tale probably featured a giant in its earlier versions, and only in a later age did that giant take on the name of the devil.

The boy born with a caul faces threats from above and below, from a monarch at the top of the social order and from the fiendish ruler of hell. Surviving the king's efforts to drown him and to murder him, the boy crosses a river into hell, where he extracts information from the devil and manages to uproot three of his golden hairs. His success is predetermined, and yet his cheerful confidence in the face of one menacing event after another establishes him as a valiant fellow who deserves his good fortune.

nce upon a time there was a poor woman who gave birth to a son. He was born with a caul,[1] which was considered good luck, and a fortune-teller predicted that he would marry the daughter of a king when he was fourteen years old. One day the king came to the village, and no one recognized him. When he asked people if anything of interest had happened in the town, they replied: "A few days ago a child was born with a caul. Fortune will smile on him no matter what he does. A fortune-teller also said that he would marry the daughter of the king when he reached the age of fourteen."

The king was irritated by the prophecy, and on top of that he had a wicked heart. He went to meet the boy's parents and pretended to be friendly and said: "You are poor people. If you let me raise your child, I will take good care of him." At first they refused, but the stranger offered them a generous amount of gold and they began to think: "Fortune has smiled on him, and this will all turn out for the best." And so they consented and gave him their child.

The king put the boy in a box[2] and rode off with him until he found some deep waters. Then he plunged the box in the water and thought: "Now I've liberated my daughter from an undesirable suitor."

The box didn't sink but ended up floating like a little ship, and not a drop of water got into it. It floated to a point that was about two miles from the king's capital city, where it got caught in a dam by a mill. Fortunately a miller's apprentice was standing near the water and saw it. Thinking that he might have found a great treasure, he pulled it toward shore with a big hook. When he opened the box, he discovered a beautiful baby boy, as hale and hearty as you can imagine. He brought him to the miller and his wife, who didn't have any children

1. *He was born with a caul.* The caul is a portion of the amnion, which sometimes covers the head of a child at birth. Superstitions about the caul as a bearer of good fortune reach back to antiquity. As late as the 1870s British newspapers posted ads offering substantial sums of money for cauls. For the hero of this tale, the caul takes on symbolic meaning, protecting him from the various assaults on his body, including the king's effort to kill him by throwing him into water.

2. *The king put the boy in a box.* In a parallel biblical moment, the mother of Moses tries to *save* her son by putting him into a basket of reeds that floats in the waters. But the king here is not aware that water is, for this boy in particular, a friendly element.

of their own and who were delighted when they saw the boy. They said: "This is God's gift to us." They took good care of the foundling, and he was raised to be virtuous and honest.

One day the king was caught in a storm, and he found shelter at the mill. He asked the miller and his wife if the boy was theirs. "No," they replied. "He's an orphan. Fourteen years ago he came floating down to the mill in a box, and our apprentice fished him out of the water." Then the king realized that it was the lucky lad he had thrown into the water, and he said: "Do you think that that fellow could take a letter to my wife, the queen? I'll be happy to give him two gold pieces as a reward."

"As the king wishes," the miller and his wife said, and they told the boy to get ready. The king wrote the queen a letter that read: "As soon as the boy bearing this letter arrives, I want you to have him killed and buried. You must take care of this before I return."

The boy got on the road to deliver the letter, but he lost his way, and when night fell he ended up in the woods. Although it was dark, he could make out a little light, and he worked his way toward it and found a hut. When he walked in, he saw an old woman sitting all alone by the fire. She was frightened when she saw the boy and asked him: "Where are you coming from and where are you going?"

"I'm coming from the mill," he replied, "and I was hoping to take a letter to the queen. But since I've lost my way in the woods, I'd be grateful if I could stay here for the night."

"You poor boy," the woman said. "You've walked into a house where robbers are living.[3] When they come home, they will kill you."

"Let come what may," the boy said. "I'm not afraid. Besides, I'm too tired to go any farther," and he stretched out on a bench and fell asleep. Not much later the robbers returned and asked in an angry tone about the stranger lying on the bench.

3. *"You've walked into a house where robbers are living."* In the Grimms' "The Robber Bridegroom," the heroine of the story also learns from an old woman that her life is in danger. But in this tale, the robbers do not represent a threat, rather the king and the devil figure as the sources of danger. "The Bremen Town Musicians" and "The Robber Bridegroom" both feature robbers who imperil the main character.

"Ah," said the old woman, "he's just an innocent child who got lost in the woods. I felt sorry for him and took him in. He has been sent to deliver a letter to the queen."

When the robbers opened the letter and read it, they discovered that the boy was to be murdered after delivering the letter. Even the hardhearted robbers felt sorry for him, and the leader tore the letter in two and composed a new one which said that the boy was to marry the princess on arrival. The boy slept undisturbed, and they let him stay on the bench until the next morning. When he woke up, they gave him the new letter and pointed him in the right direction. The queen received the letter, read it, and did exactly as it said. She ordered a splendid wedding feast, and the princess was married to the lucky lad. And because the fellow was handsome and charming, she lived with him in peace and happiness.

Some time later the king returned to his castle and saw that the prophecy had been fulfilled and that the lucky lad had married his daughter. "How could that have happened?" he exclaimed. "My letter sent very different instructions." The queen handed him the letter and told him to see for himself what was in it. The king read the contents and realized that his letter had been exchanged for another. He asked the boy what had happened to the document entrusted to him and why he had arrived with a different one.

"I wouldn't know," he replied. "Someone must have switched the letters while I was asleep in the woods."

The king was enraged and said: "It's not all going to fall in your lap like this." Whoever marries my daughter is going to have to go to hell and bring back three hairs from the devil's head. If you do as I say, you can stay married to my daughter." The king was hoping to get rid of him forever that way. But the lucky lad replied: "I will go and fetch the golden hairs.[4] I'm not afraid of the devil." And so he took his leave and set out on his journey.

4. *"I will go and fetch the golden hairs."* It is rare that a villain possesses hair made of gold, and in this case the gold seems to be little more than a signal pointing to the possibility of wealth. The pulling of the hair awakens the devil and provokes him to explain how to solve the mystery of the well and the apple tree and to provide a solution to the ferryman's dilemma. The old woman catches the devil off guard by pulling out hairs and asking him questions while he is still half asleep.

The road took him to a big town, and the guards at the gates wanted to know everything about him, what trade he practiced and what he knew.

"I know everything," the lucky lad replied.

"Then you can do us a big favor," the guards said, "and tell us why the well that stands in the marketplace has dried up. It used to overflow with wine, and now we can't even get water from it."

"You'll get your answer," he replied. "Just wait until I come back."

He went on his way and came to another town. The guard at the gates there also asked him what kind of trade he practiced and what he knew.

"I know everything," he replied.

"Then you can do us a favor and tell us why the tree in our town, which used to bear golden apples, won't even put out leaves now."

"You'll get your answer," he replied. "Just wait until I come back."

He kept walking and reached a deep river that he had to cross. The ferryman asked him what trade he practiced and what he knew.

"I know everything," he replied.

"Then you can do me a favor," the ferryman said, "and tell me why I have to keep rowing back and forth,[5] and no one relieves me."

"You'll get your answer," he replied. "Just wait until I come back."

When he reached the other side of the river, he found the entrance to hell. It was dark and sooty. The devil wasn't home, but his grandmother was sitting there in a great big easy chair.

"What do you want here?" she asked, and she didn't look all that mean.

"I'm hoping to get three golden hairs from the devil's

5. *"tell me why I have to keep rowing back and forth."* Like Charon of Greek mythology, this ferryman provides passage between the world of the living and a nether world. Doomed to keep rowing, he seeks the possibility of release from perpetual motion.

6. *"But I feel sorry for you, and I'm going to see if I can help you."* Like the giant's wife in "Jack and the Beanstalk," the devil's granny takes pity on the hero. If the male figures in the tale are greedy, predatory, untrustworthy, and duplicitous, the female figures stand ready to help the hero when he is in need.

head," he replied. "Otherwise I won't be allowed to stay married to my wife."

"That's asking a lot," she said. "When the devil comes home and finds you here, there will be hell to pay. But I feel sorry for you, and I'm going to see if I can help you."[6]

With that, she turned him into an ant and said: "Crawl into the folds of my skirt. You'll be safe there."

"Yes," he said, "that's just fine. But I'd like to get some information about three things. First, why does a well that used to overflow with wine suddenly go dry and not even give water? Second, why does a tree that used to bear golden apples stop putting out even leaves? And third, why does a ferryman have to keep rowing back and forth without anyone coming to relieve him?"

"Those are tough questions," she said. "But keep quiet and hold still. And more importantly, listen carefully to what the devil says when I pull the three golden hairs from his head."

When night fell, the devil returned home. As soon as he walked in the door he noticed that there was something in the air. "I smell, I smell the flesh of a man," he said. "Something's not quite right here." Then he looked in all the nooks and crannies, but he couldn't find anything.

His old granny scolded him. "I just finished sweeping up," she said. "Everything was in its place, and now you come along and mess it all up again. You're always smelling human flesh! Have a seat and eat your supper." When he had finished eating and drinking, he felt tired, put his head in his old granny's lap, and told her to pick out the lice from his head. Before long he had fallen asleep and began wheezing and snoring. The old woman took hold of a golden hair, pulled it out, and put it next to her.

"Ouch!" screeched the devil. "What are you doing?"

"I had a bad dream and pulled your hair."

"What was your dream about?" the devil asked.

"I dreamed that a well that once overflowed with wine had

dried up, and now even water won't flow from it. What could be the cause of that?"

"Ha, if they just knew!" the devil replied. "In the well, under a stone, a toad is sitting.[7] If they just killed it, the wine would start to flow again."

The old granny picked out a few more lice until he fell asleep and started snoring so loudly that the windows were rattling. Then she pulled out a second hair.

"Hey, what's going on?" the devil yelled in a rage.

"Don't be angry with me," she said. "I did it in a dream."

"What were you dreaming about this time?" he asked.

"I dreamed that in a certain kingdom there was a fruit tree that used to bear golden apples, but now it won't even put forth leaves. What could be the cause of that?"

"Ha, if they just knew!" the devil replied. "A mouse is gnawing on its roots. If they just killed it, the tree would soon bear golden apples again. But if the mouse continues to gnaw much longer, the whole tree will wither away. But stop bothering me with your dreams. If you disturb my sleep just one more time, I'll box your ears."

The old granny spoke soothing words to him and continued picking out lice until he fell asleep and started snoring again. Then she grabbed a third golden hair and pulled it out. The devil shot into the air with a howl and was about to give her a drubbing, but she calmed him down and said: "What can you do when you have bad dreams?"

"What did you dream this time?" he asked, because he was really curious.

"I dreamed about a ferryman who was always complaining about having to row back and forth and how no one comes to relieve him. What could be the cause of that?"

"Ha, the fool!" the devil replied. "All he has to do is put the pole in the hand of someone who comes along and wants to be rowed across. Then that guy will have to do the ferrying and he will be free."

7. *"In the well, under a stone, a toad is sitting."* The toad and the mouse both seem to be instruments of the devil, who is aware of their presence precisely because of his agency. Both animals inhabit nether regions, with the toad at the bottom of a well under a stone and the mouse in the roots of the tree.

Now that the old granny had pulled out three of his golden hairs and received answers for the three questions, she left the old dragon in peace, and he slept until daybreak.

Once the devil went on his way, the old woman took the ant out of the folds in her skirt and restored the lucky lad to his human shape. "Here are the three golden hairs," she said. "I'm sure you heard the devil's answers to your three questions."

"Yes, I did," he replied. "And I'll remember every word."

"Then that takes care of you," she said. "Now you can go on your way."

He thanked the old woman for helping him out of his predicament and left hell with a smile on his face, for everything had turned out so well for him. When he reached the river, the ferryman was waiting for the answer that had been promised him. "First row me over to the other side," the lucky chap said, "and then I will tell you how you can get some relief from your work." He reached the other side and gave him the devil's advice: "When the next person comes to be rowed to the other side, put the pole in his hand."

He went on and arrived in the town where the tree that would not bear fruit was standing. The guard was waiting for the answer to his question. He told him exactly what he had heard from the devil: "Kill the mouse that is gnawing on the roots and then the tree will bear golden apples again." The guard thanked him and gave him, as a reward, two donkeys laden with gold, and they followed him.

Finally he reached the town where the well had dried up. He told the guard exactly what the devil had said: "In the well, under a stone, a toad is sitting. If you just find it and kill it, then wine will start to flow again." The guard thanked him and gave him another pair of donkeys laden with gold.

Finally the lucky lad came back home to his wife, who was overjoyed to see him again and to hear about his success. As for the king, he brought back for him just what he had asked for: three golden hairs from the devil's head. When he saw the four donkeys laden with gold, the king was delighted and said: "Now you have fulfilled all the conditions, and you can stay married to my daughter. But, tell me, dear son-in-law, where did you get all this gold? This is an immense treasure."

"I traveled across a river," he replied, "and I took it with me. It's right on the banks of the river, where there's usually sand."

"Can I go get some for myself?" asked the king, for he was a greedy man.

"As much as you want," he replied. "There's a ferryman on the river who can row you across so that you can fill up the sacks you take with you." The greedy king left as soon as he could, and when he reached the river, he beckoned the ferryman to take him to the other side. The ferryman came and told him to climb in, and when they reached the other side, he put the pole in his hand, jumped out, and ran off. The king had to row back and forth from then on as punishment for his sins.

"And is he still rowing?"

"Of course he is! Who would take that pole from him?"

The Magic Table, the Gold Donkey, and the Club in the Sack

Fairy tales, as we all know, are about wish fulfillment, and wishes often come in sets of three. They are also often attached to mundane concerns. For many fairy-tale heroes, a full belly figures at the top of any list of desires. As Robert Darnton tells us, "to eat one's fill, eat until the exhaustion of the appetite (manger à sa faim)*, was the principal pleasure that the peasants dangled before their imaginations, and one that they rarely realized in their lives." Fairy tales, he reminds us, are often less focused on flights of fancy and fantasies of escape than on a "program for survival."*

The magic table, the gold donkey, and the club in the sack all serve to free their owners from the burden of labor. Having served their apprenticeships, the brothers are rewarded with magic objects that provide unlimited food and drink, gold in abundance, and the power to thwart enemies. Through a combination of hard work and cunning on the part of the third and youngest brother, they succeed in living happily ever after with their father. This is a tale that turns on liberation from labor rather than romance and royalty. We do not move from a modest household to a regal palace, but from home and the village to the open road. This is the ordinary world of peasant life, one that engages with issues of economic prosperity and family solidarity rather than love and marriage.

The Grimms' tale of three sons unfolds in three parts. In the first, the father is the victim of a deception, duped by the family goat into believing that his sons failed to discharge their responsibility. As the sole female character in the tale, the goat might seem to occupy the position of the absent mother, particularly since she is described as the provider of milk. Yet she remains an oddly unmotivated figure, not driven by malice or any other desire to undermine the three sons. The first phase of the tale ends in a tragic mode, with the father left at home alone, sinking into a deep depression.

The second phase of the tale moves in a tragic-comic mode, with the brothers earning their way back to prosperity by learning trades. The end of their apprenticeship marks a liberation from labor, for each receives a gift that promises an end to the daily struggle for survival. The table that sets itself with food and drink, the donkey that spits gold coins from front and behind, and the club that defeats all enemies, taken together, hold forth the promise of a utopian dream in which no effort is required at all. In this second part of the tale, the brothers are once again victims of deception, but on the third repetition of thievery, the youngest brother outwits the man who swindled his two brothers.

Part three reintroduces the goat, whose deep humiliation is put on display. With shaved head, the goat seeks shelter and manages to outfox a fox, and even a bear, but falls victim to a bee, a symbolic underdog who may not get any respect from larger animals but has size, speed, and a sting that promises to defeat those who are larger and more powerful. The coda emphasizes the triumph of the underdog and adds a final flourish to a narrative in triplicate of betrayal, loss, and restitution.

For the psychologist Karl Abraham, this particular tale represents "a triple wish fulfillment related to the three erogenous zones." The first son receives full gratification of oral desires; the second son succeeds in satisfying anal hoarding impulses; the third son, who triumphs in the end and wins the approval of his father, has reached the genital stage, characterized by potency, command, and control (along with a good measure of sadistic pleasure). To be sure, Abraham's analysis tells us more about psychoanalysis and the way it divides human development into phases, yet it still provides a point of entry into the tale that can further illuminate the tale's engagement with the troubled relationship between fathers and sons.

ong, long ago there lived a tailor who had three sons and just one goat.[1] Since the goat had to supply all four of them with milk, they made sure to take her out every day to graze somewhere and to keep her well fed. The sons took turns at this task. One day the eldest son took the goat out to the churchyard, where the tastiest grass was growing, and he let her graze and frolic to her heart's content. In the evening, when it was time to return home, he asked: "Little goat, have you had enough to eat?" The goat replied:

> "I'm really stuffed,
> Enough's enough. Mehhh, mehhh!"

"Then let's go back home," the boy said. He took her by the rope, walked her back to her stall, and tied her up.

"Well," said the old tailor. "Has the goat eaten her fill?"

"Oh, yes," the son replied. "She's so full that she doesn't want another blade of grass."

The boy's father wanted to find out for himself and so he went to the goat's stall, stroked the head of his beloved animal, and asked: "Little goat, are you really full?"

The goat replied:

1. *a tailor who had three sons and just one goat.* "There comes an old man with his three sons—" / "I could match this beginning with an old tale," we hear in Shakespeare's *As You Like It.* Tales of three sons abound in folklore, and often it is the youngest and "most stupid" of the three who surpasses the others. In this tale, the mother is absent and the relationship between father and sons is played out without maternal intervention.

"Enough to eat? Hardly a chance!
A graveyard's just a place to dance.
I didn't find a single leaf: Mehhh, mehhh!"

"Well, I never!" the tailor shouted, and he ran up the stairs to confront his son.

"You miserable liar! You tell me that the goat has eaten her fill when in fact you've let her starve!" And in his rage, he took a measuring stick from the wall and used it to chase his son out of the house.[2]

The next day it was the second son's turn to take the goat out. He found a spot for her along the garden hedge, where every kind of good grass was growing, and the goat ate every blade down to the ground. In the evening, when he wanted to get back home, he asked: "Little goat, are you full now?" The goat replied:

"I'm really stuffed,
Enough's enough. Mehhh, mehhh!"

"Well then, let's go back home," the boy said, and he led her to the stall and tied her up.

"Did the goat have enough to eat?" the old tailor asked.

"Oh, she's so full that she doesn't want another blade of grass," his son replied.

The tailor wanted to see for himself that she was full, and he went over to the stall and asked: "Little goat, are you really full?"

And the goat answered:

"Enough to eat? Hardly a chance!
A graveyard's just a place to dance.
I didn't find a single leaf: Mehhh, mehhh!"

2. *used it to chase his son out of the house.* The father's faith in the goat and his lack of trust in the boys create a rift between the two generations. The goat's duplicity leads to the sons' departure from home and to a new life where they must earn their keep.

"The godless wretch!" the tailor shouted. "Letting a good creature like that starve to death!" He ran up the stairs, and waving the stick, he chased the boy out the door.

Now it was the turn of the third son, who was anxious to do things the right way. He found some bushes with tender leaves and let the goat nibble on them. In the evening, when he wanted to go back home, he asked: "Little goat, are you full now?" The goat replied:

"I'm really stuffed,
Enough's enough. Mehhh, mehhh!"

"Well, then, come back home," the boy said, and he led her to the stall and tied her up.

"Well now," the old tailor asked. "Did the goat get enough to eat?"

"Oh, yes, she's so full that she doesn't want another blade of grass," the son replied.

The tailor didn't trust him, and he went down the stairs and asked: "Little goat, are you full now?"

The malicious animal replied:

"Enough to eat? Hardly a chance!
A graveyard's just a place to dance.
I didn't find a single leaf: Mehhh, mehhh!"

"Oh, you pack of liars," the tailor shouted. "One is more wicked and unreliable than the next! Well, you can't make a fool of me any longer." Beside himself with rage, he raced up the stairs and gave the boy such a tanning with his stick that he fled the house.

The old tailor was now alone with his goat. The next morning he went down to the stall, caressed the animal, and said: "Come along, my dear little pet. I'll take you out to graze." He picked up her rope and brought her to some green hedges and some clumps of yarrow, along with everything else that goats like to eat.

"Now you can finally feast to your heart's content," he said to her, and he let her graze until sunset. Then he asked: "Well, little goat, are you full?" She replied:

"I'm really stuffed,
Enough's enough. Mehhh, mehhh!"

"Then let's go back home," said the tailor, and he took her back to her stall and tied her up. As he was about to go, he turned around and said: "Well, now you have finally eaten your fill!" But the goat treated him no better and replied:

"Enough to eat? Hardly a chance!
A graveyard's just a place to dance.
I didn't find a single leaf: Mehhh, mehhh!"

When the tailor heard those words, he was stunned, for he now realized that he had driven his sons away for no reason at all. "Just wait!" he shouted. "Throwing you out is too mild a punishment, you ungrateful wretch! I'm going to brand you so that you won't dare show your face among honest tailors any more."

He ran up the stairs as fast as he could, took out his razor, lathered the goat's head, and shaved it until it was as smooth as the palm of his hand. And since the stick seemed too good for her,[3] he picked up his whip and gave her such a thrashing that she leaped and ran off for dear life.

The tailor was now all alone in his house,[4] and he began to feel deeply lonely. He longed to have his sons back again, but no one knew where they had gone.

The eldest son had apprenticed himself to a carpenter, and he had been eager to learn and had worked hard. When he finished his apprenticeship and was about to start his travels,

3. *And since the stick seemed too good for her.* The profusion of physical punishments in this tale connects with the club in the sack, a gift that provides retaliatory pleasure through torture for its owner. Note that the father uses a tool of his trade, the yardstick, to punish the sons. He then resorts to a whip to punish the goat, and finally, when peace has settled on the household, he still has the club in the sack, just in case.

4. *The tailor was now all alone in his house.* The father is to blame for his isolation and loneliness. Unlike the biblical tale of the prodigal son, which positions the father as a benign figure, this father drives out his sons and comes to regret it.

the master carpenter gave him a little table made of ordinary wood. There was nothing special about its appearance, but it had one special quality. If you put it down and said: "Table, set yourself!" then instantly a clean tablecloth was spread out on the good little table and a plate with a knife and fork suddenly appeared. Every inch of the table was covered with platters of roast meat and stewed meat,[5] and a big glass of red wine sparkled on the table, making your heart glow.

The young journeyman thought: "That will keep you going for the rest of your life!" and he went out into the world in high spirits and never stopped to ask whether an inn was good or bad or whether you could get food there or not. When he didn't feel like stopping at an inn, he would take the little table off his back, set it up in a meadow, in a forest, or in a field, or wherever he wanted, and say: "Set yourself!" And then everything he could ever want was right there.

At last he decided to go home to his father. He was sure that his father was no longer angry and that the old man would be glad to see him with the magic table. On the way home, he stopped one evening at an inn that was filled with a large party of travelers. They welcomed him and invited him to sit down with them and share their food; otherwise he might not get anything to eat. "No, no," said the carpenter, "I don't want to take your last few morsels. Let me invite you to be my guests."

They all started laughing and were sure that he must be joking around. But then he set his little wooden table up in the middle of the room and repeated the words: "Table, set yourself." Instantly the table was covered with all kinds of food far better than what the innkeeper could have provided, and the fragrant aroma quickly rose up to the noses of the travelers.

"Help yourselves, dear friends," the carpenter said, and when the travelers realized what he was saying, they didn't wait to be asked a second time but pulled out their knives and

5. *Every inch of the table was covered with platters of roast meat and stewed meat.* As Robert Darnton tells us, "one extravagance clearly stands out: meat. In a society of de facto vegetarians, the luxury of luxuries was to sink one's teeth into a side of mutton, pork, or beef." Note that a table that sets itself represents a fulfillment of one of the most powerful fantasies of an earlier age: having a full stomach. Darnton further tells us that the wishes of fairy-tale heroes often remain fixed "on common objects in the everyday world." His insights go far toward explaining the logic of the three objects acquired by the boys, with two providing an unending source of food and money (the redundancy is telling) and the third the means to secure and guard the first two objects.

L. Leslie Brooke, *The House in the Wood and Other Old Fairy Stories*

The table that sets itself moves into action.

fell to. They were astonished by the way new platters piled high with food would appear as soon as a dish was empty. The innkeeper watched all of this from a corner of the room, and he didn't know what to do, but he thought: "I could use a cook like that in my kitchen."

The journeyman and his companions had a good time until late at night. Finally they decided to go to bed, and the young carpenter put his magic table against the wall and retired for the night.

The innkeeper's thoughts gave him no peace that night, and he remembered that there was an old table in a storeroom that looked just like the magic table. He crept out of bed quietly and switched his table with the magic table.

The next morning the journeyman paid for his lodgings and loaded the table on his back, never dreaming that it might not be the right one. He set out on his way, and at noon he reached the house of his father, who welcomed him with joy. "Well, my dear son, what trade have you learned?" he asked.

"Father, I've become a carpenter," he replied.

"That's a good trade," the old man replied. "And what have you brought back from your travels?"

"Father, the best thing that I've brought back is this little table."

The tailor examined the table from all sides and said: "That's not really much of a masterpiece that you've got there. It looks to me like a shabby old piece of furniture."

"But it's a magic table," the son replied. "When I stand it up and tell it to set itself, the finest dishes appear out of thin air, and wine, too, that makes your heart glow. Let's invite all our friends and relatives. For once, they'll get a chance to eat and drink their fill, for the little table will give them more than enough to eat."

When the guests were all present, the son set up the table in the middle of the room and said: "Table, set yourself!"

But nothing happened, and the table stayed as empty as any ordinary table that doesn't take orders. The poor carpenter realized that someone had switched tables on him, and he was mortified by the fact that he looked just like a liar. All the relatives laughed their heads off,[6] and they had to go back home as hungry and thirsty as when they had arrived. The father took out his tools and went back to being a tailor, and the son found a job with a master carpenter.

The second son found a miller to whom he apprenticed himself. When his time was up, the master said to him: "Because you worked so hard, I'm going to give you a very special kind of donkey. But he will not draw a cart for you, and he also refuses to carry sacks."

"Then what is he good for?" asked the young journeyman.

"He spits gold," the miller replied. "If you put a cloth under him and say 'Bricklebrit,' then the good animal will spit gold pieces from the front and behind."

"That sounds like a good thing," said the journeyman, and he thanked the miller and went out into the world. Whenever he needed money, all he had to do was say "Bricklebrit" to the animal and it started raining gold pieces. He just had to pick them up. Wherever he went, the best was not too good for him, and the more expensive the better, for his purse was always full.

After traveling around for a while in the world, the second son thought: "I really should go see my father. Once he sees this gold donkey, his anger will vanish, and he'll welcome me with open arms." It so happened that he ended up in the same inn where his brother's table had been switched. He was leading his donkey by the bridle when the innkeeper offered to take the animal and tie it up. But the young journeyman said: "Don't go out of your way. I'd like to take my gray jack to the stable and tie him up myself. I want to know exactly where he is." That struck the innkeeper as odd, and he was sure that anyone who had to look after his donkey couldn't

6. *All the relatives laughed their heads off.* Once again, a betrayal leads to the humiliation of the son, and he must continue to suffer until his third brother finds the means to secure the magical objects, which arouse constant envy.

have much money to spend. But when the stranger reached in his pocket and took out two pieces of gold, telling him to get him something good, the innkeeper's jaw dropped and he ran off to get the very best fare that money could buy.

After dinner the traveler asked how much he owed, and the innkeeper, who was eager to chalk up twice what it really cost, asked him for a few more pieces of gold. The second son reached into his pocket, but he had run out of gold pieces.

"If you just wait a moment, my dear Mr. Innkeeper, I'll get some more gold pieces." And he left the room, taking the tablecloth with him. The innkeeper couldn't figure out what was going on, and he was so curious that he sneaked after him. When he saw that the traveler had bolted the door to the stall, he looked in through a knothole. The stranger spread the tablecloth under the donkey, shouted "Bricklebrit," and instantly the donkey began to spit pieces of gold from the front and the back until it was raining pieces of gold.

"Egads!" the innkeeper said. "What a nice way to mint ducats! I wouldn't mind at all having a moneybag like that."

The traveler paid up and retired for the evening. Late at night the innkeeper tiptoed into the stall, removed the master of the treasury, and left another donkey in its place.

Early the next morning, the second son left with the animal, thinking he had his gold donkey with him. He arrived at his father's house that afternoon, and the old man was glad to see him again, welcoming him with open arms.

"Well, my son, what trade have you learned?" the old man asked.

"I've become a miller," the son replied.

"What have you brought back home from your travels?"

"Nothing but a donkey."

"There are enough donkeys around here," the father said. "I wish you had brought back a goat instead."

"That may be true," the son said. "But this is no ordinary donkey. I've brought home a gold donkey, and when I say

'Bricklebrit,' then the good beast spits out a whole bundle of gold coins. Let's invite our relatives over. I'll make them all rich."

"That sounds like a great idea to me," the tailor said. "Now I won't have to torture myself any longer by being on pins and needles." And he raced off to invite the relatives over.

When everyone had gathered in the house, the miller told them to make some room. Then he spread out a cloth and brought the donkey into the room. "Just watch this," he said

Ludwig Richter, *Ludwig Bechsteins Märchenbuch*

The second son treats the donkey with fondness and reverence as he seeks a place to shelter him for the night.

and shouted: "Bricklebrit!" But what fell down had nothing to do with gold pieces, and it was plain to see that this animal understood nothing about the art of minting, for not every ass can make money.[7] The poor miller made a long face. He realized that he had been cheated and apologized to his relatives, who went home as poor as they had come. There was no way around it. The old man had to go back to his sewing, and the son hired himself out to a miller.

The third brother apprenticed himself to a turner, and since that is a trade that requires real art, his training lasted the longest. His brothers wrote and told him[8] how badly they had fared and how, on the nights of their homecomings, an innkeeper had robbed them of their magical gifts. When the turner had finished his apprenticeship and was about to start traveling, the master turner gave him a sack as a reward for all his hard work: "There's a club in that sack."

"I'll throw the sack over my shoulder, and it's bound to come in handy sometime," the turner said. "But what in the world can I do with that club? All it does is add weight to the sack."

"I'll tell you what you can do with it," the master turner replied. "If anyone ever threatens to harm you, just say: 'Club, get out of that sack!' and the club will jump right out and dance a little jig on their backs[9] so that they won't be able to move a bone in their bodies for a whole week. And the club won't let up until you say 'Club, get back in the sack!'"

The turner thanked him, slung the sack over his shoulder, and whenever anyone got a little too close or threatened him,[10] he would just say: "Club, get out of that sack!" and the club would jump out and pound the dust out of the chap's coat or jacket while it was still on his back, without waiting for him to take it off. That all happened in a flash, so that the fellow next in line had his turn before he knew what hit him.

One evening the young turner arrived at the inn where his two brothers had been swindled. He put his knapsack down

7. *not every ass can make money.* This tale, more than most in the Grimms' collection, shows signs of its origins in an oral storytelling culture for adults. The scatological humor and play on words, along with the emphasis on the trials of apprenticeships and trades, suggest that the story might have circulated among tradesmen.

8. *His brothers wrote and told him.* It is unusual to find fairy-tale characters composing letters, and this brother seems more literate than his counterparts in other tales by the Grimms. Clearly the narrator felt obliged to provide a justification for the third son's knowledge of the innkeeper's treachery.

9. *dance a little jig on their backs.* The dance performed by the club produces a form of festive violence that provides the brother with a degree of *Schadenfreude*, or pleasure at witnessing the suffering of others.

10. *whenever anyone got a little too close or threatened him.* The only way to secure the magic table and the gold donkey is with the protection offered by the club. The third and youngest brother has thus earned the most valuable among the three gifts.

on the table in front of him and started to tell about all the fabulous things he had seen in the world. "Yes," he said, "you can find magic tables, gold donkeys, and the like. They're all just fine, and I'm not saying anything bad about them, but they're really nothing compared with the treasure that I earned and that I've got right here in my sack."

The innkeeper's ears perked up: "What in the world could that be?" He thought: "The sack must be full of jewels. I really deserve to get those too, for all good things come in threes."

At bedtime the turner stretched out on the bench and used his sack as a pillow for his head. When the innkeeper was sure that his guest was fast asleep and that no one else was in the room, he went over and began to tug and pull very carefully at the sack, hoping to get it away and to put another in its place. But the turner had been waiting for him to do just that. The innkeeper was about to give a good hard tug, when the turner cried out: "Club, get out of that sack!" In a flash the little club jumped out, went at the innkeeper, and gave him a sound thrashing. The innkeeper began screaming pitifully, but the louder he screamed, the harder the club beat time on his back, until at last he fell down on the ground. Then the turner said: "Now hand over the magic table and the gold donkey, or the dance will start all over again." "Oh, no!" said the innkeeper. "I'll be glad to give you everything, if only you'll make that little devil crawl back into his sack." The journeyman answered: "This time I will, but watch out or there'll be more where that came from." Then he said: "Club, get back in the sack" and left him in peace.[11]

The next morning the turner went back home to his father, taking the magic table and the gold donkey with him. The tailor was overjoyed to see him and asked him what he had learned in foreign lands. "Dear Father," he replied, "I've become a turner."

"A trade like that requires real art," the father said. "But what have you brought back from your travels?"

11. *Then he said: "Club, get back in the sack" and left him in peace.* In his *English Fairy Tales,* Joseph Jacobs points out that this tale, like many fairy tales, has been subjected to interpretations by the so-called school of solar mythology. For them "The Master who gives the three precious gifts is the All Father, the Supreme Spirit. The gold and jewel-dropping ass is the spring cloud, hanging in the sky and shedding the bright productive vernal showers. The table which covers itself is the earth becoming covered with flowers and fruit at the bidding of the new year. . . . Then comes the thunder-cloud, out of which leaps the bolt; the rain pours down, the earth receives them, and is covered with abundance—all that was lost is recovered."

"A precious object, dear Father," the son replied. "A club in a sack."

"What?" the father cried out. "A club! Hardly worth the effort. You can make something like that out of any tree around."

"Not one like this, dear Father. When I say 'Club, get out of that sack!' the club jumps out and does a nasty little dance with anyone who's not nice to me. It doesn't stop dancing until the fellow's on the ground, begging for mercy. You see, with this club I managed to recover the magic table and the gold donkey which that scoundrel of an innkeeper took from my brothers. Now go find both of them and invite all our kinfolk. I'm going to wine and dine them and fill their pockets with gold."

The old tailor could hardly believe his ears, but he went and invited all the relatives around. The turner put a cloth down in the parlor, ushered in the gold donkey, and said to his brother: "Now, dear brother, go ahead and give him his orders." The miller said "Bricklebrit," and instantly, gold pieces fell to the cloth as if it were raining money, and the donkey didn't stop until everyone had as much as they could carry. (I can see that you wish you had been there too.)[12] Then the turner brought in the table and said: "Dear brother, talk to your table." As soon as the turner said "Table, set yourself," the table was set and covered with the most appetizing dishes. Everyone at the home of the good tailor feasted as they had never before feasted, and they all stayed until late at night, enjoying themselves and living it up. The tailor took his needle and thread, his yardstick and flatiron, and locked them up in a cupboard. He lived happily and in luxury with his three sons.

But whatever became of the goat that made the tailor chase his three sons away?[13] Well, I'll tell you. She was so ashamed of her bald head that she found a fox's home and crawled into it. When the fox came back home, a pair of big eyes flashed out at him in the darkness. He got scared and ran away. He

12. *(I can see that you wish you had been there too.)* The narrator's aside here is another reminder of the oral origins of folktales and the degree to which the fantasy in the tale is the shared fantasy of the audience.

13. *But whatever became of the goat that made the tailor chase his three sons away?* Just as the innkeeper receives his just desserts, so too the goat must get her deserved punishment. In rounding out the tale, the teller reinscribes the message delivered about how vice is punished in the end even as he shows how the quick, small, and nimble manage to defeat larger adversaries.

Arthur Rackham, *Little Brother and Little Sister and Other Tales by the Brothers Grimm*

As the donkey spits gold, the spectators watch in amazement.

met a bear, who saw that the fox had a frantic look on his face and asked: "What's the matter, Brother Fox, why are you making a face like that?"

"Oh," Redback replied, "a ferocious beast is sitting in my shelter, and he glared out at me with fiery eyes."

"I'll take care of that," the bear said, and he went over to the hole with the fox and peered in. But when he saw those fiery eyes, he too got scared and didn't want to have anything to do with the beast. Off he went. While fleeing, he met a bee who noticed that he looked upset and asked: "Bear, you look really miserable. What happened to your high spirits?"

"It's easy for you to talk," the bear said. "There's a ferocious beast with fiery eyes in old Redback's house, and we just can't get it out of there."

The bee said: "I feel sorry for you, old bear. I'm just a poor pathetic creature whom you never even bother looking at, but I think I can help you."

The bee flew into the fox's hole, landed on the goat's bald, shaved head, and stuck her so hard that she jumped up and bleated "Mehhh, mehhh," and ran out into the world like a madwoman. And to this day no one knows where she went.

Walter Crane, *Household Stories from the Collection of the Brothers Grimm*

The Elves

One of three tales designated under the title "The Elves," the tale of the shoemaker and his wife conveys a lesson encapsulated by one commentator as "It is just as important to give gifts as to receive them." The Grimms noted in their commentary the oddity of the elves departing—in this tale as in others—as soon as they are given clothes. The ending to the story seems a happy one: the shoemaker's prosperity is restored even if he must continue to work, and the elves have clothing and no longer need to labor. Ruth B. Bottigheimer has noted that "sudden and unanticipated reward after ceaseless labor seems to represent a constant dream at least among Western laborers, and probably among laboring people worldwide, a dream of eternal release from endless grinding toil." The fantasy in this tale has more to do with a strange blend of curiosity, emancipation from labor, recovery, and whimsical reciprocity that leaves everyone in the tale content, including the shoemaker's customers.

nce there lived a shoemaker who, through no fault of his own, had become so poor that all he had left was enough leather to make a single pair of shoes. That evening he cut the leather for the shoes and was planning to work on them in the morning. A man with a clear conscience, he lay down quietly in his bed, commended himself to God, and fell asleep. The next day, he said his morning prayers[1] and was about to sit down to his work when he saw that the shoes were finished and laid out on his workbench. He was so astonished that he had no idea what to say. When he took the shoes in his hands to get a closer look at them, he saw that the workmanship was perfect and that there was not a false stitch on them. It was as if the shoes were intended as a masterpiece.

Before long, a customer came in, and the man liked the shoes so much that he paid more than the usual price, and the shoemaker was now able to purchase the leather for two pairs of shoes. He cut the leather in the evening and was planning to work on them the next morning with renewed energy, but there was no need to do that. When he woke up, they were already finished. Once again he found customers for them, and they gave him so much money that he could now buy the leather for four pairs of shoes. The next morning he discovered four pairs of shoes on his bench, completely finished. And so it continued. Whatever he cut in the evening was finished by the morning, and before long he had a decent income again and had become a prosperous man.

Now it happened one evening, not long before Christmas,[2] that the man was cutting up the leather for the shoes, and before retiring, he said to his wife: "Suppose we stay up tonight and try to find out who is giving us a hand?"

The wife thought it was a good idea, and she lit a candle.

1. *he said his morning prayers.* The shoemaker's piety is stressed again and again and signals that he is deserving of the reward given to him and also protected against the pagan spirits who help him out by discharging his chores.

2. *not long before Christmas.* Christmas, as a time of giving gifts, inspires the shoemaker's wife to make presents for the elves, just as the cold weather gives her a clue about what the two sprightly men need. The religious element is repeatedly drawn in as an antidote to the pagan figures.

Then they hid behind some clothes that were hanging in a corner of the room and kept a lookout. At midnight, two tiny little naked men sat down at the workbench, took all the work that had been cut out, and began to punch, sew, and hammer so nimbly and skillfully with their little fingers that the shoemaker just stared in amazement. They didn't stop until they were completely finished with everything and the shoes were on the bench. Then they ran off in a flash.

The next morning the shoemaker's wife said: "Those little fellows have made us rich. We have to find a way to show our gratitude. They must get cold running around with nothing at all to wear. How about if I sew some little shirts, coats, vests, and breeches for them? And I can also knit a pair of stockings for each of them, and you can make them a pair of shoes."

The shoemaker said: "That sounds like a good idea to me." In the evening, when they had finished everything, they put the presents on the table where the shoemaker usually put the cut leather, and then they hid in order to see how the little men would react. At midnight they scampered in and were about to start their work when they discovered the cute little articles of clothing in place of the cut-out leather. At first they were puzzled, but then they seemed elated. They slipped quickly into their beautiful clothes, smoothed them down, and sang a little song:

"Don't we look just trim and spruce?
Here's to pleasure! We're footloose!"

They skipped, danced, and jumped over the chairs and benches. And finally they danced out the door and were never seen again. The shoemaker continued to prosper for the remainder of his life, and he succeeded whenever he tried his hand at anything.

George Cruikshank, *German Popular Stories*

The industrious elves are delighted with the clothes made for them by the shoemaker's wife, and the couple who are the beneficiaries of the elves' labors delight in witnessing their glee.

The Robber Bridegroom

The story of a young woman betrothed to a robber was the stuff of ballads, folk songs, and folktales in many European cultures. In this version of the tale, the heroine is protected by an old woman who conspires with her so that both can escape from the den of robbers. The sensationalized account of the murder of the young woman kidnapped by robbers suggests a connection to the Bluebeard story and its description of the mutilated bodies of Bluebeard's former wives. But in this tale, the heroine manages to use her narrative powers to defeat her criminal bridegroom. Like Scheherazade, who uses storytelling as an instrument for survival, the young woman recounts what she witnessed at the abode of her betrothed and provides the evidence needed to seize the man and bring him to justice. In some versions, justice comes not through the legal system, as in the Grimms' tale, but in the form of a summary execution by the heroine's father and brothers.

"The Robber Bridegroom" has formed the subject matter of many literary narratives, most notably Eudora Welty's novel of the same name and Margaret Atwood's novel Robber Bride, *which reverses the tale's gender terms. Jane Campion's* The Piano *draws on "The Robber Bridegroom" and "Bluebeard" to construct its plot. The story*

experienced a revival in Anglo-American cultures of the late twentieth century when it was taken up, along with "Bluebeard" and "Fitcher's Bird," by feminist authors, artists, and filmmakers.

nce upon a time there lived a miller who had a beautiful daughter. He wanted to be sure that she was provided for and that she married well once she was grown up. He thought: "When the right kind of man comes along and asks for her hand, I shall give her to him."

Before long a suitor turned up who seemed to be rich, and since the miller could find nothing wrong with him, he promised him his daughter. But the girl didn't care for him in the way that a girl should care for her betrothed, and she did not trust him at all. Whenever she set eyes on him or when her thoughts turned to him, she was filled with dread.

One day he said to her: "You're engaged to me, and yet you've never once visited me."

The girl replied: "I don't even know where you live."

The bridegroom told her: "My house lies deep in the forest."

The girl made all kinds of excuses and claimed that she would not be able to find the way there. But the bridegroom said: "Next Sunday you have to come over to my place. I've already invited the guests, and I'll strew ashes on the path[1] so that you can find your way through the woods."

When Sunday arrived and the girl was supposed to leave, she became dreadfully frightened, without knowing exactly why, and she filled both her pockets with peas and lentils to mark the way. She entered the woods, where she found the trail of ashes, and she followed it carefully, but every step of the way she threw some peas on the ground, first to the right,

1. *"I'll strew ashes on the path."* This strategy is familiar from "Hansel and Gretel," who use first pebbles and then breadcrumbs to mark the path home. It becomes clear by the end of the tale that the ashes provide only one-way directions to the robber's house. The ashes introduce the notion of violence and death, signaling that fire is the element in which the robber bridegroom is comfortable.

then to left. She walked almost all day long until she got to the middle of the forest, where it was really gloomy. There she saw a house standing all by itself, and she didn't like the look of it because it seemed dark and spooky. She walked in. It was deadly silent. There was not a soul in sight. Suddenly, a voice cried out:

"Turn back, turn back, my pretty young bride,[2]
In a house of murderers you've arrived."

The girl looked up and realized that the voice was coming from a birdcage[3] hanging on the wall. Once again, she heard:

"Turn back, turn back, my pretty young bride,
In a house of murderers you've arrived."

The beautiful girl walked all around the house, going from one room to the next, but it was completely empty. No one was there. Finally, she went down to the cellar, where she found a woman, as old as the hills,[4] her head bobbing up and down.

"Can you tell me if my betrothed lives here?" the girl asked.

"Oh, you poor child!" said the old woman. "How did you get here? This is a den of murderers. You think you're a bride about to be married, but the only wedding you'll celebrate is a wedding with death.[5] Look over here! I had to heat up this big pot of water for them. When you get into their hands, they'll show no mercy and will chop you into pieces, cook you, and eat you, for they're cannibals.[6] You're lost unless I take pity on you and try to save you."

The old woman hid her behind a big barrel, where no one could see her. "Be still as a mouse," she said. "Don't you dare move, or that'll be the end of you. At night, when the robbers are asleep, we'll escape. I've been waiting a long time for this moment."

2. *"Turn back, turn back, my pretty young bride."* In "Mr. Fox," a British analogue to "The Robber Bridegroom," the heroine enters a house that bears the following inscription on its doorway: "Be bold, be bold, but not too bold, / Lest that your heart's blood should run cold."

3. *the voice was coming from a birdcage.* The caged bird is an early warning device for the heroine, showing in a miniaturized form that the heroine is on the site of a prison. Unable to escape its cage, the bird, like the old woman imprisoned in the cellar, can do little more than sound a warning.

4. *a woman, as old as the hills.* In the frame narrative to Apuleius's "Cupid and Psyche" (which serves as the foundational myth for "Beauty and the Beast"), an old woman takes a young bride who has been kidnapped by robbers into her confidence. The tale can be seen as elaborating both on the hazards of marriage and on the alliances between women, young and old.

5. *"wedding with death."* When Psyche agrees to marry Cupid, her wedding preparations resemble funeral rites, for she believes that she is going to marry a monster.

6. *"for they're cannibals."* The robbers resemble the cannibalistic ogres and giants of folklore, and like the giant in "Jack and the Beanstalk," they devour intruders.

Arthur Rackham, *The Fairy Tales of the Brothers Grimm*

The old woman points out a good hiding place for the young woman who has made the mistake of entering a house of robbers.

No sooner had she spoken those words than the wicked crew returned home, dragging another girl behind them. The men were drunk, and they felt no pity when they heard her screams and sobs. They forced her to drink some wine, three glasses full, one white, one red, one yellow, and before long her heart burst in two. The robbers tore off her fine clothes, put her on the table, chopped her beautiful body into pieces, and sprinkled them with salt.

The poor girl was trembling with fear in her hiding place behind the barrel, for she now understood what the robbers had in store for her. One of them caught sight of a golden ring on the little finger of the murdered girl, and when he couldn't pull it off right away, he took an ax and chopped the finger off. The finger went flying through the air up over the barrel and landed right in the girl's lap. The robber took a candle and wanted to search for it, but he couldn't find it. One of the other robbers asked: "Have you looked over there behind that big barrel?" Just then the old woman called out: "Come and eat! You can search again tomorrow. That finger isn't going to run away."

"The old woman's right," the robbers said, and they stopped searching and sat down to eat. The old woman put a few drops of a sleeping potion into their wine. Before long, they had retired to the cellar and were snoring away in their sleep.

When the bride heard the snoring noises, she came out from behind the barrel and crawled over the sleeping bodies arranged on the ground in rows. She was terrified that she might wake one of them up, but God guided her footsteps.[7] The old woman went up the stairs with her, opened the door, and they ran as fast as they could from the den of murderers. The wind had scattered the ashes, but the peas and lentils had sprouted and showed the way in the moonlight. The two walked all night long. In the morning they reached the mill, and the girl told her father about everything that had happened.

7. *God guided her footsteps.* The allusion to God in a tale about murder, mutilation, and cannibalism sounds a false note, revealing how the tales had their origins in pagan cultures but acquired an overlay of religious piety as they were retold and recorded. Certain storytellers surely made a practice of adding asides about prayer and piety.

8. *"I will tell you about a dream I had."* The narration of the dream offers an opportunity to recap the events, outlining a miniaturized version of the larger narrative. The heroine narrates her own story, providing an unusual example of first-person narrative embedded in the traditional epic, third-person style of fairy tales.

When the day of the wedding celebration arrived, the groom appeared, as did all the friends and relatives invited by the miller. At dinner, every one there was asked to tell a story. The bride sat quietly and didn't utter a word. Finally the bridegroom said to his bride: "Don't you have anything to say, my love? You have to tell us something."

"Very well," she replied. "I will tell you about a dream I had.[8] I was walking alone through the woods and came across a house. No one was living there, but on the wall there was a cage, and in it was a bird that sang

> 'Turn back, turn back, my pretty young bride,
> In a house of murderers you've arrived.'

Then it repeated those words. My dear, I must have been dreaming all this. I walked from one room to the next, and each one was completely empty. Everything was so spooky. Finally I went down to the cellar, and there I saw a woman as old as the hills, her head bobbing up and down. I asked her: 'Does my betrothed live here?' She replied: 'Oh, you poor child, you've stumbled into a den of murderers. Your betrothed lives here, but he is planning to chop you up and kill you, and then he'll cook you and eat you up.' My dear, I must have been dreaming all this. The old woman hid me behind a big barrel, and no sooner was I out of sight than the robbers returned home, dragging a maiden behind them. They gave her three kinds of wine to drink, white, red, and yellow, and her heart burst in two. My dear, I must have been dreaming all this. Then they tore off her fine clothes, chopped her beautiful body into pieces, and sprinkled them with salt. My dear, I must have been dreaming all this. One of the robbers caught sight of a gold ring on her finger and since it was hard to pull off, he took an ax and chopped it off. The finger flew through the air up behind the big barrel and landed in my lap. And here is the finger with the ring still on it."

With these words, she pulled it out and showed it to everyone there.

The robber turned white as a ghost while she was telling the story. He jumped up and tried to escape, but the guests seized him and turned him over to the law. He and his band were executed for their dreadful deeds.

THE ROBBER BRIDEGROOM
"TURN BACK, TURN BACK, THOU PRETTY BRIDE,
WITHIN THIS HOUSE THOU MUST NOT BIDE,
FOR HERE DO EVIL THINGS BETIDE."
SWAIN SC

Godfather Death

argaret Atwood recalls that her parents probably "gnawed their nails" while she was reading, as a child, the unexpurgated Grimm, with its stories about "pieces of bodies falling down the chimney, Godfather Death, and other horrors." And indeed, the story of the poor man who makes the regrettable decision to ask Death to stand as godfather to his thirteenth child is hardly a tale appropriate for bedtime reading. But it is a story that allowed earlier generations to talk about death, compassion, love, and justice. As the great leveler, Death represented a democratic principle in a world that was ruled by strict hierarchies that divided the rich from the poor and that made life seem unjust. In their revisions to the tale, the Grimms added the phrase about the father's lack of awareness that God distributes wealth and poverty "wisely" and sent contradictory messages about social justice even as they deprived the tale of its subversive edge.

Death plays no favorites, and this particular tale is a stark reminder that even those on whom fortune smiles cannot cheat it. Rich, poor, royal, humble, young, old—all succumb to its power at last. If the magic tales give us the fulfillment of wishes and endings that take us into a happily ever after, "Godfather Death" is a stark reminder that there is a fatal ending for every fairy-tale character. "None of us is getting out of this alive," as comedian Lily Tomlin has quipped.

In his film Destiny *(1921), the Austrian film director Fritz Lang drew on the motif of the candle as a human life and the snuffing of the candle as the mark of death. His figure of Death is a haunting figure who serves as a grim reminder of our common destiny.*

There once lived a poor man who had twelve children and who had to work day and night just to feed them. When a thirteenth was born, the man was so desperate that he didn't know where to turn. Finally he ran out to the main road leading into town and decided to ask the first person he met to stand godfather. That first person turned out to be the good Lord, and he already knew what was on the man's mind. "You poor soul," he said, "I feel sorry for you. I'll hold your child at the christening, and you can be sure that I'll take care of it and make certain it finds happiness on earth."

The man asked: "Tell me who you are."

"I'm your dear Lord."

"Then I don't want you as the godfather, for you give to the rich and let the poor go hungry." The man said that because he did not know how wisely God distributes wealth and poverty.[1] And so he turned away from the Lord and kept on going. Then the devil came up to him and said: "What are you looking for? If you make me your child's godfather, I'll give him a heap of gold and all the pleasures found in the world to go with it."

The man asked: "Tell me who you are."

"I'm the devil."

1. *"The man said that because he did not know how wisely God distributes wealth and poverty."* Robert Darnton points out that, in a French version of the tale, the impiety of the man's observation is never corrected, as in this aside, and instead the French tale goes on to suggest that "cheating works very well as a way of life." The French hero manages to save the princess, marry her, and live happily ever after to a ripe old age. Eventually Death gets him, but the French tale, according to Darnton, "demonstrates that no one can cheat death, at least not in the long run. But cheating gives the Frenchman an excellent short run for his money." The German tale, by contrast, has a far darker side that reveals the complete powerlessness of the hero against death.

2. *"For you there's no difference between the rich and the poor."* The powerful contrast between God's way of treating people and Death's manner of making no distinctions based on social class reflected growing skepticism about the comforts of religion. Social justice would have to come through means other than piousness and prayer.

"Then I don't want you as the godfather," the man said. "You deceive people and lead them astray." When they had parted ways, the bony-legged figure of Death came marching up to him and said: "Let me be the godfather."

The man asked him: "Tell me who you are."

"I'm Death, and I make sure that everyone is equal."

The man replied: "You're the right man for me. For you there's no difference between the rich and the poor.[2] I'm going to ask you to be my child's godfather."

"I'm going to make your child rich and famous, for the man who has me as his friend will never lack for anything."

The man said: "The christening is next Sunday. Make sure you're there on time."

Death was there as he had promised, and he made a very proper appearance.

The boy was nearly grown up when his godfather showed up one day and told him to accompany him on a walk. He took him out into the woods, showed him an herb that was growing there, and said: "It's time for me to give you your christening present. I'm going to see to it that you become a famous physician. If you are called to the bedside of someone who is ill, I'm going to be right there. If I'm standing by the patient's head, you can speak right up and declare that you are able to cure him. And if you give him some of this herb, he will recover. But if I'm standing by the feet of the person who is ill, then the patient belongs to me, and you will have to declare that all efforts are in vain and that there is no doctor in the world who can save him. Just be careful that you never use this herb against my will, or you might find yourself in deep trouble."

Before long, the young man had become the most famous physician in the world. People would say about him: "All he has to do is look at a patient and he knows just how things stand, whether the person will recover or get worse and die." They would come from far and wide to seek his help with those who were ill. They gave him so much money that, before long, he was a rich man.[3]

One day it happened that the king of the land became ill. The physician was summoned and asked to determine whether the king had any chance of recovering. But when he arrived at the royal bedside, he saw that Death was already standing by the king's feet and that no herb on earth could save him. "If I could just cheat Death this once," the physician started thinking. "Of course he'll be annoyed with me,

3. *he was a rich man.* Wealth may improve the physician's life, but it also marks him as a target for death, which makes no distinctions between rich and poor.

Ludwig Richter, *Ludwig Bechsteins Märchenbuch*

The father of a newborn child meets Death on the road and asks him to stand as godfather to his son. Note the scarecrow in the background, with its duplication in miniature of the figure of Death.

but after all, I am his godson, and he might be willing to close one eye. I think I'll take a chance." He took hold of the patient and turned him around so that Death was standing by the king's head. Then he administered some of the herb, and the king recovered. But Death strode over to the physician, gave him a dark and sinister look, shook his finger at him, and said: "You've put one over on me. Since you're my godson, I'm going to let you get away with it this one time. But if you try it one more time, you'll be risking your own neck. Believe me, I'll take care of you myself."

Not much later, the king's daughter fell gravely ill. She was an only child, and the king wept night and day until his eyes clouded over. He proclaimed throughout the land that if anyone could save her from death, that man would become her husband and inherit the crown. When the physician went to her bedside, he discovered that Death was sitting at her feet. He should have remembered his godfather's warning, but he was so dazzled by the great beauty of the princess and by the joyous prospect of becoming her husband that he threw all caution to the winds.[4] He didn't even notice that Death was casting angry glances in his direction and that he had raised his hand to threaten him with his bony fist. He just lifted the patient up and put her head where her feet had been. Then he gave her some of the herb, and before long her cheeks became flushed, and she started coming back to life.

When Death realized that he had been cheated out of his claim a second time, he strode up to the physician and said: "Now you've had it, and it's your turn to die." And he gripped him so firmly with his ice-cold hand that resistance was impossible. Death took him into an underground cavern, where there were thousands and thousands of lights burning in endless rows. Some were large, others medium-sized, and still others quite small. At any moment some went out, and others flared up, so that the little flames were always changing as they popped up and down.

4. *he threw all caution to the winds.* The physician's failure to recognize that he is subordinate to his godfather, and that despite his privileged position as godson he too is mortal, leads to his downfall. Note that he is not satisfied with wealth and power, but now strives to marry a princess and win a crown. What is considered a legitimate goal in tales of magic becomes a mark of hubris in this tale.

Ludwig Richter, *Ludwig Bechsteins Märchenbuch*

Death raises a cautionary hand, reminding the young physician that he must not try to outsmart him by changing the position of the king's bed.

"Here you can see the candles that are the lights of human lives. The large ones belong to children, the medium-sized ones to couples in their prime, the little ones to the aged. But sometimes even children and young people only have small candles."

"Show me my candle," the physician said, and he was certain that his candle would be quite tall. Death pointed to a tiny wick that was just about to go out.

"My dearest godfather, light a new one for me. Please do that so that I can have some pleasure in life by becoming king and marrying the beautiful princess."

"I'm afraid I can't," Death said to him. "I would have to put one out before a new candle is lit."[5]

"Then put the old one on top of a new one that will begin burning as soon as the old one goes out." Death pretended to do what he had asked and reached for a big new candle. But while he was getting the new one, he deliberately had an accident because he wanted his revenge. The tiny wick collapsed and went out. Just then, the physician fell down to the ground, and then, at last, he was in the hands of Death.

5. *"I would have to put one out before a new candle is lit."* Death is chosen as the godfather precisely because of his exquisite sense of social justice. Unwilling to snuff out one life even for his godson, he points out just why he is unable to act on the physician's desire.

Fitcher's Bird[1]

Closely related to the story of Bluebeard, the serial murderer of seven wives in French folklore, "Fitcher's Bird" recounts the premarital adventures of a woman betrothed to a man who is not simply an exotic outsider but a wizard, a man with supernatural powers. In Greek and Italian variants of this tale, the Lord of the Underworld and the devil figure as the unholy bridegrooms, suggesting that the Grimms' wizard, too, has diabolical powers.

The German heroine, unlike her French counterpart in "Bluebeard," has her wits about her and proves so resourceful that she is able to engineer her own rescue, not relying on her brothers to save her. Fitcher, an expert in the art of division and a master of dismemberment, uses his chopping block to separate into pieces what was meant to be whole. The third sister must reverse this process, rejoining the dismembered parts of her sisters and restoring them to life.

The "cleverest" of the trio of sisters, the third sister also becomes the preserver of life. Not only does she defy the powers of the wizard by making her sisters whole again, she also preserves the egg, protecting it from bloodied defilement by putting it in a safe place. She then transforms herself into a hybrid creature, half human, half animal,

1. *Fitcher's Bird.* Critics have speculated that the name Fitcher derives from the German terms *Feder* or *Fittich,* meaning "feathers," "wings," although that does not clarify why the name would be used to designate the wizard as Fitze Fitcher. Feathers and wings have celestial connotations and would thus stand in precise opposition to the diabolical Fitcher.

dipping her body in honey and rolling in feathers. And to entice her bridegroom to his death, she fashions what is to function as her own double: a skull decorated with flowers and jewels, which Fitcher will believe, at least from a distance, to be his bride. The display created through the decorated skull produces a symbolic nexus linking the bride with beauty and death. The sly sister creates a second self that corresponds precisely to the desires of her groom, while she herself escapes his fatal touch by transforming herself into a thing with feathers, a living creature affiliated with lightness, safety, life, and hope. The heroine claims the powers of the magician, but she uses them to restore life rather than to produce death.

nce upon a time there was a wizard who used to disguise himself as a poor man and go begging from door to door in order to capture pretty girls. No one had any idea what he did with them, for they would disappear without a trace.

One day the wizard appeared at the door of a man with three beautiful daughters. He looked like a poor, weak beggar and had a basket strapped to his back, as if he were collecting alms. When he asked for something to eat, the eldest girl came to the door[2] to give him a crust of bread, and all he did was touch her, and she had to jump right into his basket. Then he made long legs and hurried away to bring her back to his house, which was in the middle of a dark forest.

Everything in the house was splendid. The wizard gave the girl everything she wanted and told her: "Dearest, I'm sure you'll be happy here with me, for you'll have whatever your heart desires." After a few days had gone by, he said: "I have to go on a trip and will leave you alone for a short while. Here are the keys for the house. You can go anywhere you want and

2. *the eldest girl came to the door.* An opportunist who takes advantage of a gesture of compassion, the wizard has magical powers that can be seen as a metaphor for sexual attractiveness. Note that he does not court his wife or try to seduce her with his wealth. Instead he captures her heart through magical powers.

look around at anything you want, but don't go into the room that this little key opens.[3] I forbid it under the punishment of death."

He also gave her an egg[4] and said: "Carry it with you wherever you go, because if it gets lost, something terrible will happen." She took the keys and the egg and promised to do exactly as he had told her. After he left, she went over the house from top to bottom, taking a good look at everything in it. The rooms were filled with glittering silver and gold, and she thought that she had never seen anything so magnificent. When she finally got to the forbidden door, she was about to walk right past it when curiosity got the better of her.[5] She inspected the key and found that it looked just like the others. Putting it into the lock, she turned it just a little bit and the door shot open.

Imagine what she saw when she entered! In the middle of the room there was a big basin full of blood, and in it there were chopped-up pieces of dead bodies.[6] Next to the basin was a block of wood with a gleaming ax on it. She was so horrified that she dropped the egg she was holding into the basin. Even though she took it right out and wiped off the blood, it didn't help. The stain came right back. She wiped and scraped, but it just wouldn't come off.

It wasn't long before the man returned from his journey, and the first things he asked for were the key and the egg. She gave them to him, but she was trembling, and when he saw the red stain, he knew that she had been in the bloody chamber. "You went into the chamber against my wishes," he said. "Now you will go back in against yours. Your life has reached its end."

He threw her down, dragged her into the chamber by her hair, chopped her head off on the block, and hacked her into pieces so that her blood ran down all over the floor. Then he tossed her into the basin with the others.

"Now I'll go and get the second one," said the wizard, and

3. *"don't go into the room that this little key opens."* The prohibition can be seen, as in the story of Bluebeard, as an invitation to its violation. Stories about forbidden chambers often position women as victims of curiosity, even though their curiosity is nearly always justified.

4. *He also gave her an egg.* In some versions of the story, a bloodstained key alone provides evidence for the violation of the prohibition. In others, a flower that is singed reveals that the heroine has opened the door to the forbidden chamber. Egg, key, and flower have all been read by critics as charged with symbolic (sexual) meaning, for the story is encoded with issues turning on trust and disobedience in the context of a marriage.

5. *curiosity got the better of her.* A daughter of Eve, this girl, like her sister, cannot resist the temptation to open the forbidden door. The third sister is, by contrast, "clever and sly."

6. *chopped-up pieces of dead bodies.* The wizard is connected with a diabolical death principle that divides, mutilates, and destroys.

7. *she set to work gathering all the body parts.* The third sister succeeds in reversing the murderous aggression of the wizard. She triumphs over the power of death and, as the bearer of life, also becomes the restorer of life.

8. *He no longer had any power over her and had to do her bidding.* The sister's sly and clever behavior triumphs over the magic of the wizard, and now that she knows his secrets and his past, she has power over him. The wizard is reduced to the role of servant, who must carry his own wealth back to the heroine's home.

he went back to the house dressed as a poor man begging for charity. When the second daughter brought him a crust of bread, he caught her as he had the first just by touching her. He carried her off, and she fared no better than her sister. Her curiosity got the better of her: she opened the door to the bloody chamber, looked inside, and when the wizard came back she had to pay with her life.

The man went to fetch the third daughter, but she was clever and sly. After handing over the keys and the egg, he went away, and she put the egg in a safe place. She explored the house and entered the forbidden chamber. And what did she see! There in the basin were both her sisters, foully murdered and chopped into pieces. But she set to work gathering all the body parts[7] and put them back where they belonged: heads, torsos, arms, and legs. When everything was in place, the pieces began to move and to knit back together. Both girls opened their eyes and came back to life. Overjoyed, they kissed and hugged.

On his return home, the man asked right away about the keys and egg. When he was unable to find a trace of blood on the egg, he declared: "You have passed the test, and you shall be my bride." He no longer had any power over her and had to do her bidding.[8] "Very well," she replied. "But first you must take a basketful of gold to my father and mother, and you must carry it on your back. In the meantime, I'll make the plans for the wedding."

She ran to her sisters, whom she had hidden in a little room, and said: "Now is the time when I can save you. That brute will be the one who carries you home. But as soon as you get back there, send help for me."

She put both girls into a basket and covered them with gold until they were completely hidden. Then she summoned the wizard and said: "Pick up the basket and start walking, but don't you dare stop to rest along the way. I'll be looking out my little window, keeping an eye on you."

Arthur Rackham, *The Fairy Tales of the Brothers Grimm*

Fitcher hurries off to the home of his bride, unaware that he is carrying two of the three sisters in the basket.

The wizard put the basket up on his shoulders and started walking with it. But it was so heavy that sweat began to pour down his forehead. He sat down to rest for a while, but within moments one of the girls cried out from the basket: "I'm looking out my little window, and I see that you're resting. Get a move on." Whenever he stopped, the voice called out, and he had to keep going until finally, gasping for breath and groaning, he managed to get the basket with the gold and with the two girls in it back to the parents' house.

Meanwhile the bride was preparing the wedding celebration, to which she had invited all the wizard's friends. She took a skull with grinning teeth,[9] crowned it with jewels and a garland of flowers, carried it upstairs, and set it down at an attic window, facing to the outside. When everything was ready, she crawled into a barrel of honey,[10] cut open a featherbed, and rolled around in the feathers until she looked like a strange bird that no one could have recognized. She left the house, and on her way she met some wedding guests, who asked:

> "Oh, Fitcher's feathered bird, where from, where from?"
> "From feathered Fitze Fitcher's house I've come."
> "And the young bride there, how does she fare?"
> "She's swept the house all the way through,
> And from the attic window, she's staring down at you."

She then met the bridegroom, who was walking back home very slowly. He too asked:

> "Oh, Fitcher's feathered bird, where from, where from?"
> "From feathered Fitze Fitcher's house I've come."
> "And the young bride there, how does she fare?"
> "She's swept the house all the way through,
> And from the attic window, she's staring down at you."

9. *She took a skull with grinning teeth.* The third sister offers the wizard a bride in his own image: a death's head that has been aestheticized with jewels and a garland of flowers. His true alliance is not with the living but with the dead. Fashioned with artifice, but retaining its link with nature, the skull becomes the true bride who allows the false bride to escape.

10. *she crawled into a barrel of honey.* The heroine constructs her new identity by combining sweet nourishment with celestial elements. She represents a lightness of being that moves her away from the wizard and his domestic death trap.

The bridegroom looked up and saw the decorated skull. He thought it was his bride, nodded, and waved to her. But when he got to the house with his guests, the brothers and relatives who had been sent to rescue the bride[11] were already there. They locked the doors to the house so that no one could get out. Then they set fire to it, and the wizard and his crew were burned alive.

11. *the brothers and relatives who had been sent to rescue the bride.* In the end, as in stories about Bluebeard, the brothers finish off the villain, even when it is the bride who manages to outwit her groom. The wizard, associated with diabolical powers, receives his just punishment when he is consumed by flames.

The Juniper Tree[1]

1. *Juniper Tree.* The juniper has a rich folkloric tradition. Its oil, ashes, berries, leaves, and bark are used in many cultures for healing purposes, and it is the therapeutic power of the tree that seems to make it a natural choice as the resting place for the boy. But the tree's berries were also used in earlier times, as noted by the physician Galen of classical antiquity, for contraceptive purposes and to induce abortion. In Russia the juniper tree is a birch; in England it is a rose tree.

The version of the story published in the Grimms' collection came from the pen of the Romantic artist Philipp Otto Runge (1777–1810). A master of ornamental detail and decorative art, Runge sent the Grimms a highly stylized narrative which used plattdeutsch, *or Low German, to convey the impression of "artless" narration. Runge's version of the story is the only one that weds the biological mother so closely to nature—once she becomes fertile and conceives, she is turned into a virtual prisoner of nature, subject to its laws of growth and decay. An elaborate duet coordinates the rhythms of the child's gestation period with nature's seasonal changes.*

"The Juniper Tree" has been seen as a ghoulish nursery counterpart to the Greek myth of Cronus, who devours his children in order to ensure that they will not usurp his power. It tells of powerful generational conflicts that are resolved once the harmful members of the family are expelled. Like many tales from the oral tradition, "The Juniper Tree" is relentlessly fixated on orality. It begins with the hero's mother wishing for a child while she is peeling an apple, then recounts her death in childbirth after she has gorged on juniper berries. Ingestion and gestation are, as Marina Warner

has pointed out, "so braided together in the tale . . . that it is hard to disentangle where breeding ends and eating begins, or vice versa." The stepmother decapitates the boy while he is reaching for an apple, and the boy's father feasts on his son's flesh. A millstone, the instrument used for grinding wheat, becomes a murder weapon, turned on the wicked stepmother, who perishes and is eliminated from the final scene in which father and children sit down at the table and dine together.

With its lurid descriptions of decapitation and cannibalism, "The Juniper Tree" (also known as "My Mother Slew Me; My Father Ate Me") is probably the most shocking of all fairy tales. In most versions, the central character is a boy, yet occasionally, as in the British story "The Rose Tree," a girl undergoes the transformation into a bird. The scenes of the boy's beheading by the mother and consumption by the father did not deter P. L. Travers, the British author of Mary Poppins, *from describing the tale as "beautiful," nor did they keep J. R. R. Tolkien from referring to the "beauty and horror" of the story, with its "exquisite and tragic beginning."*

The "beauty" of "The Juniper Tree" probably turns less on its aesthetic appeal than on its engagement with anxieties that fascinate us in their evocation of sheer dread. In the stepmother we find a woman who represents maternal power run mad, an incarnation of a natural force so cruel and inexorable that it heightens the weakness and helplessness of the children. In the Grimms' version, the boy is transformed back to human form and reunited with his father and sister to live in a motherless household. But in some versions, as in the Scottish "Pippety Pew," the boy remains a bird, whereas "the Goodman and his daughter lived happy and died happy."

Although the poignancy of the opening paragraph in "The Juniper Tree" is unsettled by the complexities of the biological mother's associations with nature and death, it still stands in sharp contrast to the horrors of the tale's main events, events engineered largely by the (step) mother. The biological mother is presented as a "natural" foil to the stepmother, who represents self-consciousness and artifice in its most dreaded and dreadful form. The co-presence of birth and death is inscribed in the first scene, then doubled and repeated as rebirth and murder in the body of the tale.

"The Juniper Tree" eliminates both biological mother and stepmother in the end, giving us a tableau that unites brother, sister, and father to constitute a new family. This is the same "happily ever after" we know from "Hansel and Gretel" and countless other fairy tales. "The Juniper Tree" seems to enact the process of growing away from the mother, who in our culture represents dependence and domesticity, and turning to the father, who, by virtue of his traditional absence from early child-rearing, comes to signify autonomy. By crushing the mother and joining the father, the children have been seen as "successfully" negotiating the path from dependence to autonomy. It is important to bear in mind that versions of this tale and others are sacred only as cultural documents mapping the developmental routes of another era. Enough has changed and is changing since Philipp Otto Runge recorded this tale for us to begin producing variants on this cultural story, which demonizes mothers in a powerful way and represents fathers as passive and detached.

A long time ago, as many as two thousand years ago,[2] there lived a rich man with a wife who was both beautiful and good. They loved each other dearly, but they had no children,[3] even though they longed for them. Day and night the wife prayed for a child, but still they had none.

In front of the house there was a garden, and in the garden

2. *as many as two thousand years ago.* The specification of an era is unusual in fairy tales. The figure of two thousand years anchors the tale in biblical times and suggests a connection with the birth of Christ. In light of the boy's death and resurrection, the date has a special significance.

3. *they had no children.* This fairy tale, like so many others, begins with "lack" and moves to the liquidation of the lack, which in turn produces a new motor to the plot, in this case the death of the biological mother. Like many fairy-tale couples, this one is childless, and rather than just wishing for a child, the two pray. Many couples make desperate wishes that lead to the birth of some type of animal—a hedgehog, for example, in the Grimms' story "Hans My Hedgehog."

there grew a juniper tree. Once, in the wintertime, the wife was peeling an apple under the tree,[4] and while she was peeling it, she cut her finger. Blood dripped on the snow. "Ah," said the woman, and she sighed deeply. "If only I had a child as red as blood and as white as snow!" After she had spoken those words, she was happy, for she had a feeling that something would come of it. And she went back into the house.

A month went by, and the snow melted.[5] Two months passed, and everything had become green. Three months went by, and flowers were sprouting from the ground. Four months passed, and all the trees in the woods were growing tall, with their green branches intertwining. The woods echoed with the song of birds, and blossoms were dropping from the trees. And so the fifth month went by. And when the woman sat under the juniper tree, her heart leaped for joy because the tree was so fragrant. She fell to her knees and was beside herself with happiness. When the sixth month had passed, the fruit grew large and firm, and she became very quiet. In the seventh month, she picked the berries from the juniper tree and gorged herself on them until she became miserable and was ailing. After the eighth month went by, she called her husband and, in tears, said to him: "If I die, bury me under the juniper tree." After that she felt better and was calm until the ninth month had passed. Then she bore a child as white as snow and as red as blood. When she saw the child, she felt so happy that she died of joy.[6]

The woman's husband buried her beneath the juniper tree, and he wept day after day. After a while he felt better, but he still cried from time to time. Eventually he stopped, and then he took a second wife.

The man's second wife gave birth to a daughter. The child from his first marriage was a little boy, as red as blood and as white as snow.[7] When the woman looked at her daughter, she felt nothing but love for her, but whenever she looked at

4. *peeling an apple under the tree.* The apple appears later in the story as the object of desire that leads to the boy's death. Note also the connection with the apple that is used to tempt and poison Snow White.

5. *A month went by, and the snow melted.* In this paragraph, the parallels drawn between the seasons and the child's gestation period are elaborated in a mannered style more characteristic of fiction than of fairy tales. Runge was no doubt hoping to create a poetic effect with the descriptions of nature.

6. *she felt so happy that she died of joy.* Many historians have pointed out that the high rate of mortality in childbirth may have motivated the prominence of stepmothers in fairy tales. Like Cinderella and Snow White, the little boy in this story will suffer under the cruel regime of his stepmother.

7. *as red as blood and as white as snow.* The story resembles "Snow White" in many ways, especially because its plot turns on the conflict between stepmother and child. But note that in this case, it is a little boy whose lips are as red as blood and whose skin is as white as snow. Most versions of this particular tale type do not include the background story about the death of the biological mother.

the little boy, she felt sick at heart. It seemed that no matter what he did he was in the way, and the woman kept wondering how she could make sure that her daughter eventually inherited everything.[8] The devil got hold of her so that she began to hate the little boy, and she slapped him around and pinched him here and cuffed him there. The poor child lived in terror, and when he came home from school he had no peace at all.

One day the woman went into the pantry. Her little daughter followed her and asked: "Mother, will you give me an apple?"

"All right, my dear," said the woman, and she gave her a beautiful apple from a chest that had a big heavy lid with a sharp iron lock on it.

"Mother," asked the little girl, "can brother have one too?"

The woman was irritated, but she said: "Yes, he can have one when he gets back from school."

The woman looked out the window, and when she saw the boy walking home, it was as if the devil had taken hold of her,[9] and she snatched the apple out of her daughter's hand and said: "You can't have one before your brother." Then she tossed the apple into the chest and shut it.

The little boy walked in the door, and the devil got her to whisper sweetly to him and say: "My son, would you like an apple?" But she gave him a look filled with hate.

"Mother," said the little boy. "What a scary look! Yes, give me an apple."

When the little boy bent down, the devil prompted her and *bam!* She slammed the lid down so hard that the boy's head flew off and fell into the chest with the apples. Then she was overcome with fear and thought: "How am I going to get out of this?" She went to her room and took a white kerchief from her dresser drawer. She put the boy's head back on his neck and tied the scarf around it so that you couldn't tell that

8. *make sure that her daughter eventually inherited everything.* The inheritance issue creates friction even today in many blended families. In "The Juniper Tree," anxiety about dividing the patrimony is spelled out as a key factor in motivating the stepmother's hatred of the boy.

9. *it was as if the devil had taken hold of her.* The presence of the devil as a motivating force suggests that the teller of this particular tale was influenced by religious beliefs. Note that the stepmother's duplicity is connected with a diabolical force that incarnates the spirit of division and divisiveness.

anything was wrong. Then she sat him down on a chair in front of the door and put an apple in his hand.

Later on, Little Marlene came into the kitchen to see her mother, who was standing by the fire, madly stirring a pot of hot water. "Mother," said Little Marlene, "Brother is sitting by the door and looks pale. He has an apple in his hand, and when I asked him to give me the apple, he wouldn't answer. It was very scary."

"Go back to him," the mother said, "and if he doesn't give you an answer, slap his face."

Little Marlene went back to him and said: "Brother, give me the apple."

Her brother wouldn't answer. So Marlene gave him a slap, and his head went flying off. She was so terrified that she began to howl and weep. Then she ran to her mother and said: "Mother, I've knocked brother's head right off!" And she was crying so hard that she couldn't stop.

"Little Marlene," said her mother, "what a dreadful thing you've done! But don't breathe a word to a soul, for there's nothing we can do. We'll cook him up in a stew."

The mother then took the little boy and chopped him up.[10] She put the pieces into a pot and cooked them up into a stew. Little Marlene stood by the fire and wept so hard that the stew didn't need any salt at all because of her tears.

When the father came home, he sat down at the table and said: "Where's my son?"

The mother brought in a huge dish of stew, and Little Marlene was weeping so hard that she couldn't stop.

"Where's my son?" the father asked again.

"Oh," said the mother, "he went off to the country to visit his mother's great uncle. He is planning to stay there a while."

"What's he going to do there? He didn't even say good-bye to me."

10. *The mother then took the little boy and chopped him up.* The stepmother's serving up of the boy in a stew is reminiscent of the Greek myth in which Atreus prepares a banquet for his enemy Thyestes, who unknowingly feasts on his own sons. Her deed is also reminiscent of dismemberment scenes in other fairy tales (most notably Perrault's "Bluebeard" and the Grimms' "Fitcher's Bird"). The powerful resurrection scene at the end forges a connection with the dismemberment of the Egyptian god Osiris as well as of the Greek poet Orpheus, who is torn to pieces by the maenads. In Shakespeare's *Titus Andronicus*, the title figure butchers the two men who violate and brutalize his daughter, then dishes them up to their mother.

"Well, he really wanted to go, and he asked if he could stay for six weeks. They'll take good care of him."

"Oh, that makes me so sad," said the husband. "It's not right. He should have said good-bye."

Then he began eating and said: "Little Marlene, why are you crying? Your brother will be back soon." And he said: "Oh, dear wife, this stew tastes so good! Give me some more."

The more the father ate, the more he wanted. "Give me some more," he said. "No one else can have any of it. Somehow I feel as if it's all for me."

The father kept eating, and he threw the bones under the table until he had finished everything. Meanwhile, Little Marlene went to her dresser and got her best silk kerchief. She picked up all the bones from beneath the table, tied them up in her silk kerchief, and carried them outside, where she began weeping bitter tears while she was putting the bones down in the green grass under the juniper tree. Once she had finished, she suddenly felt much better and stopped crying. The juniper tree began stirring. Its branches parted and came back together again as though it were clapping its hands for joy. A mist arose from the tree, and right in the middle of the mist a flame was burning, and from the flame a beautiful bird emerged and began singing gloriously.[11] It soared up in the air and then vanished. The tree was just as it had always been before, but the kerchief with the bones was gone. Little Marlene felt so happy and lighthearted because it seemed as if her brother were still alive. She returned home feeling content and sat down at the table to eat.

Meanwhile, the bird flew away, perched on the roof of a goldsmith's house, and began singing:

"My mother, she slew me,
My father, he ate me,
My sister, Marlene,
Gathered my bones,

11. *a beautiful bird emerged and began singing gloriously.* The boy's transformation resonates with the many mythological metamorphoses from human to bird (Procne and Philomela) but is also linked to the powerful role of birds in the Grimms' fairy tales. Like the mythical Phoenix, the boy rises up, if not from ashes then from the bones that remain from the stew. His beautiful song is as compelling as the fabled melodious cry of the Phoenix. "The Juniper Tree," with its emphasis on the power of song, was translated into the operatic medium by Arthur Yorinks, who composed the libretto for "The Juniper Tree," set to music by Robert Moran and Philip Glass in 1985, and made another operatic appearance in a less renowned version by Rodney Watkins and Patricia Debney. The pop star Bjork appears in a dramatically rescripted cinematic version of the tale which retains the title *The Juniper Tree* (2002).

Kay Nielsen, *Hansel and Gretel and Other Stories by the Brothers Grimm*

Little Marlene watches in awe as the bird, of the same hue as her dress, emerges from the flames and begins singing.

Tied them in silk,
For the juniper tree.
Tweet, tweet, what a fine bird am I!"

A goldsmith was sitting in his shop, making a chain of gold. He heard a bird singing on his roof, and he found its song very beautiful. He got up, and when he crossed the threshold, he lost his slipper. Still, he kept right on going

12. *"Here's the golden chain."* The Phoenix was said to have brilliant scarlet and gold plumage, and those colors reappear in this tale as the red shoes and golden chain purchased in exchange for song.

out into the middle of the street with only one sock and one slipper on. He was also wearing his apron, and in one hand he had the golden chain, in the other his tongs. The sun was shining brightly on the street. He stopped to look at the bird and said: "Bird, you sing so beautifully. Sing me that song again."

"No," said the bird. "I never sing a second time for nothing. If you give me that golden chain, I'll sing for you again."

"Here," said the goldsmith. "Here's the golden chain.[12] Now sing that song again."

The bird came swooping down. Grasping the golden chain in its right claw, it perched in front of the goldsmith and began singing:

"My mother, she slew me,
My father, he ate me,
My sister, Marlene,
Gathered my bones,
Tied them in silk,
For the juniper tree.
Tweet, tweet, what a fine bird am I!"

Then the bird flew off to a shoemaker's house, perched on the roof and sang:

"My mother, she slew me,
My father, he ate me,
My sister, Marlene,
Gathered my bones,
Tied them in silk,
For the juniper tree.
Tweet, tweet, what a fine bird am I!"

When the shoemaker heard the song, he ran out the door in his shirtsleeves and looked up at the roof. He had to put his hand over his eyes to keep the sun from blinding him. "Bird," he said, "you sing so beautifully." Then he called into the house: "Wife, come out here for a moment. There's a bird up there. See it? How beautifully it is singing!"

The shoemaker called his daughter and her children, his apprentices, the hired hand, and the maid. They all came running out into the street to look at the bird and to admire its beauty. It had red and green feathers, and around its neck was a band of pure gold, and the eyes in its head sparkled like stars.

"Bird," said the shoemaker, "sing that song again."

"No," said the bird, "I never sing a second time for nothing. You have to give me something."

"Wife," said the man, "go up to the attic. On the top shelf you'll find a pair of red shoes. Get them for me."

His wife went and got the shoes.

"Here," said the man. "Now sing that song again."

The bird came swooping down. Taking the shoes in its left claw, it flew back up on the roof and sang:

"My mother, she slew me,
My father, he ate me,
My sister, Marlene,
Gathered my bones,
Tied them in silk,
For the juniper tree.
Tweet, tweet, what a fine bird am I!"

When the bird had finished the song, it flew away. It had the chain in its right claw and the shoes in its left, and it flew far away to a mill. The mill went "clickety-clack, clickety-clack, clickety-clack." Inside the mill sat twenty of the miller's men, hewing a stone, "hick-hack, hick-hack, hick-hack." And the mill kept going "clickety-clack, clickety-clack, clickety-clack." And so the bird went and perched on a linden tree outside the mill and sang:

"My mother, she slew me . . ."

And one of the men stopped working.

"My father, he ate me . . ."

And two more stopped working and listened.

"My sister, Marlene . . ."

Then four men stopped working.

"Gathered my bones,
Tied them in silk . . ."

Now only eight were still hewing.

"For the . . ."

Now only five.

" . . . juniper tree."

Now only one.

"Tweet, tweet, what a fine bird am I!"

The last one stopped to listen to the final words. "Bird," he said, "you sing so beautifully! Let me hear the whole thing too. Sing that song again."

"I never sing the second time for nothing. If you give me the millstone, I'll sing the song again."

"If it belonged to me alone," he said, "I would give it to you."

"If the bird sings again," the others said, "it can have the millstone."

Then the bird swooped down, and the miller's men, all twenty of them, set the beam to and raised up the stone. "Heave-ho-hup, heave-ho-hup, heave-ho-hup." And the bird stuck its neck through the hole, put the stone on as if it were a collar, flew back to the tree, and sang:

"My mother, she slew me,
My father, he ate me,
My sister, Marlene,
Gathered my bones,
Tied them in silk,
For the juniper tree.
Tweet, tweet, what a fine bird am I!"

When the bird had finished its song, it spread its wings. In its right claw was the chain, in its left claw the shoes, and round its neck was the millstone. Then it flew away, far away to the house of its father.

The father, mother, and Little Marlene were sitting at the table in the parlor, and the father said: "How happy I am! My heart feels so light."

"Not me," said the mother. "I feel frightened, as if a big storm were on its way."

Meanwhile, Little Marlene just sat there weeping. The bird flew up, and when it landed on the roof, the father said: "How happy I'm feeling. And outside the sun is shining so brightly! I feel as if I'm about to see an old friend again."

"I don't," said the woman. "I'm so scared that my teeth are chattering, and I feel as if there's fire running through my veins." She tore at her bodice to loosen it.

Little Marlene sat there weeping. She held her apron up to her eyes and cried so hard that it was completely soaked with tears. The bird swooped down to the juniper tree, perched on a branch, and sang:

13. *"the air smells like cinnamon."* The Phoenix was believed to live for close to five hundred years. When its death approached, it made a nest of aromatic branches and spices, set them on fire, and was consumed in the flames.

"My mother, she slew me . . ."

The mother stopped up her ears and closed her eyes, for she didn't want to see or hear anything, but the roaring in her ears was like the wildest possible storm, and her eyes burned and flashed like lightning.

"My father, he ate me . . ."

"Oh, Mother," said the man, "there's a beautiful bird out there, and it's singing so gloriously. The sun is shining so warmly, and the air smells like cinnamon."[13]

"My sister, Marlene . . ."

Little Marlene put her head in her lap and just kept crying and crying. But the husband said: "I'm going outside. I've got to see this bird close up."

"Oh, don't go," said the wife. "It feels as if the whole house is shaking and about to go up in flames!"

But the husband went out and looked at the bird.

"Gathered my bones,
Tied them in silk,
For the juniper tree.
Tweet, tweet, what a fine bird am I!"

After finishing its song, the bird dropped the golden chain, and it fell right around the man's neck, hanging perfectly from it. He went inside and said: "Just look at that fine bird out there! It gave me this beautiful golden chain, almost as beautiful as the bird is."

The woman was so terrified that she fell right down on the floor, and the cap she was wearing came off her head. And once again the bird sang:

> "My mother, she slew me . . ."

"Oh, if only I were a thousand feet under the ground so that I wouldn't have to listen to this!"

> "My father, he ate me . . ."

Then the woman fell down again as if dead.

> "My sister, Marlene . . ."

"Oh," said Little Marlene. "I want to go outside and see if the bird will give me something too." And she went out.

> "Gathered my bones,
> Tied them in silk . . ."

And the bird tossed her the shoes.

> "For the juniper tree.
> Tweet, tweet, what a fine bird am I!"

Little Marlene felt lighthearted and happy. She put on the new red shoes and came dancing and skipping into the house.

"Oh," Little Marlene said. "I was so sad when I went out, and now I feel so cheerful. What a fine bird that is out there. It gave me a pair of red shoes."

The woman jumped to her feet, and her hair stood straight on end like tongues of flame. "It's as if the world were coming to an end. If I go outside, maybe I'll feel better too."

The woman went over to the door and *bam!* The bird dropped the millstone on her head[14] and crushed her to death. The father and Little Marlene heard the crash and went outside. Smoke, flames, and fire were rising up from

14. *The bird dropped the millstone on her head.* Many critics have associated the millstone that crushes the stepmother with a biblical millstone that drowns those who injure the young and the innocent: "Whoever receives one such child in my name receives me; but whoever causes one of these little ones who believe in me to sin, it would be better for him to have a great millstone fastened around his neck and to be drowned in the depth of the sea" (Matthew 18:5). The millstone, which is ordinarily used to grind grain for making bread, becomes here a weapon used to eliminate the figure often associated with nourishment.

Warwick Goble, *The Fairy Book*

The bird, whose feathers match the colors of his half-sister's cape and dress, emerges in all his glory from the flame in the tree. The bird's plumage, the girl's tresses, and the tree's branches create a dramatic effect, linking the girl with the bird.

the spot, and when they vanished, little brother was back, standing right there. He took his father and Little Marlene by the hand, and the three of them were filled with joy. Then they went back in the house, sat down at the table, and dined.[15]

15. *sat down at the table, and dined.* The trio at the end partakes of a meal, almost as if it were a sacrament, recalling the sacrilege of the stew served up to the father. Here, the dining ritual renews and restores the new family, although for some critics it is seen as an allegorical staging of the consolidation of patriarchal power.

The Six Swans

The story of a girl who disenchants her brothers through silence and sewing is among the most powerful in the collection, yet it has not become part of the canonical group of tales known to the Anglo-American world. Hans Christian Andersen's "Wild Swans" offers a fuller, literary elaboration of the story, with eleven boys and a girl named Eliza, who must gather nettles, break them to pieces until they become flax, then spin and weave eleven coats with long sleeves. Eliza is also enjoined to remain silent; otherwise the first word she utters will pierce the hearts of her brothers "like a deadly dagger."

Once again, as in "Little Brother and Little Sister," there are two parts to the story, with the first charting the sojourn of the king's children in the woods, the second tracing the sister's efforts to disenchant her brothers even as she is persecuted by an evil mother-in-law. What is fascinating about the story is its positioning of the single girl as heroic rescuer of her brothers. Through her beauty, silence, and sewing, she succeeds in attracting a king and breaking the spell cast on her brothers. She also manages to found a new family at the same time that she draws the wayward brothers back to live with her family. The beleaguered heroine's triumph over black magic through per-

sistence in domestic craft must surely have been an appealing topic for the women spinning, sewing, and mending while these tales were told.

king went hunting one day out in a vast forest. He was so intent on pursuing his quarry at one point that none of his men could keep up with him. When it began to grow dark, he reined in his horse and stopped to look around. He realized then that he was lost. He looked hard for a way out of the forest, but he couldn't find one anywhere. While he was searching, he encountered a doddering old woman who shook her head from side to side as she walked up to him: she was a witch.

"Good woman," he said, "can you show me the way out of this forest?"

"Of course I can, Your Highness," she replied. "I can let you know how to get out, but there's one little condition that goes with it. If you don't satisfy it, you'll never leave this forest, and you'll die of hunger."

"What's the condition?" the king asked.

"I have a daughter," the old woman said. "She's as beautiful as any woman on earth and deserves to be your wife. If you decide to make her your queen, I will show you the way out of these woods."

The king agreed to the condition, for he feared for his life, and the old woman sent him into her hut, where her daughter was sitting by the hearth. She welcomed the king as if she had been expecting him. He could see that she was very beautiful, but for some reason he didn't like her, and he couldn't look at her without cringing. But he went ahead and got on his horse with the daughter, and the old woman showed him the path out of the woods. When the king arrived at his royal palace, the wedding was celebrated.

The king had been married once before, and he had seven children from his first wife, six boys and a girl, whom he loved more than anything else in the world. He was afraid that the new stepmother might treat them badly or even harm them, and so he sent all of them out to a solitary castle deep in the woods. It was so remote and the path to it was so hard to find that he would have had trouble finding it himself if a Wise Woman had not given him a ball of yarn with magical properties.[1] When he tossed the ball to the ground, it unwound on its own and showed him the path.

The king had been spending so much time with his beloved children that the queen began taking note of his long absences. She was curious and wanted to find out what he was doing out there all alone in the woods. She bribed the servants with money, and they not only disclosed his secret, they also told her about the ball of yarn that you needed to find the path.

The queen could find no peace until she had found out where the king was hiding the yarn. She then sewed little white shirts of silk, and since she had learned witchcraft from her mother, she stitched a magic spell into them.

One day when the king went out hunting, she took the little shirts and went into the woods. The ball of yarn showed her the path through the forest to the house. The children, who could see someone approaching from the distance, believed that their father was on his way, and filled with joy, they ran to meet him. Suddenly the queen threw a shirt over each one of them, and when it touched them, they turned into swans[2] and flew high up over the trees.

The queen went back home, filled with glee, thinking that

1. *if a Wise Woman had not given him a ball of yarn with magical properties.* The ball of yarn is reminiscent of the ball of thread given by Ariadne, daughter of King Minos, to Theseus so that he can find his way back out of the Labyrinth after slaying the Minotaur. But this ball of yarn leads both into the forest and back out of it.

2. *they turned into swans.* European folklore is rich in stories about the metamorphosis of swans and seals into beautiful maidens who leave the air and waters to settle down with a mortal, bear children, then return to their native habitat. Here, it is boys who are turned into birds that, for all their beauty and freedom, represent a state of captivity.

Warwick Goble, *The Fairy Book*

The queen has cast spells on six shirts and thrown them over the boys, who are instantly transformed into swans that fly away into the woods.

3. *She didn't dare to get into any one of them.* Like Snow White and Cinderella, the girl comes across a cottage, but is so well mannered that she doesn't disturb any of the beds in it. Instead, she is prepared to sleep on the floor, in hiding, in case anyone returns home.

she had gotten rid of the stepchildren. But as it turned out, the girl had not left the house with her brothers, and the queen didn't know that she existed.

The next day the king went into the forest to visit his children, but only the girl was there. "Where are your brothers?" the king asked.

"Dear Father," she replied, "they've all gone away and left me here alone." And she told him how she had stood at the window and watched her brothers fly away high up over the trees. She even showed him the feathers that she had found in the yard, which she had picked up after they left. The king was distraught, but it never dawned on him that his wife was responsible for this wicked deed. He was afraid that the girl would be taken from him as well, and he was planning to take her back home with him. But the daughter was terrified of the stepmother and asked the king if he would stay just this one night in the castle.

The poor girl was thinking: "I can't live here any longer. I've got to go out and find my brothers." At nightfall she left and fled straight into the woods. She walked all night long, and the next day as well, until she was too worn out to go on. When she found a little hut, she entered it and discovered a room with six little beds in it. She didn't dare get into any one of them[3] but crawled underneath one and was hoping to spend the night stretched out on the hard ground.

Just about the time that the sun was setting, she heard a whirring of wings and saw six swans come flying in through the window. They settled on the ground and huffed and puffed until all their feathers dropped to the ground, and then their swan skins came off as if they were nothing but shirts. The girl took a good look at them, and suddenly she realized that they were her brothers. She was overjoyed to see them and came crawling out from under the bed. The brothers were just as excited to see their little sister, but their joy was short-lived.

"You can't stay here for long," they told her. "This is a robber's den. If they come back and find you, they'll kill you."

"Can't you protect me from them?" their sister asked.

"No," they replied. "We only get to remove our swan skins for a quarter of an hour in the evening. For that short time we take on our human form, but then we're turned back into swans."

The sister wept and said: "Can't anyone break the spell?"

"Oh, yes," they replied, "there's a way to do it, but it's just too hard. For six years you would have to go without speaking or laughing. You would have to spend all that time sewing six shirts for us from star flowers. If a single word came out of your mouth, all your work would be for nothing."

Just as the brothers finished explaining what had to be done, their quarter of an hour was up, and they returned to their shape as swans and flew out the window.

The girl had decided to set her brothers free no matter what, even at the cost of her life. She left the little hut, went deep into the woods, climbed up a tree, and slept there all night long. The next morning she went into the woods to collect star flowers, and she began sewing. She didn't have anyone to talk to, and she had no desire to laugh. All she did was sit there and attend to her work.

One day, after she had spent a lot of time in the woods, the king of the land was hunting in the forest,[4] and some of his men discovered the tree where the girl had been spending her time. They called out to her and asked: "Who are you?" But she didn't reply.

"Come down here to us," they said. "We won't hurt you."

The girl just shook her head. They kept asking questions until finally she threw her golden necklace down to them,[5] thinking that it would satisfy them. But they wouldn't stop and so she tossed down her belt, and when that did no good, her garters, until finally she had gotten rid of everything that she could manage to do without. She was left there with nothing on but her shift.

4. *the king of the land was hunting in the forest.* Each of the two episodes in the story begins with a king hunting in the forest, first the girl's father who loses his way in the woods but finds a new (false) bride, then a new king who never loses his sense of orientation and discovers a (true) bride.

5. *she threw her golden necklace down to them.* Like the princess in "The Frog King" and the miller's daughter in "Rumpelstiltskin," the girl tries to liberate herself from the hunters by offering jewels or clothing. The opportunity for risqué humor in retellings of the tale becomes evident as we learn about how the girl tosses down her belt and garter. It is unlikely that the women who dictated the stories to the Grimms would have taken advantage of those opportunities to indulge in the kind of off-color humor that appears in some versions of "Little Red Riding Hood" when the girl takes off her garments one by one before getting into bed with the wolf.

The huntsmen refused to make any kind of trade, and they ended up climbing the tree, carrying the girl down, and taking her to the king. The king asked her: "Who are you and what were you doing in that tree?"

The girl refused to answer. The king asked her the same question in every language he knew, but she remained as mute as a stone. He was greatly moved by her beauty, and he felt overwhelmed by a deep love for her. Putting his cloak around her, he mounted his horse and rode off with her to his castle. He dressed the girl in royal garments that made her beauty shine like the sun, but he still couldn't get a word out of her. He seated her next to him at the table, and he was so enamored of her modest manner and good breeding that he declared: "I want to marry this woman alone, and I'm not interested in any other woman on earth." A few days later, their marriage was celebrated.

The king's mother was an evil woman,[6] and she was not at all happy with the marriage. She never missed a chance to speak ill of the young queen. "Who knows where that little hussy came from!" she would say. "How can someone who can't even talk be good enough to marry a king?"

A year later, when the queen gave birth to her first child, the old woman took it away and smeared blood on the queen's mouth while she was sleeping. Then she went straight to the king and accused the mother of eating her baby. The king refused to believe what she said and wouldn't let anyone touch his wife.

For her part, the queen would sit quietly sewing her shirts, paying attention to nothing else. When she gave birth again, this time to a beautiful baby boy, the treacherous mother-in-law played the same trick, but the king still refused to believe what she claimed.

"She is just far too good and too kind to do a thing like that," he said. "If she could talk and were able to defend herself, it would be plain as day that she's innocent."

6. *The king's mother was an evil woman.* The French version of "Sleeping Beauty" by Charles Perrault also concludes with an episode in which an evil mother-in-law kidnaps children and tries to implicate their mother in their murder. In the end, she too is sentenced to death, receiving the punishment intended for her daughter-in-law.

When the old woman stole the newborn baby a third time and accused the queen of killing it, and when the queen still failed to utter a word to defend herself, the king had no choice but to turn her over to a judge, who sentenced her to death by fire.

The day on which the sentence was to be carried out was exactly the last day of the six years during which she had not been able to speak or laugh and had devoted herself to breaking the magic spell cast on her dear brothers. The six shirts were finished, and all that was missing was the left sleeve on one of them.

When the queen was led to the stake, she had the shirts over her arm. She was already up there at the stake and someone was just coming to light the fire, when she looked up and saw the six swans flying through the air toward her. She knew that they would soon be freed, and her heart swelled with joy. The swans flew right over to her and landed close enough so that she could toss the shirts on them. At the moment when the shirts touched them, the swan skins vanished and there were her brothers standing right before her: strong, fit, and handsome. Only the youngest was missing an arm, and in its place there was a swan's wing.

The queen and her brothers couldn't stop hugging and kissing. Finally the queen spoke to the king, who was utterly confused by what was happening. "Dear husband," she said, "now I can finally speak and let you know that I am entirely innocent and that all those accusations were false." She told him about how the old woman had stolen away the children and kept them in hiding. To the king's great joy, the children were brought back, and the evil mother-in-law was sentenced to death at the stake.[7] She burned to ashes.

The king and the queen lived in peace and happiness for the rest of their days with the six brothers of the queen.

7. *the evil mother-in-law was sentenced to death at the stake.* The villain's punishment, however severe, is no worse than what she planned for the tale's protagonist. The fact that she burns to ashes signifies a definitive end to her reign of terror.

BRIAR ROSE[1]

P. L. Travers, author of Mary Poppins, *noted that the "idea of the sleeper, of somebody hidden from mortal eye, waiting until the time shall ripen has always been dear to the folkly mind," and she offered an inventory of legendary sleepers: Snow White in her glass coffin, Brunhilde behind the wall of fire, Charlemagne in France, King Arthur on the Isle of Avalon, and Frederick Barbarossa in his mountain domain in Thuringia. Andrew Lang, editor of a famous series of fairy-tale anthologies, suggested that "the idea of a long sleep may possibly have been derived from the repose of Nature in winter," but most readers of "Sleeping Beauty" will not think of spring when the prince awakens the heroine with a kiss.*

Sleeping Beauty is the fabled passive princess who awaits liberation by a prince. Deprived of agency, she resembles the catatonic Snow White, who can do nothing more than lie in wait for Prince Charming. Yet critics often forget that she is also an adventurer, a curious child who, when finally left to her own devices, explores the castle, discovers something new, and seeks to try it out, even though the consequences are grave. The clichéd view of fairy-tale heroines as purely passive creatures also overlooks the many clever and resource-

1. *Briar Rose.* The Grimms' title, *Dornröschen*, is sometimes translated literally as "Little Briar Rose." Note that the name encapsulates both thorns and the rose, thus capturing the suffering and beauty of religious and erotic passion. Perrault's French title is "Sleeping Beauty in the Wood." In their annotations, the Grimms referred to the figure of Brunhilde and the wall of flames that surrounds her.

ful girls and women who are able to liberate themselves from danger. Anthologies by Kathleen Ragan, Angela Carter, Alison Lurie, and Ethel Johnston Phelps have resurrected older stories about strong, courageous, and resilient heroines who rescue themselves and others, thus providing weighty evidence that not all princesses lie in wait for Prince Charming.

The earliest recorded version of "Sleeping Beauty" appears as "Troylus and Zellandine" in a fourteenth-century prose narrative called Perceforest. *The Grimms' story of Sleeping Beauty is considered a truncated version of Giambattista Basile's "Sun, Moon, and Talia" (1636) and Charles Perrault's "Sleeping Beauty in the Wood" (1697). In Basile's story, Talia (whose name derives from the Greek word* Thaleia, *meaning "the blossoming one") gets a tiny piece of flax under her fingernail and falls down dead. The king who discovers Talia in an abandoned castle is already married, but he is so overcome with desire for her that he "plucks from her the fruits of love" while she is still asleep. Talia is awakened from her deep sleep when one of the two infants to which she gives birth—exactly nine months after the king's visit—sucks the piece of flax from her finger. When the king's wife learns about Talia and her two children, Sun and Moon, she orders their deaths, but she herself perishes in the fire she prepares for Talia, and the others live happily ever after.*

Perrault's "Sleeping Beauty in the Wood" is awakened when a prince kneels before her, and the two carry on a love affair that produces a daughter named Aurora and a son named Day. Although the prince marries Sleeping Beauty, he is soon summoned to battle and entrusts his wife and children to the care of his mother, who is descended from a "race of ogres." The mother's cannibalistic inclinations get the better of her, but a compassionate steward spares the lives of mother and children, substituting animals for the humans. In the end, the queen, caught by her son in the act of trying to do away with his family, flings herself headfirst into a vat filled with "toads, vipers, adders, and serpents."

The Grimms' "Sleeping Beauty" has a narrative integrity that has made it more appealing than Basile's story and Perrault's tale,

Jennie Harbour, *My Book of Favourite Fairy Tales*

at least to audiences in the United States. In this version of the story, P. L. Travers tells us, it is as if "the tale itself, through its own energy and need, had winnowed away everything but the true whole grain. . . . The story emerges clear, all essence." The second phase of action in the Italian and French versions features postmarital conflicts that, according to some folklorists, constitute separate narratives. It is not at all unusual for the tellers of tales to splice stories together to produce a narrative that charts premarital conflicts as well as what happens in the not so happily-ever-after.

Tchaikovsky's ballet The Sleeping Beauty *was first performed in 1890. In 1958 Disney Studios released a cinematic version of the tale (the least successful of its fairy-tale adaptations). Perpetually rewritten and adapted, the story has been retold, most recently, as a Holocaust tale by Jane Yolen (*Briar Rose*), as a postmodern pastiche of fairy-tale romance by Robert Coover (*Briar Rose*), and as a sadomasochistic romance narrative by Anne Rice (*The Claiming of Sleeping Beauty*, written under the pseudonym A. N. Roquelaure).*

ong, long ago there lived a king and a queen. Day after day they said to each other: "Oh, if only we could have a child!"[2] But nothing ever happened. One day, while the queen was bathing, a frog crawled out of the water, crept ashore, and said to her: "Your wish shall be fulfilled. Before a year goes by, you will give birth to a daughter."

The frog's prediction came true,[3] and the queen gave birth to a girl who was so beautiful that the king was beside himself with joy and arranged a great feast. He invited relatives, friends, and acquaintances, and he also sent for the Wise Women of the kingdom, for he wanted to be sure that they would be kindly disposed toward his child. There were thirteen

2. *"Oh, if only we could have a child!"* The inability to conceive often leads fairy-tale couples to make reckless promises or to engage in outlandish bargains. In "Briar Rose," the parents' lack of foresight appears only at the festivities celebrating the birth of a daughter. The longing for a child can be read as the desire for renewal, transformation, and rejuvenation.

3. *The frog's prediction came true.* In the Grimms' first version of the story, a crab makes the prophecy, hence the hazards of reading too much into the fact that a frog makes the prediction about the birth of a child and is therefore a symbol of fertility in fairy tales. Yet it is significant that a creature arises from the depths to announce the impending birth.

Wise Women in all, but since the king had only twelve golden plates for them to dine on, one of the women had to stay home.

The feast was celebrated with great splendor, and when it drew to a close, the Wise Women bestowed their magic gifts on the girl.[4] One conferred virtue on her, a second gave her beauty, a third wealth, and on it went until the girl had everything in the world you could ever want. Just as the eleventh woman was presenting her gift, the thirteenth in the group appeared out of nowhere. She had not been invited, and now she wanted her revenge.[5] Without so much as a greeting or even a glance at anyone there, she cried out in a loud voice: "When the daughter of the king turns fifteen, she will prick her finger on a spindle and fall down dead." And without another word, she turned her back on those assembled and left the hall.

Everyone was horrified, but just in the nick of time the twelfth of the Wise Women stepped forward. She had not yet made her wish. Although she could not lift the evil spell, she could temper it, and so she said: "The princess will not die, but she will fall into a deep sleep that will last for a hundred years." The king, who was intent on preventing any harm from coming to his child, sent out an order that every spindle in the entire kingdom was to be burned to ashes.

As for the girl, all the wishes made by the Wise Women came true, for she was so beautiful, kind, charming, and sensible that everyone who set eyes on her could not help but love her. On the very day that the princess turned fifteen, the king and the queen happened to be away from home, and the girl was left all alone. She wandered around in the castle, poking her head into one room after another, and eventually she came to the foot of an old tower. After climbing up a narrow, winding staircase in the tower, she ended up in front of a little door with a rusty old key in its lock.[6] As she turned the key, the door burst open to reveal a tiny little room, in which an old woman was sitting with her spindle, busily spinning flax.

4. *the Wise Women bestowed their magic gifts on the girl.* In Perrault's version and in one version recorded by the Grimms, fairies provide the gifts. But the Grimms eventually turned the eight fairies in the French tale into thirteen Wise Women. In *Perceforest*, three goddesses (Lucina, Themis, and Venus) are invited to celebrate the birth of Zellandine. Themis becomes enraged that there is no knife at her plate and utters the curse that Venus undoes in part by promising to arrange for a rescue. Fairies, Wise Women, and goddesses—all these women can be seen as kin to the Fates and the World Mothers, with powers that change depending on circumstances: "They curse and bless with equal gusto" according to P. L. Travers. The gifts given by the Wise Women promise to turn the Grimms' Briar Rose into an "ideal" woman—virtuous, beautiful, and wealthy. In Perrault's version, the girl is given beauty, an angelic disposition, grace, the ability to dance perfectly, the voice of a nightingale, and the ability to play instruments.

5. *She had not been invited, and now she wanted her revenge.* The resentment of the slighted Wise Woman calls to mind the wrath of Eris, goddess of discord, who when not invited to the wedding feast of Peleus and Thetis exacted her revenge by throwing the notorious Apple of Discord, marked with the words "For the Fairest," among the assembled wedded guests. The elaborate debates and negotiations over the Apple of Discord eventually led to the Trojan War.

6. *a little door with a rusty old key in its lock.* Note that Briar Rose's curiosity—her desire to see what is behind the door and her fascination with the spindle—gets her into trouble. By contrast, the prince is rewarded for his curiosity, which takes the form of the desire to find the fabled

castle in which Briar Rose slumbers. Many critics have commented on the plethora of sexual symbols that follow the opening of the door: the curse, the spindle that jumps about, and the pricking of the finger.

7. *"I'm spinning flax."* The spindle or distaff is associated with the Fates, who "spin" or measure out the span of life. Spinning is also an activity that fostered female storytelling, and the spinning of flax often crossed over from the storytelling context into the story itself. The German term for spinning has a secondary meaning associated with fantasizing and building castles in the air. As standard symbols for female domesticity, the spindle and distaff were sometimes carried before the bride in wedding processions of an earlier age. The Grimms' *German Mythology* points out the powerful connection between spindles and domesticity.

8. *she had pricked her finger.* The story of Briar Rose has been thought to map female sexual maturation, with the touching of the spindle representing the onset of puberty, a kind of sexual awakening that leads to a passive, introspective period of latency. Bruno Bettelheim tells us that the story communicates the view that "a long period of quiescence, of contemplation, of concentration on the self, can and often does lead to highest achievement." Joseph Campbell, who in *The Power of Myth* insists that fairy tales are for children, notes that the tales are often about girls who resist growing up: "At the crisis of that threshold crossing she's balking. So she goes to sleep until the prince comes through all the barriers and gives her a reason to think it might be nice on the other side after all. Many of the Grimms' tales represent the little girl who is stuck. All of these dragon killings and threshold crossings have to do with getting past being stuck."

"Good afternoon, Granny," said the princess. "What are you doing here?"

"I'm spinning flax,"[7] the old woman replied, and she nodded to the girl.

"What is that thing bobbing about so oddly?" asked the girl, and she put her hand on the spindle, for she too wanted to spin. The magic spell began to take effect at once, for she had pricked her finger[8] on the spindle.

The instant she felt the prick on her finger, she slumped down on the bed that was in the room, and a deep sleep came over her. The sleep spread through the entire castle.[9] The king and the queen, who had just returned home and were entering the hall, fell asleep, and their attendants along with them. The horses fell asleep in the stables, the dogs in the courtyard, the doves on the roof, the flies on the walls, and yes indeed, even the fire flickering in the hearth died down and fell asleep, and the roast stopped sizzling, and the cook, who was about to pull the hair of the kitchen boy because he had done something stupid, let go and fell asleep. The wind also died down so that not a leaf was stirring on the trees outside the castle.

Soon a hedge of briars began to grow all around the castle. Every year it grew higher until one day it surrounded the entire place. It had grown so thick that you could not even see the banner on the turret of the castle. Throughout the land, stories circulated about the beautiful Briar Rose, for that was the name given to the slumbering princess. From time to time a prince would try to force his way through the hedge to get to the castle. But no one ever succeeded, because the briars clasped each other as if they were holding hands, and the young men who tried got caught in them and couldn't pry themselves loose. They died an agonizing death.[10]

After many, many years had passed, another prince appeared in the land. He heard an old man talking about a briar hedge that was said to conceal a castle, where a wondrously beautiful princess named Briar Rose had been sleeping for a hundred

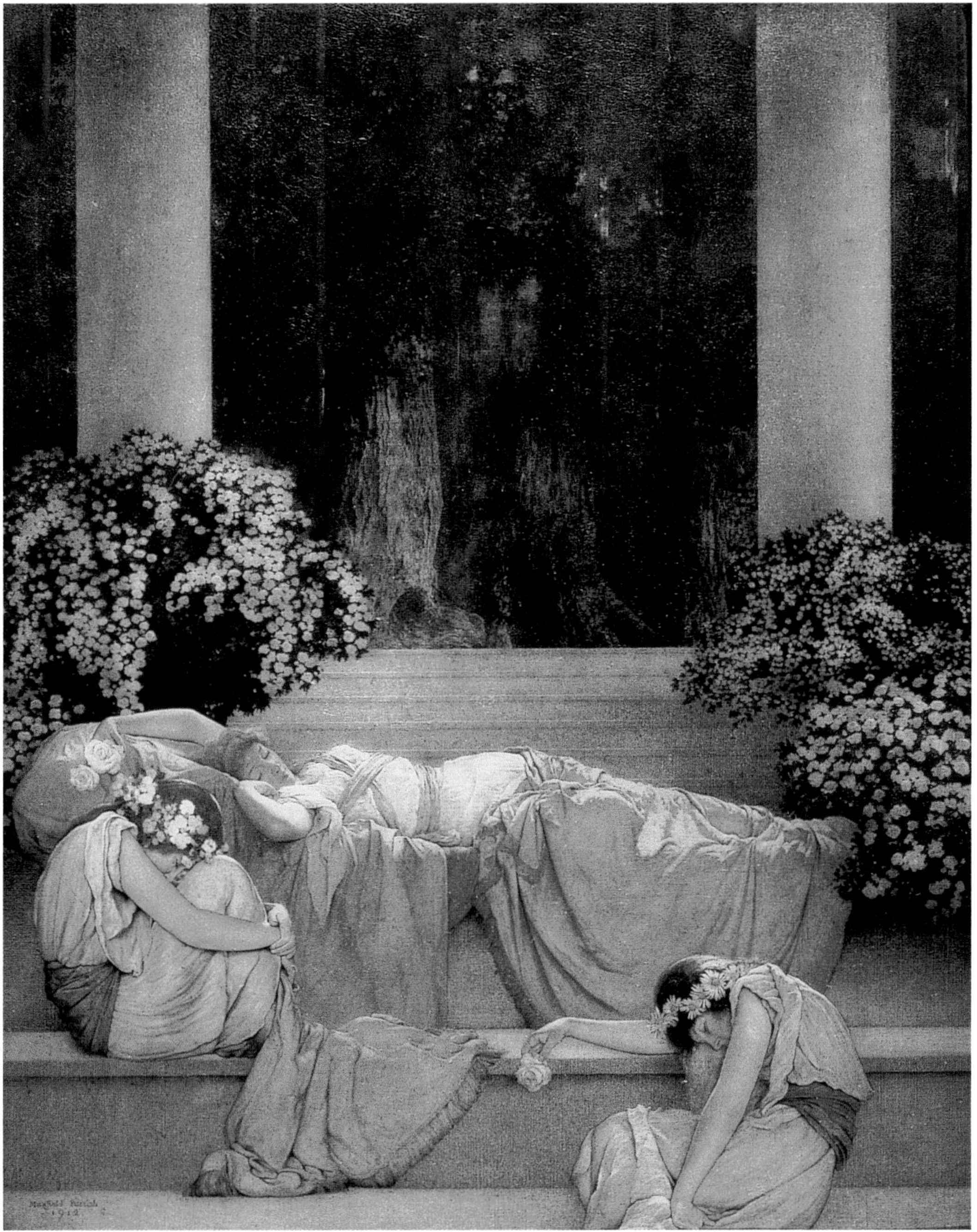

Maxfield Parrish, *Collier's* Magazine

For the cover of a 1912 *Collier's* magazine, Parrish produced a sensuous Sleeping Beauty, draped across a staircase topped by classical columns. The two ladies-in-waiting, with their floral wreaths, contribute to the extraordinary compositional balance of the painting. Fusing the classical with the gothic, Parrish produces an eerily beautiful tableau.

years, and with her the king, the queen, and the entire court. The old man had learned from his grandfather that many other princes had tried to make their way through the briar hedge, but they had gotten caught on the briars and perished in horrible ways. The young man said: "I am not afraid. I am going to find that castle so that I can see the beautiful Briar Rose." The kind old man did his best to discourage the prince, but he refused to listen.

It so happened that the term of one hundred years had just ended, and the day on which Briar Rose was to awaken had arrived. When the prince approached the briar hedge, he found nothing but big, beautiful flowers. They opened to make a path for him[11] and to let him pass unharmed; then they closed behind him to form a hedge.

In the courtyard the horses and the spotted hounds were lying in the same place fast asleep, and the doves were roosting with their little heads tucked under their wings. The prince made his way into the castle and saw how the flies were fast asleep on the walls. The cook was still in the kitchen, with his hand up in the air as if he were about to grab the kitchen boy, and the maid was still sitting at a table with a black hen that she was about to pluck.

The prince walked along a little farther, over to the great hall, where he saw the entire court fast asleep, with the king and the queen sleeping right next to their thrones. He continued on his way, and everything was so quiet that he could hear his own breath. Finally he got to the tower, and he opened up the door to the little room in which Briar Rose was sleeping. There she lay, so beautiful that he could not take his eyes off her, and he bent down to kiss her.

No sooner had the prince touched Briar Rose's lips than she woke up,[12] opened her eyes, and smiled sweetly at him. They went down the stairs together. The king, the queen, and the entire court had awoken, and they were all staring at each other in amazement. The horses in the courtyard stood

9. *The sleep spread through the entire castle.* The whimsical elaboration that follows this statement was added by the Grimms to the first edition of their collection.

10. *died an agonizing death.* Wilhelm Grimm added descriptions of the death throes of the suitors to the first printed edition of the tales.

11. *They opened to make a path for him.* This prince does not have to kill any giants or slay any dragons in order to win his bride. There is no glass mountain to be climbed or sieve-bottomed vessel to be filled with water. His timing is impeccable, however, illustrating how good fortune often trumps heroic feats in fairy tales.

12. *No sooner had the prince touched Briar Rose's lips than she woke up.* In Perrault's version, Sleeping Beauty is awakened when the prince drops to his knees. Many versions of "The Frog King" now end in the manner of "Sleeping Beauty," with the princess kissing the frog (and thereby transforming him into a prince) rather than hurling him against the wall. As in the legend of the Grail, when the Fisher King recovers from his ailment, the courtiers too are rejuvenated and the land is transformed.

Warwick Goble, *The Fairy Book*

Sleeping Beauty appears as if on display, with draperies behind her, a canopy above her, and a richly embroidered blanket covering her. The prince is about to wake her by kneeling before her, while a small dog watches with anticipation in the foreground.

up and shook themselves. The hounds jumped to their feet and wagged their tails. The doves pulled their heads out from under their wings, looked around, and flew off into the fields. The flies began crawling on the walls. The fire in the kitchen flickered, flared up, and began cooking the food again. The roast started to sizzle. The cook slapped the boy so hard that he let out a screech. The maid finished plucking the hen.

The wedding of Briar Rose and the prince was celebrated in great splendor, and the two lived out their days in happiness.

26

SNOW WHITE[1]

ore than Beauty in "Beauty and the Beast," Snow White has become the quintessentially fair—both beautiful and just—heroine of fairy tales. The innocent, persecuted heroine par excellence, she succeeds in living happily ever after despite the plots designed by her wicked stepmother. Named after only one of the three colors that characterize her beauty (skin white as snow, lips red as blood, hair black as ebony), she is often connected with the purity and innocence that our culture associates with the color white. But the term "snow" adds another dimension to her characterization, deepening the meaning of her innocence. Snow suggests cold and remoteness, along with the notion of the lifeless and inert, yet it also comes down from the heavens. And Snow White in the coffin does indeed become not only pure and innocent but also passive, comatose, and ethereally beautiful.

Bruno Bettelheim, in exploring some of the alternate versions of "Snow White" recorded by the Brothers Grimm, came to the conclusion that the story turns on "the oedipal desires of a father and daughter, and how these arouse the mother's jealousy which makes her wish to get rid of the daughter." The oedipal entanglements, he argues, come to be disguised in the version chosen by the Grimms,

1. *Snow White.* Only the Grimms' version of the story alludes to the heroine's complexion in her name. Their fair-skinned heroine became, through the Disney film, an icon of feminine beauty for the latter half of the twentieth century. *Sneewittchen,* Snow White's name in Low German, is a diminutive form and can be literally translated as "Little Snow White." Disney's film title, by including the seven dwarfs with Snow White, dilutes the importance of the heroine and shifts the tale's center of gravity from the relationship between the heroine and her wicked stepmother to the relationship between the heroine and her seven comic sidekicks.

which turns the biological mother into a stepmother and relegates the father to the judgmental voice in the mirror.

The many versions of "Snow White" heard by the Grimms suggest the richness of folkloric variation and remind us how we have allowed stories that once circulated freely to ossify into definitive versions. The Grimms describe one version of "Snow White" in which a count and countess drive by three mounds of snow and the count wishes for a girl as white as the snow. After passing three ditches filled with red blood, he wishes for a girl with cheeks as red as the blood. Finally, three ravens fly overhead and he wishes for a girl with hair as black as the ravens. The couple discovers on the road a girl exactly like the one the count longs for, and they invite her into their carriage. The count immediately has tender feelings for the girl. The countess, however, cannot abide the girl and schemes to get rid of her. She drops her glove and orders Snow White to retrieve it, and then orders the coachman to drive off as speedily as possible. In a related version, the countess tells Snow White to gather roses and then deserts the girl, leaving her to fend for herself in the woods.

Walt Disney's Snow White and the Seven Dwarfs *(1937) has so overshadowed other versions of the story that it is easy to forget that the tale is widely disseminated across a variety of cultures. The heroine may ingest a poisoned apple in her cinematic incarnation, but in Italy she is just as likely to fall victim to a toxic comb, a contaminated cake, or a suffocating braid. Disney's queen, who demands Snow White's heart from the huntsman who takes her into the woods, seems restrained by comparison with the Grimms' evil queen, who orders the huntsman to return with the girl's lungs and liver, both of which she plans to eat after boiling them in salt water. In Spain the queen is even more bloodthirsty, asking for a bottle of blood stoppered with the girl's toe. In Italy she instructs the huntsman to return with the girl's intestines and her blood-soaked shirt. The dwarfs are sometimes miners but sometimes compassionate robbers, thieves, bears, wild men, or ogres. Disney's film has made much of Snow White's coffin being made of glass, but in other versions of the tale that coffin is made of gold, silver, or lead or is jewel encrusted. Although it is*

Jennie Harbour, *My Book of Favourite Fairy Tales*

often displayed on a mountaintop, it can also be set adrift on a river, placed under a tree, hung from the rafters of a room, or locked in a room and surrounded with candles.

"Snow White" may vary tremendously from culture to culture in its details, but it has an easily identifiable, stable core in the conflict between mother and daughter. In many versions of the tale, the evil queen is the girl's biological mother, not a stepmother. (The Grimms, in an effort to preserve the sanctity of motherhood, were forever turning biological mothers into stepmothers.) The struggle between Snow White and the wicked queen so dominates the psychological landscape of this fairy tale that Sandra Gilbert and Susan Gubar, in a landmark book of feminist literary criticism, proposed renaming the story "Snow White and Her Wicked Stepmother." In The Madwoman in the Attic, *they describe how the Grimms' story stages a contest between the "angel-woman" and the "monster-woman" of Western culture. For them the motor of the "Snow White" plot is in the relationship between two women, "the one fair, young, pale, the other just as fair, but older, fiercer; the one a daughter, the other a mother; the one sweet, ignorant, passive, the other both artful and active; the one a sort of angel, the other an undeniable witch."*

Gilbert and Gubar, rather than reading the story as an oedipal plot in which mother and daughter become sexual rivals for approval from the father (incarnated as the voice in the mirror), suggest that the tale mirrors our cultural division of femininity into two components, one that is writ large in our most popular version of the tale. In Disney's Snow White and the Seven Dwarfs, *we find these two components fiercely polarized in a murderously jealous and forbiddingly cold woman on the one hand and an innocently sweet girl accomplished in the art of good housekeeping on the other. Yet the Disney film also positions the evil queen as the figure of gripping narrative energy and makes Snow White so dull that she requires a supporting cast of seven to enliven her scenes. Ultimately it is the stepmother's disruptive, disturbing, and divisive presence that invests the film with a degree of fascination that has facilitated its wide-*

spread circulation and allowed it to take such powerful hold in our own culture.

Children reading this story are unlikely to make the interpretive moves described above. For them, this will be the story of a mother-daughter conflict, which, according to Bruno Bettelheim, offers cathartic pleasures in its lurid punishment of the jealous queen. Once again, as in "Cinderella," the good mother is dead, and in this story the only real assistance she offers is in her legacy of beauty. Snow White must contend with a villain doubly incarnated as beautiful, proud, and evil queen and as ugly, sinister, and wicked witch. Small wonder that she is reduced to a role of pure passivity, a "dumb bunny" as the poet Anne Sexton put it. In its validation of murderous hatred as a "natural" affect in the relationship between daughter and (step)mother and its promotion of youth, beauty, and hard work, "Snow White" is not without problematic dimensions, yet it has remained one of our most powerful cultural stories. In 1997, filmmaker Michael Cohn drew out the dark, Gothic elements of the story in his Grimm Brothers' Snow White*, starring Sigourney Weaver.*

nce upon a time in the middle of winter, when snowflakes the size of feathers were falling from the sky, a queen was sitting and sewing by a window with an ebony frame. While she was sewing, she looked out at the snow and pricked her finger with a needle.[2] Three drops of blood fell onto the snow. The red looked so beautiful against the white snow that she thought: "If only I had a child as white as snow, as red as blood, and as black as the wood of the window frame."[3] Not long after that, she gave birth to a little girl who was white as snow, red as blood, and black as ebony, and she was called

2. *pricked her finger with a needle.* A similar motif appears in "Briar Rose," when the heroine finds a spindle, pricks her finger, and falls into a deep sleep. In this case, the wound precipitates the wish for a child, and it is almost as if the queen has, by wishing herself to be with child, succeeded in becoming pregnant.

3. *"as black as the wood of the window frame."* Sandra Gilbert and Susan Gubar see the mother as a figure trapped by the ebony frame, just as the second queen is later trapped by the magic mirror. Whereas the mother is confined indoors, sewing, the second queen is mobile and wily, but locked in a state of narcissistic desire. Note that one queen looks through a transparent surface, and the other is captivated by an opaque surface that reflects her own image back to her. That Snow White is put on aesthetic display in a glass coffin seems to refer back to both the window and the looking glass.

Snow White. The queen died shortly after the child was born.[4]

A year later, her husband, the king, married another woman. She was a beautiful lady, but proud and domineering, and she could not bear the thought that anyone might be more beautiful than she was. She owned a magic mirror, and whenever she stood in front of it to look at herself, she would say:

"Mirror, mirror, on the wall,
Who's the fairest one of all?"[5]

The mirror would always answer:

"You, O Queen, are the fairest of all."

Then she was happy, for she knew that the mirror always spoke the truth.

Snow White was growing up, and with each passing day she became more beautiful. When she reached the age of seven,[6] she had become as beautiful as the bright day and more beautiful than the queen herself. One day the queen asked the mirror:

"Mirror, mirror, on the wall,
Who's the fairest one of all?"

The mirror replied:

"My queen, you may be the fairest here,
But Snow White is a thousand times more fair."

When the queen heard these words, she began to tremble, and her face turned green with envy. From that moment on, she hated Snow White,[7] and whenever she set eyes on her,

4. *The queen died shortly after the child was born.* The Grimms added the prefatory episode about Snow White's birth and about her mother's death to later editions of their collection. In the 1810 manuscript version of "Snow White," there is only one queen, and she is both biological mother and persecutor.

5. *"Who's the fairest one of all?"* The voice in the mirror may be viewed as a judgmental voice, representing the absent father or patriarchy in general, which places a premium on beauty. But that voice could also be an echo of the queen's own self-assessment, one that is, to be sure, informed by cultural norms about physical appearances.

6. *When she reached the age of seven.* In earlier centuries, especially before the onset of public education, childhood was of a much shorter duration, with the child integrated into the adult world of work even before the onset of puberty. Still, Snow White's youth is difficult to square with the fact that she marries at the end of the story, particularly since there are no markers of aging. Most illustrations for the story depict her as an adolescent or young adult approaching an age suitable for marriage.

7. *she hated Snow White.* The tale turns on the (sexual) rivalry between stepmother and daughter, with Snow White positioned as the classic "innocent persecuted heroine" of fairy tales. "Snow White" has been read as a story that plots the trajectory of normal female maturation (in symbolic terms) and maps a case study of maternal jealousy in its most pathological form.

her heart turned cold like a stone. Envy and pride grew as fast as weeds in her heart. By day or by night, she never had a moment's peace.

One day she summoned a huntsman and said: "Take the child out into the forest. I don't want to set eyes on her ever again. Bring me her lungs and her liver as proof that you have killed her."

The huntsman obeyed and took the girl out into the woods, but just as he was taking out his hunting knife and about to take aim at her innocent heart, she began weeping, and she pleaded with him for her life. "Alas, dear huntsman, have mercy. I promise to run into the woods, and I'll never come back again."

Snow White was so beautiful that the huntsman took pity on her and said: "Just run off, you poor child."

"The wild animals will devour you before long," he thought. He felt as if a great weight had been lifted from his shoulders, for at least he would not have to kill the girl. Just then, a young boar ran by him, and the huntsman stabbed it to death. He removed the lungs and liver and brought them to the queen as proof that he had murdered the child. The cook was told to boil them in brine, and the wicked woman ate them up,[8] thinking that she had consumed Snow White's lungs and liver.

The poor child was now all alone in the vast forest. She was so frightened that she just stared at all the leaves on the trees and had no idea where to turn. She started running and raced over sharp stones and through thorn bushes. Wild beasts hovered around her at times, but they did her no harm. She ran as far as her legs would carry her. When night fell, she discovered a little cottage and went inside to rest. Everything in the house was tiny and indescribably dainty and spotless.[9] There was a little table, with seven little plates on a white cloth, each with its own little spoon. And then there were seven little knives and forks, and seven cups. Against the wall

8. *the wicked woman ate them up.* Like the witches and ogres of folklore, the queen engages in cannibalistic acts, hoping that by incorporating her stepdaughter, she will also acquire her beauty.

9. *Everything in the house was tiny and indescribably dainty and spotless.* Unlike Disney's seven dwarfs, these men are models of tidiness whose home provides a cozy haven. Like Hansel and Gretel, Snow White finds shelter in the woods, and she also is subjected to another threat in her new home.

Jennie Harbour, *My Book of Favourite Fairy Tales*

were seven little beds in a row, each made up with sheets as white as snow. Snow White was so hungry and so thirsty that she ate a few vegetables and some bread from each little plate and drank a drop of wine from each little cup. She didn't want to take everything away from one of the places. Later, she was so tired that she tried out the beds, but they did not seem to be the right size. The first one was too long, the second too short, but the seventh one was just right,[10] and she stayed in it. Then she said her prayers[11] and fell fast asleep.

It was completely dark outside when the owners of the cottage returned. They were seven dwarfs who spent their days in the mountains,[12] mining ore and digging for minerals. They lit their seven little lanterns, and when the cottage was no longer dark, they saw that someone had been there, for not everything was as they had left it.

The first dwarf asked: "Who's been sitting in my little chair?"

The second one asked: "Who's been eating from my little plate?"

The third asked: "Who's been eating my little loaf of bread?"

The fourth asked: "Who's been eating from my little plate of vegetables?"

The fifth asked: "Who's been using my little fork?"

The sixth asked: "Who's been using my little knife to cut things up?"

The seventh asked: "Who's been drinking from my little cup?"

The first dwarf turned around and saw that his sheets were all wrinkled and said: "Who has been sleeping in my little bed?"

The others came running, and each shouted: "Someone's been sleeping in my bed too."

When the seventh dwarf looked in his bed, he saw Snow White lying there, fast asleep. He shouted to the others who

10. *but the seventh one was just right.* Like Goldilocks, Snow White tries out different possibilities and finds the bed that is just right for her, in this case a signal that she has found an appropriate refuge.

11. *said her prayers.* The Grimms, intent on producing a "manual of manners," made sure that Snow White said her prayers before falling asleep.

12. *seven dwarfs who spent their days in the mountains.* Associated with earth, the dwarfs are hardworking creatures who lead an existence on the social periphery, yet who show compassionate hospitality to the orphaned girl. Unlike Disney's dwarfs, the Grimms' dwarfs are not differentiated from each other and have no names. Their diminutive stature makes them sexually unthreatening, even as their sevenfold admiration for Snow White's beauty magnifies her attractiveness. In some versions of the tale, the men in the forest are robbers who offer Snow White shelter.

came running and who were stunned when they raised their seven little lanterns to let light shine on Snow White.

"My goodness, my goodness!" they all exclaimed. "What a beautiful child!"

The dwarfs were so delighted to see her that they decided not to wake her up, and they let her keep sleeping in the little bed. The seventh dwarf slept for one hour with each of his companions until the night was over.

In the morning, Snow White woke up. When she saw the dwarfs, she was frightened, but they were friendly and asked: "What's your name?"

"My name is Snow White," she replied.

Warwick Goble, *The Fairy Book*

Surrounded by the seven dwarfs, who seem both pleased and bewildered by her presence, Snow White discusses the opportunities for co-existence. The bedding and furniture give the scene a contemporary look.

13. *"If you will keep house for us."* In carrying out domestic chores, Snow White moves into a new developmental stage, demonstrating her ability to engage in labor and to carry out the terms of a contract. No longer a child, she is preparing herself for the state of matrimony.

"How did you get to our house?" asked the dwarfs.

Snow White told them how her stepmother had tried to kill her and how the huntsman had spared her life. She had run all day long until she had arrived at their cottage.

The dwarfs told her: "If you will keep house for us,[13] cook, make the beds, wash, sew, knit, and keep everything neat and tidy, then you can stay with us, and we'll give you everything you need."

"Yes, with pleasure," Snow White replied, and she stayed with them.

Snow White kept house for the dwarfs. In the morning, they would go up to the mountains in search of minerals and gold. In the evening, they would return, and dinner had to be ready for them. Since the girl was by herself during the day, the good dwarfs gave her a stern warning: "Beware of your stepmother. She'll know soon enough that you're here. Don't let anyone in the house."

After the queen had finished eating what she believed were Snow White's lungs and liver, she was sure that she was once again the fairest of all in the land. She went up to the mirror and asked:

> "Mirror, mirror, on the wall,
> Who's the fairest of them all?"

The mirror replied:

> "You're the fairest here, dear Queen,
> But Little Snow White, though far away
> With the seven dwarfs in her hideaway
> Is now the fairest ever seen."

When the queen heard these words she was horrified, for she knew that the mirror never lied. She realized that the huntsman must have deceived her and that Snow White was still alive. She thought long and hard about how she could get rid of Snow White. Unless she herself was the fairest in the land, she would never be able to feel anything but envy. Finally, she came up with a plan.[14] By staining her face and dressing up as an old peddler woman, she made herself completely unrecognizable. In that disguise, she traveled beyond the seven hills to the home of the seven dwarfs. Then she knocked on the door and called out: "Pretty wares for a good price."

Snow White peeked out the window and said: "Good day, old woman. What do you have for sale?"

"Nice things, pretty things," she replied. "Staylaces in all kinds of colors," and she took out a silk lace woven of many colors.

"I can let this good woman in,"[15] Snow White thought, and she unbolted the door and bought the pretty lace.

"Oh, my child, what a sight you are. Come, let me lace you up properly."

Snow White wasn't the least bit suspicious. She stood in front of the old woman and let her put on the new lace. The old woman laced her up so quickly and so tightly that Snow White's breath was cut off,[16] and she fell down as if dead.

"So much for being the fairest of them all," the old woman said as she hurried away.

Not much later, in the evening, the seven dwarfs came home. When they saw their beloved Snow White lying on the ground, they were horrified. She wasn't moving at all, and they were sure she was dead. They lifted her up, and when they saw that she had been laced too tightly, they cut the staylace in two. Snow White began to breathe, and little by little she came back to life. When the dwarfs heard what had happened, they said: "The old peddler woman was none other than the wicked queen. Be on your guard, and don't let anyone in unless we're at home."

When the wicked woman returned home, she went to the mirror and asked:

14. *she came up with a plan.* Sandra Gilbert and Susan Gubar try to move against the grain of conventional interpretations, which focus on the queen as the source of evil. They view the queen as the consummate "plotter, a plot-maker, a schemer, a witch, an artist" and as a woman who is "witty, wily, and self-absorbed as all artists traditionally are." It is the queen who becomes the center of narrative energy, advancing the action and providing powerfully attractive twists and turns to the plot.

15. *"I can let this good woman in."* Snow White, like many fairy-tale heroines, violates a prohibition. But in her case, as with Briar Rose and other heroines, the violation results in punishment rather than serving as the pathway to adventure, as is true for many fairy-tale heroes.

16. *The old woman laced her up so quickly and so tightly that Snow White's breath was cut off.* Snow White's attraction to staylaces and combs, along with the fact that she is easily duped, have been seen as signs of her immaturity. But Snow White seems to be less "dumb bunny" than innocent child who falls victim to the stepmother's duplicity. The stepmother traps Snow White by donning disguises and by mimicking nurturing behavior.

"Mirror, mirror, on the wall,
Who's the fairest of them all?"

The mirror replied as usual:

"You're the fairest here, dear Queen,
But Little Snow White, though far away
With the seven dwarfs in her hideaway
Is now the fairest ever seen."

When the queen heard those words, the blood froze in her veins. She was horrified, for she knew that Snow White was still alive. "But this time," she said, "I will dream up something that will destroy you."

Using all the witchcraft in her power, she made a poisoned comb. And then she changed her clothes and disguised herself once more as an old woman. She traveled beyond the seven hills to the home of the seven dwarfs, knocked on the door, and called out: "Pretty wares at a good price."

Snow White peeked out the window and said: "Go away, I can't let anyone in."

"But you can at least take a look," said the old woman, and she took out a poisoned comb and held it up in the air. The child liked it so much that she was completely fooled and opened the door. When they had agreed on a price, the old woman said: "Now I'll give your hair a good combing."

Poor Snow White suspected nothing and let the woman go ahead, but no sooner had the comb touched her hair than the poison took effect, and the girl fell senseless to the ground.

"There, my beauty," said the wicked woman, "now you're finished." And she rushed away.

Fortunately, the dwarfs were on their way home, for it was almost nighttime. When they saw Snow White lying on the ground as if dead, they suspected the stepmother right away. They examined her and discovered the poisoned comb. As

soon as they pulled it out, Snow White came back to life and told them what had happened. Again they warned her to be on her guard and not to open the door to anyone.

At home, the queen stood in front of the mirror and said:

"Mirror, mirror, on the wall,
Who's the fairest of them all?"

The mirror answered as before:

"You're the fairest here, dear Queen,
But Little Snow White, though far away
With the seven dwarfs in her hideaway
Is now the fairest ever seen."

When the queen heard the words spoken by the mirror, she began trembling with rage. "Snow White must die!" she cried out. "Even if it costs me my life."

The queen went into a remote, hidden chamber in which no one ever set foot and made an apple full of poison. On the outside it looked beautiful—white with red cheeks[17]—and if you saw it, you craved it. But if you took the tiniest bite, you would die. When the apple was finished, the queen stained her face again, dressed up as a peasant woman, and traveled beyond the seven hills to the home of the seven dwarfs.

The old woman knocked at the door, and Snow White stuck her head out the window to say: "I can't let anyone in. The seven dwarfs won't allow it."

"That's all right," the peasant woman replied. "I'll get rid of my apples soon enough. Here, I'll give you one."

"No," said Snow White. "I'm not supposed to take anything."

"Are you afraid that it's poisoned?" asked the old woman. "Here, I'll cut the apple in two. You eat the red part, I'll eat the white."

17. *white with red cheeks.* Note that the physical description of the apple coincides with the description of Snow White. Ever since the Garden of Eden, apples have been invested with powerful symbolic significance.

The apple had been made so craftily that only the red part of it had poison. Snow White felt a craving for the beautiful apple, and when she saw that the peasant woman was taking a bite, she could no longer resist. She put her hand out the window and took the poisoned half. But no sooner had she taken a bite than she fell to the ground dead. The queen stared at her with savage eyes and burst out laughing: "White as snow, red as blood, black as ebony![18] This time the dwarfs won't be able to bring you back to life!"

At home, she asked the mirror:

> "Mirror, mirror, on the wall,
> Who's the fairest of them all?"

And finally it replied:

> "O Queen, you are the fairest in the land."

The queen's envious heart was finally at peace, as much as an envious heart can be.

When the dwarfs returned home in the evening, they found Snow White lying on the ground. Not a breath of air was coming from her lips. She was dead. They lifted her up and looked around for something that might be poisonous. They unlaced her, combed her hair, washed her with water and wine, but it was all in vain. The dear child was gone, and nothing could bring her back. After placing her on a bier, all seven of them sat down around it and mourned Snow White. They wept for three days. They were about to bury her, but she still looked like a living person with beautiful red cheeks.

The dwarfs said: "We can't possibly put her into the cold ground." And so they had a transparent glass coffin made that allowed Snow White to be seen from all sides. They put her in it, wrote her name on it in golden letters,[19] and added that she was the daughter of a king. They brought the coffin up to

18. *"White as snow, red as blood, black as ebony!"* White, red, and black are among the most prominent colors in fairy tales, along with gold and silver. Green, as Max Lüthi has pointed out, is conspicuously absent from the fairy-tale palette. The stepmother's invocation of the first queen's fantasy about her child points to the underlying identity of the biological mother and the evil queen. Fairy tales often split the maternal figure into two components: a good, dead mother and a mobile, malicious stepmother. Children are thereby able to preserve a positive image of the mother even as they indulge in fantasies about maternal evil.

19. *wrote her name on it in golden letters.* Snow White becomes an object that is put on aesthetic display. Like the title of a painting in a museum, her name is written in golden letters, and she becomes something of a tourist attraction.

Kay Nielsen, *Hansel and Gretel and Other Stories by the Brothers Grimm*

Preserved in a glass coffin, Snow White has the pallor and look of death. The seven dwarfs keep guard in a setting that places the coffin on display.

the top of a mountain, and one of them always remained by it to keep vigil. Animals also came to mourn Snow White, first an owl, then a raven, and finally a dove.[20]

Snow White lay in the coffin for a long, long time. But she did not decay, and she looked just as if she were sleeping, for she was still white as snow, red as blood, and had hair as black as ebony.

One day the son of a king was traveling through the forest and came to the cottage of the dwarfs. He was hoping to spend the night there. When he went to the top of the mountain, he saw the coffin with beautiful Snow White lying in it, and he read the words written in gold letters. Then he said to the dwarfs: "Let me have the coffin. I will give you whatever you want for it."

The dwarfs replied: "We wouldn't sell it for all the gold in the world."

He said: "Make me a gift of it, for I can't live without being able to see Snow White. I will honor and cherish her as if she were my beloved."

The good dwarfs took pity when they heard those words, and they gave him the coffin. The prince ordered his servants to put the coffin on their shoulders and to carry it away. It happened that they stumbled over a shrub, and the jolt freed the poisonous piece of apple lodged in Snow White's throat.[21] She came back to life. "Good heavens, where am I?" she cried out.

The prince was thrilled and said: "You will stay with me," and he told her what had happened. "I love you more than anything else on earth," he said. "Come with me to my father's castle. You shall be my bride." Snow White had tender feelings for him, and she departed with him. The marriage was celebrated with great splendor.

Snow White's wicked stepmother had also been invited to the wedding feast. She put on beautiful clothes, stepped up to the mirror, and said:

20. *first an owl, then a raven, and finally a dove.* Ronald Murphy has pointed out that the three birds bring together the symbolic avian creatures of Greek mythology, Germanic lore, and Christian iconography and reflect the Grimms' desire to produce a synthetic new mythology.

21. *the jolt freed the poisonous piece of apple lodged in Snow White's throat.* This accidental awakening stands in sharp contrast to the kiss (borrowed from "Sleeping Beauty") that awakens Snow White in Disney's animated film version. Although the prince has shown his devotion to Snow White, it is ultimately by sheer chance that Snow White comes back to life.

"Mirror, mirror, on the wall,
Who's the fairest of them all?"

The mirror replied:

"My Queen, you may be the fairest here,
But the young queen is a thousand times more fair."

The wicked woman let out a curse, and she was so paralyzed with fear that she didn't know what to do. At first she didn't want to go to the wedding feast. But she never had a moment's peace after that and had to go see the young queen. When she entered, Snow White recognized her right away. The queen was so terrified that she just stood there and couldn't budge an inch. Iron slippers had already been heated up for her over a fire of coals. They were brought in with tongs and set up right in front of her. She had to put on the red-hot iron shoes[22] and dance in them until she dropped to the ground dead.

22. *red-hot iron shoes.* In the Disney film version, the queen is pursued to the edge of a cliff and falls to her death. The Grimms' queen is subjected to a painful and humiliating death, one that puts her on display in the same way that Snow White was exhibited as the consummate beautiful woman. Note, however, that the queen's tortured dance stands in sharp contrast to Snow White's immobilization in the coffin. The queen is presented as a cowardly figure who shows no sign of repentance, unlike some fairy-tale villains who regret their evil ways. Hans Christian Andersen's "Red Shoes" features a heroine who nearly dances to death after she willfully wears red shoes to church.

Rumpelstiltskin

umpelstiltskin goes by many names. Titeliture, Purzinigele, Batzibitzili, Panzimanzi, and Whuppity Stoorie are just a few of his sobriquets. Whether he makes an appearance as Ricdin-Ricdon in a French tale, Tom Tit Tot in a British tale, as Gilitrutt in Iceland, as Rompetailtailskin in Louisiana, or as Tambutoe in African-American folklore, his essence and function remain much the same. Not so with the tale's heroine. Although she is almost always a young girl of humble origins, her other attributes and abilities change dramatically from one tale to the next. In some versions of the story she is hopelessly lazy and often gluttonous to boot; in others she is a hard worker, a diligent daughter who can spin heaps upon heaps of straw or who can spin straw into gold, even without the assistance of a helper. In one of the versions of "Rumpelstiltskin" recorded by the Grimms, for example, the heroine needs help because she is "cursed" with the gift of spinning flax to gold, unable to produce "a single flaxen thread."

What makes "Rumpelstiltskin" particularly troubling for those who seek moral guidance for children in fairy tales is the way in which its plot turns on deception and greed. The miller tricks the king into thinking that his daughter can spin straw into gold; the miller's daughter misleads the king; the king marries because he lusts after gold. Finally, the queen not only dodges the terms of the contract drawn up with Rumpelstiltskin but also engages in a cruel game of playing dumb as she rehearses various names before pronouncing the one that will release her from a dreadful pact made in a moment of desperation. The cast of characters is neither clever, resourceful, nor quick-witted. To the contrary, all seem rash, irresponsible, and recklessly opportunistic. And the queen's only real triumph seems to be the identification of "The Name of the Helper," as the story is known to folklorists.

"Rumpelstiltskin" is almost universally known in cultures that depend on spinning for the garments they wear. Spinning, according to the German philosopher Walter Benjamin, who wrote an essay about old-fashioned storytelling, produces more than textiles—it is also the breeding ground for texts, creating the endless stretch of time that demands relief through storytelling. Well into the nineteenth century, spinning and storytelling were powerfully associated, as in a German calendar of 1850, quoted by Ruth B. Bottigheimer: "Father's smoking his pipe, mother's sitting and spinning, / Grandma's telling about nixie and elfenkind, / About Thumbling and Snow-White and about the magic bear." "Rumpelstiltskin" shows us how the straw of domestic labor can be transformed into the gold that captures the heart of a king. It is a tale that thematizes the labor that gives birth to storytelling, suggesting in turn that there is an even exchange between the life-giving labors of the queen and the life-saving labors of the diminutive gnome. Spinning straw to gold,

Rumpelstiltskin is less demonic helper than agent of transformation, a figure who becomes heroic in his power to help someone save face and to demonstrate compassion. Is it any wonder that many versions of his story show him as a sprightly figure who hightails it out of the palace on a spoon rather than as a vicious gnome who tears himself in two when his name is discovered?

Once upon a time there lived a miller who was very poor but who had a beautiful daughter. One day it happened that he was given an audience with the king, and in order to appear as a person of some importance,[1] he said to him: "I have a daughter who can spin straw into gold."

"Now there's a talent worth having," the king said to the miller. "If your daughter is as clever as you say she is, bring her to my palace tomorrow. I will put her to the test."

When the girl arrived at the palace, he put her into a room full of straw, gave her a spinning wheel and a spindle,[2] and said: "Get to work right away. If you don't succeed in spinning this straw into gold by tomorrow morning, then you shall die." And the king locked the door after he went out and left her all alone inside.

The poor miller's daughter sat there in the room and was completely perplexed. She didn't have the slightest idea how she was going to spin straw into gold. She felt so miserable that she started crying. Suddenly the door opened and a little gnome walked right in and said: "Good evening, Little Miss Miller's Daughter. Why are you in tears?"

"Oh dear," the girl answered. "I'm supposed to spin that straw into gold, and I have no idea how it's done."

1. *in order to appear as a person of some importance.* Boasting about a child is what generally sets the plot of Rumpelstiltskin stories in motion. The exaggerated claims of an ambitious parent lead to a crisis for the child. The prelude to the tale can take one of two basic forms. When it operates with the opposition lazy/diligent, it shifts into the comic mode of the folktale. A mother, for example, boasts that her daughter can spin five skeins a day, when in reality her sole achievement consists of eating five pies in a single sitting. The tale then takes humorous turns that are never really life threatening for the heroine. When the Rumpelstiltskin story operates with the opposition natural/supernatural in its prelude, the tale slips into the melodramatic mode of fairy tales, depicting situations in which the stakes are always high and a heroine whose morale is low. A father boasts about his daughter's supernatural powers, for example, and the daughter is then placed in a situation of real crisis, as in the Grimms' version of the tale.

2. *gave her a spinning wheel and a spindle.* In rural communities, spinning or sewing could be something of a marriage test, for an adept worker might be a welcome source of added income. In the Grimms' "The Spindle, the Shuttle, and the Needle," an orphan wins a prince through her extraordinary domestic competence in the household arts. "The Odds and Ends," another tale in their collection, shows a bridegroom trading his attractive, but "lazy and slovenly," betrothed for a serving maid with a reputation for being a "good hard worker." Yet there are also tales in the collection, for example "The Horrid Spinning of Flax," which condemn spinning as a deforming activity. The heroine avoids enslavement to spinning by seeking out three misshapen hags, confronting her husband with them, and attributing each of the women's deformi-

The gnome asked: "What will you give me if I do it for you?"[3]

"My necklace," the girl replied.

The gnome took the necklace, sat down at the spinning wheel, and whirr, whirr, whirr,[4] the wheel spun three times and the bobbin was full. Then he put another bundle of straw up, and whirr, whirr, whirr, the wheel spun three times and the second bobbin was full. He worked on until dawn, and by then the straw had been spun and all the bobbins were full of gold.

At the crack of dawn, the king made his way to the room. When he saw all that gold, he was astonished and filled with joy, but now he lusted more than ever for that precious metal. He ordered the miller's daughter to go to a much larger room, one that was also filled with straw, and he told her that if she valued her life she would spin it all into gold by dawn. The girl had no idea what to do, and she began to cry. The door opened, as before, and the gnome reappeared and asked: "What will you give me if I spin the straw into gold for you?"

"I'll give you the ring on my finger," the girl replied. The gnome took the ring, began to whirl the wheel around, and by dawn he had spun all of the straw into glittering gold. The king was pleased beyond measure at the sight of the gold, but his greed was still not satisfied. This time he ordered the miller's daughter to go into an even larger room filled with straw and said: "You have to spin this to gold in one night. If you succeed, you will become my wife."

"She may just be a miller's daughter," he thought, "but I could never find a richer wife if I were to search for one the world over."

When the girl was all by herself again, the gnome appeared for the third time and asked: "What will you give me if I spin the straw for you again?"

"I have nothing left to give you," the girl replied.

"Then promise to give me your first child, after you become queen."[5]

ties to one step in the process of spinning. Ruth B. Bottigheimer points out that Wilhelm Grimm tried to put "a good face" on spinning but that spinning tales "communicate the grim reality" of the household chore.

3. *"What will you give me if I do it for you?"* The nature of the task in this tale usually takes the form of spinning, but there are some variants that require the helper to undertake architectural feats (putting a spire on a church) or take on farm duties (curing a dying sow).

4. *whirr, whirr, whirr.* It is not hard to imagine that this tale had its origins in spinning rooms, where the labor thematized in the tale provided acoustic effects that embellished the tale.

5. *"Then promise to give me your first child, after you become queen."* Escalating demands are typical of fairy-tale helpers. They ask for something trivial to start with, then move to something that is beyond the norm of an economy of bartering. The helper or donor quickly moves into the role of villain.

"Who knows what may happen before that?" thought the miller's daughter. Since she was desperate to find a way out, she promised the gnome what he had demanded, and, once again, he set to work and spun the straw into gold.

When the king returned in the morning and found everything as he wished it to be, he made the wedding arrangements, and the beautiful miller's daughter became a queen.

A year later, the miller's daughter gave birth to a beautiful child. She had forgotten all about the gnome, but one day he suddenly appeared in her room and said: "Give me what you promised."

The queen was horrified, and she offered the gnome the entire wealth of the kingdom if only he would let her keep the child. But he replied: "I prefer a living creature to all the treasures in the world."[6] The queen's tears and sobs were so heartrending that the gnome took pity on her. "I will give you three days," he declared. "If by then you can guess my name,[7] you can keep your child."

All night long the queen racked her brains, thinking of all the names she had ever heard. She dispatched a messenger to inquire throughout the land if there were any names she had forgotten. When the little man returned the next day, she began with Casper, Melchior, and Balthasar and recited every single name she had ever heard. But at each one the little man said: "That's not my name."

The next day she sent the messenger out to inquire about the names of all the people in the neighborhood, and she tried out the most unusual and bizarre names on the little man: "Do you happen to be called Ribfiend or Muttonchops or Spindleshanks?"[8] But each time he replied: "That's not my name."

On the third day the messenger returned and said: "I couldn't find a single new name, but when I rounded a bend in the forest at the foot of a huge mountain, a place so remote that the foxes and hares bid each other goodnight, I came

6. *"I prefer a living creature to all the treasures in the world."* Rumpelstiltskin's desire for something "living" links him with demonic creatures that make pacts with mortals in order to secure living creatures. At the heart of all versions of "Rumpelstiltskin" is the contract made between an innocent young girl and a devilish creature, a misshapen gnome of questionable origins who is probably one of the least attractive of fairy-tale figures. Yet Rumpelstiltskin comes off rather well in a world where fathers tell brazen lies about their daughters, marriages are based on greed, and young women agree to give up a first-born child. He works hard to hold up his end of the bargain made with the miller's daughter, shows genuine compassion when the queen regrets the agreement into which she has entered, and is prepared to add an escape clause to their contract even though he stands to gain nothing from it.

7. *If by then you can guess my name.* Rumpelstiltskin's challenge to the queen reminds us of the power of names and how the name taboo came about. In ancient religions, naming the gods compelled them to respond to worshippers, hence the taboo against invoking their names. Knowing the name of your antagonist represents a form of control, a way of containing the power of the adversary and of having influence over his soul. Since names are a vital part of personal identity, revealing your name can be dangerous. In numerous myths and folktales, there is a prohibition against asking the name of the beloved, and violation of the taboo often leads to flight or transformation into an animal. Joseph Jacobs points out, in his notes to "Tom Tit Tot" (the British Rumpelstiltskin) that "the class of name-guessing stories" is probably "a 'survival' of the superstition that to know a man's name gives you power over him, for which rea-

son savages object to tell their names." "It may be necessary," he adds, "to explain to the little one that Tom Tit Tot can only be referred to as 'that,' because his name is not known until the end."

In *The Hobbit*, Bilbo uses the strategy of riddling talk to disguise his name, for that is "the way to talk to dragons, if you don't want to reveal your proper name (which is wise), and don't want to infuriate them by a flat refusal (which is also very wise)." The Chinese princess named in the title of Puccini's opera *Turandot* (1926) is challenged to identify the name of the man who has solved her riddles.

8. *"Ribfiend or Muttonchops or Spindleshanks."* The naming of possible names offers the opportunity for comic associations from both storyteller and listeners. It is easy to imagine the audience calling out names in response to the queen's efforts to identify the name of the gnome.

9. *"Tomorrow I brew, today I bake."* Rumpelstiltskin's chant, by connecting feasting with the securing of the child, hints at cannibalism. The chant varies from one version to the next. In Louisiana, the verse takes the following form: "Today I burn, tomorrow I shall bloom. / What luck! The queen's child will come take my place. / No one knows what my name is. / My name is Rompetailtailskin."

George Cruikshank,
German Popular Stories

In a rage, Rumpelstiltskin stamps his right foot into the ground, while the queen and her courtiers (one holding the child that is at stake) look on with no sympathy at all for the gnome.

across a little hut. A fire was burning right in front of the hut, and a really strange little man was dancing around the fire, hopping on one foot and chanting:

> 'Tomorrow I brew, today I bake,[9]
> Soon the child is mine to take.
> Oh what luck to win this game,
> Rumpelstiltskin is my name.' "

You can imagine how happy the queen was to hear that name. The gnome returned and asked: "Well, Your Majesty, who am I?"

The queen replied: "Is your name Conrad?"

"No, it's not."

"Is your name Harry?"

"No, it's not."

"Could your name possibly be Rumpelstiltskin?"

"The devil told you that, the devil told you!" the little man screamed, and in his rage he stamped his right foot so hard that it went into the ground right up to his waist. Then in his fury he seized his left foot with both hands and tore himself in two.

Kay Nielsen, *Hansel and Gretel and Other Stories by the Brothers Grimm*

An enraged Rumpelstiltskin, dressed in vibrant reds, begins to tear himelf in two. The serenity of the courtiers, expressed in the perfect symmetries of the composition, is disrupted by the mad gnome.

THE GOLDEN BIRD

If the female protagonists of fairy tales are often as good as they are beautiful, their male counterparts often appear to be as young and naïve as they are stupid. The fathers of fairy-tale heroes are perpetually frustrated by the unrivaled obtuseness of their sons. If asked the question "Who is the stupidest of them all?" most fairy-tale fathers would reply: "My youngest son." That youngest son often receives a name tailored to his level of intelligence: Numbskull, Dummy, or Simpleton. Yet that son is also the son who, for all his lack of wit and cunning, ends up triumphing over his older and cleverer siblings. The hero of "The Golden Bird" is not only considered a simpleton, he also has trouble following the instructions of his best advisor. "You don't really deserve my help," the fox declares in frustration after his sage advice has been disregarded on no less than three occasions.

The hero of "The Golden Bird" has few admirable qualities. He steals his way to success, kidnaps a princess against her will, and repeatedly turns a deaf ear to good advice. In fairy tales the world over, the least likely boy to succeed paradoxically becomes the most likely successor to a kingdom. Aladdin, the prototype of the undeserving hero who lives happily ever after, begins his rise to wealth and power under less than auspicious circumstances: "From his earliest years Aladdin was a headstrong and incorrigible good-for-nothing." When he persists in his idle ways and refuses to learn a trade, his father, "grieving over the perverseness of his son," falls ill and dies. Or ponder Jack of beanstalk fame and the way in which he stumbles into wealth and riches, tossing beans out the window after he has traded the family cow for a handful of seeds.

Merit rarely counts in fairy tales about boys; good fortune is everything. And yet critics of this story have strained to find admirable qualities in the third son who triumphs against the odds. One commentator sees in "The Golden Bird" a "profound praise of placidity" and describes the tale as extolling the virtues of being "good-natured and agreeable" but only "at the appropriate time," since those qualities do not always stand the hero in good stead. What becomes evident from this tale is that the third son is simply the chosen one, and even when he makes mistakes, he will manage to find "complete happiness."

long time ago there lived a king who had a beautiful garden of delights right behind his castle. In it grew a tree that bore golden apples. As soon as the apples became ripe, they were counted, but the very next morning one of them was missing.[1] The king heard about it right away, and he gave orders to have the tree guarded at night.

The king had three sons, and he sent the oldest into the garden at nightfall. Around midnight, however, the boy was overcome by sleep, and the next morning another apple was missing. On the following night, the second son kept watch, but he fared no better. When the clock struck midnight, he fell asleep, and the next morning another apple was missing. Now it was the turn of the third son to keep watch. He was willing and eager, but the king didn't have a great deal of

1. *but the very next morning one of them was missing.* The missing apple serves as the initial lack in this version of the story. Other variants tell of a king who is becoming ill or blind and who sends his sons out in search of a bird that resembles the Phoenix.

faith in him[2] and felt sure that he would do even worse than his brothers. Finally, however, he gave his permission.

The boy stretched out under the tree, kept watch, and fought off going to sleep. When the clock struck twelve, something began stirring in the air, and he caught sight of a bird flying toward him. Its golden feathers glittered in the moonlight when it landed on the tree. The bird had just plucked an apple from the tree when the boy shot an arrow at it. The bird managed to escape, but the arrow grazed it, and one of its golden feathers fell to the ground. The boy picked it up, brought it to the king the next morning, and told him what had happened that night. The king summoned his councilors, and they all agreed that a feather like that was worth more than the entire kingdom.[3] "If the feather is indeed that valuable," the king said, "then a single one just isn't enough. I have to get my hands on that bird, and I'll do anything to catch it."

The eldest of the three sons set out in search of the bird. He was a clever fellow, and so he was sure that the golden bird would soon be in his possession. After traveling for a while, he caught sight of a fox at the edge of a forest,[4] and he raised his gun and took aim. The fox cried out: "Hold your fire! I can give you some good advice if you don't shoot. I know that you're searching for the golden bird. Tonight you're going to reach a village where there are two inns on opposite sides of the road. One of them will be lit up brightly, and you'll see people having a good time. But don't spend the night there. Stay at the other one, even though it may not look inviting."

"How can a dim-witted animal like that give sensible advice!" the prince thought, and he pulled the trigger. But he missed the fox, who stretched out his tail and sped off into the forest. Then he continued on his journey, and in the evening he reached the village where there were two inns on opposite sides of the street. In one there was singing and dancing; the other one looked gloomy and dilapidated.

2. *but the king didn't have a great deal of faith in him.* The youngest son is positioned as the boy who is seen by his parent as wanting in the qualities possessed by the older boys. The Grimms noted that this son was called Dummy (*Dummling*) in a version told to them.

3. *they all agreed that a feather like that was worth more than the entire kingdom.* The value of the feather points to the possibility that the bird is a folkloric cousin of the mythological Phoenix, which renews itself once it burns to ashes. Some versions of the tale feature a white dove that is transformed, at the end of the tale, into a princess.

4. *he caught sight of a fox at the edge of a forest.* The fox, nimble and crafty, makes a perfect helper figure. A little gray man figures in some versions of the tale as helper, and when the hero speaks the words "God bless you," the gray helper is transformed back to his normal human form.

"I would be a fool to stay at the shabby old inn and to pass up the nice one," he thought. And so he went into the inn where things were festive, lived it up, and completely forgot about the bird, about his father, and about every piece of advice he'd ever gotten.

After some time had passed, and it became evident that the eldest son was not going to return home, the second set out to look for the golden bird. Like the eldest, he too met the fox, and he received the same good advice that he then disregarded. He reached the two inns and saw his brother at the window of the one in which there was much carousing. When his brother called out to him, he couldn't resist, and once he was inside, he got lost in a life of pleasure.[5]

More time went by, and now the youngest son wanted to go out and try his luck, but the king was dead set against it. "It's no use," he declared. "He has even less of a chance than his brothers of finding the golden bird, and if something happens to him, he won't know how to manage, for he's never been the brightest." But finally, since the boy gave him no peace, he let him go.

The fox was there again, at the edge of the forest. He pleaded for his life and offered good advice in exchange for it. The boy had always been good-natured, and he said: "Don't worry, little fox, I would never think of harming you."

"You won't regret it," the fox replied, "and if you climb up on my tail, I can get you where you're going much faster." The fox raced off as soon as the boy was on his back, and away they went up hill and down dale, so swiftly that the wind began to whistle through the boy's hair.

When they reached the village, the boy alighted, and he followed the advice given by the fox. Without pondering it for a moment, he decided to stay in the shabby inn, where he got a good night's rest.

The next morning, when he left the village, he saw the fox again, who said: "I'm going to tell you what you have to

5. *he got lost in a life of pleasure.* The two older brothers seem to land in a village version of the legendary Mountain of Venus, which draws wanderers into a life of pleasure, leading them to forget the missions on which they embarked.

6. *"Don't take the bird out of its plain cage."* The command issued by the fox has no clear logic, but once it is violated, the hero is faced with new challenges that lead to ever more desirable prizes. The boy's repeated violation of prohibitions does not seem to militate against his final triumph.

George Cruikshank, *German Popular Stories*

Holding on to his hat, the hero of the tale has found an ideal form of transport on the tail of a fox as he makes his way to destinations that will enable him to carry out the tasks required to win a princess and inherit a kingdom.

do next. If you keep walking down this road, you'll reach a castle. There will be a whole company of soldiers lying on the ground, but don't pay any attention to them, because they'll only be sleeping and snoring away. Just walk right through their ranks and go straight into the castle. When you walk through all the rooms, you'll reach a chamber where there will be a golden bird in a wooden cage. Next to the cage there'll be an empty golden cage hanging there just for show. But watch out! Don't take the bird out of its plain cage[6] and put it in the splendid-looking one. You'll run into trouble if you do." With these words, the fox stretched his tail out, and the prince climbed back on it. They raced up hill and down dale, so swiftly that the wind began to blow through the boy's hair.

When the prince reached the castle, he found that everything was exactly as the fox had told him. He walked into the chamber and found the golden bird sitting in a wooden cage. Next to it was a golden cage. Three golden apples were scattered around the room. Thinking that it would be ridiculous to leave the beautiful bird in the plain and ugly cage, he opened the door, grabbed the bird, and put it into the golden cage. That instant the bird let loose a piercing scream. The soldiers were roused from their sleep and came rushing in. They took the boy off to prison. The next day he was brought to trial, and when he confessed to everything, he was sentenced to death. But the king promised to spare his life under one condition: He would have to bring him a golden horse that could run faster than the wind. If he managed to bring him the horse, the golden bird would be his reward.

The prince started out on his journey, but his spirits were low and he felt miserable. Where in the world was he going to get a golden horse? Just then he met up with his old friend the fox, who was right there on the road.

"See what happens when you don't pay attention to my advice! But all is not lost. I'm still going to help you, and I'll tell you how to find the golden horse. You will have to keep going down this road until you come to a castle. There'll be a stable there with the horse in it. In front of the stable, you'll see grooms lying on the ground, but they will be sleeping and snoring away, so you can go right ahead and get the golden horse. But make sure that you put the plain leather saddle with wooden trim on the horse and not the golden one hanging nearby, or you'll be in for trouble." The fox stretched his tail out, and the prince climbed back on it. The two raced up hill and down dale, so swiftly that the wind began to blow through the boy's hair.

Everything happened as the fox said it would. The boy reached the stable where the golden horse was kept. He was about to put the plain saddle on the horse when he thought: "It would be a shame to put a plain saddle on a horse that really deserves better." No sooner had the golden saddle touched the horse than the beast began to neigh. The grooms were roused from their sleep, and they seized the boy and threw him into prison. The next morning he was sentenced to death, but the king promised to spare his life and to give him the golden horse if he could just bring him the beautiful princess living in the golden castle.

With a heavy heart, the boy got on the road again. To his great joy he met the faithful fox once again. "I should really leave you to your own devices," the fox said, "but I feel sorry for you, and I'm going to help you beat your bad luck. If you follow this path, you will reach the golden castle. You will get there in the evening, and at night, when everything's quiet, the beautiful princess will go into the bathhouse to take her evening bath. When she walks in, run over to her and give her a kiss. She'll have to follow you, and you can take her with you. But you mustn't let her take leave of her parents, or you're in for trouble."

The fox stretched out his tail, and the prince got back on it. They went up hill and down dale until the wind went whistling through his hair. When he got to the golden castle, it was just as the fox said it would be. He waited until midnight when everyone was fast asleep, and then, when the beautiful maiden was on her way to the bathhouse, he jumped out and gave her a kiss. She told him that she would be glad to leave with him, but she wept and pleaded with him to let her say good-bye to her parents. At first he refused, but she just kept on weeping and fell to her knees, and finally he gave in. But just as the maiden was approaching her father's bed, every-

Arthur Rackham, *Hansel and Gretel and Other Tales by the Brothers Grimm*

The hero of the tale races off to his next stop, and the obliging fox willingly transports him, despite the hero's repeated failures to heed the fox's advice.

7. *"You will have to get rid of the mountain that is blocking the view."* The impossible task assigned as the fourth and final challenge differs from the other three in that it requires Herculean strength rather than cunning. Similar tasks are required of heroes in other tales, when they must, for example, empty a lake with a pail that has holes in it.

one else in the castle woke up and the boy was captured and thrown into prison.

The next day the king said to him: "You have forfeited your life, but I'll give you one chance at a pardon: You will have to get rid of the mountain that is blocking the view[7] from my windows, and you will have to do it in a week. If you succeed, you shall have my daughter as your reward."

Right away the prince began digging and shoveling without pausing for a moment. But when he saw how little he had accomplished and how all his work was really in vain, he fell into a state of deep gloom and gave up hope.

On the evening of the seventh day, the fox appeared and said: "You don't really deserve my help, but never mind, and just go take a nap. I'll do the work for you."

The next morning the prince woke up and looked out the window only to discover that the mountain had vanished. His heart was filled with joy, and he raced over to see the king to let him know that he had completed the task. Whether the king liked it or not, he had to keep his word and give him his daughter.

The prince and the princess set out together, and before long they met the faithful fox. "It's true that you have won the real prize," he said, "but the golden horse really ought to go with the princess from the golden castle."

"How can I manage that?" the boy asked.

"I'll tell you how," the fox replied. "First of all, you'll have to bring the beautiful maiden to the king who sent you to the golden castle. There will be great rejoicing, and they'll be so happy to give you the golden horse that they'll bring it right out. Mount the horse right away and be sure to shake hands with everyone as you're taking leave. At the very end, shake the hand of the beautiful princess, and once her hand is in yours, swing her up to the saddle and gallop off. No one will be able to catch you, since you'll be riding a horse that runs faster than the wind."

Everything went as planned, and the prince carried off the beautiful princess on the golden horse. The fox went with them and said to the boy: "Now I'm going to help you get the golden bird too. When you get near the castle where the bird is, let the princess dismount, and I'll take care of her. Then you will want to ride on the golden horse into the courtyard of the castle. When they see you, they will be overjoyed, and they'll bring out the golden bird. Once you have the cage in your hands, gallop back to us and come get the princess."

The plan went smoothly once again, and the prince was about to ride home with his treasures when the fox said: "And now you must reward me for my help."

"What do you wish for in return?"

"When we reach the woods over there, just shoot me and chop off my head and paws."

"That would be real gratitude," the prince said. "I'm afraid that I can't possibly do as you wish."

"If you won't do it, then I will have to leave you. But before I go, I'm going to give you one more good piece of advice. Be on your guard about two things:[8] don't buy any gallows meat and never sit down on the edge of a well." And with that the fox ran into the forest.

The prince thought: "He's really a strange old fellow with all kinds of bizarre ideas. Who in the world would think of buying gallows meat! And I've never really longed to sit on the edge of a well."

The prince rode on with the beautiful maiden, and the path took him through the village in which his two brothers had decided to live. There was a great clamor and uproar in the town, and when he asked what was going on, he was told that two fellows were going to be strung up. When he got closer, he realized that the two men were his brothers, who had been up to all kinds of mischief and had squandered everything they owned. He asked if there was any chance they could be released. "Well, if you're willing to buy their freedom," he

8. *"Be on your guard about two things."* The cryptic nature of the advice is a near guarantee that the hero will fail to heed it. The advice about sitting on the edge of the well connects the fairy tale to the story of Joseph and his brothers, for there too, the elder brothers throw the youngest into an opening in the ground.

was told. "But why in the world would you want to waste your money on setting those scoundrels free?"

He didn't think twice about it,[9] but just paid up, and once they were released, all four of them went on the road together.

After some time had passed, they arrived in the forest where the prince had first met the fox, and since it was cool and pleasant there and the sun had been beating down on them, both brothers said: "Let's stop here at this well and rest for a while. We can have something to eat and drink."

The prince agreed, and while they were talking he forgot himself, and suspecting nothing, he sat down at the edge of the well. The two brothers saw their chance and pushed him backward into the well, captured the princess, and took the horse and the bird back home to their father.

"Not only are we bringing him the golden bird," they said. "We also have the golden horse, and we've kidnapped the princess from the golden castle." There was much rejoicing when they returned home, but the horse refused to eat, the bird would not sing, and the princess just sat around and wept.

It turned out that the youngest brother had not perished. The well happened to be dry, and when he fell, he landed on soft moss without injuring himself. But he couldn't figure out how to get out of the well. The fox was there and stood by him in his trouble even now. He jumped down into the well and scolded the boy for ignoring his advice.

"I can't help myself," he said. "I'm still going to help you get out of here."

The fox told the prince to grab on to his tail and hold tight until they got back up to the top. "You're still not completely out of danger," the fox said. "Your brothers weren't sure that you were dead, so they stationed sentries all around the woods, and they've been ordered to shoot you on sight."

On the way, the prince saw a poor man, and he decided to exchange clothes with him[10] before going to the king's court.

9. *He didn't think twice about it.* Like many fairy-tale heroes and heroines, the king's son is magnanimous, seeking to produce harmony rather than promoting rivalry.

10. *he decided to exchange clothes with him.* Like Odysseus, the king's son returns home in disguise. The princess, like the nurse in *The Odyssey*, recognizes him, even in his beggar's clothing.

No one recognized him, but all of a sudden the bird began to sing, the horse started eating again, and the beautiful princess stopped crying. The king was mystified and asked: "What is going on?"

The princess said, "I'm not sure, but I was so sad before and now I'm happy. I feel as if my true betrothed were around here somewhere."

The princess told the king everything that had happened, even though the brothers had threatened to kill her if she revealed anything. The king ordered everyone in the castle to appear before him. The young prince also came, dressed as a man wearing rags. The princess recognized him at once and fell into his arms. The wicked brothers were seized and executed, and the prince married the beautiful princess and was appointed heir to the throne.

But what happened to the poor fox? Many years later, the prince was walking in the forest and he met the fox, who said to him: "Now you have everything that you could ever want. As for me, I have no end of bad luck, and yet it is in your power to liberate me." A second time he pleaded with the prince to shoot him dead and to chop off his head and paws. This time he did it, and as soon as the deed was done, the fox turned into none other than the brother of the beautiful princess, who was finally released from the spell that had been cast on him. And now nothing more was wanting, and for the rest of their lives, the happiness of all three was complete.

The Three Feathers

This story of a dummy who triumphs over his older, wiser siblings never entered the Western fairy-tale canon, but it gives us the classic configuration of three sons who vie for their father's inheritance. The two elder brothers are never really differentiated from each other: both reveal themselves to be, despite their reputations for cleverness, inept and underhanded. Dummy triumphs, less because of his innate intelligence, kindness, or resourcefulness than because of his alliance with nature and his sheer good luck. The youngest, and therefore historically also the last in line for an inheritance, he manages to emerge as ruler, despite the efforts of his brothers to block his ascension to the throne.

The animal bride, another figure that has receded from our folkloric imagination, also figures prominently in this tale. Note that the youth's bride is drawn from the realm of amphibians, hybrid creatures that inhabit the lands and the seas. The fairy tale stages the marriage of high and low, of a king's son who occupies the top of the social ladder and a toad that dwells in the nether regions.

Because the hero of this fairy tale does not show any special merit, he can provide special inspiration to child listeners and readers, who identify with the vulnerability and incompetence of the third son. As Bruno Bettelheim puts it, "a small child, bright though he may be, feels himself stupid and inadequate when confronted by the complexity of the world which surrounds him." Every child feels like the youngest and least respected in the family: "This is why many fairy tales begin with the hero being depreciated and considered stupid."

The third and youngest son becomes a child allied with nature, possessing a certain grace that allows him to descend into nether regions where a toad, among the most lowly and repulsive creatures, fulfills the function of donor and presents him with gifts that are so beautiful that they have an otherworldly quality to them. Dummy has become the chosen one, a hero who attains the rank of monarch but who also has the power to conjure works of art with a transcendent quality to them.

nce upon a time there lived a king who had three sons. Two of them were sharp and clever, but the third didn't have much to say, and he was considered dim-witted. Everyone called him Dummy.[1] When the king became old and weak, he started worrying about which of his sons should inherit the kingdom.[2] He summoned all three of them one day and said: "I want you to go out into the world. Whoever brings back the most splendid carpet[3] will become king after my death." Just to make sure that his sons wouldn't start quarreling with each other, he took them to a place in front of the castle, blew three feathers into the air,[4] and said: "Choose a feather and follow its flight." One feather flew to the east, the other to the west, and the third flew straight ahead, but it didn't go very far before landing on the ground. One brother went to the right, the other to the left, and both brothers made fun of

1. *Everyone called him Dummy.* The youngest son, who is often also the most naïve in a trio of boys, must bear a name that designates his position as social inferior: Numbskull, Simpleton, or Dummy.

2. *which of his sons should inherit the kingdom.* Many of the Grimms' fairy tales had their origins in a culture that endorsed primogeniture, with the oldest son inheriting the family land and wealth. Here, the king decides that he shall base his decision about the line of royal descent on the son who can fulfill the task he sets.

3. *"Whoever brings back the most splendid carpet."* "Carpet" can be understood as an intricate weaving and therefore can be connected with the three Fates and their handicraft. The fact that it is both "beautiful" and "fine" suggests that it is a work of art as much as a practical object.

4. *blew three feathers into the air.* Some versions of the tale show the father shooting three arrows into the air, and the direction of those arrows determines the path of each son. What is important here is the fact that the feathers are not human artifacts but belong instead to nature, which determines the right course for each of the three sons.

5. *climbed down the stairs.* Dummy's descent represents a journey into a well-like netherworld. He ventures into terra incognita, while the two brothers remain earthbound, searching only in predictable arenas.

Dummy, who was going to have to stay right where the third feather had fallen.

Dummy sat down and was feeling miserable. But suddenly he noticed that there was a trapdoor right next to his feather. He lifted it up, discovered a staircase, and climbed down the stairs.[5] There he found another door, knocked on it, and heard a voice crying out from inside:

"Little maiden, green and tiny,
Hop toad, hop up, greenback shiny,
Hop right here, land on the floor,
Quick, hop home, who's at the door?"

The door opened up, and he saw a big, fat toad sitting there, surrounded by many, many little toads. The large toad asked what he desired, and the boy replied: "I am looking for the world's most beautiful and splendid carpet." The toad cried out to one of the young ones and said:

"Little maiden, green and tiny,
Hop toad, hop up, greenback shiny,
Hop right here, land on the floor,
Bring me the box for the boy at the door."

The young frog fetched the box, and the big frog opened it up and handed Dummy the carpet that was in it. It was more beautiful and fine than anything that could have been woven by human hands. Dummy thanked the frog and climbed back up the stairs.

The two other brothers were sure that their younger brother was way too stupid to ever find anything and bring it back. "Why should we even bother going to the trouble of searching around?" they thought. And they snatched some coarse fabric from the first shepherd's wife they ran into and took it home to the king. Around the same time, Dummy arrived home, carrying the beautiful carpet he had received. When the king saw it, he was astonished and said: "If we play by the rules, then my youngest son is entitled to the kingdom."

The two older brothers were fuming, and they told their father that he could not possibly let Dummy, who was clueless about absolutely everything, become king. They pleaded with him to set a new test. Finally, the father said: "Whoever brings me the most beautiful ring[6] will inherit my kingdom." And he went outside with his sons and blew three feathers into the air, and once more, the boys were to follow their flight. The two oldest boys, as usual, went east and west, but the feather of the youngest flew straight ahead and fell down right at the trapdoor in the ground. Dummy walked back down the stairs to the big fat toad and said that he needed to have the most beautiful ring in the world. The toad asked to have the same large box brought in and gave the boy a ring with diamonds that sparkled. It was so beautiful that no goldsmith on earth could possibly have fashioned it. The two older brothers thought it was hilarious that Dummy was going off to look for a ring, and they decided that they didn't need to make any effort at all. They pulled the nails out of an old carriage ring and brought it to the king. When Dummy showed him the golden ring, the father said once again: "The kingdom belongs to him!"

But the two brothers tortured the king until he finally established a third test, announcing that whoever brought home the most beautiful woman would inherit the kingdom. The king blew the three feathers into the air, and they flew in the same directions as before.

Dummy went at once to the big fat toad and said: "Now I'm supposed to bring home the most beautiful woman."

"Aha!" the toad replied. "The most beautiful woman in the world! She doesn't happen to be here right now, but you'll still be able to find her." And with that the toad gave him

6. *"Whoever brings me the most beautiful ring."* The rug, as a rectangular woven object, stands in contrast to the ring, a circular object set with stones.

a yellow turnip that had been hollowed out and that had six little mice harnessed up to it.

Dummy got worried and asked: "What am I supposed to do with that?"

The toad replied: "Just put one of my little toads into the turnip."

Dummy chose one of the little toads from the group at random[7] and seated her in the yellow turnip. As soon as she sat down, she turned into a fabulously beautiful young woman, and the turnip was transformed into a coach drawn by the horses that had once been mice. He gave the woman a kiss, drove off at a fast clip with the horses, and returned to see the king.

Not much later, the two brothers arrived home. They had not taken the trouble to search for beautiful women but had just picked out the first decent peasant women they encountered. When the king saw them, he said: "After I die, the kingdom will belong to my youngest son." But the two older sons made such a racket that the king almost lost his hearing: "We are not going to allow Dummy to become king." They demanded a new test that would favor the one whose wife could jump through a ring[8] that had been placed in the middle of the hall. They thought: "That will come easily to these peasant women, for they're strong, but that delicate young lady will leap to her death." The king agreed to that test as well. The two peasant women jumped, and they made it through the ring, but they were so clumsy that they fell and broke their stout arms and legs. Then the beautiful woman that Dummy had brought home jumped, and she soared through the ring as gracefully as a fawn. From then on it was useless to try for another challenge. Dummy received the crown, and he ruled with great wisdom for many, many years.

7. *chose one of the little toads from the group at random.* Dummy can clearly do no wrong and makes the right choice even when he seems to be acting in arbitrary fashion.

8. *the one whose wife could jump through a ring.* The tale adds a fourth to the usual three tests, the last test requiring the wife of the hero to demonstrate her mettle. Many brides in this situation are required to display their skills in the domestic arts, but this animal bride, once a toad, will clearly win any contest that tests the ability to leap or jump.

Kay Nielsen, *Hansel and Gretel and Other Stories by the Brothers Grimm*

The youngest of three sons watches as the toad he chose drives off in a carriage drawn by six mice. The mice, the turnip-carriage, and the toad are about to undergo a dramatic transformation.

The Golden Goose

This tale of three sons combines a story about the attractions of a golden goose, about a princess who cannot laugh, and about a series of impossible tasks. Dummy, the youngest and most naïve of three brothers, is also the only one who shows any compassion. He shares his food with a little gray man and is rewarded repeatedly for his small act of kindness.

Simone de Beauvoir's description of the stereotypical fairy-tale hero reminds us of the degree to which the Grimms' protagonists deviate from what is seen as a norm. "In song and story, the young man is seen departing adventurously in search of woman; he slays the dragon, he battles giants." Yet in the Grimms' entire collection there are only a few giant killers and dragon slayers, and some of them are named, like the hero of "The Golden Goose," Dummy. "Silly," "useless," "foolish," and "simple": these are the terms used to characterize many of the boys who go out into the world in search of wealth and power. But it is precisely their lack of guile and their simplicity that proves enabling. Dummy, unlike his "clever" brothers who reflect on the consequences of dividing their food, spontaneously shares what he has. Once he exhibits compassion, he can do no wrong, and he is both singled out for good fortune and armed with a donor/helper for the tasks that lie ahead.

The gift of the golden goose leads to what folklorists call "incremental repetition," in which each new event builds on the previous one. In "The Golden Goose," we witness the cumulative effect of the new additions to the chain of people attached to the goose, but we never see the release of the figures. Instead Dummy rises to the challenge of making the princess laugh by parading before her the people holding on to his goose. Putting cupidity (and the vanity of efforts to arrest it) on display, the line of figures produces a carnivalesque effect that gets the desired laugh from the solemn princess.

Dummy still has three impossible tasks to fulfill, and once again, with help from the little gray man in the woods, he manages to empty the cellar full of wine, make the mountain of bread vanish, and produce a ship that sails on land and on water. Oddly, it is not the production of excess but the consumption of excess that brings him the crown. And the hybrid ship, with its ability to navigate both earth and seas, seems an odd climax to the series of tasks. But the hero of "The Golden Goose" excels in the production of the kind of humor that was vital to the storytelling tradition in earlier centuries. If he himself is neither trickster nor prankster, his ability to stage folly and vanity produces results both for himself and for the audience listening to the tale.

Once there lived a man who had three sons, and the youngest, who was called Dummy, was forever belittled, mocked, and disdained. One day, the oldest of the three decided to go into the forest to chop some wood. Before he left, his mother gave him a tasty pancake and a bottle of wine to make sure he would not get hungry or thirsty. When he reached the forest, he met a little old gray man,[1] who wished him good day and said: "I'm really hungry and thirsty. Would you mind giving me a piece of that pancake in your knapsack and a sip of that wine?" The clever son said: "If I give you some of my pancake and wine, then there won't be anything left for me. Be off with you." And he left the little man standing there while he went on his way. Later, when he started cutting down a tree, he missed his aim and the ax cut right into his arm. And so he had to go home and have it bandaged. That was all the little gray man's doing.

Next the second son went into the woods, and his mother gave him, as she had given the eldest, a pancake and a bottle of wine. He too met the little old gray man, who asked for a little piece of the pancake and a sip of the wine. The second son too replied with great logic: "Whatever I give you, I won't have for myself. Be off with you." He left the little man standing there and went on his way. His punishment was not long in coming. He whacked a tree a few times, and then struck himself in the leg so that he had to be carried home.

At last Dummy said: "Father, let me go out into the forest to chop some wood." The father replied: "Your brothers tried it and got injured. Better leave it alone, especially since you don't know the first thing about chopping wood." But Dummy pleaded with him until finally he said: "Go ahead, we all learn from our injuries."

Dummy's mother gave him a pancake that had been made of water and baked in the ashes,[2] and she added a bottle of sour beer. When he got to the forest, he met the little old gray man too, who greeted him and said: "Will you give me a piece of your pancake and a drink out of your bottle? I'm so hungry and thirsty."

Dummy replied: "All I have is an ashcake and sour beer. But if you don't mind, let's sit down together and eat it." They sat down, and when Dummy took out his ashcake, it had turned into a tasty pancake, and the sour beer had become

1. *a little old gray man.* A test of compassion, posed early on in the tale, determines whether the hero is eligible to carry out "impossible tasks." The tester figure is also often the helper or donor that the hero later encounters. In this case, the helper takes the form of a diminutive male figure, but the helper can also be an old woman, and in many cases animals as well.

2. *baked in the ashes.* The ashes in which the pancake is baked are reminiscent of the ashes in which Cinderella has to take refuge. Dummy is a male Cinderella, but he does not have to sit at home in the ashes, and instead, with a little prodding, manages to leave home and seek his fortune.

good wine. They ate and they drank, and then the little man said: "Since you have a kind heart and are willing to share what you have, I am going to grant you good fortune. See that old tree over there? If you chop it down, you'll find something in the roots."[3] And the little man left.

Dummy went over and chopped the tree down, and when it fell, he found in its roots a goose with feathers of pure gold. He picked the goose up and took it with him to an inn, where he was planning to spend the night. The innkeeper happened to have three daughters. They saw the goose and were curious to know more about the wondrous bird.[4] They were all hoping to pluck one of its golden feathers, and the eldest thought: "I'll find one way or another to get one of those feathers."

When Dummy left the inn for a while, she grabbed the goose by its wings, but her finger and hand stuck fast. Not much later the second sister came, and all she could think of was how to get a golden feather. But as soon as she touched her sister, she stuck fast to her. Finally the third sister came with the same plan. The two others screamed: "Stay away, for heaven's sake, stay away." But since she had no idea why she was supposed to stay away, all she thought was: "If they can touch the goose, so can I," and she ran over to them, but as soon as she touched her sister, she too got stuck fast. And so they had to spend the night with the goose.

The next morning Dummy picked the goose up in his arms and left, without worrying at all about the three girls who were stuck to it. They had to run behind him, to the left or to the right, whichever way he happened to be going. While crossing a meadow they met the parson, who, when he saw the procession, said: "You should be ashamed of yourselves, you horrid girls. Running after that young fellow through the meadows! Is that proper behavior?" And he grabbed the youngest to pull her away, but when he touched her, he too got stuck and had to run with them. Before long the sexton

3. *"If you chop it down, you'll find something in the roots."* The myths about Yggdrasil and other world trees reveal how the roots of trees are invested with magical qualities. In "The Juniper Tree" too, magical creatures emerge from trees, though in that tale the bird emerges from the mist surrounding the tree.

4. *were curious to know more about the wondrous bird.* Curiosity generally gets women in trouble, and here the curious sisters find that their desire to touch the goose and to pluck a feather from it produces real discomfort and distress.

came by and saw the parson, who looked like he was pursuing three girls. He was shocked and cried out: "Hey there, Reverend, where are you going so fast? Don't forget about the christening we have today," and he ran after him, grabbed his sleeve, and also got stuck. As the five of them trotted along, they met two farmers leaving the fields with their hoes. The pastor called out to them, hoping that they could release him and the sexton. But as soon as they touched the sexton, they got stuck, and now seven of them were running after Dummy and his goose.

Later that day, they came to a city where there was a king with a daughter so solemn that no one could get her to laugh. And so the king had decreed that whoever could make her laugh could also marry her.[5] When Dummy heard that, he went with his goose and his retinue to the princess, and when she saw those seven people running along in a chain, she couldn't contain herself and burst out laughing. Dummy claimed her as his wife, but the king didn't particularly want him as a son-in-law, and he began raising all kinds of objections. First of all, he decided that Dummy would have to find

5. *whoever could make her laugh could also marry her.* The solemn princess provides the opportunity in this tale and others for comic relief. The hero's pranks do not always succeed on the first try, and sometimes he or other suitors must make many efforts before getting the princess to laugh.

Walter Crane, *Household Stories from the Collection of the Brothers Grimm*

The hero leads a parade of five, who march through the streets, stuck fast to one another.

George Cruikshank, *German Popular Stories*

Observers watch in delight as the hero parades through the streets, golden goose in hand, followed by the sister who sticks fast to the goose and those behind her.

a man who could drink an entire cellar full of wine. Dummy had a feeling that the little gray man might be able to help him, and he went out into the forest to the place where he had chopped down the tree. There was a man sitting there who looked completely downcast. Dummy asked him why he was so depressed. He answered: "I've got such a huge thirst that it's impossible to quench. Cold water just doesn't agree with me, and I've emptied a whole barrel of wine, but that's just a drop in the bucket."

"I can help you there," Dummy said. "Come along with me, and you can drink your fill."

He took him to the king's cellar, and the man started drinking eagerly from the great hogsheads. He drank and he drank until his sides ached, and before the day was over he had managed to drink an entire cellar full of wine.

Once again Dummy claimed his bride, but the king was annoyed at the idea that his daughter would be hitched to a dolt like that, whom everyone called Dummy, and he set another condition. Dummy would have to find a man who could eat a mountain of bread. Dummy didn't hesitate for long and went right back into the woods. He found a man sitting in the exact same place who was tightening a belt around his belly, making a long face, and saying: "I just ate a whole oven full of bread, but what good is that when you're as hungry as I am. My belly just won't fill up, and I have to strap it up tight, or else I'll starve to death." Dummy was happy to hear that and said: "Get up and come with me. You'll finally get to eat your fill." He took him to the king's court, to a place where all the flour in the kingdom had been transported so that a huge mountain of bread could be made. The man who had been out in the woods sat down before it, started to eat, and before the day was over, the mountain had vanished.

For the third time, Dummy wanted to claim his bride, but the king set another condition and demanded a ship that could sail on land and on water. "As soon as you come sailing along in it," he said, "I will give you my daughter as your wife." Dummy went straight back to the forest, and there was the little old gray man to whom he had given his cake. He said: "I drank for you, and I ate for you, and now I'm also going to give you the ship. I'm doing all this because

Kay Nielsen, *Hansel and Gretel and Other Stories by the Brothers Grimm*

The princess watches with pleasure as the hero passes before her with his entourage.

you were kind to me and showed compassion." He gave him a ship that could sail on land and on water, and when the king saw it, he could no longer deny him his daughter. The marriage was celebrated, and after the king died, Dummy inherited the kingdom and lived in great happiness with his wife for many days.

Furrypelts[1]

Cinderella," which traces a rags-to-riches trajectory and shows how an innocent young girl survives the persecutions of a wicked stepmother, has become the most prominent story in our pantheon of fairy tales. Put on screen by Disney, it has found special favor in a culture that endorses social mobility and self-invention. While its star continues to rise, its companion piece in the Grimms' collection, "Furrypelts" (also known as "Thousandfurs" and "Allfurs"), languishes, unfamiliar to all but the most ardent fairy-tale enthusiasts.

If "Cinderella" tells of the problems that arise for children when a father takes a new wife who sees the children as rivals for her husband's affections, "Furrypelts" shows what happens when a father does not want to find a wife outside the family and settles on his own daughter as the only suitable bride. In the Grimms' tale, the mother of the heroine is seen as complicit in engineering the marriage, for she decrees that her husband shall not marry anyone who is not as beautiful as she is.

The heroine of "Cinderella" may suffer from an absence of maternal love and affection, but the heroine of "Furrypelts" suffers from an excess of paternal love and affection. In her story, mothers and step-

1. *Furrypelts.* The Grimms' title "Allerleirauh" can be translated as "All Kinds of Pelts." Allerleirauh has many folkloric cousins, including the British Catskin and Cap o' Rushes as well as the French Donkeyskin and the Italian Doralice, in Straparola's *Facetious Nights.*

mothers are entirely absent, allowing the father to give free rein to the erotic pursuit of his daughter. That our own culture has suppressed the theme of incestuous desire even as it indulges freely in elaborate variations on the theme of maternal malice is not surprising on a number of counts. Since tales such as "Furrypelts" make for disturbing reading matter for adults, it hardly seems advisable to put them between the covers of books for children.

"Furrypelts" raises the charged issue of incestuous desire and places the heroine in serious jeopardy, but as a result, it furnishes a rare stage for creative action, opening the possibility for displaying resourcefulness and survival skills. Unlike Cinderella, who endures humiliation at home and is empowered only through the gifts she receives, the heroine of "Furrypelts" is mobile, active, and clever. She begins with a strong assertion of her own desires by resisting the paternal declaration: "Tomorrow our wedding will be celebrated." Fleeing the household, she moves out into an alien world that requires her to be inventive, energetic, and enterprising if she is to reestablish herself and to reclaim her royal rank. To be sure, her resourcefulness is confined largely to sartorial and culinary arts, but these were, after all, the two areas in which women traditionally distinguished themselves. Furrypelts dazzles with her dress, and she successfully uses her cuisine to draw the king into romance.

The literary source for the Grimms' tale, Carl Nehrlich's novel Schilly *(1798), begins with the flight of the heroine from a cruel stepmother, not from a menacing father. Allerlei-Rauch becomes the target of her stepmother's wrath because of the attentions of a suitor, to whom she becomes betrothed. She is abandoned in the woods, rescued by hunters, and obliged to polish boots and clean the kitchen in the castle where she takes up residence. By putting the ring given to her by her betrothed into the soup served up to him, she ensures her recognition and marries the duke of the castle.*

The story of "Furrypelts," for all its complications and moments of discomfort, provides a remarkable opportunity for thinking through father-daughter relationships and for showing how a young woman can make the daring leap from home, striking out on her own and making new familial connections.

nce upon a time there lived a king whose wife had golden hair, and she was so beautiful that it was impossible to find her equal anywhere on earth. It so happened that she fell ill, and when she realized that she was going to die, she called the king to her bedside and said: "If you decide to wed after my death, you must promise that you will only marry a woman as beautiful as I am, with golden hair like mine."[2] When the king had agreed, she closed her eyes and died.

For a long time the king was inconsolable, and he never even gave a thought to taking another wife. At length, however, his councilors said: "Things cannot continue like this. The king has to remarry so that we will have a queen." Messengers were sent far and wide to search for a bride whose beauty would be equal to that of the dead queen. But there was no one like her in the whole wide world, and even if they had succeeded in finding such a woman, she would not have had golden hair like the queen's. And so they failed to accomplish their mission and returned home.

The king had a daughter who was as beautiful as her dead mother and who had golden hair like hers. She was now grown up, and this king turned to her one day and realized that she looked exactly like his wife. He was seized with a passionate love for her. He told his councilors: "I have decided to marry my daughter, for she is the living image of my dead wife, and I shall never find another bride like her.

When the councilors heard these words, they were aghast

2. *"you must promise that you will only marry a woman as beautiful as I am, with golden hair like mine."* Other versions of the tale use a similar strategy to lift the blame for the desired marriage from the father to the mother. The incestuous proposal on which the plot turns is attributed to the collusive mother, who seems invested in making sure that the only candidate for marriage is her own daughter. In some versions of this story, the mother decrees that the king can only marry the woman whose finger fits her own wedding band, and that woman turns out to be the couple's daughter.

and said: "God has forbidden a man to marry his daughter.[3] Nothing good can come from sin, and the kingdom will be dragged down to perdition with you."

The daughter was horrified when she heard about her father's plans, but she was sure that she could change his mind. She said to him: "Before I fulfill your wish, I will have to have three dresses: one as golden as the sun, a second as silvery as the moon, and a third as bright as the stars. In addition, I will need a cloak made of thousands of kinds of pelts and furs,[4] with a snippet taken from every animal in your kingdom."

"He can't possibly get me all those things," she thought, "and trying will distract him from his wicked intentions."

But the king was not at all discouraged, and he ordered the most skilled maidens in his realm to weave three dresses, one as golden as the sun, one as silvery as the moon, and a third as bright as the stars. His huntsmen had to capture all the animals in the kingdom and take a snippet of fur from each one. From those pieces, a cloak was made of thousands of pieces of fur. When everything was ready, the king brought out the cloak, spread it in front of her, and said: "Tomorrow our wedding will be celebrated."

When the princess realized that there was no chance that her father would have a change of heart, she made up her mind to flee. That night, while everyone was sleeping, she got up and took out three of her most precious possessions:[5] a golden ring, a little golden spinning wheel, and a golden bobbin. She put the three dresses—the dresses of the sun, moon, and stars—into a nutshell and put on the cloak of a thousand furs. She used soot to blacken her hands and face. Then she commended herself to God and slipped out the door. She walked all night long until she reached a large forest. By that time she was so tired that she just crawled into a hollow tree and fell asleep.

When the sun rose, she was still fast asleep and continued

3. *"God has forbidden a man to marry his daughter."* The councilors act as a kind of chorus, pointing out that the father's desires run counter to God's will and are sinful. It is entirely possible that the Grimms added this line to ensure that no one would imagine that they condoned the king's proposal. Joseph Jacobs, in his annotations to a British analogue, points out that the "unsavoury motif of the Unnatural Father" is said to have its home in England, but he notes with relief: "There are only very slight traces of the story in these islands nowadays, while it abounds in Italy, which possesses one almost perfect version of the formula."

4. *"a cloak made of thousands of kinds of pelts and furs."* Furrypelts's coat connects her with nature and with the creatures in the forest where she finds refuge. The gross animal nature in the form of the cloak masks a spiritual power with a deep connection to nature. The three dresses are affiliated with celestial bodies (sun, moon, and stars) and point to a connection with the heavens as well as with the creatures on earth.

5. *she got up and took out three of her most precious possessions.* Furrypelts will later use these dainty objects to signal her royal heritage when she makes a bread soup for the king. Princesses who bake or cook their way to success often "sign" their products with rings from their fingers or with miniature spindles and spinning wheels. These dainty golden objects betray the fact that it is no mere kitchen drudge who has prepared the culinary delight.

Kay Nielsen, *Hansel and Gretel and Other Stories by the Brothers Grimm*

The cloak of animal skins cannot conceal the beauty of Furrypelts, who is illuminated by light that radiates from no evident source.

6. *"you'll be good for work in the kitchen."* Like Cinderella, Furrypelts is consigned to the kitchen and forced to labor as a drudge. She conceals her royal descent in part to avoid paternal pursuit, but also in part to invite the king to court her.

sleeping until broad daylight. It just so happened that the king to whom the forest belonged was out hunting that day. When his dogs got to the tree, they started sniffing it and barked loudly as they ran around it. The king said to his huntsmen: "Why don't you take a look and see what kind of animal is hiding in there." The huntsmen did his bidding, and when they returned they said: "We've never seen anything like the really strange animal that's lying in the hollow of the tree. Its coat is made up of thousands of different furs, and it's curled up, fast asleep."

"Try to capture it alive and then tie it to the carriage and we'll take it back with us," the king said.

When the huntsmen grabbed hold of the girl, she woke up in a fright and cried out: "I'm just a poor girl who's been abandoned by her father and mother. Have pity on me and take me with you."

"Furrypelts," they said, "you'll be good for work in the kitchen.[6] Come with us, and we'll give you a job sweeping the ashes." And so they put her in the carriage and drove back to the royal castle. There they settled her in a little den under the stairs, where daylight never reached, and they told her: "This will be your living room and bedroom." Then they sent her to the kitchen where she was made to do all the dirty work, carrying water and wood for the fire, keeping the fires going, plucking the chickens, cleaning vegetables, and sweeping the ashes.

For a long time Furrypelts led a wretched life. Ah, fairest princess! What will become of you!

One day a ball was held at the castle, and Furrypelts asked the cook: "May I go up for a while to watch? I'll stay behind the door."

"Just go ahead, but remember that you have to be back here in a half hour to clean up the ashes," the cook said.

And so Furrypelts took her little oil lamp, went over to her den, took off her cloak of furs, and washed the soot off her hands and face, revealing her full beauty to the world. Then she opened up the nutshell and took out the dress that shone like the sun. And she went up to the ball. Everyone there stepped aside when she walked in, and they all assumed that she was a princess, for no one recognized her. The king came up to her, gave her his hand, and all the while he was dancing with her, he was thinking in his heart: "I've never set eyes on anyone as beautiful as she is."

When the dance was over, Furrypelts curtseyed, and before the king knew it she had vanished, and no one had any idea where she had gone. The guards keeping watch were summoned and interrogated, but no one had seen her.

Furrypelts had raced off to her little den, removed her dress, blackened her hands and face, put on the cloak of furs, and had turned back into her old self. When she returned to the kitchen to get back to her work sweeping the ashes, the cook said: "That can wait until tomorrow. I'd like you to cook the king's soup, because I want to take a look upstairs too. But don't you dare let a hair fall into the soup or you'll never get anything to eat again."

The cook left, and Furrypelts made a soup for the king, a bread soup that was as good as she could make it. When she had finished, she went into her little den to retrieve the golden ring, which she put right in the bowl into which she had ladled the soup. When the ball was over, the king sent for his soup, and he ate it up. It tasted so good that he could not stop talking about how delicious it was. When he got to the bottom of the bowl, he found a golden ring and couldn't figure out how it had landed there. He sent for the cook, who was terrified when he got the order to appear before the king and said to Furrypelts: "You must have let a hair fall in the soup. If it's true, I'll box your ears."

When the cook appeared before the king, the king asked who had prepared the soup. The cook replied: "I did." But the king said: "That can't be true. It tasted different and was much better than usual." Then the cook replied: "I guess I have to admit it. It was Furrypelts, not I, who cooked the soup." The king said: "Go tell her to come see me."

When Furrypelts got there, the king asked: "Who are you?"

"I'm a poor child who has neither father nor mother."

Then he continued with his questioning: "Why are you here in my castle?"

"The only thing I'm good for is having boots thrown at my head."[7]

He then asked: "Where did you get that ring that was in my soup?"

"I don't know anything about a ring," she replied.

And so the king couldn't get any answers to his questions and had to let her go.

After some time there was another ball, and as before, Furrypelts asked the cook for permission to go up and take a look. He replied: "All right, but be sure to come back in a half hour to cook that bread soup that the king likes so much."

Furrypelts ran over to her little den, washed up as fast as she could, removed the dress that was silvery as the moon from the nutshell, and put it on. Then she went upstairs, looking like a princess. The king approached her and was overjoyed to see her again. Just then the music sounded, and the two danced together. When the dance was over, Furrypelts vanished into thin air, and the king couldn't tell where she had gone. She raced over to her little den and turned herself back into her old self and went to the kitchen to cook the bread soup. When the cook was upstairs, she took out the golden spinning wheel and put it in the bowl and poured the soup over it. It was taken to the king who ate it and found that it tasted just as good as before. He summoned the cook who had to admit that Furrypelts had made the soup this time too. Furrypelts had to appear before the king again, but all

7. *"The only thing I'm good for is having boots thrown at my head."* In some versions of the tale, the heroine must blacken boots in addition to her other household chores.

she said was that she was there so that boots could be thrown at her head and, also, that she knew nothing about that little golden spinning wheel.

When the king gave a ball for the third time, everything happened as before. But the cook said: "You must be a witch, Furrypelts, for you're always putting something into the soup that makes the king like it better than the soup I cook for him." But since Furrypelts pleaded with him, he let her go to the ball anyway for a little while. This time she put on the dress that glittered like the stars and walked into the ballroom. The king danced once again with the beautiful maiden and believed she was even more beautiful than before. While he was dancing, he put the golden ring on her finger without her being aware of it. He also ordered that the musicians play longer than before. When the music came to an end, he tried to grab her hands and hold on tight to her, but she tore herself away and ran so fast into the crowds that she vanished before his very eyes. She ran as fast as she could over to her little den under the stairs, but since she had stayed longer than the usual half hour, she didn't have time to take off the beautiful dress and just threw the cloak of furs over it. She was in such a big hurry that she didn't manage to blacken herself completely. One finger remained white.

Furrypelts ran into the kitchen, made the bread soup for the king, and as soon as the cook left, she put the golden bobbin in it. When the king found the golden bobbin at the bottom of his bowl, he called for Furrypelts. He noticed the white finger right away and also saw the ring that he had put on her finger while they were dancing. He grabbed her hand and held it tight. When she tried to work herself free and run off, the cloak of furs opened up a tiny bit, and he could see the dress of stars glittering under it. The king took off the cloak and tore it from her head to reveal her golden hair.[8]

8. *The king took off the cloak and tore it from her head to reveal her golden hair.* The violence that opened the narrative is repeated in this final scene, in muted fashion to be sure. This second king is not kin but also less than kind. When Furrypelts is said to be "more beautiful than anyone ever seen on earth," the ending nods once again in the direction of the introduction.

There she stood in her full glory, which could no longer be concealed. And when she wiped the soot and ashes off her face, she was more beautiful than anyone ever seen on earth. The king said: "You are my beloved bride, and we shall never part." The wedding was celebrated, and they lived happily until they died.

32

JORINDA AND JORINGEL

This fairy tale about two young people who lose their way in the woods was adapted from the autobiography of the German writer Johann Heinrich Jung-Stilling. The Grimms report that they had once heard an oral version of the tale, which they did not record. In Jung-Stilling's autobiography, the listeners react by noting that the story is too frightening to tell in the nighttime.

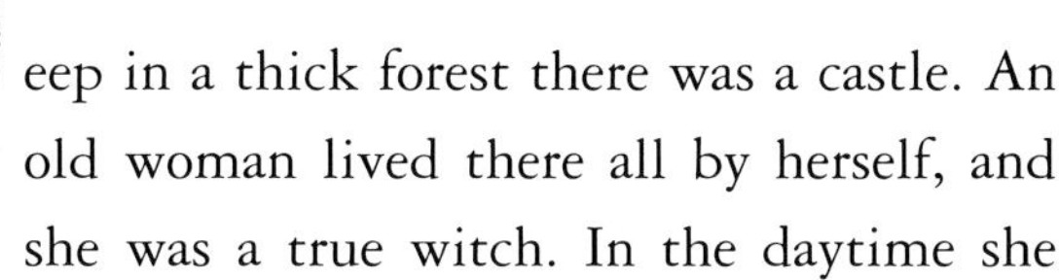

Deep in a thick forest there was a castle. An old woman lived there all by herself, and she was a true witch. In the daytime she would turn herself into a cat or a night owl, and at night she would return to her human form. She was able to lure wild game and birds into her house, and, once she killed them, she would cook or roast them. If anyone came within a hundred feet of the castle, they would freeze on the spot and be unable

Wanda Gág, *More Tales from Grimm*

to move until she made up her mind to break the spell. If any innocent girls entered the magic circle, the witch would turn them into birds and lock them up in cages kept in one of the rooms of the castle. She had collected somewhere close to seven thousand rare birds, all locked in those cages up in the castle.

There was once a girl named Jorinda, and she was more beautiful than any other girl in the world. She and a handsome boy named Joringel were betrothed to each other. They were planning to marry soon, and they enjoyed nothing more than spending time together. One day they wanted some time for themselves, and they decided to take a walk in the woods. "Just make sure we don't come too close to the castle," Joringel said. It was a beautiful evening, and the bright sunshine streaming between tree trunks lit up the deep green in the forest, while a turtledove perched in tall beech trees sang plaintively. Jorinda began to weep, and she sat down in the sun and sighed. Joringel began to sigh as well, and they felt nearly as sad as if they had been condemned to die. They looked around them in confusion, for they no longer knew the way home. The sun was still partly above the mountain, and partly hidden by it. Joringel looked through the greenery and could see the wall of the

Arthur Rackham, *The Fairy Tales of the Brothers Grimm*
"By day she made herself into a cat."

Wanda Gág, *More Tales from Grimm*

old castle just steps away. He was horrified and deeply worried. Jorinda began to sing a tune:

"My little bird with a ring so red,
Sings sorrow, sorrow, and pain.
It sings about my little dove's death,
Sings sorrow, Sor—zickety, zickety, zick."

Joringel looked at Jorinda. She had been turned into a nightingale[1] that was singing "Zickety, zickety." A night owl with flashing eyes flew around her three times and screeched three times, "Shoo, whoo, whoo, whoo." Joringel was unable to move. He had become like a statue, unable to shed tears, speak, or move his hands and feet.

Once the sun had set, the owl flew into a bush, and a moment later a gnarled old woman emerged from it. She was

1. *She had been turned into a nightingale.* The nightingale is a songbird of reddish-brown plumage found in Great Britain, Asia, Africa, and Europe. Although it sings both day and night, the nocturnal refrain is considered unusual, since few other birds sing at night. The bird has enjoyed a robust literary life, first appearing in Ovid's story of Philomela, a girl who is turned into a nightingale. John Keats's "Ode to a Nightingale" celebrates the expressive power and transcendent beauty of the bird's melody. And in Oscar Wilde's "The Nightingale and the Rose," the bird impales itself on a thorn in order to transform a white rose into a red one.

scrawny with yellow skin, big red eyes, and a crooked nose, the tip of which touched her chin. Muttering to herself, she captured the nightingale and walked off with it perched on her hand. Joringel could not protest or stir from his spot, and the nightingale was gone. Later, when the woman returned, she said in a muffled voice: "Greetings, Zachiel![2] When the moon shines on the cage, set him free, Zachiel, just at the right time." And Joringel was set free. He fell to his knees before the old woman and pleaded with her to bring Jorinda back, but she told him that he would never be reunited with her and left him. He cried out, he sobbed, he moaned, but it was pointless.

"Oh! Oh! What is to become of me?" In the end, Joringel had to leave, and he reached an unfamiliar village, where he worked for a long time tending sheep. Sometimes he would walk around the castle there, but he never came too close to it. One night he had a dream about finding a blood-red flower[3] with a big, beautiful pearl in it. He picked the flower and took it to the castle. Everything he touched with the flower was disenchanted. And then he dreamed that the flower helped him get Jorinda back again.

When he awoke the next morning, he began to wander up hill and down dale, looking for the flower. Early in the morning on the ninth day of his search, he found the blood-red flower. In its center he saw a large drop of dew, as bright as the finest pearl. When he arrived at the castle and was within a hundred feet of it, he was not frozen in place but was able to keep walking right up to the gate. His heart leaped for joy, and when he touched the gate with the flower, it flew open. He walked in and passed through the courtyard, listening carefully for the sound of birds. Suddenly he was able to hear them, and he kept walking until he found the room in which the enchantress kept her seven thousand cages, and there she was feeding her birds. When she caught sight of Joringel, she flew into a real rage,

2. *"Zachiel!"* The name may be related to Zadkiel, the archangel associated with freedom, benevolence, and mercy.

3. *a blood-red flower.* In *Heinrich von Ofterdingen*, a novel by the German Romantic poet Novalis, the protagonist is in search of a blue flower that will signal redemption and renewal of the world.

Arthur Rackham, *The Fairy Tales of the Brothers Grimm*
". . . Or a screech owl."

scolding and spitting on him with all the venom she could muster. But she could not get closer than two feet from him. Instead of paying any attention to her at all, he began looking at all the birds in the cages. There were several hundred nightingales in them. How could he possibly find Jorinda among them?

While he was looking through the cages, he noticed that the old woman had snatched one little cage on the sly and was making her way to the door. In a flash he flew over to her, touched the cage and then the witch with the flower. Never again would she be able to cast spells. Jorinda was standing there, looking as beautiful as ever, and she threw her arms around him. After turning all the other birds back into girls, Joringel went back home with Jorinda, and they lived together in happiness for a long, long time.

Wanda Gág, *More Tales from Grimm*

33

The Old Man and His Grandson

The Grimms drew this story from Johann Heinrich Jung-Stilling's autobiographical novel of 1778. The poignant tale is inspired by the fourth commandment, and, like Hans Christian Andersen's "The Emperor's New Clothes," pays homage to the wisdom of children.

There once lived a very old man, so old that his eyes were failing him, his ears could no longer hear, and his knees trembled. When he sat at the table, he could hardly hold his spoon and spilled soup on the cloth—sometimes it would even run out the side of his mouth. His son and daughter-in-law found that disgusting, and they made the old man sit in a corner behind the stove. They brought him his food in an earthenware bowl, and very little on top of that. When he looked over at the table, he grew sad and his eyes filled with tears.

Arthur Rackham, *The Fairy Tales of the Brothers Grimm*

"The Old Man had to sit by himself, and he ate his food from a wooden bowl."

One day his hands were trembling so hard that he dropped his bowl, and it fell to the ground and broke. The young woman scolded him, but he did not say a word and only sighed. For a few pennies, she bought him a wooden bowl, and from then on he had to eat from it.

One day they were all at home, and the man's four-year-old grandson was on the floor playing with some little pieces of wood. "What are you making?" his father asked. "I'm making a little trough," he answered, "and Father and Mother can eat from it when I am grown." The man and his wife looked at each other, and tears came to their eyes. From then on, they made sure that the old grandfather sat and ate with them at the table. And never again did they say a word if he happened to spill a little something here and there.

The Singing, Soaring Lark

A hybrid of "Beauty and the Beast" and "East o' the Sun and West o' the Moon," the Grimms' tale about a girl's marriage to a monster and the rescue of her husband offers a splendid example of a courageous, resourceful, and loyal heroine. Not only is she willing to face the ferocious creature to whom her father has promised her, she is also willing to save her husband from a second spell of enchantment cast on him. Traveling to the ends of the earth, she appeals to nature in her quest to find her husband and bring him back home. The sun, the moon, and the four winds aid in her efforts.

The French literary critic Jacques Barchilon has observed that in the Grimms' tale, the lion as beast is "a charming surprise." In fact, he adds, "a lion as a beast that Beauty will eventually disenchant is certainly less repulsive than the indescribably fearful and dangerous beast of Mme Leprince de Beaumont's version." The Grimms' lion, he points out, probably inspired Jean Cocteau's celebrated 1946 film La Belle et la Bête *as well as Angela Carter's short story "The Courtship of Mr. Lion." As for Beauty, she never receives a name in the Grimms' tale; we know her only as the youngest of three daughters and the one most devoted to her father. If she were to be named, the attributes most fitting would be courageous, persistent, and loyal.*

There once lived a man who was planning to take a long journey. As he was bidding his three daughters farewell, he asked them what he could bring back for them. The oldest of the three asked for pearls, the second wanted diamonds, and the third said: "Father dear, I should like to have a singing, soaring lark."[1] "If I find one, you shall have it," her father replied. And he kissed all three girls and left.

When the time came for him to return home, he had already bought pearls and diamonds for the two older girls, but he had searched in vain for the singing, soaring lark that his youngest daughter wanted. That pained him no end, for she was his favorite child. The path home took him through a forest, in the midst of which was a splendid castle. Near the castle there stood a tree, and right at the very top of the tree he saw a lark, singing and soaring.

"Aha," he cried out with joy, "you've come at just the right time," and he asked his servant to climb up the tree and catch the creature. But when he walked over to the tree, a lion suddenly leaped to his feet, shook himself, and roared so loudly that the leaves in the tree began to tremble. "If anyone tries to steal my singing, soaring lark," he shouted, "I'll eat him up."

The man said: "I didn't realize that the bird was yours. Please spare my life. I'd be happy to make amends and give you plenty of gold for my release."

The lion replied: "The only way you can save yourself is to promise to give me whatever your eyes first meet when you

1. *"I should like to have a singing, soaring lark."* The daughter's request for a bird is unusual, since her counterpart in "Beauty and the Beast" tales usually asks for a rose, one that blooms in the winter. The bird's song and ability to soar through the air are emblematic of the heroine's spunk and spirit. Like the rose, which has iconic significance as a symbol of beauty and is thereby related to the girl Beauty, the bird is emblematic of the heroine's character.

return home.[2] If you agree to that, I'll spare your life and give you the bird as a gift for your daughter into the bargain."

"That could turn out to be my youngest daughter," the man said, and he refused the offer. "She loves me more than the others, and she always runs to meet me when I come back home."

The man's servant was becoming anxious, and he said: "Maybe it won't be your daughter after all. It could just as well be a cat or a dog that you first see." And so the man let himself be persuaded to accept the offer, and he took the singing, soaring lark and promised the lion to give him whatever creature he first met on returning home.

When the man arrived home and walked into his house, the first person whom he met was none other than his beloved youngest daughter. She came running up to him, hugged him and kissed him, and when she saw that he had brought back a singing, soaring lark for her, she was beside herself with joy. But her father could not share her pleasure, and he began to weep, saying. "My dear child, I paid a high price for that little bird. I had to promise you to a ferocious lion, and once he gets you, he'll tear you to pieces and gobble you up." He told her about everything that had happened and begged her not to go, no matter what. She consoled him by saying: "Father dearest, if you made a promise, you will have to keep it.[3] I am willing to go, and maybe I can appease the lion and return home safe and sound."

The next morning she got directions to the castle from her father and went on her way, feeling confident as she entered the forest. The lion was in reality an enchanted prince. By day he was a lion and all his courtiers were also lions, but at night they all returned to their natural, human form. When she arrived, they gave her a warm welcome and invited her into the castle. At nightfall, the lion was a handsome man, and the two were married in a splendid ceremony. They lived

2. *"promise to give me whatever your eyes first meet when you return home."* This passage is reminiscent of the biblical Jephthah's fatal vow that he will sacrifice the first living thing he meets when returning home (Judges 11). It is of course his daughter whom he meets first. The motif also appears in the Grimms' "Maiden without Hands."

3. *"if you made a promise, you will have to keep it."* In "The Frog King," it is the father who reminds the daughter of the importance of keeping promises. Here, the daughter incarnates the virtue of self-sacrifice as well as a sense of duty. She is the one teaching the lessons.

happily together, and all day long they slept, while at night they stayed awake.

One day her husband came to her and said: "Tomorrow your elder sister is getting married, and there's going to be a celebration at your father's house. If you would like to attend, my lions can escort you." When she arrived home, there was great rejoicing, for everyone believed that she had been torn to pieces by the lion and was no longer alive. But she told them that she was married to a very handsome man and that she was quite happy. She stayed at home for the wedding celebration and then returned to the woods. When the second daughter married and she was once again invited to the wedding, she told the lion: "I don't want to go alone this time. Why don't you come with me?" But the lion said that it was too risky. If just a ray of candlelight hit him,[4] then he would be transformed into a dove and would have to spend seven years flying with doves.

"Oh," she said, "please come with me. I'll protect you and make sure that no light falls on you." And so they left together and took their little child along with them. She had a room constructed with walls so strong and thick that no light could shine through them, and her husband was going to stay there when the candles were lit for the wedding. But the door was made of green wood, and it split and developed a crack that no one noticed.

The marriage was celebrated with great splendor, but when the procession, with all its torches and candles, passed by the hall, a mere hair's breadth of light fell on the prince, and at the very instant the light hit him, he was transformed. When she returned and started looking for him, she could not find him anywhere, and all that she could see was a white dove. The dove said to her: "I have to spend the next seven years flying around in the world. But every seven paces you walk, I am going to let fall a drop of red blood and a white

4. *If just a ray of candlelight hit him.* In "Cupid and Psyche," the story to which "Beauty and the Beast" is usually traced, Psyche drops hot wax from a candle on Cupid, and he flees. It is her curiosity, in the form of a desire to see the beloved, that accounts for his flight. Here, the beam of light that falls on the husband is purely accidental.

Arthur Rackham, *The Fairy Tales of the Brothers Grimm*

The heroine, whose trials begin when she asks for a bird and who is later aided by a dove, wears a dress with birds embroidered on it. She is escorted by the lion-beast of the tale and his entourage.

feather. They will show you the path, and if you follow my track, you will be able to break the spell."

Then the dove flew out the door, and she followed it. Every seven steps a drop of red blood and a little white feather fell to the ground to show her the way. And so she went farther and farther into the wide world, never looking back and never pausing, and the seven years were almost over. Then she was happy, for it seemed as if they would soon be set free. But in fact they had a long way to go before it was over.

One day, while she was following the dove, not a single feather fell to the ground and there wasn't a drop of red blood anywhere, and when she looked up, the dove had disappeared. And since she was quite certain that human beings would not be able to help her, she climbed up to the sun[5] and said: "You shine into every nook and cranny. Have you seen a white dove anywhere?" "No, I haven't," the sun said, "but I'm going to give you a little box that you can open if you ever get into trouble."

She thanked the sun and kept going until evening, and when she saw the moon, she asked: "You shine all night long over hill and dale. Have you seen a white dove anywhere?" "No, I haven't," the moon replied, "but I'm going to give you this egg, which I want you to break if you ever get into trouble."

She thanked the moon and kept going until the night wind began rising up and blowing in her direction. She said to the wind: "You blow over all the trees and under every leaf. Have you seen a white dove anywhere?" "No, I haven't," the night wind said. "But I'll ask the three other winds if they have seen a white dove." The east wind and the west wind said that they had seen nothing, but the south wind said: "I saw the white dove, and it flew over to the Red Sea and turned back into a lion, for the seven years were up. The lion is fighting a dragon, and the dragon is an enchanted princess." The night wind said to her: "I'm going to give you some advice. Go over to the Red Sea and there, on the right bank, you will find

5. *she climbed up to the sun.* In many tales, young women make journeys to the sun, the moon, and the winds or stars. These cosmic excursions produce dresses or objects that are tendered as bribes to a false bride in exchange for the chance to arrange an intimate meeting with a prince. The sun, the moon, and the stars also appear in fairy tales where the heroine is less adventurous. Furrypelts, for example, demands dresses that are as golden as the sun, as silvery as the moon, and as glittering as the stars.

some tall reeds growing. Count them, and then cut down the eleventh one and use it to smite the dragon. If you do that, the lion will be able to vanquish it, and both will return to their human forms. Then turn around, and you will find a griffin on the shore of the Red Sea. Climb up on its back with your beloved. The bird will carry you back home across the sea. I'm going to give you a nut which you should drop while you're flying over the sea. It will sprout, and out of the water will rise a huge nut tree which the griffin can rest on, because if it doesn't have a chance to rest, it won't have the strength to carry you across the sea. If you forget to drop the nut, the bird will let you fall into the sea."[6]

She went and she found everything was as the night wind had told her. She counted the reeds on the shore, cut down the eleventh one, and when she used it to smite the dragon, the lion was able to vanquish it. And then both returned to their human form. But as soon as the princess, who had been the dragon, was disenchanted, she took the youth by the arm, climbed on the griffin's back, and rode off with him. The poor girl had wandered so far, and now she was all alone. She sat down and cried.[7] But finally she summoned her courage and said: "I'll keep going as far as the wind blows and as long as the rooster crows, until I find him at last." And she covered great distances until she finally reached the castle where the two were living. There she heard that there was going to be a feast to celebrate the marriage of the two. But she said: "God will help me,"[8] and she opened the little box that the sun had given her. In it was a dress that shone like the sun itself. She removed it from the box, put it on, and went to the castle. Everyone there, including the bride, looked at her with astonishment, and the bride liked the dress so much that she thought it would make a good wedding dress. She asked if it might be for sale.[9] "Not for money or gold," she replied, "but for flesh and blood."

6. *"If you forget to drop the nut, the bird will let you fall into the sea."* Usually a warning as explicit as this one goes unheeded and the hero or heroine must face the consequences. But given the perpetual bad luck of this heroine, she is exempt from the usual course of events.

7. *she sat down and cried.* It is not uncommon for even the most enterprising hero or heroine to sit down and have a good cry. The weeping is emblematic of the grief and sadness they feel, and it gives the character an opportunity to pause before moving on to a new phase of action. Since fairy tales habitually externalize inner states, the weeping is the only truly significant way to capture the depth of the character's sorrow or distress.

8. *"God will help me."* Despite the fact that the tale relies on magic, the Grimms included several religious allusions, with one at the end of the story referring to God's lifting of the spell. The overlay of piety seems out of place in a narrative about dragons, cosmic helpers, and dresses that shine like the sun.

9. *She asked if it might be for sale.* The true bride is often able to lure the false bride into a bargain that will allow her access to her lost husband. The objects she has are often made of gold, which arouses the desire for wealth and plays to the false bride's cupidity.

The bride asked what she meant by that, and she said: "Let me sleep for one night in the chamber where your groom is staying." The bride was unwilling, but she really wanted the dress, and so she finally consented, but a servant had slipped the prince a sleeping potion. At night when the youth was sleeping, she was taken into his bedchamber. She sat at his bedside and said: "I followed you for seven years, and I went to the sun, the moon, and the four winds to find you. I helped you in the battle with the dragon. Have you forgotten me completely?"

The prince was sleeping so soundly that he thought that the wind was just stirring in the branches of the fir trees. At daybreak, she was escorted out and had to give up the dress of gold. When she had failed once again, she became despondent and went out to the meadow, where she sat down and cried. While she was there, she remembered the egg that the moon had given her. She cracked it open and out came a mother hen with twelve chicks, all completely golden. They ran in circles, cheeped, and crawled under their mother's wings, and you can't imagine a more charming sight. Then she got up and herded the hen and her chicks across the meadow until she came to the window of the bride, who was so enchanted by the sight of the little chicks that she came right down and asked if they were for sale. "Not for money or gold, but for flesh and blood. Let me spend one night in the chamber where the groom is sleeping." The bride consented and was planning to deceive her as she had the night before. When the prince went to bed, he asked his servant about the rustling and murmuring that he had heard the night before. The servant told him how he had been forced to give him a sleeping potion because a poor girl was secretly spending the night in his room. Tonight he had been told to give him the potion again.

The prince said: "Pour the drink out behind my bed." At night the girl was escorted in, and when she began to talk about her sad plight, he recognized the voice of his beloved wife. He jumped up and said: "Now I am truly set free. It's as if I'd been dreaming, for a strange princess bewitched me so that I would forget you. But at just the right moment God has lifted the spell." That night they slipped away from the castle secretly, for they were afraid of the princess's father, who was a wizard. They climbed on the griffin's back, and he flew them over the Red Sea, and while they were flying across it, she dropped a nut down, and a tall nut tree rose up. The bird rested in its branches, and then it brought them back home, where they found their child who had grown up and become a handsome lad. And they lived happily until the end of their days.

The Goose Girl

Widely disseminated in European countries, "The Goose Girl" takes the heroine from home to a new family, where she must unmask a pretender to the throne and reestablish her identity as true bride and heir to the throne. The goose girl rises to the challenges of deceptions and betrayals, finding a way to give voice to her complaint. In place of the tests of humility and compassion found in tales about boy heroes, "The Goose Girl" shows us a heroine who suffers a series of humiliations at the hands of a servant and bides her time. But she is also a girl who a deep connection to nature—with her horse Falada, with the geese that endow her with a epithet, and with the winds that aid her in diverting Conrad.

Like many stories pitting a false bride against a true bride, this tale contrasts the trickery of the maid, or false bride, with the virtue of the princess, or true bride. While the goose girl seems, at first blush, to lack the powers of her male counterpart in "Roswal and Lillian" (the tale of a prince who, although deceived by his steward, triumphs over his adversary in a tournament) and appears to exercise little more than patience, the spells she casts reveal that she has a powerful connection to nature. When Conrad begins to make a nuisance of himself, she calls on the winds to help her divert him, and they come to her rescue. Although her connection with Falada, the talking horse, is somewhat cryptic, it is clear that the goose girl understands the importance of beheading the animal so that some creature will utter the words she has sworn not to speak.

In "Germany, a Winter Fairy Tale," the poet Heinrich Heine expressed the profound effect the story had on him as a child:

> *"How my heart used to beat when the old nurse told how*
> *The king's daughter, in days now olden,*
> *Sat alone on the desert heath,*
> *While glistened her tresses so golden.*
>
> *Her business was to tend the geese*
> *As a goose girl, and when at nightfall*
> *She drove the geese home again through the gate*
> *Her tears would in piteous plight fall."*

Wronged by a cruel and arrogant impostor, the goose girl does not seek revenge. Rather she retreats into nature, developing her powers to ward off threats (Conrad's advances) at a less momentous level, and finally builds a relationship that helps to uncover the truth and restore her to her lofty social rank. The chambermaid's punishment is self-imposed: the usurper pronounces her own sentence and becomes the source of her own undoing.

There once lived an old queen whose husband had died some years back, and she had a beautiful daughter. When the princess was of the right age, she was betrothed to a prince who lived far away. The time of the marriage drew near, and the princess was preparing to travel to the distant kingdom. Her mother packed all manner of precious utensils and vessels, jewelry and goblets, gold and silver. She loved her daughter with all her heart and wanted to give her everything she needed for a royal dowry. She made sure there was a chambermaid to accompany the bride on her journey and to deliver her to the groom. Both had horses for the journey. The princess's horse was named Falada[1] and was able to talk.

When it was time to part, the mother went to her bedroom, took a little knife, and cut her finger until it bled. Then she held a little white handkerchief under her finger while three drops of blood[2] fell on it. She gave the handkerchief to her daughter with the words: "Dear child, take good care of this. You will need it on your journey."

Mother and daughter bid farewell with great sorrow in their hearts. The princess put the handkerchief in her bodice, mounted her horse, and rode off to her betrothed. After they had been on the road for an hour, she felt a fierce thirst and told her maid: "If you dismount here, you can take the cup that you've brought along and get me some water from this brook. I'm really thirsty."

"If you want something to drink," the maid replied, "go get it yourself. You can just go to the brook, bend over, and get a drink. I'm not going to wait on you."

The princess was so thirsty that she dismounted, bent over the brook, and drank from it. And so she wasn't able to drink from the golden cup[3] that the maid had with her. "Dear Lord," she sighed. The three drops of blood replied: "If your mother knew what was happening, it would break her heart." But the princess was not proud; she got back on her horse and said nothing.

The two rode on for several miles, but it was a hot day and the sun was beating down on them. The princess was getting thirsty again. When they came to a stream, she called her maid once more and said: "Can you dismount and bring me

1. *Falada.* The Grimms connect the name of the horse with Valantin, Valantis, or Valatin, the name of Roland's horse in the *Chanson de Roland.* Tacitus reports that horses were thought to predict the future, and in many northern countries they were hung on walls to ward off enemies or the plague.

2. *three drops of blood.* In "Snow White," the three drops of blood that fall on the snow are connected with birth, the arrival of a daughter, rather than with separation and departure. The handkerchief with the three drops of blood represents a symbolic bond between mother and daughter, assuring the survival of the daughter so long as the mother is alive. A French version of the tale elevates the significance of the handkerchief by calling the tale "The Cloth with the Three Drops of Blood."

3. *the golden cup.* The gold of the princess's hair will later reprise the gold of the cup, signs of the princess's aristocratic descent and beauty. The golden cup figures in an episode displaying the princess's degradation; the golden hair comes into play in an episode exhibiting the princess's empowerment.

some water in my golden cup?" She was willing to overlook the cruel words spoken earlier by the maid.

The maid replied even more arrogantly than before: "If you're thirsty, go ahead and get a drink. I'm not going to wait on you."

The princess was so thirsty that she got off her horse, sat down by the edge of the stream, wept, and said: "Dear God!" And once again the drops of blood replied: "If your mother knew what was happening, it would break her heart."

The princess bent down so far to get a drink from the stream that the handkerchief with the three drops of blood slipped out of her bodice and fell into the water. She was feeling so anxious that she never even noticed it, but the maid saw the whole thing and was elated that she now had power over the bride, who, without those drops of blood, had become weak and powerless. When the princess was about to get back on her horse Falada, the maid said: "I'm going to ride on Falada, and you can have my old nag." The princess couldn't do anything about it. With harsh words, the maid ordered her to remove her royal clothing and to put on her own plain ones. Finally she had to swear on a stack of bibles that she would never breathe a word of this to anyone at court. If she had not made this pledge, the maid would have killed her on the spot. Falada saw everything and remembered it well.

The chambermaid climbed up on Falada, and the true bride mounted the wretched nag, and they rode on until they finally arrived at the royal palace. There was great rejoicing over their arrival, and the prince ran out to meet them and helped the maid dismount, for he was sure that she was his bride. He escorted her up the stairs, and the true princess was left standing down below. The old king was looking out the window and noticed that someone was waiting in the courtyard. He could see how fine, delicate, even beautiful she was,[4] and he went straight to the royal apartment to ask the bride about the girl who had arrived with her and was now waiting down in the courtyard. "Oh, I met her on the way here and

4. *He could see how fine, delicate, even beautiful she was.* The "old queen" and the "old king" form a counterpart to the younger couple in the tale. The old king's attentiveness to the child seems to hint that the tale has an oedipal dimension, with the daughter leaving her mother and catching the attention of the "old king" before she moves on, matures, and marries the prince.

brought her along to keep me company. Give her some work to keep her busy." But the old king didn't have any work for her, and he couldn't think of any, so he said: "There's a young fellow here who tends the geese. She can help him out." And so the true bride had to help tend geese with a boy named Conrad.

Before long the false bride said to the young king: "Dearest husband, I beg you to do me a favor."

"Gladly," he replied.

"Send for the knacker[5] and have him cut off the head of the horse that brought me here. On the way here that beast really got on my nerves." The truth was that she was afraid that the horse might start talking and tell everyone how she had behaved around the princess.

And so the day finally came when the faithful Falada was going to die. The true princess learned what was going to happen, and she made a deal in secret with the knacker. She would give him some money if he did her a small favor. In town there was a large dark gateway through which she passed every morning and evening with the geese. She asked him to nail Falada's head to the wall of the gateway so that she would be able to see it every day. The knacker promised to do that, and when he cut off the horse's head, he nailed it to the wall of the gateway.

Early in the morning, when the princess and Conrad were driving the flock beneath the gateway, she would say as she was passing by:

"Alas, poor Falada, hanging up there."

And the horse's head would reply:

"Princess, princess, down and out,
If your mother found this out,[6]
There's no doubt—her heart would break."

5. *"Send for the knacker."* In an earlier age, knackers were prominent figures, men who bought useless animal carcasses or slaughtered animals, usually horses, that were no longer productive. Dealing with death, they were often considered unclean and uncouth. The loss of the handkerchief, the clothes, and finally the horse leaves the goose girl bereft of her possessions and identity.

6. *"If your mother found this out."* Falada, like the handkerchief, ventriloquizes the grief of the mother.

George Cruikshank, *German Popular Stories*

The goose girl summons the winds to send Conrad's hat into the air, while she combs her golden hair out in the meadows where she is tending geese until the time that her royal descent becomes known.

The two continued on their way out of town, and they drove the geese into the country. When they came to a meadow, the princess sat down and let her hair down, which was like pure gold. When Conrad saw how her hair was glittering, he was fascinated and wanted to pull a few strands out for himself, but she chanted the words:

> "Blow, winds, blow![7]
> Send Conrad's hat into the air,
> Flying here and flying there.
> While I comb and braid my hair.
> Blow, winds, blow!"

7. *"Blow, winds, blow!"* The princess's chant is, as Ruth B. Bottigheimer points out, something like a spell that she casts. The girl's power derives from her "queenship over nature, which one may consider a legacy from her mother." Like Cinderella, who is able to summon birds to help her and who acquires magic gifts from a tree, the goose girl seems closely allied with nature.

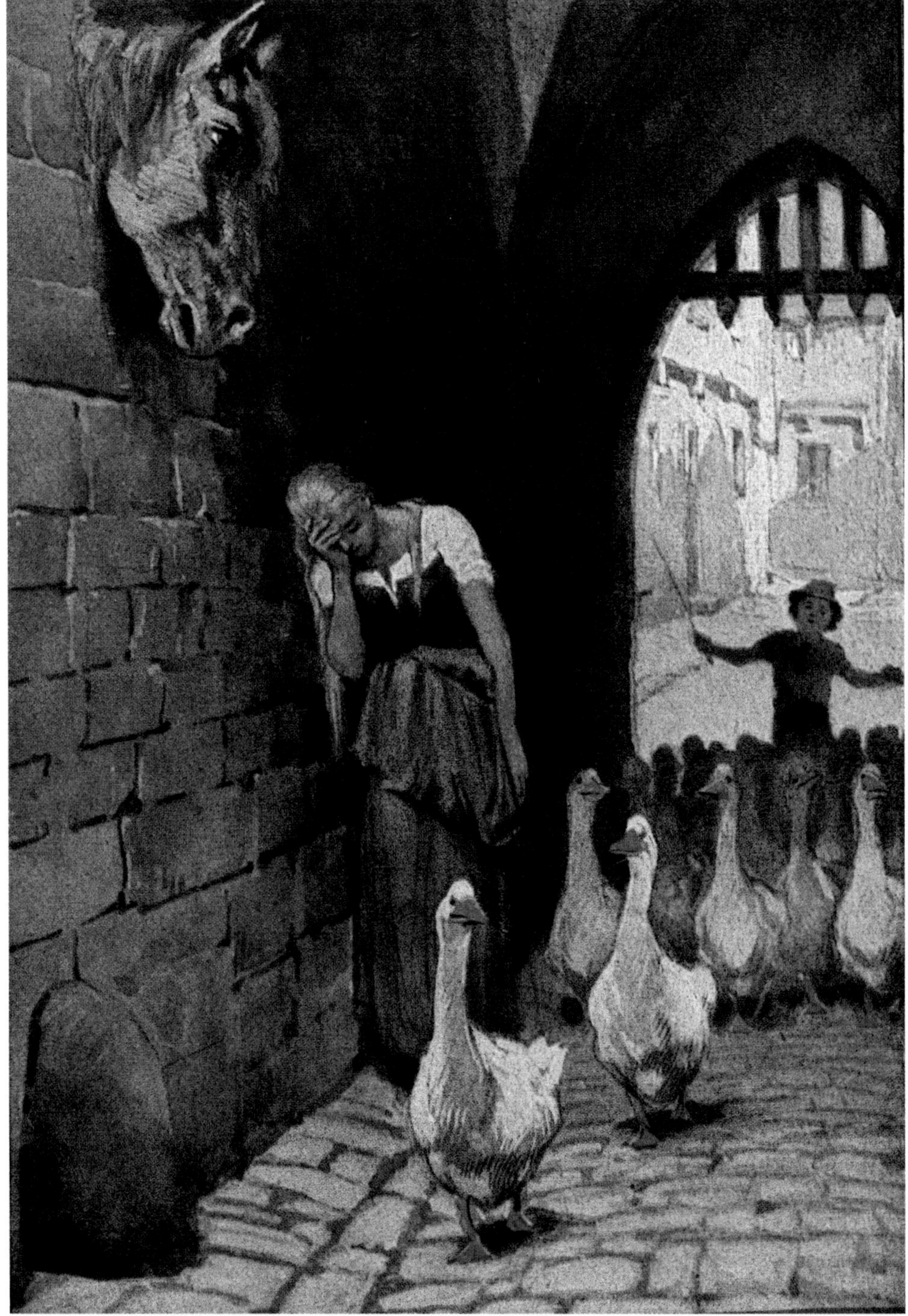

Paul Hey, *Die schönsten Kindermärchen der Brüder Grimm*

The head of the horse Falada watches as the princess suffers the humiliation of tending geese and taking them out to the meadow with Conrad.

A wind came up so strong that it sent Conrad's hat flying into the air and he had to run after it. By the time he returned, she had finished combing her hair and had put it up in a bun so that he couldn't pull out a single strand of it. That made him angry, and he wouldn't talk to her. And so they tended the geese until evening, when they returned home.

The next morning, they were driving the geese out through the dark gateway again, and the maiden said:

"Alas, poor Falada, hanging up there."

And Falada replied:

"Princess, princess, down and out,
If your mother found this out,
There's no doubt—her heart would break."

Out on the meadow she sat down in the grass again and began to comb her hair. Conrad saw it and wanted to grab some of it, but she quickly began chanting:

"Blow, winds, blow!
Send Conrad's hat into the air,
Flying here and flying there.
While I comb and braid my hair.
Blow, winds, blow!"

The wind began to blow, and it sent Conrad's little hat into the air so that he had to go running after it. And when he returned, she had managed to put her hair up in a bun so that he couldn't grab any of it. And so they tended the geese until night fell.

In the evening, after they had returned home, Conrad went to the old king and said: "I don't want to tend geese any longer with that girl."

Kay Nielsen, *Hansel and Gretel and Other Stories by the Brothers Grimm*

A personified blast of wind blows Conrad's hat into the distance, forcing him to run after it, while the goose girl combs her golden tresses.

"Why not?" asked the old king.

"Oh, she's just so annoying."

The king ordered him to explain what was going on between the two of them. Conrad told him that in the morning, when the two of them would drive geese under the dark gateway, there was a horse's head nailed to the wall. The girl always spoke to it and would say:

> "Alas, poor Falada, hanging up there."

And the horse's head would reply:

> "Princess, princess, down and out,
> If your mother found this out,
> There's no doubt—her heart would break."

Conrad told the king about everything that had taken place on the meadow and how he would have to go chasing after his hat.

The old king ordered Conrad to go ahead and herd the geese the next day. But in the morning he hid behind the dark gateway and heard how the girl would talk to Falada's head. Then he went out to the meadow with the two of them and hid behind a bush. There he saw with his own eyes the goose girl and the goose boy coming along with the herd. After a while the girl sat down, undid her braids, and her hair glittered like gold. Then she started chanting:

> "Blow, winds, blow!
> Send Conrad's hat into the air,
> Flying here and flying there.
> While I comb and braid my hair.
> Blow, winds, blow!"

A gust of wind came along and carried Conrad's hat off so swiftly that he had to run after it. The maid then started quietly combing and braiding her hair. The king saw the whole thing, and he left without anyone noticing him. When the goose girl returned home in the evening, he summoned her and asked why she had done all those things.

"I can't possibly tell you that, and I can't pour my feelings out to anyone, for I swore on a stack of bibles never to tell anybody. I would have been killed otherwise."

The king implored her to tell him more, and he wouldn't stop asking, but it was no use, he couldn't get anything out of her. Finally he said: "Maybe you can't reveal anything to me, but how about talking to this old iron stove?"[8] and then he walked away.

The princess crawled into the iron stove and started weeping and wailing. She poured her feelings out and said: "Here I sit, abandoned by the whole world, even though I'm the daughter of a king. A false maid forced me to remove my royal clothing, and now she has taken my place with my bridegroom. And here I am, forced to do menial work as a goose girl. If my mother knew about this, her heart would break in two."

The old king was standing outside with his ear to the stovepipe, and he heard every word she said. He came back into the room and told the girl to get out of the oven. He ordered her to appear in royal garments, and she was so beautiful that it seemed like a miracle had taken place. The old king summoned his son and revealed to him that he was with the wrong bride. The true bride, the former goose girl, was standing right there before him; the other one was just a chambermaid. The young king was elated when he saw that his real bride was both beautiful and virtuous.

A great festival was arranged, and all the king's friends—indeed everyone in the land—were invited. The bridegroom sat at the head of the table, with the princess to one side of him, the maid to the other. The maid was dazzled by the princess and didn't recognize her with all her radiant jewelry.

8. *"how about talking to this old iron stove?"* The stove, as inanimate object, is exempt from the oath taken by the princess. Connected to the hearth or center of the household, the stove might also be linked, through its domestic warmth, to a reassuring maternal presence. "Oven-confession" (*Ofenbeichte*) is a term used in children's games, when a secret is articulated but not communicated.

After they had feasted and everyone was in good spirits, the old king put a riddle to the maid: What would a woman deserve if she had betrayed a gentleman in this way and that? He went on to tell the whole story of what had happened, and then he asked: "What punishment does this woman deserve?" The false bride said: "She deserves to be stripped naked[9] and put into a barrel studded on the inside with sharp nails. Then two white horses[10] should be harnessed up to the barrel and made to drag it through the streets until she is dead."

"You're the one I've been talking about, and that will be the punishment carried out on you!" the king said. And while the punishment was being imposed, the young king married the true bride, and both ruled the kingdom in peace and joy.

9. *"She deserves to be stripped naked."* The maid chooses her own punishment and thus makes herself, rather than those who inflict the punishment, guilty of vicious retribution. These kinds of vivid punishments are not unusual in folklore from many different cultures.

10. *two white horses.* It is not by chance that the false bride chooses horses, doubles of Falada, to inflict the punishment.

36

The Water of Life[1]

1. *The Water of Life.* The Fountain of Youth has been the source of imaginative inspiration for centuries. Herodotus identified Ethiopia as its location. Alexander the Great was said to have crossed the Land of Darkness to find the spring that would restore youth. In *The Travels of Sir John Mandeville*, the Fountain of Youth was located in India. For the Spanish, the Caribbean island of Bimini became a site of wealth, prosperity, and waters that could endow men with eternal youth. Ponce de Léon's name was associated with the Fountain of Youth, even though he never mentioned the search specifically in his travel writings. Jorge Luis Borges's short story "The Immortal" describes the search for the Fountain of Death by immortals who are weary of living forever.

he Grimms created a composite tale from various sources and included variant forms of this tale in notes to their collection. One version did not include a princess and ended with a contest among the three brothers, with the youngest crossing a blanket made of gold to emerge as winner. In another version a fisherman plays the role of the dwarf. And in a third the youngest brother has to slay a dragon with seven heads in order to acquire the Water of Life from a beautiful princess. Legends about rejuvenating waters are legion, and this tale captures the ambivalence of sons who want to prolong the life of their father but are also eager to inherit his wealth and kingdom.

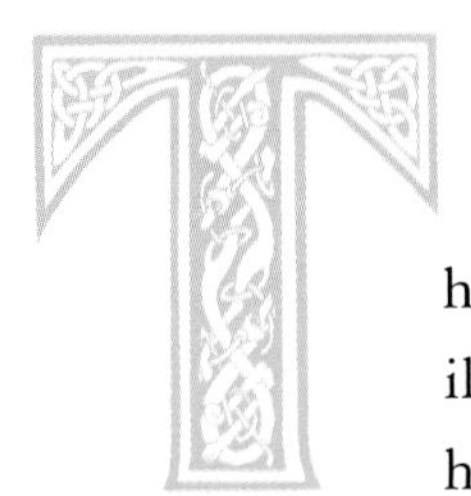

here once lived a king, and one day he fell so ill that no one in the kingdom believed that he would recover. His three sons were deeply saddened. They spent some time in the gardens of the palace and were weeping when an old man appeared and asked why they were so troubled. They told him that their father, the king, was so ill that he would surely die, for nothing could heal him.

"I know a remedy," the old man said. "It is the Water of Life. If he could drink it, he would regain his health, but it's difficult to find."

The eldest son said, "I will find a way." And he went to see the dying king and asked for permission to seek the Water of Life, since that alone would cure him.

"No," the king said. "It's far too dangerous a task, and I would rather die." The son pleaded for so long that the king finally gave his consent. The prince was all the while thinking, "If I find the Water, then my father will love me the best, and I shall inherit the entire kingdom."

And so he departed. After riding for a while, he met a dwarf who called out to him, "What's the rush?"

"You stupid twerp," the prince said contemptuously.[2] "That's none of your business." And he kept riding. The dwarf was furious and put a curse on him. The prince rode onward through a mountain gorge, and the farther he traveled, the more narrow the pass became until finally there was so little space that he was trapped. It was impossible to turn around or to dismount, and so he found himself wedged in.

At home, the ailing king waited in vain for his son, but he did not return. And so the second son said, "Father, let me ride out to find the Water." He thought to himself, "If my brother is dead, then I will inherit the kingdom." At first the king did not want to let him go, but in the end he gave in. The prince took the same route as his brother and met the same dwarf, who stopped and asked why he was in such a hurry. "You stupid twerp," said the prince. "That's none of your business." And he traveled on without looking back once. The dwarf cursed him too, and he ended up in a mountain gorge, trapped like his brother and unable to move. That's what happens to the proud.

2. *the prince said contemptuously.* Pride, arrogance, and rude behavior are often punished in fairy tales. Old women, dwarfs, and figures in disguise test the generosity and kindness of male and female figures alike. It is often the two eldest in a trio of siblings who fail the test of hospitality and kindness, while the youngest shares a crust of bread, gives directions, or engages in other ways with the humble characters encountered on the road.

When the second son also failed to return, the youngest offered to go out into the world and bring back the Water. Eventually the king let him go too. When he met the dwarf and was asked why he was in such a rush, he stopped to talk and answer his question. "I am searching for the Water of Life, for my father is dying."

"Do you know where to find it?"

"No," the prince replied.

"Because you have behaved kindly and not used the haughty words of your faithless brothers, I am going to give you some advice about how to find the Water of Life. You'll find it gushing in a fountain set in the courtyard of an enchanted castle. You will never make it in unless I give you an iron wand and two loaves of bread. Strike the iron gate of the castle three times with the wand, and it will fly open. Inside you will find two lions with gaping jaws, but if you toss a loaf of bread to each, they will quiet down. Then you will have to hurry and fetch some of the Water of Life before the clock strikes twelve, otherwise the gate will shut and you will be locked in."

The prince thanked him, took the wand and the bread, and went on his way. When he arrived at the castle, everything was just as the dwarf said it would be. The gate flew open at the third stroke of the wand, and when he had pacified the lions with the bread, he walked into the castle and found a majestic hall, with enchanted princes seated in it. He took the rings from their fingers, and picked up a sword and a loaf of bread and took them with him. Then he reached a room in which a beautiful maiden was standing. She was overjoyed when she saw him, kissed him, and told him that he had set her free and now had earned her entire kingdom as his reward. If he returned in a year, then they would be able to celebrate their marriage. She also told him where to find the fountain with the Water of Life and reminded him to hurry and draw the water before the clock struck midnight.

The prince walked farther into the castle and found a room with a beautiful freshly made bed in it. He was so tired that he decided to rest for a while. He lay down and fell asleep. When he woke up, the clock was striking a quarter to twelve. He jumped up in a panic, ran back to the fountain, and drew water from it with a cup that he found nearby. Then he raced off as fast as he could. The clock struck twelve just as he was passing through the iron gate, and the gate slammed shut with such force that it took off a piece of his heel.[3]

All the same, he was glad that he had found the Water of Life. On the way home, he met the dwarf once more, and this time he said, after seeing the sword and the bread: "You've succeeded in obtaining some real treasures. You'll be able to defeat an entire army with that sword, and the bread will always be there, no matter how much of it you eat."

But the prince didn't want to return home to his father without his brothers, and he said: "My dear dwarf, can't you tell me where my two brothers are? They set out in search of the Water of Life before me, and they never returned."

"They are trapped between two mountains," said the dwarf. "I used a spell to keep them there because they were so proud." The prince pleaded with the dwarf until finally he agreed to release them but not without a warning. "Beware of them," he said. "They have evil hearts."

When the prince saw his brothers, he was thrilled to be reunited with them. He told them about his adventures and how he had found the Water of Life and was now bringing back a cupful of it, as well as about how he had rescued a beautiful princess, who was going to wait a year for him and then they were going to marry and he would rule over a vast kingdom. They rode on together for a while and reached a country plagued by war and famine. The situation was so dire that the king was sure he would die before long. The prince went to him and gave him the bread so that he could feed all his people and relieve their hunger. The prince even

3. *a piece of his heel.* The loss of a part of the heel may be a fleeting allusion to Achilles's heel and how that body part became a source of vulnerability. In Greek mythology, Achilles's mother, Thetis, took her son to the River Styx and dipped his body into the waters to make him invincible. Holding him by the heel, she left that body part vulnerable when the waters failed to wash over it. Achilles dies from a poisoned arrow lodged in his heel. The prince loses a piece of his heel but survives the perfidy of his brothers.

Arthur Rackham, *The Fairy Tales of the Brothers Grimm*

"Good Dwarf, can you not tell me where my brothers are?"

gave him the sword with which he was able to vanquish the enemy armies and live in peace and tranquillity. Then the prince took back his sword and his loaf, and the brothers rode onward. They passed through two more countries plagued by famine and war, and each time the prince gave the kings his magical bread and sword. And so, in all, he saved three kingdoms.

Next they boarded a ship and sailed across the seas. During the voyage the two elder brothers plotted against the younger: "Our younger brother has found the Water of Life without our help. That means that our father will turn over to him the kingdom to which we are entitled, and he will rob us of any possible happiness." They longed for revenge and figured out how to do away with him.[4] They waited until he was fast asleep one day, and then they poured the Water of Life into their own cup and filled his with bitter salt water.

When they arrived back home, the youngest brother brought the ailing king his cup, expecting him to recover once he drank from it. But no sooner had the king taken a sip from the cup than he became more ill than ever. While he was bemoaning his condition, the two elder sons came in and blamed the youngest for trying to poison him. They brought in the true Water of Life and handed it to the king. All he took was a sip, and he could feel his illness melting away. Suddenly he was as strong and healthy as he had been in his youth.

The two brothers spoke to the youngest and made fun of him, adding: "You may have found the Water of Life, but you did all the work and we reaped the rewards. You should have been smarter and kept your eyes open. We took it away from you on the boat, while you were sleeping. In a year's time, one of us will go to claim the beautiful princess. And don't you dare say a word, for Father won't believe you no matter what. If you say so much as a single word, you're done for, but if you keep quiet, we'll let you live."

4. *and figured out how to do away with him.* The treachery of the brothers evokes the story of Joseph and his brothers, who are also anxious about their patrimony and throw Joseph down a well and then sell him into slavery.

5. *"The king has ordered me to kill you."* Like Snow White, the prince is so appealing that he softens the heart of the huntsman, who releases him rather than murdering him.

The old king was angry with his youngest son and was sure that he had tried to kill him. He summoned his ministers and, in secret, had them sentence the boy to be shot.

One day the prince, who suspected no evil, went out hunting, and the king's huntsman was ordered to accompany him. Once they were alone out in the forest, the king's hunter looked so sorrowful that the prince asked him, "My dear huntsman, what is the matter?"

The huntsman replied, "I can't tell you, and yet I should."

The prince said, "Speak up, and, no matter what it is, I will forgive you."

"Well," said the huntsman. "The king has ordered me to kill you."[5]

The prince was stunned and said, "My dear huntsman, let me live. I'm going to give you my royal garments, and I will take your lowly clothing in exchange."

"Gladly," the huntsman said. "I would never have been able to shoot you in any case." The two exchanged clothing, and the huntsman returned home. The prince traveled deeper into the forest.

Sometime later, three wagons loaded with gold and precious stones pulled up at the castle. They had been sent to the youngest son by the three kings who had defeated their enemies with the prince's sword and fed their people with his bread. They had been delivered as a token of gratitude. The old king thought to himself, "Is it possible that my son was innocent?" He said to his courtiers, "If only he were still alive. How wrong I was to have him killed."

"He is still alive," the huntsman said. "I didn't have the heart to carry out your command."

A weight fell from the king's heart, and he proclaimed in all the kingdoms that his son was free to return and that he was back in favor with the king.

Meanwhile, the princess had built a glittering road made of gold, and it led right up to her castle. She told her guards that whoever came riding straight down the middle of that road would be the right man for her and should be allowed to enter. But anyone who rode on the side of the road would not be the right man and should not be admitted.

When the year was almost up, the eldest brother decided to get a head start and to try to pass himself off as her savior. He was hoping to win her as his wife and get the kingdom in the bargain. He rode forth, and when he saw the beautiful golden path leading to the castle, he thought, "It would be a shame to ride on such a beautiful road." And he veered off the road to the right and rode alongside it. When he reached the gate, the guards told him that he was not the right man and that he would be better off leaving.

Soon thereafter the second prince started out, and when he reached the golden road and his horse set a hoof down on it, he thought: "It would be a real shame to put nicks in this road." And he veered off the road to the left and rode alongside it. When he arrived at the gate, the guards told him that he was not the right man and that he would be better off leaving.

When an entire year had passed, the third son decided to leave the forest, travel to his beloved, and forget his sorrows with her. He rode off and was so absorbed in thoughts about how he would soon be with her that he did not even see the golden road. His horse rode straight down the path, and when he reached the gate, it flew open. The princess welcomed him joyfully and told him that he was her savior and lord of the kingdom. There was much rejoicing when the marriage was celebrated. After the wedding was over, the princess told him that his father had sent for him and pardoned him. He rode home and revealed to his father how he had kept quiet about the brothers and how they had betrayed him. The old king was ready to punish them, but they had already boarded a ship and sailed away. And they never returned as long as they lived.[6]

6. *they never returned as long as they lived.* The two evil brothers are spared the punishments of Cinderella's stepsisters, whose eyes are pecked out by doves.

37

The Poor Miller's Boy and the Cat

Walking the tightrope between adult entertainment and primer for children, this tale, with its innocent boy and seductive feline, is filled with possibilities for bawdy improvisations, but it also reveals how a fellow who discharges the tasks assigned to him can marry a princess and live in a castle of silver and gold.

Ruth B. Bottigheimer points out that "nearly every image and metaphor in 'The Poor Miller's Boy and the Cat' can be read erotically." She points to the use of the term "reward," the many references to clothing and a state of undress, and the delayed gratification at work in the tale. A resourceful raconteur would surely know how to use body language, verbal flourishes, and conspiratorial winks to create a tale guaranteed to keep the attention of an adult audience. And yet we are also in the realm of the simpleton who must, against the odds, win for himself a bride and a kingdom. With its plainspoken moral—"So don't let people tell you that a simpleton will never amount to anything in life"—the tale reassures small children that, even if they are the target of constant jokes, they will one day rise above their lowly station to earn the rewards they deserve.

There was once a miller who had neither wife nor children. He lived in his mill with three hired hands,[1] who had been with him for a long time. One day, he said to them: "I'm getting old, and it won't be long before I'm ready to retire and just sit by the fire. I want the three of you to go out into the world and see who can bring back the finest horse. The victor will get my mill, as long as he agrees to take care of me until my death."

The youngest of the hired hands was an apprentice, and the two others thought that he was really stupid and didn't deserve to have a chance at getting the mill. It turned out that he didn't even want it. But all three started out together, and when they arrived at the first village, the two of them said to stupid Hans: "Why don't you stay here? You're never going to find a horse." But Hans decided to go with them, and when night fell they found a cave where they could all sleep. The two clever ones waited until Hans had fallen asleep.[2] Then they got up and ran off, leaving him all alone. They thought that they had made a pretty smart move, but—just you wait—better not start gloating yet!

When the sun rose and Hans awoke, he was lying in a dark cave. He looked around and cried out: "Dear God, where in the world am I?" He got up, scrambled his way out of the cave, and went into the woods. "Here I am, all alone and on my own," he thought. "How will I ever find that horse?"

As he was walking along, deep in thought, he met a little tabby cat, who turned to him and asked in a friendly manner: "Hans, where are you going?"

"Oh, never mind, there's no way you can help me."

"I happen to know just what you're looking for," the little cat said. "You're trying to find a really fine-looking horse. If you come with me and serve me faithfully for seven years, I

1. *with three hired hands.* Another version recorded by the Grimms tells of a man with three *sons*, each of whom competes to bring back the finest horse. The two older brothers are so contemptuous of their younger brother that they return home with a blind horse and a lame horse. When the youngest (Dummling) wins the first competition, the brothers demand a second, then a third. The brothers must bring back the best shirt, and finally, the best loaf of bread. The tale further relates the youngest son's adventures with his bride, who was once a turtle.

2. *The two clever ones waited until Hans had fallen asleep.* Reminiscent of the scene in which the parents of Hansel and Gretel abandon their children, this tale also resonates, like many tales of three brothers, with the story of Joseph and his brothers.

will give you one that is more beautiful than anything you have ever seen."

"Now there's an unusual cat," Hans thought. "But I'd like to see if what she says is true."

The cat took him to her enchanted castle, where there were all kinds of other cats who were her servants. They leaped and bounded up and down the stairs and were always cheerful and high-spirited. In the evening, when Hans and the cat sat down to have dinner, three of the kittens gave a concert. One played the double bass; another played the fiddle; and a third put a trumpet to her lips, puffed up her cheeks, and blew as

Hermann Vogel,
Kinder- und Hausmärchen gesammelt durch die Brüder Grimm

Dejected, Hans wipes the tears from his eyes while the cat offers him encouraging words about his prospects.

hard as she could. After they finished dining, the table was cleared and the cat said: "Hans, how about dancing with me?"

"No," he replied, "I don't dance with kitty cats. I never have, and I never will."

"Take him up to his bedroom," the cat said to her servants. One of them lit the way to his bedroom;[3] another took off his shoes; a third removed his stockings; and a fourth blew out the light.

The next morning the servants returned and helped him get out of bed. One put on his stockings; a second fetched his shoes; a third washed his face; and a fourth used her tail to dry his face. "That feels nice and soft," Hans said.

Hans was also given some work to do, and every day he went to chop some firewood with an ax made of silver, a saw, wedges made of silver, and a mallet of copper.[4] He stayed close to home, and he just chopped wood day in and day out. There was plenty of good food and drink, but he never saw anyone but the tabby cat and her servants.

One day the tabby cat said to him: "Go over and mow my meadow, and then get the hay ready," and she gave him a scythe made of silver and a whetstone made of gold and told him to return them in good condition when he was finished. Hans did exactly as he was told. When he finished the work, he brought the scythe, the whetstone, and the hay back home and asked the tabby whether she was ready to give him his reward.

"No, not yet," said the cat. "You still have one more task before you. Over there you'll find some building materials made of silver, an ax, a square, and a lot of other things you'll need, all made of silver. I want you to build me a cottage."[5] Hans went ahead and built the little house, and he told her he was finished, but he still didn't get his horse. The seven years had passed so quickly that it was like just half a year. Finally, the cat asked if he wanted to see her horses.

"Oh, yes," said Hans. And the cat opened the door to the little house, and lo and behold, there were twelve horses, and

3. *One of them lit the way to his bedroom.* The detailed description of how Hans retires for the night and how the cats help him undress, and then dress again, must have provided the opportunity for comic pantomime, especially in light of Hans's comment "That feels nice and soft" after one of the cats dries off his face.

4. *with an ax made of silver, a saw, wedges made of silver, and a mallet of copper.* These instruments have their counterparts in the miniature spindles, bobbins, and spinning wheels made of gold in stories about young women seeking the right marriage partner. The miniature objects often land in dough or bowls of soup. Here, the tools of the carpenter's trade are ennobled by the precious metals out of which they are made.

5. *"I want you to build me a cottage."* The "faithful service" of Hans becomes evident in his willingness to provide fuel for the fire, hay from the meadows, and shelter in the form of the cottage.

Hermann Vogel,
Kinder- und Hausmärchen gesammelt durch die Brüder Grimm

The cats pamper Hans, taking off his shoes and socks, combing his hair, and scrubbing his face.

what proud horses they were! His heart leaped for joy when he saw how sleek and shiny their coats were. The cat offered him food and drink and then said: "Go home now. I'm not going to give you your horse yet, but I will bring it to you in three days."

The cat showed Hans how to get back to the mill, and he set out on the road. Since the cat had not given him anything new to wear, he had to wear the tattered clothing in which he had arrived,[6] and everything had become way too small for him in the seven years he had spent there. When he arrived home, the two other hired hands were there. Each of them had come back with a horse, but one was blind and the other was lame. They asked him: "Hans, where is your horse?"

"It will be here in three days," he replied.

They started laughing and said: "Oh, yes, where are you going to be getting that horse? He'll turn out to be some fine animal!"

Hans went into the miller's house, but the miller said that he was too scruffy and unkempt to sit at the table. If someone walked in and saw him, it would be humiliating for him. They gave him something to eat outside, and when they went to sleep at night, the two others refused to give him a bed. He had to crawl into the place where the geese were kept and lie down on some hard straw.

When he woke up the next morning, the three days were already up, and a carriage drew up with six horses that were as sleek as they were beautiful. A servant brought a seventh horse which was the gift for the poor miller's apprentice. A dazzlingly beautiful princess stepped out of the carriage and went into the mill. The princess was none other than the little tabby cat whom poor Hans had served for seven years.

The princess asked the miller about his apprentice. The miller told her: "He's so filthy that we can't let him come into the mill. He has to stay in the place where the geese sleep."

6. *he had to wear the tattered clothing in which he had arrived.* As is customary, the youngest son returns home as a beggar, often wearing clothes that conceal the imminence of his social elevation.

Hermann Vogel,
Kinder- und Hausmärchen gesammelt durch die Brüder Grimm

The dazzlingly beautiful princess arrives at the mill with a steed to rescue the Cinderella-like Hans from abject poverty.

The princess asked him to bring out the apprentice at once. And so they went to get him, and he had to hold his overalls together to keep from exposing himself. The princess's servant unpacked splendid garments and began bathing and dressing Hans, who looked as handsome as a king as soon as he was fully clothed. Then the maiden asked to see the horses that the hired hands had brought back, the blind one and the lame one. She told her servant to bring in the seventh horse. When the miller saw it, he declared that he had never ever seen a horse like that in his land.

"And that's the one the apprentice brought back," she said.

"In that case, he gets the mill," said the miller. But the princess said that she would give him the horse and that the miller could just keep the mill for himself.[7] She took faithful Hans by the hand and got into the coach with him and drove off. First they drove to the little cottage that he had made with silver tools, and it had turned out to be a huge castle. Everything in it was made of silver and gold. Then the two married, and he was so rich, so very rich, that he had more than enough money for the rest of his life. So don't let people tell you that a simpleton will never amount to anything in life.

7. *the miller could just keep the mill for himself.* Hans becomes completely independent, without any need for an inheritance. At the beginning of the tale, we learn that he is not really invested in winning the mill—"he didn't even want it." Thus, by the end the mill becomes superfluous.

38

Four Artful Brothers

nlike stories about mothers and (step)daughters, tales about fathers and sons often describe boys leaving home to make their fortune in the wide world. If it is a trio of boys, they often stand in a relationship of rivalry, with each vying for success in ways that will enable him to return home triumphant. The quartet of sons in this tale are pitted against each other as they seek to learn a trade that will prove their superiority to the other brothers. The sons are described as "kunstreich," a German term that signals enterprising cleverness as well as artfulness. Although they fail to win the hand of the princess, they each succeed in earning half a kingdom and live happily ever after and in peace with their father and brothers.

J. K. Rowling's "Story of Three Brothers" in Harry Potter and the Deathly Hallows *is told to wizard children and was evidently inspired by Chaucer's "Pardoner's Tale." The three objects collected by the brothers in Rowling's tale become the Deathly Hallows, the most powerful magical artifacts in Harry Potter's world. In the Grimms' tale, each of the brothers is endowed with a supernatural skill, and three receive magical instruments.*

nce there was a poor man with four sons. He said to them, when they were all grown up: "My dear children: you will now have to go out into the world, for I have nothing to give you. Go out on the road and travel to foreign lands. Learn a trade and try to find some success in the world."

The four brothers prepared themselves for a journey, took leave of their father, and went out together to the town gate. After they had walked for a while, they reached a crossing, with roads leading in four different directions. The eldest said: "Now we will have to part, but four years from now, let's meet right here. In the meantime, we shall all try our luck."

Each brother went his way. The eldest met a man who asked him where he was going and what he had in mind to do.

"I'm hoping to learn a trade," he replied.

The man said, "Come with me, and I'll turn you into a thief."[1]

"No," he replied. "That's not an honest trade, and I'm more than likely to end up dangling from the gallows."

The man said, "Oh, you don't have to worry about the gallows. I will teach you how to take things that no one else can touch, and I'll also show you how to do that without ever getting caught."

That was good enough for the son, and so he was trained as a thief and became so adroit that nothing belonging to anyone else was safe if he wanted it.

The second brother met a man who asked him the same question about what kind of trade he had in mind for the future.

"I haven't the slightest idea," he replied.

"Then come with me and learn to be a stargazer.[2] Nothing beats that as a trade, because no one can hide a thing from you."

1. *"I'll turn you into a thief."* Many heroes of fairy tales are expert liars and thieves, among them Puss in Boots and Jack from "Jack and the Beanstalk." The eldest brother is far more scrupulous than Puss or Jack about taking what belongs to others. His artfulness as a thief is presented as more of a sleight-of-hand operation than a challenge to property rights.

2. *"learn to be a stargazer."* While the three other brothers learn trades that require manual dexterity or sleight-of-hand skills, the second brother develops his visual skills and is the least bound to material objects. At the end of his apprenticeship, he receives a special instrument to enhance his vision even further. The sons receive three gifts in all: a telescope, a gun, and a needle.

The brother liked that idea and became so adept as a stargazer that, once he had finished his apprenticeship and was about to move on, his master gave him a telescope and said: "You will now be able to see everything that happens on earth and in the skies. Nothing can be hidden from you."

A hunter took the third brother on as apprentice and gave him expert instruction in all there was to know about hunting. As a farewell gift, he presented him with a gun and said: "It never misses. Whatever you aim at, you will be sure to hit."

The youngest brother also met a man who spoke with him about his plans and asked: "Wouldn't you enjoy working as a tailor?"

"I'm not so sure about that," the boy replied. "Why would I want to spend my life hunched over, day in and day out, first working a needle, then an iron."

"You really don't know much about being a tailor," the man said. "With me you'll learn the trade in ways that you'll find agreeable and respectable, and the work may even bring you great honor."

The brother was persuaded and went with the man to learn about tailoring from the bottom up. When it was time to say farewell, the man gave him a needle and said: "You can use this to mend whatever you want, whether it's something soft as an egg or hard as steel. You will also be able to put it back together again so that not even a seam will show."

The four designated years went by, and the brothers all met at the crossroads. They embraced, kissed each other, and then returned home to their father.

The overjoyed father said, "Well, well, it looks like the wind has blown you back to me at last."

The sons explained what had happened to each of them and how they had each learned different trades. As they sat under a large tree in front of their home, the father said: "I'm going to put each of you to a test to find out what you have

Arthur Rackham, *The Fairy Tales of the Brothers Grimm*

"So the four Brothers took their sticks in their hands, bade their Father good-by, and passed out of the town gate."

learned." Then he looked up and said to the second son: "In the crown of this tree there's a chaffinch's nest right between two branches. Tell me how many eggs are in it?"

The stargazer took out his telescope, looked up, and said: "There are five in all."

The father turned to the eldest and said: "Bring the eggs down from the tree without disturbing the mother bird who is busy hatching them." The artful thief climbed up the tree and snatched the five eggs from under the mother bird, who did not notice a thing and continued to sit peacefully in the nest. The father took the eggs and put one in each corner of the table and one in the middle and said to the hunter: "I want you to break all five eggs with a single shot."

The hunter took aim, and, just as his father had ordered, he broke all five eggs in two with a single shot. He must have owned some kind of powder than can round corners.

"Now it's your turn," the father said to the fourth son. "I want you to mend the eggs, as well as the chicks inside them, so that the shot will not have done them any harm." The tailor took out his needle and sewed just as his father had asked. Once he was done, the thief had to take the eggs back up the tree and return them to the nest without the mother bird noticing anything. When the chicks hatched a few days later, they crawled out and each had a thin red line around the neck, exactly in the place where the tailor had done his work.

"Well, well," the old man said to his sons, "I can hardly give you too much praise. You've made good use of your time and learned some astonishing skills. I can't really tell who deserves the most praise. The next time you have a chance to apply your talents, we will have the answer."

Not long after that, there was a great uproar in the land, for the king's daughter had been carried off by a dragon. Day and night, the king was in anguish about her, and he announced that whoever rescued her could also have her for his bride. The four brothers met and talked about what had happened:

Arthur Rackham, *The Fairy Tales of the Brothers Grimm*

"The King's only daughter had been carried off by a Dragon."

"This is our chance to show what we can do." They decided to travel together and free the king's daughter.

"Before long I will find out where she is," the stargazer said, and he looked through his telescope and said, "I have already spotted her. She is very far away, sitting on a rock in the ocean, and right next to her is the dragon guarding her." He went to the king and asked for a ship, and the four brothers sailed across the ocean until they reached the rock. The princess was right there on the rock, and the dragon was fast asleep with his head in her lap. The hunter said: "I don't dare shoot, for I might kill the beautiful maiden."

"Then I'll try my luck," the thief said, and he tiptoed over so quietly and stole her away so nimbly that the dragon didn't notice a thing and just kept on snoring. The brothers rushed back to the ship with her and headed for the open seas, but the dragon, who had awoken and discovered that the Princess was gone, raced after them and came flying through the air, snorting angrily. The dragon was hovering right over the ship and about to swoop down when the hunter took aim and shot it right in the heart. The beast fell down dead, but it was so huge and powerful that it smashed the ship to pieces on its way down. The brothers were in luck and salvaged a few planks from the ship. They floated aimlessly on the waters for a while. Once again, their lives were at risk, but the tailor did not waste any time, and he took his miraculous needle and sewed the planks together with a few swift strokes. Then he got on the raft and collected all the different parts of the ship, mending them so skillfully that the boat was seaworthy in no time, and they could all sail back home safely.

When the king set eyes on his daughter again, he was overjoyed and said to the four brothers: "One of you shall have her as his bride, but you will have to decide among yourselves which one it is to be." A fierce quarrel broke out among them, for each made a claim on the princess. The stargazer said: "If I had not spotted the princess, then all your talents would have been in vain. That's why she should be mine."

The thief said, "A lot of good your vision would have done if I had not stolen her out from under the dragon. That's why she should be mine."

The hunter said: "You would all have been torn apart by the monster, right along with the princess, if my bullet had not hit its mark. That's why she should be mine."

The tailor said: "And if I had not used all my skills to repair the ship, then you would have died a miserable death by drowning. That's why she should be mine."

The king decided that he had heard enough. "You all have just arguments, but you can't all marry my daughter. And so, no one will marry her, but I will reward each of you with half a foreign kingdom."

The brothers were satisfied with that decision, and they said: "You're right. It's better to have nothing than set us against each other." Each one of them received half a kingdom, and they lived happily with their father[3] as long as it pleased God.

3. *lived happily with their father.* Like Jack, the brothers return home to live happily ever after, in this case with a father who had been unable to provide them with a patrimony. Seeking a fortune in the world by becoming an apprentice or a journeyman was the fate of most sons whose fathers did not own land. And the younger sons in a family often inherited nothing in countries with primogeniture customs in place.

The Worn-Out Dancing Shoes

This tale also goes by the name "The Twelve Dancing Princesses" and was available to the Grimms in several variants, one of which features a shoemaker's apprentice who releases a princess from a spell cast on her, and another in which a soldier who acquires a magic cloak and boots pursues three princesses whose shoes are torn apart every night. Folklorists Iona and Peter Opie point out that the "do-or-die terms offered to candidates for a princess's hand are not uncommon in popular literature, but Victorian editors found their harshness unacceptable. . . . Andrew Lang disposed of the unsuccessful candidates as unobtrusively as possible, stating that when the morning came they had all disappeared, and no one could tell what had become of them."

The tale is disseminated across European countries, and its best known analogue is probably "Kate Crackernuts," which recounts the rescue by Kate of an invalid prince who is obliged to attend underground dances on a nightly basis. If the princesses in the Grimms' tale seem to enjoy their nightly escapades, their counterparts in other versions of the tale seem beholden to a dark spirit from nether regions, who compels them to dance on a nightly basis.

nce upon a time there lived a king who had twelve daughters, and one was more beautiful than the next. They all slept in one large room, and their beds stood side by side. When they would retire for the night, the king would shut the door to their bedroom and lock it tight. But when he returned to open the door in the morning, he found that the shoes of the princesses were worn out from dancing, and no one could figure out how this could keep happening. Finally, the king proclaimed that whoever found out where his daughters were dancing at night could choose one of them for his wife and would become king after his death. But if anyone came forward and failed to uncover anything within three days and nights, then he would lose his life.

It wasn't long before a prince came along who decided to try his luck. He was received with a warm welcome, and in the evening he was conducted to a room adjacent to the bedroom of the princesses. A bed was prepared for him, and he was told to keep watch and find out where the girls went dancing. Just to make sure that the princesses didn't do anything in secret or go somewhere else, the door of the room that led to his was kept open. But the eyelids of the prince became heavy as lead, and before he knew it, he was fast asleep. When he awoke in the morning, all twelve princesses had spent the night dancing, for their shoes were right there with holes in the soles. On the second and third nights, the same thing happened, and then the king had no mercy and ordered the prince's head chopped off. Many men followed him and wanted to try their luck too, but one after another, they lost their lives.

Now it happened that an old soldier who was wounded

and could no longer serve in the army[1] was headed to the city where the king dwelt. Along the way, he met an old woman[2] who asked him where he was going.

"To tell you the truth, I don't really know," he said, and then he added in jest: "I wouldn't mind finding out how the king's daughters wear out their shoes. Then I could become king."

"It's really not that hard," the old woman said. "Just don't have any of the wine that they bring you in the evening. Pretend that you're fast asleep."

Then she gave him a little cloak and said: "If you put this on, you'll be invisible[3] and you'll have no trouble following the princesses."

After receiving the good advice, the soldier began to think seriously about the venture, and he screwed up his courage to present himself to the king as a suitor. He was welcomed just as warmly as the others had been and was given royal garments to wear. In the evening, when it was time to go to sleep, he was conducted to the antechamber, and just as he was getting ready to go to bed, the oldest of the princesses came and brought him a beaker of wine. But the soldier tied a sponge under his chin, and he let the wine run down into it and didn't drink a single drop. Then he lay down, and after a while he began to snore as if he were sound asleep. The twelve princesses heard him, and they burst out laughing. The oldest said: "There's another one who could have done better things with his life."

Then they all got up, opened chests, cabinets, and closets, and took out all kinds of splendid clothes. They groomed themselves in front of the mirrors, rushed to and fro, and could hardly wait for the ball. But the youngest said: "You're all so excited. I don't know about you, but I have a strange feeling and am worried that something bad is going to happen to us."

"You silly goose," the oldest said. "You're always nervous.

1. *an old soldier who was wounded and could no longer serve in the army.* That fairy tales are like magnets, picking up bits and pieces of the social realities in which they are told, becomes evident from the presence of a retired soldier in a tale with princesses, magic cloaks, and an underground paradise.

2. *Along the way, he met an old woman.* In most episodes like this one, the hero is subjected to a test of compassion before he is given the magical objects that help him accomplish the test set by a king.

3. *"If you put this on, you'll be invisible."* The cloak of invisibility is rare in fairy tales. Its origins can be traced to the "Tarnkappe," or hat that makes its wearer invisible.

Have you already forgotten how many princes have been here before? I didn't really need to give that soldier a sleeping potion. Even if I hadn't given it to him, that oaf would never have woken up."

When they were all ready, they took a good look at the soldier before leaving. But his eyes were shut tight, and since he was neither moving nor stirring, they were sure that the coast was clear. Then the oldest went over to her bed and tapped on it. It sank right down into the ground, and they all climbed down the opening, one after another, with the oldest going first. The soldier, who was watching everything, lost no time in putting on the cloak and followed in the steps of the youngest. Halfway down the stairs, he stepped on her dress and she was so startled that she cried out: "What's going on? Who's holding my dress?"

"Don't act like a fool," the oldest girl said. "You just caught it on a nail."

They went all the way down the stairs, and when they reached the bottom they were standing in a marvelous avenue of trees, where the leaves were all made of silver[4] and glittered and sparkled. The soldier thought: "You'd better take a piece of evidence with you." When he broke off a branch, the tree made a tremendous cracking sound.

"Something's wrong. Did you hear that noise?" the youngest girl shouted.

"Those are just gun salutes, for we'll soon be setting our princes free," the oldest insisted.

They soon reached another avenue of trees, where all the leaves were made of gold, and then a third, where they were made of pure diamonds. The soldier broke a branch off each one, and the cracking sound was so loud that each time the youngest princess was startled and felt afraid. But the oldest kept insisting that the sounds were nothing but gun salutes.

The princesses walked on and reached a huge lake with twelve boats on it. In each of the boats there was a handsome

4. *where the leaves were all made of silver.* In the Sumerian epic of Gilgamesh, the hero makes his way through the underworld into the garden of the gods where, after crossing the waters of death, he finds jewel-encrusted vines and bushes.

Kay Nielsen, *In Powder and Crinoline: Old Fairy Tales*

The princesses, clothed in enchanting garments, make their way to the ball, along with the invisible soldier who follows them to their nocturnal destination.

prince. All of them had been waiting for the twelve princesses, and each one took a princess in his boat. The soldier went aboard with the youngest princess.

"I'm not sure what's going on, but the ship is much heavier than usual, and I have to row with all my might to get it moving."

"It must be the hot weather," the youngest princess said. "I'm feeling a little warm too."

On the other side of the lake there was a beautiful, brightly lit castle, with drums and trumpets making merry music within. They rowed over to the palace, entered, and each of the princes danced with his sweetheart. The soldier was invisible, but he danced along as well, and whenever a princess picked up a glass of wine, he would drink it and drain it dry before it reached her lips. The youngest princess started worrying about this too, but the oldest told her to keep quiet.

They all danced until three in the morning, when all the shoes were worn through, and they had to stop. The princes rowed them back across the lake, and this time the soldier sat in the first boat with the oldest princess. The princesses took leave of their partners on the banks of the lake, and they promised to return the following night. When they reached the stairs, the soldier ran ahead of them and got into bed. And when the twelve girls came dragging wearily in, he was snoring so loudly again that they all heard it and said: "We don't have to worry about him." Then they took off their beautiful dresses, put them away, placed the worn-out shoes under the bed, and went to sleep.

The next morning the soldier decided not to say anything but wanted to witness the strange events again, and he went with them for a second and then a third night. Everything happened as on the first night, and each time they danced until the shoes fell apart. The third time he took a glass as a piece of evidence.

The hour came when he was to bear witness, and he took

Kay Nielsen, *In Powder and Crinoline: Old Fairy Tales*

The princess dances with one of the suitors in this illustration for a retold version of the Grimms' tale about twelve princesses who wear out their dancing shoes.

with him the three branches and the cup and went to the king. The twelve princesses were waiting behind the door and listening to what he would say. When the king asked: "Where did my twelve daughters wear out their shoes?" he replied: "In an underground palace with twelve princes." And he reported what had happened and produced the evidence.

The king called for his daughters and asked them if the soldier was telling the truth. They realized that they had been exposed and that trying to deny it would do no good. They had to admit everything.

The king asked the soldier which of his daughters he wanted as wife. He replied: "I'm not so young any more. How about the oldest?" The wedding was celebrated on that very day, and the king promised that the soldier would inherit the kingdom after his death. As for the princes, they were compelled to remain under a spell for exactly the number of nights that they had danced with the princesses.

The Star Talers[1]

1. *Taler:* The taler was first minted as a silver coin in 1519 in Joachimthal, where substantial amounts of silver had been discovered. The taler remained the main unit of currency until 1871, when the mark was introduced.

he tale was told from "dim" childhood recollections, but it also has literary origins in a novel by the eighteenth-century German writer Jean Paul. Originally entitled "The Poor Child," it bears a resemblance to Hans Christian Andersen's later "The Little Match Girl," which ends, however, with the death of the child, right after she has a vision of her grandmother welcoming her into heaven. Andersen knew the Grimms' collection, but he may have been inspired by native lore.

Paul Hey, *Die schönsten Kindermärchen der Brüder Grimm*

The barefoot heroine stoops to collect the stars that have fallen from the heavens and turned into coins.

There was once a little girl who had lost her father and mother[2] and who was so poor that she no longer had a room to live in, nor a bed to sleep in, and in the end there was nothing she could call her own but the clothes on her back and a crust of bread that some kind soul had given her. But she was both good and devout, and when she was abandoned by everyone, she put her faith in God and went out into the countryside.

There she met a poor man who said to her: "Please give me something to eat. I'm so hungry." She handed him the entire crust of bread,[3] saying, "May the Lord bless it for you," and she continued on her way.

Then she met a child who complained to her: "My head is so cold. Can you give me something to cover it with?" The girl took off her cap and gave it to the child.

She walked a little farther and met another child who didn't have a jacket and was freezing, and so she gave her jacket to the child. Farther on, another child begged for her dress, and she gave that away too. At length she made her way into a forest. It was dark by then, and another child came and asked for her shift. The kind-hearted girl thought: "It's dark outside. Since no one can see you, you can give your shift away too," and she took it off and gave it away.[4]

She was standing outside with nothing left whatsoever, when stars began to fall from the sky, and they were shiny new talers. Even though she had just given her shift away, she had a new one on, and it was made of the finest linen. She gathered the talers into her lap, and for the rest of her life she was rich.

2. *who had lost her father and mother.* Completely on her own, the little girl becomes the prototypical fairy-tale heroine, a girl who is bereft of family and must find a way to establish a new family.

3. *She handed him the entire crust of bread.* The girl passes the first character test, a test of compassion, by giving up all that she has left to eat.

4. *she took it off and gave it away.* The heroine is more self-abnegating than most fairy-tale figures, who are required to share their last crust or to give it away, but who manage to keep the clothes on their backs.

The Nixie in the Well

The Grimms heard this story from Marie Hassenpflug, a friend of their sister Charlotte, who contributed a good number of the canonical tales to the collection. She was of Huguenot background, and the tales she provided were largely connected with French traditions.

Two children, a brother and a sister, were playing next to a well, and they fell into it while at play. At the bottom of the well there lived a water nixie, and she said: "Now that I've caught you, I'm going to make you work hard for me." And she took them away with her.

She gave the girl nastily tangled flax to spin, and forced her to carry water in a bottomless keg. The boy had to chop down a tree with a blunt ax. All they had to eat were dumplings that were hard as rocks. The children were so eager to escape that they made a plan to leave when the nixie was in church one Sunday, and off they ran.

When church let out, the nixie realized that the chickens had flown the coop, and she pursued them, making leaps and bounds. The children could see her coming in the distance, and the girl flung a brush behind her. It grew into a huge mountain with thousands upon thousands of bristles, but the nixie worked hard to get a footing and sure enough she made it over the mountain. When the children caught sight of her, the boy threw a comb behind him, and it grew into a huge mountain with thousands upon thousands of teeth, but the nixie managed to grab hold of them and made it across. Then the girl threw a looking glass behind her, which turned into a glass mountain so slippery that it was impossible to cross. And the nixie thought: "I'm going to run home and get my ax and chop the mountain in two." But by the time she returned and chopped up the glass, the children had already made their escape, and the water nixie had to trudge back and slip into her well.

Snow White and Rose Red

Wilhelm Grimm added this tale to the collection in 1837 (it had previously appeared only in the annotations to the 1822 edition). The tale derives from Caroline Stahl's "The Ungrateful Dwarf" and was retold by Wilhelm Grimm, who was so attached to the story that he included it in the Compact Edition of the tales. Most same-sex siblings in fairy tales are hostile to each other, but Snow White and Rose Red are remarkable exceptions to this rule. Positioned as opposites, with one associated with winter, the other with summer, they are nonetheless more like twins in terms of behavior, both serving as models of compassion and kindness. These are not the "kind" and "unkind" sisters common in European folklore. The two girls not only run the household, carrying out the domestic chores assigned to them, they also help those in need, no matter how terrifying or repellent they may be.

The two male figures, the gentle bear and hateful dwarf, present stark contrasts in both appearances and essences. Tolerant, amicable, and good-natured, the bear, even before his transformation, seems an ideal companion. The dwarf, who ranks among the most ill-tempered figures in the Grimms' collection, swears, steals, and embraces the vice that is the cardinal sin of the folklore world: ingratitude. For Bruno Bettelheim, this particular tale implies that there are "both friendly and disgusting aspects to our natures, and when we rid ourselves of the latter, all can be happiness. At the story's end the essential unity of the protagonists is restated by Snow-White's marrying the prince, and Rose-Red his brother."

For other critics, this particular story held a special appeal for the Grimms because it focused on the close relationship between two siblings who live with their mother alone in the forest. As Jack Zipes points out, "The girls, not unlike the Brothers Grimm, are like night and day but are inseparable and supportive of one another." For him, the tale resonates powerfully with the lives of the Grimms: "The treasures of a realm are restored to the rightful owners. The girls enter into new unions but remain inseparable. Their mother, as cultivator of their home and heritage, remains with them, and their tradition flourishes."

Although it is illuminating to look at the tale in psycho-sexual terms, as does Bettelheim, or to consider it from a biographical perspective, as does Zipes, it is also useful to consider the appeal of this particular tale for collectors who hoped to provide children with models of good behavior. Snow White and Rose Red serve their mother diligently, becoming experts in the art of good housekeeping. They have an outrageously high tolerance for insufferable behavior; they occasionally engage in mischief, but only within playful limits; and they value family above all else. Even marriage cannot divide the siblings, who marry brothers and continue living with their mother. For all that, the dwarf, in his frenzied rages and maddening lack of appreciation, becomes a powerfully attractive antidote to the "peace" and "happiness" of married life, giving rise to all kinds of mishaps and adventures. Male figures clearly have a greater behavioral range than do the three women in this story, who delight in cultivating their ability to be kind, compassionate, and industrious in carrying out household chores.

here once lived a poor widow, all alone in a little cottage, and in front of the cottage there was a garden with two rosebushes growing in it, one with white roses and the other with red. The widow had two children who resembled the rosebushes. One was called Snow White, the other Rose Red. No two children had ever been as kind and devout, and as helpful and cheerful, as they were. Snow White was more quiet and gentle than Rose Red. Rose Red liked to frolic in the fields and on the meadows, looking for flowers and catching butterflies. Snow White, on the other hand, liked to stay at home with her mother, helping out with the housework, or reading out loud to her mother when all the work was done.

The two children liked each other so much that they would always clasp hands when they went out together. When Snow White would say: "We'll never leave each other," Rose Red would answer "Not as long as we live," and their mother would chime in by saying "You must always share whatever you have." They would often go into the woods to pick red berries, and they never had to worry about the animals, for they made friends with them right away. Rabbits nibbled at cabbage leaves from their hands; deer would graze beside them; stags bounded right by them; and birds would perch on branches near them and sing all the songs they knew. No harm ever came to the girls. If it got late while they were in the forest, they would lie down next to each other on the moss and sleep until dawn. Their mother knew what they were doing and never worried about them.

Once when they spent the night in the woods and the rising sun woke them up, they saw right before them a beautiful child wearing a glittering, white dress. The child stood up and looked at them in a friendly way, but said nothing and went into the forest. When they looked around, they realized that they had been sleeping near a cliff and would surely have fallen off the edge if they had just gone a few steps farther in the darkness. Their mother told them that the child must have been the angel that watches over good children.

Snow White and Rose Red kept the cottage so tidy[1] that it was always a pleasure to look at. In the summertime Rose Red took care of the house, and every morning she would put a bouquet of flowers, with one rose from each of the bushes, at her mother's bedside. In the wintertime Snow White lit the fire and hung the kettle over the hearth. The kettle was made of brass and had been scoured so clean that it glittered like gold. In the evening, when snowflakes were falling to the ground, the mother would say: "Snow White, go and bolt the door." Then they would all sit around the hearth, and the mother would take out her spectacles and read to them from a big book. The two girls would listen while they were spinning. A little lamb lay on the floor beside them, and behind them a little white dove was on its perch with its head tucked under its wing.

One evening, while they were sitting peacefully at home, someone started knocking at the door as if he wanted to be let in right away. The mother said: "Quick, Rose Red, go and open the door. It may be a wayfarer seeking shelter." Rose Red went to the door and unbolted it. She was sure it was going to be some poor soul, but it wasn't at all. It was a bear, and he thrust his big black head right through the doorway. Rose Red screamed and backed off. The little lamb bleated, the dove fluttered into the air, and Snow White hid behind her mother's bed.

The bear began to speak, and he said: "Don't be afraid. I'm not going to hurt you. I'm half-frozen from the weather, and all I want to do is get warm."

"You poor fellow," said the mother. "Lie down by the hearth, but just make sure that your fur doesn't catch fire."

1. *Snow White and Rose Red kept the cottage so tidy.* The Grimms' portrait of the idyllic family scene is extraordinary in its emphasis on cleanliness as a condition for domestic bliss. The lamb and the dove at the hearth add a touch of kitsch to the portrait, but even their presence cannot mask the fact that there is a missing father in this family idyll. A. S. Byatt has pointed out that Dorothea and Rosamond in *Middlemarch* resemble Snow White and Rose Red: "Dorothea is white, has a nun-like quality, and is compared (ironically) to the Blessed Virgin . . . Rosamond's name itself is rose-red, Rosa Mundi, the rose of the world, another way of referring to the Virgin, of course."

Jennie Harbour, *My Book of Favourite Fairy Tales*

Snow White, Rose Red, and their mother recoil in fear when they are approached by the half-frozen bear that seeks shelter with them.

Then she called out: "Snow White, Rose Red, come back out. The bear isn't going to hurt you, he means no harm." And the two girls came out and little by little the lamb and the dove too, for they were no longer afraid. The bear said: "Children, would you mind beating my fur a little to get the snow off it." And the girls fetched a broom and swept the snow off his coat. Then he stretched out in front of the hearth, and feeling completely content, he began to rumble blissfully.

It didn't take long for the girls to get used to their awkward guest, and he soon had to put up with all kinds of mischief from them. They would tug at his fur, walk on his back with their feet, and roll him back and forth, or else they would beat him with a hazel branch, and when he growled they would start laughing. The bear was a good sport about it all, but if they took things too far, he would shout: "Children, spare me!

Snow White and Rose Red,
You'll beat your suitor till he's dead."

When it was time to go to sleep and everyone was ready for bed, the mother said to the bear: "You are very welcome to spend the night at the hearth. Then you'll be protected from the cold and the harsh weather." At daybreak the two children let him go outside, and he ambled across the snow into the forest. From then on, the bear would arrive every evening at the exact same time. He would lie down at the hearth and let the children tease him as much as they wanted. They had become so accustomed to his arrival that the door was never bolted until their big black friend had returned.

When spring arrived and everything outside was turning green, the bear announced one morning to Snow White: "I'm going to have to leave and won't return until the summer is over."

"Where are you going, dear bear?" Snow White asked.

"I have to go back to the woods to guard my treasures against the evil dwarfs.[2] In the winter, when the ground is frozen, they have to stay underground and can't work their way up. But now that the sun has warmed up the ground and thawed everything out, they can break through, come above ground, look around, and steal. Whatever they get their hands on and carry off to their caves isn't so easy to recover."

Snow White felt sad to see the bear go. When she unbolted the door for him and he was squeezing through it, his coat caught on the latch and some of his skin came off. Snow White could have sworn that she saw gold shimmering through, but she wasn't completely sure. The bear hurried off, and soon he disappeared into the woods.

After a while the mother sent the two children into the woods to gather brushwood. They discovered a huge tree that had been felled, and right next to it something was jumping up and down in the grass, but they couldn't figure out what it was. When they got closer, they realized that it was a dwarf with a wizened old face and a very long beard that was white as snow. The end of his beard had gotten caught in the crack

2. *"guard my treasures against the evil dwarfs."* Like the miners in "Snow White," the dwarfs in this tale inhabit underground regions, but rather than being in a relationship of harmony with nature, they are in a fractious relation with it. These dwarfs seem to be close kin to the trolls of Scandinavian lore.

of a tree trunk, and the gnome was racing back and forth like a little dog on a chain and couldn't figure out what to do. He stared at the two girls with his fiery red eyes and screamed: "What are you standing there for! Can't you come over here and help me!"

"What happened to you, my dear little man?" asked Rose Red.

"You stupid nosey goose," he replied. "I wanted to split this tree trunk to get some firewood[3] for my kitchen. If we use big logs to heat our little dinners, they burn right up. We don't have the huge portions that you uncouth, greedy folks all wolf down. I just drove the wedge in the exact right spot, and everything would have gone according to plan, but the stupid piece of wood was too smooth and it popped right out. The cleft closed right up with my beard in it. Now my beautiful white beard is caught in the tree trunk, and I can't get out of here. And you silly baby-faced girls just sit there and laugh. How nasty you both are!"

The girls pulled as hard as they could on the beard, but it was stuck tight.

"I'll run and get help," Rose Red said.

"You crazy dolts," the dwarf snarled. "You want to go get help and bring other people over here? You're already two too many. Don't you have any better ideas?"

"Why are you so impatient?" asked Snow White. "I can help you," and she pulled out a little pair of scissors from her pocket and cut the tip of the beard off. As soon as the dwarf realized that he was free, he grabbed his sack, which was lying between the roots of the tree and was filled with gold, lifted it up, and muttered to himself: "Ill-mannered brats! Cutting off a piece of my elegant beard! The devil take you!" With that he threw his sack on his shoulders and left, without so much as a glance at the children.

Not much later Snow White and Rose Red were planning to catch some fish for dinner. When they got near the brook,

3. *"I wanted to split this tree trunk to get some firewood."* Despite the dwarf's insistence that he and his kinsmen require only small portions, the episode itself puts his greed on display. The girls look for brushwood in the forest, but the dwarf does violence to nature, cutting down a tree.

Warwick Goble, *The Fairy Book*

Snow White and Rose Red struggle to free the dwarf from the claws of an eagle that is about to fly off with him.

they saw something that looked like a huge grasshopper hopping toward the brook and about to jump in. They ran to get a closer look and recognized the dwarf.

"Where are you going?" asked Rose Red. "You're not planning to jump in the water, are you?"

"How can you think I'm such a big idiot?" screamed the dwarf. "Can't you tell that that damned fish is trying to pull me into the water?"

The dwarf had been sitting there fishing, and unluckily for him, the wind had tangled his beard with the line. When a big fish bit, right after his beard got caught, the scrawny little chap didn't have the strength to pull the fish out of the water. Once the fish had the upper hand, it began to pull the dwarf into the water. The dwarf was clutching on to the grass and rushes, but it was no use, he had to follow the movements of the fish and was just about to get dragged into the water. The girls arrived at just the right moment, and they held on to him while they were trying to free his beard from the line. But it was in vain: the beard and the line were hopelessly tangled. The only thing they could do was to take out the little pair of scissors again and cut the beard, leaving a little bit of it on the fishing line. When the dwarf realized what was going to happen, he screamed at them: "Is that how you disfigure people, you nasty little toads? It wasn't enough to clip the end of my beard, now you've cut off the best part of it. I'm ashamed to show my face at home. I hope that you have to use your legs sometime soon and that the soles of your shoes go missing." With that he grabbed a sack of pearls that he had hidden in the rushes, dragged it away, and disappeared beneath a rock.

One day the mother sent the girls into town to buy needles and thread, along with laces and ribbons. Their path took them across a heath that had big rocks strewn all over it. Suddenly they caught sight of a huge bird soaring above them. It circled them on the way down and swooped down on a rock

4. *He wanted to continue with his foul language.* The dwarf's language is reminiscent of the speech of the title character in the tale "The Jew in the Brambles." Both constantly utter oaths and denounce their interlocutors.

not too far away from them. A moment later they heard a pitiful cry of distress and ran in the direction of the voice. To their horror they realized that the eagle had seized the dwarf and was about to fly off with him. The kindhearted children grabbed on to the little man and held tight, struggling with the eagle until it finally let go of its prey.

The dwarf was just recovering from his fright when he screamed: "Can't you treat me with a little more care? You pulled so hard at my thin little jacket that it's practically in pieces and full of holes. You evil little clods!" Then he picked up a sack full of diamonds and slipped under a rock to get back to his cave. By now the girls were accustomed to his lack of gratitude, and they continued on their way, finishing their errands. On the way home, when they were crossing the heath, they surprised the dwarf, who had just emptied his sack of jewels on a spot he had cleared out. He had not imagined that someone might be passing by so late in the day. The evening sun was shining on the sparkling stones so that their colors glimmered and glowed magnificently. The children stopped in their tracks and gazed at the stones.

"Why are you standing there gaping at my stones," the dwarf screamed, and his ash gray features turned scarlet with rage. He wanted to continue with his foul language,[4] but a loud growling filled the air and a black bear dashed out of the woods onto the heath. The dwarf jumped up in fright and would have made his usual getaway if the bear had not gotten so close. He cried out in terror: "My dear Mr. Bear, please spare my life. I promise to give you my treasures—just look at these beautiful diamonds lying on the ground. Give me my life! Why would you want to eat a pitiful, scrawny fellow like me? You'll hardly even notice that I'm between your jaws. Just take a look at those two wicked girls. They're as fat as young quails and will make tasty morsels. Go after them, for God's sake!" The bear paid no attention to what he was saying

Jennie Harbour, *My Book of Favourite Fairy Tales*

The dwarf has emptied his sack of jewels and uses "foul language" when he discovers that he has been caught off guard by Snow White and Rose Red.

and gave the wicked creature a single blow with his paw, and after that the dwarf didn't move.

The girls had fled, and the bear called after them: "Snow White and Rose Red, don't be afraid. Wait for me, and we can walk together." The girls recognized the voice and stopped in their tracks. When the bear caught up with them, his skin fell off, and he stood there suddenly as a handsome man, dressed in gold. "I am the son of a king," he said, "and that wicked dwarf stole my treasures and turned me into a wild bear forced to roam the forest. Only his death could break the spell. Now he's gotten the punishment he deserved."

Snow White married the prince and Rose Red married his brother, and they shared the great wealth that the dwarf had gathered in his cave. The mother lived for many years with her children in peace and happiness. She brought with her the two rosebushes, which she planted in front of her window, and every year they bore the most beautiful flowers, white and red.

Jennie Harbour, *My Book of Favourite Fairy Tales*

The Golden Key

In his novel Shadowland, *Peter Straub retells the story of the golden key and provides a sequel to it: "Every story in the world, every story ever told, blew up out of the box. Princes and princesses, wizards, foxes and trolls and witches and wolves and woodsmen and kings and elves and dwarves and a beautiful girl in a red cape, and for a second the boy saw them all perfectly, spinning silently in the air. Then the wind caught them and sent them blowing away, some this way and some that."*

The locked casket in this story does not contain the evils associated with Pandora's box but, more likely, the wonders of storytelling. Positioned as the final tale in the Grimms' collection, "The Golden Key" might also have worked well as the introductory tale. The story resonates with many other tales: "The Star Talers" and "The Little Match Girl" both begin with children exposed to the elements. And like Bluebeard's wife, the boy in this story finds a key to a space that is, if not forbidden, at least not a personal possession. The aura of mystery and wonder surrounding the contents of the casket perfectly captures the frisson we feel when, for example, we look through

Keats's "magic casements, opening on the foam / Of perilous seas, in faery lands forlorn."

ne day during the winter, when the snow was piled high, a poor boy was sent out with his sled to get some wood. He gathered what he could and put it on his sled, but it was so cold that, instead of going straight home, he decided to make a fire to warm himself up. While he was clearing a space and

Wanda Gág, *Tales from Grimm*

After a boy finds a key in the snow, he discovers the casket it can open.

Wanda Gág, *Tales from Grimm*

The casket contains sheafs of paper with the stories in the collection, according to one illustrator.

getting the snow out of the way, he found a golden key. And since he was sure that where there was a key there must also be a lock, he started scraping away at the ground and found an iron casket.

"Oh, I hope that the key fits the lock!" he thought. "There must be precious things in the casket." He couldn't find a keyhole anywhere, but finally he noticed that there was a small opening, so tiny that you could hardly see it. He tried the key, and it fit perfectly. Now he's started turning it, and we'll just have to wait until he finishes unlocking the casket and lifts the lid. Then we'll know what kinds of wonderful things can be found in it.

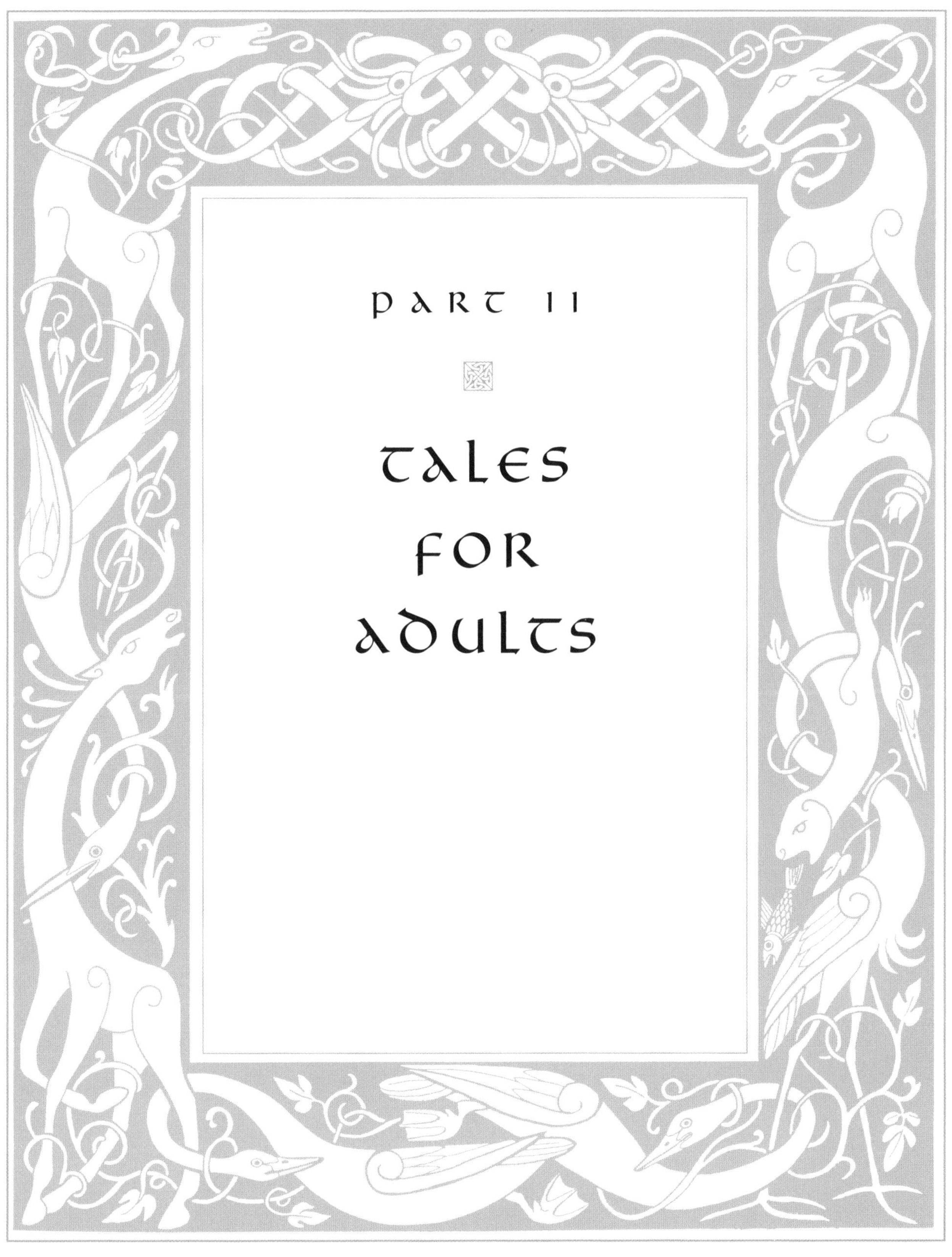

PART II

TALES FOR ADULTS

The Jew in the Brambles

There was once a rich man who had a hardworking and honest servant. This fellow was the first to get out of bed in the morning and the last into bed at night. If there was any unpleasant work to be done that no one was willing to touch, he went ahead and did it. And yet he was always in good spirits, content with his lot, and he never complained. When a year had passed, his master had still not given him any wages, because he had a plan: "This is working well, because it will not only save me money but also keep him from leaving my service." The servant didn't say a word. He continued to work for another year, and when he got no wages the second time, he still didn't complain and stayed on. When a third year had gone by, the master thought over the situation, reached into his pockets, but came up empty. At that point the servant finally spoke up: "Master," he said, "I've served you faithfully for three years. Now it's time to do your part and pay me what you owe me. I'd like to go out into the world and travel for a while." The old skinflint replied: "Yes, my good man, you've served me without complaint, and in exchange I plan to be generous with you." He reached into his pockets, counted out three pennies, and said to the servant: "Here is a penny for every year you worked. You won't get this generous a wage from any other master." The faithful servant, who didn't know much about money, accepted the windfall, thinking: "Now that my pockets are full, I won't have to worry or wear myself down with hard work."

Away the servant went, up hill and down dale, skipping along and singing to his heart's content. It happened that he was walking past some bushes when a gnome jumped out and addressed him: "Where are you headed, my lucky lad? I see that you're not burdened with any cares."

"Why in the world should I be glum?" the servant replied. "I've got plenty of cash. There's three years' worth of wages jingling in my pockets."

"Just how big is your treasure?" the gnome asked.

"You're wondering how much I've got? Three pennies in hard cash, no more, no less."

"Listen to me," said the gnome. "I'm a poor, needy man. Give me those three pennies. I can't work anymore, but you're young and can still make a living."

The servant had a kind heart and felt sorry for the gnome. He handed over the three pennies and said: "Go ahead and take them, in God's name. I'll certainly manage without them."

The gnome replied: "I can see that you have a kind heart, and so I am going to grant you three wishes, one for each penny that you gave me, and they will all come true."

"Aha," the servant exclaimed. "I can see that you're one of those miracle workers! Well, if that's the case, then I will wish first for a bird gun that will hit everything I aim at. Next I'll wish for a fiddle that will make everyone dance when I start playing it. And third, I wish that whenever I ask someone for a favor, they won't be able to refuse me."

"Your three wishes have been granted," the gnome said, and he reached into the bushes, and just imagine, the fiddle and the bird gun were right there as if on command. He gave them to the servant and said: "Whenever you ask anyone for a favor, they won't be able to refuse it."

"Well, what more could you want?" the servant said to himself, and he went on his merry way. Before long he met a Jew with a long goatee who had stopped to listen to the song of a bird perched up high on a tree branch.

"What a divine creature," he cried out. "That little bird has such an awfully loud voice! If only it belonged to me! If someone could just catch it for me!"

"If that's all you want," said the servant, "I'll bring that bird down in no time." And he aimed his gun so accurately that the bird fell down into the brambles.

"You dirty dog," the servant said to the Jew, "go get that bird for yourself now."

"If you drop the 'dirty,'" said the Jew, "then the dog will go fetch it. You hit the bird, and I'll go retrieve it." And he got down on all fours and began to work his way into the thicket of brambles. When he was right in the midst of the bushes, the servant decided to make mischief. He took out his fiddle and started playing. The Jew lifted his feet and started dancing around; and the longer the servant played, the wilder the dance became. The brambles tore his shabby coat, combed his goatee, and scraped and scratched him all over.

"Good heavens," the Jew cried out, "what's the meaning of all that fiddling? Would you kindly stop! I'm not interested in dancing."

The servant paid no attention at all and thought to himself: "You've skinned people plenty of times. Now the brambles can give you a scraping." He kept on playing, and the Jew had to keep jumping higher until bits of his coat were left hanging on the thorns.

"Ouch and double-ouch," the Jew cried out. "I'll give the gentleman whatever he wants if he just stops fiddling. Even a whole sack of money."

"If you're that generous," said the servant, "then I'll be glad to stop my music. But I have to admit that your dancing has real style." And with that he took the sack of money and went on his way.

The Jew stood there and held his tongue as he watched the servant disappear and fade from sight. Then he screeched at the top of his lungs: "You're a miserable excuse for a musician! You beer-hall fiddler! Just wait until I catch you alone. I'll chase you down until the soles of your shoes come off! You scamp, put a nickel in your mouth so you can say you're worth five cents." And the Jew hurled every insult he could think up. When he had finally let off some steam and was feeling better, he hurried into town to talk to the judge.

"Your Honor, I've got nothing but aches and pains. A wicked man robbed me in broad daylight on the road. Look what he's done to me! A stone on the ground would take pity. My clothes are torn to shreds. I've got scrapes and scratches all over my body! My paltry assets have been taken off in a sack. My precious ducats, one more beautiful than the next. For God's sake, throw the rascal into jail."

The judge asked: "Did a soldier slash you with his sword?"

"God forbid!" the Jew replied. "The fellow wasn't carrying a sword, but he did have a gun slung over his shoulder and a fiddle hanging around his neck. The rascal will be easy to recognize."

The judge sent out his men in search of the servant, whom they tracked down easily since he was in no rush, and they found the sack of gold on him. When he was brought before the judge, he said: "I didn't touch the Jew, and I didn't take his money. He gave it to me of his own free will so that I would stop my fiddling, which he just couldn't stand."

"Good God," the Jew shouted. "He's lying through his teeth." The judge didn't believe the servant either and said: "That's an unlikely story. No Jew would do that." And he sentenced the good servant to death by hanging for highway robbery. When he was being escorted away, the Jew shouted after him: "You layabout, you no-good musician, you're finally going to get what you deserve." The servant climbed calmly up the ladder with the hangman, but on the top rung he turned around and said to the judge: "Grant me one last favor before I die."

"As long as you don't ask me to spare your life," the judge replied.

"Not in your life," the servant declared.

"Just let me play my fiddle one last time."

The Jew stirred up a great commotion: "For God's sake, don't let him do that, don't let him do it."

But the judge said: "Why shouldn't I allow him this one small pleasure? I'll grant his wish, and that's that." Even if he had wanted to, he wouldn't have been able to deny the request, because of the gift bestowed on the servant.

The Jew cried out: "Help me! Help me now! Tie me up, tie me down!"

The good servant took the fiddle from around his neck and tucked it under his chin. With the first stroke of his bow, everything began to shake and quake, the judge, the clerks, and the executioner, who dropped the rope that he was going to use to tie down the Jew. With the second stroke, everyone got on their feet, and the executioner let go of the servant and started getting ready to dance. At the third stroke, everyone jumped high in the air and began dancing. The judge and the Jew were in the front row and kicked the highest. Before long everyone was dancing, even the people who had been drawn just by curiosity to the market. Young and old, fat and thin, were all mixed up. Even the dogs stood up on their hind legs and started hopping. The longer the servant played, the higher the dancers jumped until finally they were hitting each other on the head and beginning to screech with pain. At length, the judge, who was completely out of breath, cried out: "I'll spare your life. Just stop that fiddling."

The good servant let himself be persuaded to stop playing, hung the fiddle back around his neck, and climbed down the ladder. He walked over to the Jew, who was lying on the ground, gasping for breath. "You scoundrel! Now just admit where you got that money or I'll get my fiddle out and start playing again."

"I stole it! I stole it!" he screamed. "And you earned it honestly."

The judge had the Jew taken to the gallows and hanged as a thief.

Of the three tales in the Grimms' collection that contain Jewish figures, the two that feature anti-Semitism in its most virulent form were included in the Compact Edition designed for young readers. "The Jew in the Brambles" and "The Good Bargain" were featured prominently, whereas "The Bright Sun Will Bring It to Light," a tale that illustrates the compulsion to confess in the case of a young man who murders a Jew for his money, was not included.

Why would the Grimms include these stories in a collection that they repeatedly describe as reflecting the "purity" and "innocence" of the folk, particularly since nothing like these tales exists in the other major nineteenth-century collections of German fairy tales? Ruth B. Bottigheimer has pointed out that Wilhelm Grimm's friendship with members of the conservative Christian-German Society in Berlin may have been symptomatic of a deep strain of anti-Semitism and that the German Legends *published by the Grimms intensifies that suspicion because of its inclusion of two tales about bloodthirsty Jews. Furthermore, a dream recorded by Wilhelm Grimm in 1810 recycles motifs from "The Jew in the Brambles," suggesting that the tale resonated powerfully with him on an unconscious level.*

In their annotations to "The Jew in the Brambles," the Grimms point out that other versions of the tale stage a conflict between a servant and a monk, making it clear that, when faced with the option of including an anti-clerical tale or an anti-Semitic tale, they chose the latter. A French version of the tale known as "The Three Gifts," a variant of the tale type folklorists designate as "The Dance among the Thorns," describes the fortunes of a boy who is persecuted by his wicked stepmother. After demonstrating compassion for those less fortunate, the boy is granted three wishes, and he proceeds to ask for a crossbow that will always hit its target and a flute that will force everyone who hears it to dance. The third wish is directed at his cruel stepmother, who is forced to let loose a "loud fart" whenever she sneezes. When a priest reprimands him for humiliating his stepmother, the boy sends the priest into a bramble patch to fetch a bird shot down by his crossbow. No sooner has the priest stepped into the brambles than the boy takes out his flute and strikes up a tune on it. The priest begins to whirl and dance so rapidly that his cassock gets caught in the thorns and is torn to shreds. Efforts to mobilize the legal system to punish the boy are in vain—the hero takes out his flute, forcing the priest, clerk, and justice of the peace to dance to his tune.

As in the Grimms' tale, the hero uses his instrument to stage a violent display of burlesque comedy, one that operates with a double economy resulting in the punishment of the enemy and the release of the hero. But "The Jew in the Brambles" adds a third element: the extraction of a "confession" from the Jew: "I stole it! I stole it!" the Jew shouts, desperate to stop dancing. "And you earned it honestly." With those self-incriminating words, the Jew is taken to the gallows and hanged as a thief, even though it is the "rich" master in the tale's introduction who is described as a "skinflint" and who cheats the "honest" servant out of three years' wages. That the Jew becomes the scapegoat for the master's miserliness and swindling of his servant is evident, yet it seems equally clear that "The Jew in the Brambles" fails to offer a critique of that scapegoating and instead legitimizes it in its final tableau. In its repeated use of the attribute "good" to describe the servant, the false accusations ring true as a global accusation of all Jews as thieves. The Jew in the story is never seen as victim but as the deserving target of punishment.

Illustrations for the story, even when they were included in editions clearly intended for children, focus on the scene of punishment, providing stereotypical images of the Jew and unabashedly presenting the scene of torture as a carnivalesque spectacle provoking laughter rather than pity.

This tale was included in many English editions of the tale for audiences of children and appeared as late as 1936 under the title "The Magic Riddle," in Grimms' Fairy Tales: A New Translation by Mrs. H. B. Paul, Specially Adapted and Arranged for Young People.

George Cruikshank, *German Popular Stories*

All must dance to the fiddler's tune as he begins to play at the gallows, while the Jew in the tale exhorts the fiddler to cease.

Arthur Rackham, *The Fairy Tales of the Brothers Grimm*

Coins fall to the ground as the Jew dances as hard as he can.

Arthur Rackham, *The Fairy Tales of the Brothers Grimm*

Rackham seems at pains to depict the Jew in as grotesque a form as possible.

CHARLES ROBINSON, *The Big Book of Fairy Tales*

The Jew is forced to go into contortions while he is being tortured by the music.

L. LESLIE BROOKE,
The House in the Wood and Other Old Fairy Stories

The Jew, purse in hand, tries to persuade the boy to stop fiddling.

Mother Trudy

Once upon a time there lived a little girl who was stubborn and inquisitive, and whenever her parents told her to do something, she refused. How could things possibly go well for her? One day she said to her parents: "I've heard so much about Mother Trudy. I'd like to go visit her. They say that her house is quite strange and that odd things happen there. That's made me really curious about her."

The girl's parents gave her strict orders not to go near the house, and they told her: "Mother Trudy is an evil woman, who does wicked things. If you go to see her, you're no longer our daughter."

But the child paid no attention to what her parents said and went to see Mother Trudy anyway. When she arrived at the house, Mother Trudy asked her: "Why are you so pale?"

"I saw something that really scared me."

"What did you see?"

"On your staircase I saw a black man."

"That was just the charcoal burner."

"Then I saw a green man."

"That was just a huntsman."

"And then I saw a blood red man."

"That was just the butcher."

"Oh, Mother Trudy, I was so scared. I looked through the window and couldn't see you, but I did see a devil with a fiery head."

"Aha!" she said. "Then you saw the witch in all her finery. I've been hoping that you would come here, and I've been waiting for a long time. You can provide me with some light."

And with that, she turned the girl into a block of wood and threw it on the fire. And when it was blazing, she sat down beside it, warmed herself up, and said: "Now that really does give off a nice bright light."

In this cautionary tale warning of the consequences of stubbornness and curiosity, the parents and Mother Trudy, although not allied with each other, triumph over the child. Failure to heed parental warnings leads to the girl's incineration, and Mother Trudy cheerfully warms herself at the blazing fire. The three figures—a black man, a green man, and a red man—are probably kinsmen of the three horsemen that the Russian folklore heroine meets in tales about the witch Baba Yaga. But in the German tale, the girl does not return from her escapade, and she perishes at the home of the witch.

The Hand with the Knife

There once lived a girl who had three brothers. The boys meant everything to their mother, and the girl was always put at a disadvantage and treated badly. Every day she had to go out to a barren heath to dig peat, which was used for cooking and heating. A dull old tool was all she had for that nasty work.

The little girl had an admirer, an elf who lived in a hill near her mother's house. Whenever she passed by that hill, the elf would stretch his hand out of a boulder and hold out a very sharp knife that had special powers and could cut through anything. She was able to dig out the peat quickly with that knife, go home with the required amount, and when she got to the boulder, she tapped on it twice. The hand would then reach out to take back the knife.

When the mother began to notice how quickly and effortlessly the girl brought home the peat, she told the brothers that someone else had to be helping her with the work, otherwise it wouldn't be possible. The brothers stealthily followed her and saw how she got the magical knife, then caught up with her and forced her to give it to them. They headed back, struck the rock as the girl had done, and when the good elf stretched his hand out, they cut if off with his own knife. The bloody arm pulled back, and because the elf believed that his beloved had betrayed him, he was never seen again.

Published as the eighth tale in the first edition of the stories, this story was excised from the collection by 1819, when the second edition was released. Jacob Grimm translated the tale, which had Scottish origins and had appeared in a volume on the superstitions of Scotland, with the following commentary: "One of these (stories) which I have heard sung *by children at a very early age, and which is just to them the Babes in the Wood, I can never forget. The affecting simplicity of the tune, the strange wild imagery and the marks of remote antiquity in the little narrative, gave it the greatest interest to me, who delights in tracing back poetry to its infancy."*

The story begins like many of the fairy tales in the Grimms' collection, with a disadvantaged child sent out to perform impossible labors. The violent act of the brothers, carried out against a figure who is clearly benevolent, does not square with the rules of other tales in the collection.

How Children Played Butcher with Each Other

First Version

In a city called Franecker located in West Friesland, it happened that young children aged five and six, both boys and girls, were playing together. And they decided that one boy should be the butcher, another boy should be the cook, and a third should be the pig. Next they decided that one little girl should play the cook, another was to be the assistant to the cook. The assistant was supposed to catch the blood from the pig in a little basin so that they could make sausages from it. The butcher, as had been agreed, chased after the boy who was playing the pig, pulled him down to the ground, and cut his throat with a little knife. The assistant to the cook caught the blood in her little basin. A councilor who happens to be passing by sees the whole miserable spectacle. He dashes off with the butcher, takes him up to the house of the mayor, who immediately calls a meeting of all councilors. They deliberated at length on the matter and had no idea what to do, for they realized that it had all been child's play. One of them, a wise old man, ventured the opinion that the chief judge should put a nice red apple in one hand and a guilder in the other and that he call the child in and stretch both hands out to him. If the child took the apple, he would be declared innocent. If he took the guilder, he would be killed. This was done: the child, laughing, reached out for the apple and was therefore not subjected to any kind of punishment.

SECOND VERSION

A man once slaughtered a pig while his children were looking on. When they started playing in the afternoon, one child said to the other: "You be the little pig, and I'll be the butcher," whereupon he took an open blade and thrust it into his brother's neck. Their mother, who was upstairs in a room bathing the youngest child in a tub, heard the cries of her other child, quickly ran downstairs, and when she saw what had happened, drew the knife out of the child's neck, and in a rage, thrust it into the heart of the child who had been the butcher. She then rushed back to the house to see what her other child was doing in the tub, but in the meantime it had drowned in the bath. The woman was so horrified that she fell into a state of utter despair, refused to be consoled by the servants, and hanged herself. When her husband returned home from the fields and saw this, he was so distraught that he died shortly thereafter.

*These tales may seem to deviate dramatically from the form of the fairy tale, but bearing in mind that the German term for fairy tales (*Märchen*) is a diminutive form of the word for "news," these two reports, which read almost like newspaper accounts, conform to the nature of the genre.*

The first of the two accounts appeared in the Berliner Abendblätter*, a short-lived newspaper edited by the writer Heinrich von Kleist. The incident was based on a published report from 1555 and interested Kleist because of the test at the end of the narrative, with the child declared innocent because he has not yet attained an understanding of symbolic thinking. The second account was first published in 1600 in a volume in Latin. The two tales were published only in the first edition of the* Children's Stories and Household Tales. *Achim von Arnim, a friend and collaborator, wrote to the Grimms: "I've already heard one mother complaining that the piece about the child who slaughters another child is in {your collection}, and for that reason she won't let her children read it." Wilhelm Grimm defended himself by insisting that the tale had an important cautionary function: "My mother used to tell the story about the butchering when I was young, and it made me careful and apprehensive about child's play." The second of the two versions reads like an anti-Märchen, a tale that recounts a chain of events leading from one disaster to another.*

Hans Dumm

Once there was a king who lived happily with a daughter who was his only child. This princess unexpectedly gave birth to a child, and no one knew who the father was. The king had no idea what to do. Finally he ordered the princess to go to church with the child. There the child was to be given a lemon, and the person to whom it handed the lemon would be declared father of the child and husband of the princess. So it came to pass, but orders were given that no one but good-looking people should be admitted to the church.

Now in this city there lived a short, misshapen, hunchbacked fellow who was not terribly bright and who was therefore called Hans Dumm. Somehow he pressed himself into the crowd and managed to make his way unseen into the church. When the child was supposed to give away the lemon, it handed it to Hans Dumm. The princess was in shock. The king was so outraged that he put his daughter and the child, along with Hans Dumm, out to sea in a sealed cask. The cask floated on the waters, and once they were alone the princess started complaining and said: "You think you're so clever, you disgusting hunchback, but you're to blame for my misfortune. Why did you force your way into the church? You can't possibly have anything to do with the child."

"Oh yes I do," Hans Dumm replied. "I sure do have something to do with it. After all, I once wished that you would have a child, and whatever I wish for comes true."

"If that's really the case, then why don't you wish us something to eat?"

"Happy to oblige," Hans Dumm replied. But he ended up wishing for a bowl piled high with potatoes.

Once they had eaten their fill, Hans Dumm said: "Now I'm going to wish us a beautiful ship!" and as soon as the words were out of his mouth, they found themselves in a fabulous ship. Everything they could want was there in abundance. The pilot steered straight for land, and when they got out, Hans Dumm said: "Now I want a castle right over there." Suddenly a magnificent castle appeared, with servants in golden uniforms who led the princess and her child into the castle. When they got to the middle of the hall, Hans Dumm said: "Now I'm going to wish that I were a smart young prince!" All at once his hump was gone, and he turned into a handsome, tall, and amiable young man. He greatly pleased the princess and became her husband.

For a long time they lived happily. Then one day the old king rode out into the woods, lost his way, and arrived at the castle. He was quite astonished by it, for he had never seen it before, and rode through the gates. The princess recognized her father immediately, but he didn't recognize her. After all, he thought that she had perished at sea a long time ago. She was a fabulous hostess, and when he made plans to go home, she secretly put a goblet of gold in one of his bags. Once he had ridden off, she sent a couple of servants after him. They stopped him and searched him. When they found the goblet of gold in his bag, they took him back with them. He swore to the princess that he had not stolen it and that he had no idea how it had ended up in his bag.

"As you can see," she said, "you shouldn't jump to conclusions about a person's guilt." And she revealed that she was his daughter. The king was overjoyed, and they all lived happily together. After his death, Hans Dumm became king.

The Grimms noted that this tale had appeared in two Italian collections of fairy tales, and they may also have been aware of a literary version based on a French tale. But it was surely more than the literary nature and foreign origins of the tale that discouraged them from including it in the second edition of the Children's Stories and Household Tales. *Hans Dumm, with his extraordinary magical powers and ability to make all his wishes come true, may be a cheerful young man, but he is every young woman's nightmare. The princess, first the victim of Hans Dumm, then of a rancorous father, serves as the voice of reason in the tale, teaching her father a lesson about justice even as she ends up living happily ever after with the man who impregnated her simply by wishing her with child.*

The Evil Mother-in-Law

Once upon a time there lived a king and a queen, and the queen had a wicked and evil mother-in-law. When-the king went off to war, the old queen had her daughter-in-law locked up in a musty room in the cellar, and her two little boys were locked up with her. One day she thought: "I would love to eat one of the two children," whereupon she summoned the cook and had him go down to the cellar to get one of the little boys and slaughter him and prepare him for cooking.

"What kind of sauce should I prepare?" asked the cook.

"A brown one," the old queen replied.

The cook went down to the cellar and said: "Oh my queen, the old queen wants me to slaughter and cook your son tonight."

The young queen was distraught and said: "Why can't you just take a baby pig instead? You can cook it up just as she wanted and tell her that it's my child."

The cook did as she had instructed and presented the roasted suckling in a brown sauce: "Here's the child." And the old queen ate it up with a hearty appetite.

Soon the old woman thought: "The flesh of that child was just so delicate and tasty, I'll just have to eat the other one too." She summoned the cook, sent him to the cellar, and had him slaughter the second son.

"In what kind of sauce should I cook him?"

"A white one," the old queen replied.

The cook went downstairs and said: "Now the old queen has ordered me to slaughter and cook your second little son." The young queen said: "Take a suckling pig and cook it the way she likes."

The cook did just that and presented the suckling pig to the old woman in a white sauce, and she ate it with an even heartier appetite.

Finally, the old woman thought: "Now the children are in my body, and I can eat the young queen herself." She summoned the cook and ordered him to prepare the young queen.—

(Fragment: The third time the cook slaughters a young hind. But now the young queen has a lot of trouble keeping her children from crying, and the old woman will realize that they are still alive, etc.)

* * *

This episode was included among the fragments at the end of the collection and appeared in the first edition of the tales. We do not have to read long and far in other folklore collections to learn how the queen and her children fare. In Perrault's "Sleeping Beauty," we find that the story of the wicked mother-in-law begins at the point where most latter-day versions of the story end. Perrault's mother-in-law comes from "a race of ogres," and she has "the greatest difficulty in the world keeping herself from pouncing" on her grandchildren. After devouring what she believes to be the two grandchildren and their mother, she prowls around the castle one day in search of human flesh and hears her grandchildren weeping. Enraged, she fills a huge vat with vipers, toads, and serpents and is about to throw her kin and the cook-accomplice into the vat when the king returns. The mother-in-law ends up in the vat and is devoured by the reptiles in it. If the king regrets her death ("after all she was his mother"), he finds ample consolation in his wife and children. A similar episode is found in Giambattista Basile's seventeenth-century collection of Neapolitan tales.

It is not difficult to understand why the Grimms did not make the effort to find a fuller version of this tale or to reconstruct the fragment and turn it into a sequel to their "Briar

Rose." The unsavory subject matter was clearly not appropriate for a volume that was turning into a book for children, and the fact that the tale existed in a fuller version in French and Italian stories did not add to the appeal. "The Evil Mother-in-Law" went the way of "Bluebeard," "Puss-in-Boots," and other stories that bore too close a resemblance to French literary sources.

The Children Living in a Time of Famine

There once lived a woman who fell into such deep poverty with her two daughters that they didn't even have a crust of bread left to put in their mouths. Finally they were so famished that the mother was beside herself with despair and said to the older child: "I will have to kill you so that I'll have something to eat."

The daughter replied: "Oh, no, dearest Mother, spare me. I'll go out and see to it that I can get something to eat without having to beg for it."

And so she went out, returned, and brought with her a small piece of bread that they all ate, but it was too little to ease the pangs of hunger.

And so the mother said to the other daughter: "Now it's your turn."

But she replied: "Oh, no, dearest Mother, spare me. I'll go out and get something to eat without anyone noticing it."

And so she went out, returned, and brought with her two small pieces of bread. They all ate them, but it was too little to ease their pangs of hunger. After a few hours, the mother said to them once again: "You will have to die, otherwise we'll all perish."

The girls replied: "Dearest Mother, we'll lie down and go to sleep, and we won't rise again until the Day of Judgment." And so they lay down and slept so soundly that no one could awaken them. The mother left, and not a soul knows where she is.

A summary of a seventeenth-century written account of a mother who threatened to kill and devour her daughters so that she could survive a famine, "The Children Living in a Time of Famine" is less fairy tale than sensational news story. It is telling, however, that the Grimms elected to include this kind of account in their collection. Clearly, for them there was no distinct dividing line between the fiction of fairy tales and the facts of everyday life, or at least the most sensationalistic aspects of everyday life. What really distinguishes this report from fairy tales is the absence of magic and the sudden appearance of a way out—a way for the two sisters to rescue themselves from the cannibalistic ogre who is their mother. But the many faces of maternal evil in fairy tales no doubt led the Grimms to believe that this account did not deviate radically from fairy-tale narratives.

The Stubborn Child

There once lived a stubborn child, and he never did what his mother told him to do. And so our dear Lord did not look kindly on him and let him become ill. Doctors could not cure him, and before long he was lying on his deathbed. His coffin was being lowered into the grave and they were about to cover it with earth when suddenly one of his little arms emerged and reached up into the air. They pushed it back in again and covered the coffin with more earth, but it was no use. The little arm kept reaching out of the grave. Finally, his mother had to go to the grave and strike the little arm with a switch. After she did that, the arm withdrew, and the child finally began to rest in peace beneath the earth.

"Eigensinnig," *the German term for stubborn, suggests a strong will, a desire to have things your own way. In their annotations, the Grimms point to superstitious beliefs surrounding children who strike their parents—they evidently are not able to rest in peace and their arms emerge periodically from the grave to make beating gestures. This tale appears today in the*

standard collections of Grimms' fairy tales, and, like "The Jew in the Brambles," remains of historical interest, even if it is not appropriate as a story for children. Some child readers, nonetheless, find this tale fascinating, and it has been viewed by some adult readers as a tale for mothers who need reassurance that the process of grieving for a child that has died must find an end. The German version of the tale does not specify the gender of the child.

The Rose

Once upon a time there lived an old woman who had two children. Every day the youngest had to go into the forest to fetch wood. Once, when he had gone very far into the forest, he met a small, but sturdy, child who worked hard to help him find wood and bring it right up to the house. The child vanished in the blink of an eye. The boy told his mother all about what had happened, but she didn't believe him. Later the boy brought his mother a rose and told her that the beautiful child had given him the rose and would come again when it was in full bloom. The mother put the rose in water. One morning the child did not get out of bed. The mother went over to the child's bed and discovered that he had died. But he looked peaceful. And the rose was in full bloom that morning.

The ten legends for children appended to the two hundred tales in the Children's Stories and Household Tales *are more religious tales than fairy tales. One tale replicates the structure of the kind and unkind girls, with Saint Joseph as the figure who rewards and punishes. A second tells of twelve starving brothers who are rescued by angels to become the twelve apostles. A third tells of a widow with five children whose sister refuses to share food with*

her. When the sister's husband, who is "as rich as a gold mine," cuts a slice of bread, blood gushes from the loaf. He rushes over to the sister's house and finds her praying and holding her two surviving children. She refuses the offer for food and expires with the two children before his eyes. These tales, like "The Rose," were designed to provide comfort and consolation to those living in hard times, with the promise of a glorious afterlife that would compensate for earthly hardships. A motif from this tale appears in Maurice Sendak's illustrations for Wilhelm Grimm's tale "Dear Mili."

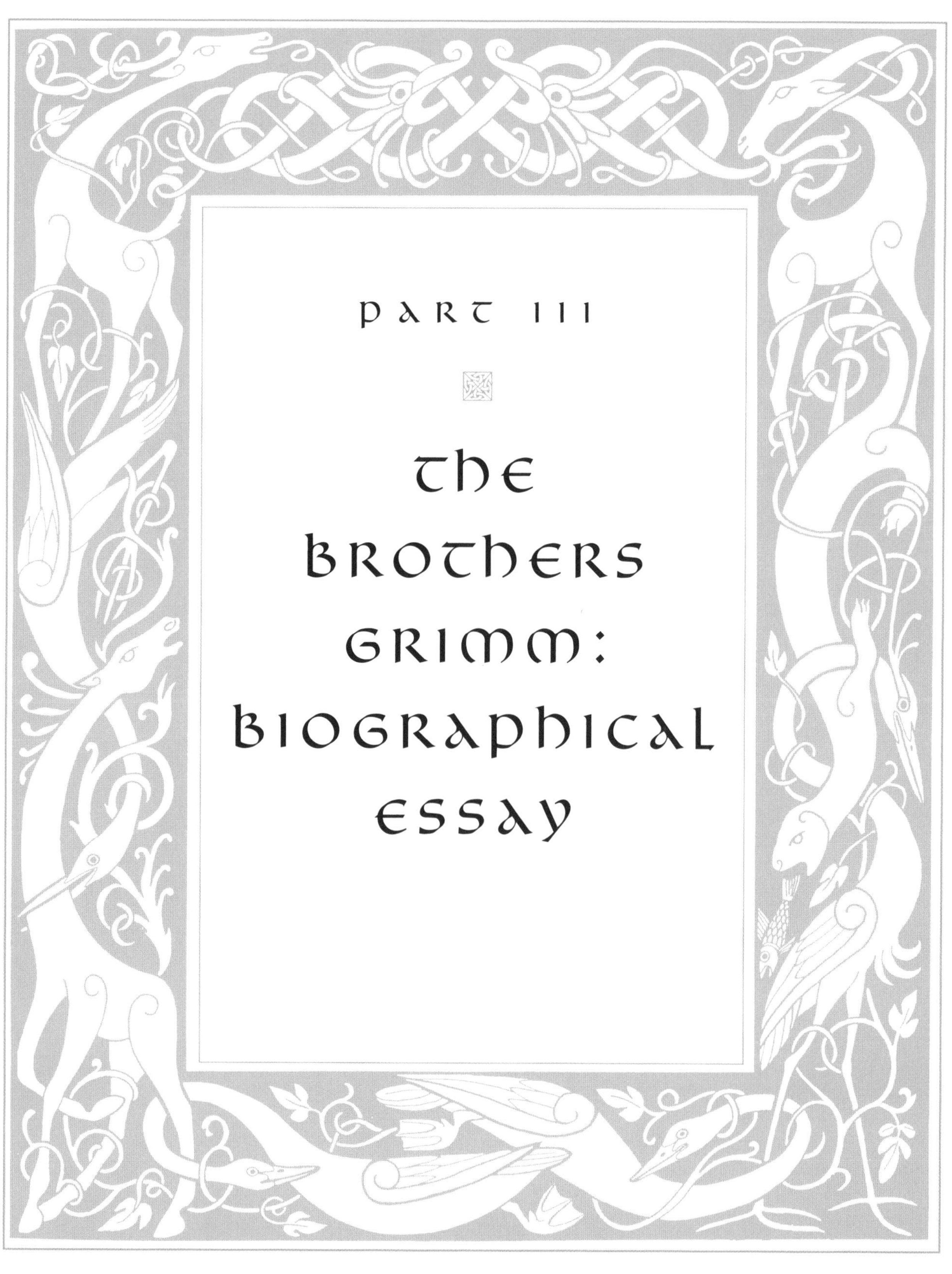

PART III

The Brothers Grimm: Biographical Essay

Jacob and Wilhelm Grimm

"Silence was their real element. . . . I remember how as a child I would walk about in the studies of my father and 'Apapa,' as we children called Jacob Grimm. All you could hear was the scratching of their pens, and sometimes Jacob's frequent little coughs. When writing, he bent down close over the paper, the ends of his quills were cut off short, and he wrote quickly and with excitement. . . . My father left the goose quills unplucked, and he wrote more deliberately. The facial features of both were in constant motion: their eyebrows would move up and down, at times they stared into space. Often they would get up, take out a book and turn the pages. I cannot imagine that anyone would dare interrupt this sacred silence." Wilhelm Grimm's son, Herman, captured in this vignette what the Grimms are perhaps best known for: a passion for scholarly matters and a collaborative vigor that began when they were young and continued into old age. Dedicating their lives to philology, literature, and history, Jacob and Wilhelm Grimm collected texts, studied them, annotated them, compared them, and engaged in their analysis. Their lives form a tribute to the pleasures and challenges of scholarly pursuits. Laboring next to each other for most of their lives, they collaborated on volumes that laid the foundations for the study of German language, literature, and folklore and that set the standard for scientific research in those fields.

"Many are the fairy tales and myths," Jack Zipes has observed, "that have been spread about the Brothers Grimm." For some, Jacob and Wilhelm Grimm are cultural heroes, men who pioneered the study of philology and folklore in Germany and who left a remarkable legacy in the volumes they published during their lifetimes. As the scholar Murray Peppard puts it, "the fairy tale brothers lifted the musty veil obscuring Germany's past and wove it into a magic web that captured the imagination of all Europe." For others, the Grimms were proto-fascists who promoted nationalistic sentiment and values that are unacceptable to us today. The distinguished American folklorist Richard M. Dorson underscored the link between what the Grimms published and what the Nazis found appealing: "In the wake of the Grimms, late nineteenth-century nationalists extolled the brothers and their Märchen for helping acquaint Germans with a sense of folk unity and historical past. Under the Nazis the originals of the tales with their bloodletting and violence were reintroduced."

The brothers' philological achievements (launching the *German Dictionary*, producing the *German Grammar*, collecting fairy tales and legends, and editing Old High German and Middle High German texts), their accomplishments in the arena of public service (as professors, diplomats, and librarians), and their political engagement (most prominently as members of a group protesting the dissolution of parliament and revocation of constitutional rights in Hannover) have come to be dwarfed by their folkloric legacy.

Born in Hanau in 1785 and 1786, Jacob and Wilhelm Grimm were the oldest of six children. In his autobiography, Wilhelm recalled his childhood home—its garden wall, a peach tree that blossomed every year, and the old church at the center of town. The family was solidly middle class: Philipp Wilhelm Grimm, the boys' father, was scribe and district magistrate in the town of Steinau, near Kassel, where he was given a generous salary and a comfortable home for his family. In the mornings, Jacob and Wilhelm received instruction in geography, history, and botany from their tutor Herr Zinckhahn; in the afternoon they attended private lessons in French and Latin. Jacob, who was being groomed for legal studies, received special lessons in law from his father. Still, there remained time for childhood games, and both brothers write at length in their autobiographical accounts about hide-and-seek, marbles, snowball fights, arts and crafts, along with afternoons devoted to long walks in the meadows or watching swallows build nests. It was, as the brothers recalled, an idyllic period in their lives. "I can still recall," Wilhelm wrote many years later, "how the two of us, Jacob and I, would walk hand in hand past the market in the city to our French teacher, who lived next to the church. We would stand gazing in childish delight at the golden rooster on top of the tower, watching it turn in the wind."

The "collector spirit," or *Sammlergeist,* was a quality that both brothers cultivated early in life. Wilhelm not only collected insects and butterflies but also drew sketches of them in his notebook. Jacob and Wilhelm both made a habit of copying passages from books, preserving them for later perusal. These hobbies foreshadowed their joint interest in collecting legends, myths, folktales, folk songs, and proverbs, along with the thousands and thousands of citations that were gathered as part of their project for a German dictionary.

In 1796 Philipp Wilhelm Grimm, described by his son Jacob as "hard-working, methodical, and affectionate," came down with pneumonia and died. In an autobiographical statement penned in 1831, Jacob Grimm still had vivid memories of the black coffin in which his father was carried to the cemetery. Without a government pension, Dorothea Grimm was forced to draw on savings to support herself and her six children. She moved from the comfortable home in Steinau with Jacob, Wilhelm, and their three younger brothers (Carl, Ferdinand, and Ludwig) and sister Lotte to a more modest dwelling. The following year, Henriette Zimmer, Dorothea's sister, invited the two older boys to live with her in Kassel so they could attend the prestigious Lyceum Fredericianum. Wilhelm, the more physically fragile of the two brothers, suffered under the strict educational regimen and struggled periodically with bouts of colds and asthma. Jacob, more physically robust, was troubled by social slights that he and his brother had to endure. It was in Kassel that Jacob developed a keen sense of social justice and a devotion to democratic rule in all spheres of life.

Both brothers graduated from the lyceum at the head of their classes, but both also had to request special dispensation to study law at the University of Marburg. Their work ethic was unparalleled, and material hardship served to spur their efforts. In his autobiography, Jacob observed that "poverty is an inducement to diligence and hard work—it protects from many a distraction and inspires a healthy sense of pride based on the consciousness of one's own merits by contrast to what is bestowed on others for their rank or wealth." In Marburg the brothers launched their legal studies, with Jacob enrolling at the university in 1802 and Wilhelm beginning his studies the following year. The year-long separation weighed heavily on the brothers, who were accustomed to sharing everything, including a single bed. Living modestly—only members of the aristocracy and rich landowners were given stipends, much to Jacob's dismay—they were more absorbed by their studies than by concerns for material comfort. While other students gambled, played cards, dueled, and rode horseback, they remained dedicated to the curriculum.

Under the tutelage of Friedrich Karl von Savigny, founder of the historical school of law, the brothers discovered the importance of philological studies and historical research. In Savigny's library, they had a chance to browse books and manuscripts from an earlier era and to indulge their love of matters both literary and historical. When Jacob published his *German Grammar*, he dedicated the volume to Savigny, whose lectures had modeled the scientific method of research for him and his brother. In Marburg the Grimms also discovered Romantic literature, reading such authors as Ludwig Tieck and Friedrich Schlegel with enthusiasm, and working through texts from the Middle Ages, to which they would later return in their scholarly studies. When asked to go on an outing, Jacob often refused, saying that he intended to "take a walk in literature."

Savigny invited Jacob to accompany him to Paris as his research assistant at the university, where he was writing a history of Roman law in the Middle Ages. Jacob's letters to Wilhelm reveal his avid interest in the culture and politics of the French capital. Fluent in French, Jacob was offered a position at the Hessian War Ministry in 1806 and quickly accepted with the hope of providing support for his brother, mother, and siblings. Separation was not easy, and Jacob wrote from Paris that he hoped the two would never again part ways: "If at any time in the future one of us should be sent away, the other must give notice at once. We are so accustomed to being together that the mere thought of separation causes me deep distress." Forced to wear a stiff uniform with powdered wig and high collar and to perform mind-numbing work, Jacob was nonetheless prepared to carry out his duties in exchange for a modest salary. Political events produced momentous changes, and that same year Kassel became the capital of the new kingdom of Westphalia, ruled by Napoleon's youngest brother, Jérôme.

During the years of the Napoleonic occupation, Jacob Grimm reflected on the gradual shift in his interests from law to literature: "I consider myself qualified to seek a position in the public library in Kassel, especially since I had some practice in the reading of manuscripts and reasonable familiarity with the history of literature through private study. I also felt that I would make stronger progress in that field, rather than in the field of French law, which I detested, and into which our entire system of jurisprudence was about to be transformed." Jacob sensed that the pursuit of legal studies had been determined less by intellectual inclination than by a sense of filial responsibility. Wherever there were books, he felt at home, and the position of librarian and archivist, with its low-key social dimension and opportunities for immersion in reading, had a powerful appeal for him. "My uncle loved books," Herman Grimm observed, capturing Jacob's real passion in life.

Jacob's efforts to secure a position in Kassel were finally successful in 1808, when King Jérôme offered him a position as royal librarian in Napoleonshöhe, formerly known as Wilhelmshöhe. Just weeks before the appointment, Dorothea Grimm died, leaving Jacob and Wilhelm to manage family matters and to care for their four siblings. The new position provided financial stability and was something of a sinecure, requiring only a few hours a day of cataloging new entries. Jacob had ample time to use the resources of the Royal Library to pursue his own research interests, even after he was made auditor to the Council of State.

It was during Jacob's tenure at the War Ministry and at the Royal Library that the brothers launched their efforts to collect folklore. These were not easy years for the Grimms, and in 1809 Wilhelm's health had declined so dramatically that he was sent to Halle for treatment with the famed physician Johann Christian Reil. The costly "magnetic" treatments lasted nearly six months and significantly depleted the family resources. Years later, Wilhelm described the precarious state of his health in his autobiography: "To the shortness of breath which made climbing a few steps a terrible burden and the constant fierce pains in my chest were now added a heart condition.

The pain, which felt like a fiery arrow was being shot repeatedly through my heart, left me with a constant sense of anxiety. Sometimes I experienced violent palpitations. . . . I was not completely distraught by my illness, and when things were tolerable, I was able to work, even finding some pleasure in it."

The plan of Clemens Brentano, a close friend to both brothers, to issue a volume of folktales inspired the Grimms to collect oral tales in the region of Kassel and to identify written versions of tales. This was a period of unprecedented productivity in the lives of the brothers, and they published volumes on songs, ballads, tales, and in 1812, the first installment to the *Children's Stories and Household Tales*. Their turn to older German literature and to folklore can be seen in some ways as a form of passive resistance, a quiet protest to the Napoleonic occupation, in its effort to establish the basis for a German cultural identity. Wilhelm wrote in his autobiography about the political dimension he perceived in the scholarly turn taken in their work: "The days marking the collapse of all previously existing establishments will never be forgotten. . . . The zeal with which we pursued our studies in older German helped overcome our spiritual depression. . . . Undoubtedly the world situation and the need to withdraw into the tranquillity of scholarship contributed to the reawakening of the long-forgotten literature, but we were not just seeking solace in the past, we also hoped that the course on which we had embarked would contribute somehow to the return of a better day."

For the Grimms, the fairy tales published in 1812 and 1815 represented the "last echoes of ancient myths." These stories belonged to a pagan past, and it was the duty of scholars everywhere to preserve what had been passed down from one generation to the next as faithfully as possible. "In the fairy tales," Wilhelm Grimm wrote in his preface to a collection of Danish ballads, "a world of magic is opened up before us, one which still exists among us in secret forests, in underground caves, and in the deepest sea, and it is still visible to children. . . . [These fairy tales] belong to our national poetic heritage, since it can be proved that they have existed among the people for several centuries." What attracted the Grimms to folklore was not only its historical value but also its poetic core. The ancient myths and modern fairy tales captured existential mysteries and truths higher than those articulated by philosophers and scholars.

The year 1813 witnessed the end of French occupation, and in the following year Jacob was appointed to the Hessian Peace Delegation and spent time in the diplomatic service in both Paris and Vienna. After the peace treaties were signed, Jacob returned home and joined Wilhelm as librarian in the Royal Library in Kassel. For more than a decade the Grimms worked side by side, pursuing their scholarly mission, publishing massive volumes with such titles as *German Legends, German Grammar, Ancient German Law,* and *German Heroic Legends*. Jacob Grimm's *German Grammar* alone took up 3,854 pages. These were the years that Jacob was to refer to as "the quietest, most industrious, and perhaps also the most fruitful period" of his life.

But much as the brothers are often idealized as scholarly soul mates who labored side by side to produce extraordinarily learned tomes, their relationship was not without friction. In 1822 Wilhelm wrote to his friend Achim von Arnim about Jacob's temperament, explaining why his brother was not suited for an academic post: "He has neither the desire nor the composure for communicating and presenting in class. In fact he is generally both excited and belligerent and is therefore not well suited for communal activities where each person has his place. He tends by nature to engage in criticism, and he has nurtured this tendency, so that he always sees the worst side of things first. . . . I often worry about this condition, but then he is also extremely sensitive, often believing that he has been abandoned or neglected. He acts unhappy about that, but in fact he is the one who alienates people with his testy nature." The less industrious of the two brothers, Wilhelm conceded that he had few real scholarly ambitions and that he had spent most of his life "submitting" to his brother's will in things.

Jacob remained a bachelor his entire life. In 1825 Wilhelm married Dorothea Wild, the daughter of a pharmacist in Kassel and the great-granddaughter of a famous philologist. Wilhelm considered the marriage "God's best blessing." The brothers lived in the same household and continued as librarians until 1829, when the first librarian of the Royal Library died and the elector of Kassel failed to appoint either of the two to the vacant post. The elector, who had greeted a copy of the first volume of

Jacob's *German Grammar* with the observation that he hoped the author was not neglecting his official duties, turned down the Grimms' applications for the promotion. Jacob and Wilhelm resigned their positions and traveled to Göttingen, where Jacob accepted a post as professor of German linguistics and law and as head librarian, and where Wilhelm was appointed librarian and then professor. The university library in Göttingen had the largest and finest collection in Hesse, and it became the first lending library in Germany. The elector is said to have remarked on the Grimms' departure: "So the Grimms are leaving. What a loss! They have never done anything for me." But within a matter of weeks, he began to understand the real loss in prestige his kingdom had suffered, and he made a belated offer to the Grimms, who had by then already committed themselves to the move to Göttingen.

In 1837 King Ernst August II succeeded to the throne of Hannover and made it his first duty of business to dissolve parliament and to revoke the constitution of 1833. All civil servants were required to swear a personal oath of allegiance. The Grimms, along with five other renowned professors, signed a protest document in which they reaffirmed their loyalty to the constitution of 1833 and rejected the notion that the king could revoke it. All seven were dismissed from their posts just a few weeks later, and three of the professors, among them Jacob Grimm, were ordered to leave the kingdom within three days or go to prison. The "Göttingen Seven," as the dissident professors were called, became renowned for their protest against tyranny. In a public address to students and professors, Jacob cited Martin Luther: "The freedom of Christian men must give us the courage to resist our ruler if it turns out that he acts against the spirit of God and if he offends human rights." Forced into exile, Jacob was obliged to leave Göttingen. "It is not the arm of justice but sheer power that forced me to leave the country," Jacob wrote in an essay on his dismissal from the university. Still, the majority of the Grimms' university colleagues sided with the monarch and offered no resistance to the royal decrees. The protest marked a real watershed in the lives of the Grimms, for, at the time, their stand was not considered at all heroic by many. Savigny, for example, remained on cordial terms with the Grimms, but his refusal to endorse their actions carried with it a silent reproach. There were efforts to raise money on behalf of the brothers, but there were also many who blamed the seven professors for the academic troubles that plagued Göttingen in the years following the protest. The king of Hannover remained untroubled by his actions, famously remarking that all you needed was money to secure the services of "dancers, whores, and professors."

Wilhelm Grimm soon joined Jacob in Kassel, where the brothers both received a warm reception. But with no secure source of income, they had to rely on occasional earnings and on friends. Still, the Grimms managed to continue their scholarly efforts, launching the *German Dictionary,* the German equivalent of the *Oxford English Dictionary*. In 1838 they announced their venture in a newspaper published in Leipzig: "It is one of the gifts of human nature to be able to discover sweetness in what is bitter and to find fruit in privation. Jacob and Wilhelm Grimm, assailed at the same time by the same fate, after a long and fruitless wait for a German state to appoint them to some post, have found the courage to assure and strengthen their future. They are undertaking a great German Dictionary . . . which will contain the vast wealth of our fatherland's language from Luther to Goethe." The vast enterprise demanded an extraordinary commitment to labors that were exacting and often tedious—"words seemed to emerge from every nook and cranny." At times they seemed engaged in an effort that required, as they themselves put it, the focused concentration and Herculean effort of chopping wood for the better part of the day.

In 1840 the king of Prussia offered the brothers a generous stipend at the University of Berlin and at the Academy of Sciences, where they were to continue work on their dictionary. "The king's generosity," Jacob observed, "will allow us the leisure needed to complete our task." The brothers moved with Dorothea and the three children to more capacious living quarters in the Prussian capital.

During the Revolution of 1848, Jacob Grimm was elected to parliament, but hopes for reform dwindled as the Grimms watched one compromise after another erode the possibility of democratic rule. The brothers retired from active politics, and Jacob retired from his academic position in 1848, with Wilhelm following his example four years later. In the remaining years of their lives, they continued work on their monumental *German Dictionary,* getting as far as the letter *F* and the word *Frucht* ("fruit").

With so many projects containing the term *Deutsch* ("German"/"Germanic") in the title, the Grimms could easily be seen as promoting nationalistic aims. Yet the brothers' preoccupation with Germanic traditions was less symptomatic of chauvinistic zeal than of an effort to mobilize linguistics, history, and folklore to understand a culture. In many ways, the Grimms were more cosmopolitan than nationalistic, for they were always eager to use a comparative approach to identify cultural differences and what gave rise to them. Wilhelm Grimm studied Danish ballads, songs, and folktales, in addition to translating Scottish songs. Jacob translated *Reynard the Fox* and compared Low German, French, Dutch, and Latin variants of the epic. The brothers collaborated on a translation of *The Elder Edda* and on Old French and Old English epics and romances. Their correspondents included Sir Walter Scott in Scotland, the translator Edgar Taylor in England, the Norwegian folklorists Peter Christian Asbjørnsen and Jørgen Moe, and the folklorist Alexander Afanasev in Russia.

In 1859 Wilhelm Grimm died at age 73 of complications from heart and liver ailments. In his eulogy, Jacob referred to his brother as the *Märchenbruder*, or fairy-tale brother, suggesting that he was both the ideal brother and also the brother who had done the lion's share of the work on the *Children's Stories and Household Tales*. Jacob continued work on the *German Dictionary*, at times writing in bed, with a pillow propping him up. He died four years later in 1863. At the request of the brothers, their tombstones in Berlin bear the simple inscriptions "Here lies Wilhelm Grimm" and "Here lies Jacob Grimm."

PART IV

OTHER MATTERS

Prefaces to the First Two Editions of the Grimms' Children's Stories and Household Tales

The Grimms' *Children's Stories and Household Tales* appeared in two volumes, the first in 1812, the second in 1815. Each volume had its own preface, penned by Wilhelm Grimm but drawing on the shared wisdom of the brothers on folklore. For the second edition of the tales, Wilhelm Grimm elaborated on the plot conventions, stereotypical characters, and stylistic features of German folklore. Although there is some overlap between the prefaces of 1812 and 1815 and the second revised version, I include all three documents here, for they offer powerful insights into the spirit of the Grimms' collecting efforts and their views about the symptomatic character of folklore. Occasionally the florid language, effusive style, and arcane allusions obscure the Grimms' meaning, but in most cases we get a candid look at what the brothers sought to achieve with their collection.

The Grimms' reverence for the folk and for its every creative expression is reflected in these prefaces. Extolling the virtues of *Volkspoesie*, a poetry that captures the voice of the people, they assert the close ties between it and *Naturpoesie*, the poetry of nature. The Grimms insisted that they had not tampered with the words they heard. To the contrary, they had aimed for fidelity to both the letter and spirit of the voices they heard. "We tried to collect these tales in as pure a form as possible," they declared. "No details have been added or embellished and changed." The claim is probably an honest one, but by 1819 the Grimms had changed their tune about their collecting methods. They no longer insisted on fidelity to the letter (as it were) but to the spirit of the tales they heard. They claimed to have resisted the temptation to add episodes or to improve on what they heard, but they also conceded that the "phrasing" of each text was mainly their own. More important, for the second edition of the *Children's Stories and Household Tales*, they freely admitted that they had taken care to eliminate "every phrase not appropriate for children." The brothers had originally planned to produce a contribution to the "history of poetry" and had had no intention of publishing "a volume for entertainment." But in the end Wilhelm Grimm could not resist giving in to popular demand and expectations rather than worrying about scholarly standards and methods. The brothers were collecting at a time when folklore did not exist as a discipline, and they were more or less inventing the rules of the collection as they went along. With each new edition of the tales, the brothers tried to produce texts that had a certain narrative integrity and stylistic unity and that erased the off-color humor of tales told around the fireside when the children were asleep. The tales lost some of their sensationalistic verve, but they also gained in readability and accessibility for broader audiences. The household tales were now more than adult entertainment—they were to provide diversion for children as well as their parents.

The prefaces reveal the great sense of national pride the Grimms took in the poetry of the people. They also show the brothers' familiarity with other traditions—French, Italian, and Scandinavian—and their respect for other national collections. To be sure, the Grimms understood their collection as a foundation stone for the construction of German national identity, yet they were also aware that folkloric traditions, for all their local color and cultural specificity, revealed a certain universality, at least among European nations. Their respect for native lore of other regions and their sympathetic and sensitive exploration of foreign traditions reveal a cosmopolitan stance that was absent from their nationalist admirers in the first half of the twentieth century.

Preface to Volume I of the First Edition of Children's Stories and Household Tales

Kinder- und Hausmärchen. Gesammelt durch die Brüder Grimm. Berlin, in der Realschulbuchhandlung, 1812.

When a storm or some other calamity from the heavens destroys an entire crop, it is reassuring to find that a small spot on a path lined by hedges or bushes has been spared and that a few stalks, at least, remain standing. If the sun favors them with light, they continue to grow, alone and unobserved, and no scythe comes along to cut them down prematurely for vast storage bins. But near the end of the summer, once they have ripened and become full, poor devout hands seek them out; ear upon ear, carefully bound and esteemed more highly than entire sheaves, they are brought home, and for the entire winter they provide nourishment, perhaps the only seed for the future. That is how it all seems to us when we review the riches of German poetry from earlier times and discover that nothing of it has been kept alive. Even the memory of it is lost—folk songs and these innocent household tales are all that remain. The places by the stove, the hearth in the kitchen, attic stairs, holidays still celebrated, meadows and forests in their solitude, and above all the untrammeled imagination have functioned as hedges preserving them and passing them on from one generation to the next. These are our thoughts after surveying this collection. At first we were convinced that much had been lost in this area too, and that the only tales still left were the ones we already knew, which others tell in different forms (as is always the case). But ever on the watch for everything that *still* remains of this poetry, we also wanted to get to know these different versions, and much that was new came to light unexpectedly. Even though we were not able to make broad inquiries, our collection grew so much from year to year that now, after some six years have passed, it seems rich to us. We realize, of course, that we may still be missing a great deal, but we are also gratified by the thought that we have the most and the best of the lot. Everything has been collected, with a few exceptions as noted, from oral traditions in Hessen and in the Main and Kinzig regions of the Duchy of Hanau, from where we hail. For that reason, we have happy memories about every single tale. Few books have been produced with so much pleasure, and we are delighted to thank publicly all those who had a part in it.

It is probably just the right time to gather these tales, since those who have been making an effort to preserve them are becoming ever harder to find (to be sure, those who know them still know a great deal, because people may die, but the stories live on). The custom of telling tales is, however, on the wane, just as all the cozy corners in homes and gardens are giving way to an empty splendor that resembles the smile with which one speaks of these tales—a smile that looks elegant but costs so little. Where the tales still exist, they live on and no one worries about whether they are good or bad, poetic or vulgar. We know them and we love them just because we happen to have heard them in a certain way, and we like them without reflecting on why. Telling these tales is an extraordinary custom—and this too the tales share with everything immortal—that one must like it no matter what others say. At any rate, one quickly discovers that the custom persists only in places where there is a warm openness to poetry or where there are imaginations not yet deformed by the perversities of modern life. In that very spirit, we do not intend to praise these tales or even to defend them against opposing views: their very *existence* suffices to protect them. Anything that has succeeded in bringing so much pleasure so often, and has at the same time inspired and instructed, carries its own inner justification and must have issued from the eternal wellspring that bedews all life, even if it is only a single drop enclosed by a small, protective leaf, yet shimmering in the rosy dawn.

These stories are suffused with the same purity that makes children appear so wondrous and blessed to us: they have the same bluish white, flawless, shining eyes (that small children so love to grab at),[1] which are as big as they will ever get, even as other parts of the body remain delicate, weak, and awkward for use on earth. Most of the events in these stories are so basic that many readers will have encountered them in real life, but, like all things true to life, they appear fresh and moving. Parents have no food left, and, as a result, have to cast out their children, or a hard-hearted stepmother makes them suffer[2] and would like to see them die. Or siblings find themselves all alone in the woods, the wind frightens them, they are afraid of wild animals, but they stand by each other with the loyalty you would expect. Little Brother knows how to find his way back home again, or, if he has been bewitched, Little Sister leads him around in the form of a fawn and collects greens and mosses for his bed; or she sits silently and sews him a shirt of star flowers to break a magic spell. The entire range of this world is clearly defined: kings, princes, faithful servants and honest tradesmen, above all fishermen, millers, colliers, and herdsmen (those who have stayed close to nature) make an appearance; everything else is alien and unknown to that world. As in myths that tell of a golden age, all of nature is alive; the sun, the moon, and the stars are approachable, give gifts, and can even be woven into gowns; dwarfs mine metals in the mountains; mermaids leap in the water; birds (doves are the most beloved and the most helpful), plants, and stones all speak and know just how to express their sympathy; even blood can call out and say things. This poetry exercises certain rights that later storytelling can only strive to express through metaphors. The easy, innocent familiarity between large and small is indescribably endearing, and we get more pleasure from a conversation between the stars and a poor child abandoned in the woods than from hearing the music of the spheres. Everything beautiful is golden and strewn with pearls; there are even golden people living there; misfortune, by contrast, is a dark power, a dreadful cannibalistic giant who is, however, vanquished, since a good woman who knows just how to avert misfortune stands ready to help. These narratives always end by opening the prospect of boundless happiness. Evil is also neither inconsequential nor something close to home, and not something very bad, to which one could grow accustomed, but something terrible, black, and wholly alien that you cannot even get near. The punishment of evil is equally terrifying: snakes and poisonous reptiles devour their victims, or the evil person dances to death in red-hot iron shoes. Many things have their own obvious meanings: a mother gets her real child back just when she manages to get a laugh out of the changeling that familiar spirits have substituted for her own child; the life of a child similarly begins with a smile and continues in joy, and when it smiles in its sleep, angels are talking with it. A quarter hour of each day is exempt from the power of magic, and then the human form steps forth in freedom, as if no power could envelop us completely. Every day offers moments when man can rid himself of everything that is false and can see clearly; on the other hand, the magic spell is never completely broken, and a swan's wing is left in place of an arm. Or because a tear was shed, an eye is lost with it. Or worldly cleverness is humbled, and the numbskull alone, ridiculed and despised by everyone, yet pure of heart, has good fortune. In these features we can see the basis for the moral precept or for the relevant object lesson that can be derived so readily from these tales; it was never their purpose to instruct, nor were they made up for that reason, but a moral grows out of them, just as good fruit develops from healthy blossoms without help from man. The proof of all authentic poetry is that it is never without some connection to real life and returns to it, just as clouds return to their place of birth once they have watered the earth.

The essence of these stories seems to us as follows: outwardly they resemble all folktales and legends. Never fixed and always changing from one region to another, from one teller to another, they still preserve a basic core. They are, however, clearly distinguishable from *local folk legends*, which are attached to real places or historical figures, and of which we have not included any examples here, although we have collected a good many and intend to publish them at a later date. We have often included several variants of one and the same tale owing to the pleasingly distinctive tone of the variations; the less significant we have put in an appendix; but all in all we have collected as faithfully as was possible for us. It is also clear that these tales were forever being created anew as time went on, but for just that reason their core must be very old. The age of some can be shown to be almost three centuries, for there are allusions to them in Fischart and Rollenhagen (which are noted where appropriate), but beyond doubt they are older than that, even if lack of evidence makes direct proof impossible. There is only one sure piece of evidence, and it is built on the tales' connections with heroic epics and indigenous animal fables. But this is not the right place to go into details. We have said something about this matter in the appendix.

The closeness of the poetry to the earliest and simplest forms of life accounts for its widespread diffusion. There is not a single culture that does without it. Even the Negroes of West Africa entertain their children with stories, and Strabo expressly says the same thing about the Greeks. (In the end, one will find similar attestations among others, which goes to show just how highly these tales were esteemed by those who understand the value of a voice speaking directly to the heart.) This explains another most remarkable circumstance, and that concerns the widespread diffusion of the German tales. In that respect, they not only match the heroic stories of Siegfried the dragon slayer, but even surpass them, for we find these tales, and precisely these tales, throughout Europe, thus revealing a kinship among the noblest peoples. In the north, we know only the Danish heroic ballads, which contain much that is pertinent here, even if in the form of songs, which are not quite appropriate for children since they are meant to be sung. But here too the dividing line can hardly be drawn with greater precision than for the more serious historical legend, and there are actually areas of overlap. England has the Tabart collection, which is not very rich, but what treasures of oral narratives must still exist in Wales, Scotland, and Ireland! Wales has a real treasure just in its *Mabinogion* (now in print). Similarly, Norway, Sweden, and Denmark have retained their riches; the southern countries less so. We know of nothing from Spain, but a passage from Cervantes leaves no room for doubt about the existence and telling of tales.[3] France must surely have more than what was published by Perrault, who treated them as children's tales (not so his inferior imitators, Aulnoy, Murat); he gives us only nine, although these are the best known stories and also among the most beautiful. The merit of his work rests on his refusal to add things and on his decision to leave the stories unchanged, aside from minor details. His manner of presentation deserves special praise for being as simple as was possible for him. There is really nothing more difficult than using the French language to tell children's stories in a naïve and simple manner, that is, without any pretentiousness, for the language in its current state transforms itself almost spontaneously into epigrammatic remarks and finely honed dialogue (just look at the conversation between Riquet à la houpe and the stupid princess, as well as at the end of "Petit Poucet"); sometimes the tales are unnecessarily long and drawn out. A study about to be published holds that Perrault invented these tales and only through him (born 1633, died 1703) did they reach the people. It also maintains that an imitation of Homer appears in the story of Tom Thumb, which allegedly has the aim of making Ulysses' plight when confronted with Polyphemus understandable to children. Johanneau had a more accurate view on this matter. The older Italian collections are richer than all the others. First and foremost the *Nights* of Straparola, which contains many good things, but especially *The Pentamerone* of Basile, as well known and beloved in Italy as it is rare and unknown in Germany. Written in the Neapolitan dialect, it is in every respect an excellent work. The content is almost entirely without gaps and without inauthentic additions. The style is replete with fine turns of phrase and sayings. To translate it in a lively way requires a Fischart[4] and his age; we plan to make all this clear in the second volume of the present collection, in which everything furnished by foreign sources will find a place.

We have tried to collect these tales in as pure a form as possible. In many, the narrative flow is interrupted by rhymes and lines of verse which sometimes clearly alliterate but are never sung during the telling of a tale. Precisely these are the oldest and best tales. No details have been added or embellished or changed, for we would have been reluctant to expand stories already so rich by adding analogies and allusions. They cannot be invented. A collection of this kind has never existed in Germany. The tales have almost always been used as the stuff of longer stories, which have been expanded and edited at the author's pleasure. To be sure, they had some value for that purpose, but what belonged to children was always torn out of their hands, and nothing was given back to them in return. Even those who kept children in mind could not resist mixing in mannerisms of contemporary writing; there was hardly ever enough diligence in collecting so that only a few tales, picked up by chance,[5] were published. Had we been fortunate enough to be able to tell the stories in a specific dialect, then they would no doubt have gained much; here we have one of those cases where a high degree of development, refinement, and artistry in language misfires, and where one feels that a purified literary language, as effective as it may be for other purposes, has become brighter and more transparent, but also more insipid and would have failed to capture the essentials.

We bequeath this book to well-meaning hands and cannot help but think of the powerful blessing that dwells in them. We hope that the book will remain completely unknown to those who begrudge poor and modest souls these small morsels of poetry.

KASSEL, *October* 18, 1812

ENDNOTES

1. Fischart, *Gargantua*, 129b, 131b.

2. The situation appears here often and is probably the first cloud to rise on each child's horizon, evoking the first tears, which people fail to see, but that angels count. Flowers have even acquired their names in this way; the Viola tricolor is called "little stepmother" because each of its yellow leaves has a slender green leaf beneath it that holds it up. Those are said to be the chairs given by a mother to her own happy children; the two stepchildren stand mournfully above in dark violet, and they have no chairs.

3. —y aquellas (cosas) que à ti te deven parecer profecias, no son sino palabras de consejar, ocuentos de viejas, como aquellos del cavallo sin cabeça, y de la varilla de virtudes, con que se entretienen al fuego las dilatadas noches del invierno. Colloq. Entre cip. Y Berg.

4. With the language of his day and with his admirable memory, what a much better book of tales he could have produced had he recognized the value of a true, unadulterated recording.

5. *Musäus* and *Naubert* used as material what we have called local legends; the far more admirable *Otmar* used only those; an *Erfurt* collection of 1787 is weak, a *Leipzig* collection of 1799 hardly belongs here, even though it is not all bad; a collection from *Braunschweig* of 1801 is the richest of these, although in a very different tone. There was nothing for us to take from the latest *Büsching* collection, and it should be expressly noted that a collection published a few years ago by our namesake *A. L. Grimm* in Heidelberg under the title *Children's Tales* was not done very well and has absolutely nothing to do with us and with our work.

The recently published *Winter Tales* by Father *Johann* (Jena at Voigt 1813) only has a new title and actually appeared ten years ago.

They have the same author as the Leipzig collection. Peter Kling is his name, and he has written both books in the same manner. Only the sixth and part of the fifth tale are of value; the others have no substance and, apart from a few details, are hollow inventions.

We ask those who have the opportunity and the desire to help us to improve the details of this book, to complete its fragments, and especially to collect new and unusual animal fables. We would be most grateful for such information, which is best sent to the publisher or to bookstores in Göttingen, Kassel, and Marburg.

Preface to Volume II of the First Edition of the **Children's Stories and Household Tales**

Kinder- und Hausmärchen. Gesammelt durch die Brüder Grimm. Berlin, in der Realschulbuchhandlung, 1815.

Even with the heavy pressures of time, this second volume of household tales moved along substantially more quickly and easily than the first. This was in part because it had earned itself friends who supported it, in part because those who would have liked to support it earlier now clearly perceived the what and how of it; also we were favored by the kind of luck that looks to be chance but that generally accompanies the efforts of diligent, persevering collectors. Once you become accustomed to looking for something, you find it far more frequently than can be imagined, and that is the case in general with folk customs and manners, as with folk sayings and anecdotes.

We owe the lovely Low German tales from the principalities of Paderborn and Münster to a deed of special good will and friendship. The intimate tone of the dialect in them is especially auspicious in light of their internal integrity. Out in the celebrated regions of German freedom, the tales have continued to serve as an almost regular Sunday pastime in many places. In the mountains the shepherds tell a story that is also known in the Harz region and probably indigenous to every mountainous region: the story of Kaiser Rotbart, who lives there with his treasures, and also of the race of giants known as Hühnen and how they throw their hammers to each other from mountain peaks that lie hours apart from each other. There are many things there that we were planning to publish elsewhere. The region remains rich in ancient customs and songs.

One of those happy pieces of good fortune was the acquaintance with a peasant woman from the village of Zwehrn near Kassel. Through her we acquired a good part of the tales published here along with a number of additions to the first volume. They can therefore be counted as genuinely Hessian. This woman, still vigorous and not much over fifty, is called Viehmann. She has a firmly set, pleasant face with bright, clear eyes and was probably beautiful when she was young. She has these stories clearly in mind, a gift which she says is not given to everyone. Many people cannot memorize anything at all. She narrates carefully, confidently, and in an unusually lively manner, taking great pleasure in it. At first she speaks spontaneously, then, if you ask, she will repeat what she has said very slowly so that, with a little practice, it can be transcribed. In this way, much was taken down *verbatim* and no one will fail to recognize its authenticity. Those who believe that oral narratives are routinely falsified, that they are not carefully preserved, and that long recitations are, as a rule, impossible, should have the chance to hear how precisely she stays with each story and how keen she is to narrate correctly. When she retells something, she never changes its essence and corrects errors as soon as she notices them, even if it means interrupting herself. Devotion to tradition is far stronger among people who always adhere to the same way of life than we (who tend to want change) can understand. For that reason, oral narratives, which have stood the test of time, have a certain intimacy and inner effectiveness that other things, which may on the surface seem more dazzling, rarely attain. The epic basis of folk poetry resembles the color green as one finds it throughout nature in various shades: each satisfies and soothes without ever becoming tiresome.

The true value of these tales must really be set quite high: they put our ancient heroic poetry in a new light that could not have been produced in any other way. Briar Rose, who is put to sleep after being pricked by a spindle, is really Brunhilde, put to sleep after being pricked by a thorn—not the one in the *Nibelungenlied*, but the Old Norse one herself. Snow White sleeps peacefully with the same glowing red colors of life on her cheeks as Snæfrid, the most beautiful woman of all, at whose coffin sits Harald the Fair-Haired. Like the faithful dwarfs, he keeps watch over and guards the maiden in suspended animation. The piece of apple stuck in her throat is a special fruit with soporific powers. The story of the golden feather that is dropped by a bird and for which a king sends out search parties the world over is the tale of King Mark in "Tristan," to whom a bird brings the golden hair of a princess, for whom he then develops a longing. We have a better understanding of why Loki sticks fast to a huge eagle once we have read the tale of the golden goose that both men and women stick to when they touch it. Who does not recognize Sigurd's own story in the evil goldsmith, the talking bird, and the episode recounting the eating of a heart? This volume offers other towering and overpowering tales (to some extent they are already in the poem) of Sigurd and his youth—tales that bring welcome assistance to the difficult task of interpreting the treasure that is to be divided up. Nothing is more reliable or more secure than what flows from two sources that were separated at an early date and later joined in a single river bed. These folktales have kept intact German myths that were thought to be lost, and we are firmly convinced that if a search were conducted in all the hallowed regions of our fatherland, long neglected treasures would transform themselves into fabulous treasures and help to found the study of the origins of our poetry. It works the same way with the many dialects of our language. In them a large part of the words and peculiarities that we had long held to be defunct live on undetected.

The aim of our collection was not just to serve the cause of the history of poetry. It was also our intention that the poetry living in it be effective, bringing pleasure wherever it could, and that it therefore become a manual of manners. In this context, it has been noted that this or that might prove embarrassing and would be unsuitable for children or offensive (such as the naming of certain situations and relations—there are those who do not even want them to hear bad things about the devil) and that parents might not want to put the book into the hands of their children. That concern might well be appropriate in certain cases, and then one can easily choose selections. On the whole, it is really unnecessary. Nature itself is our best witness, for she has let these flowers and leaves grow in these colors and shapes. Whoever fails to find them right for certain needs, unknown to nature, can pass right by them, but ought not to demand that they therefore be colored and cut in a different fashion. To put it another way: rain and dew benefit everything on earth. Whoever is afraid to put plants outside because they are too delicate and could be injured, instead preferring to moisten them indoors can hardly demand an end to the rain and dew. Everything that is natural can also be healthy, and that is what we should be after. Incidentally, we do not know of a single healthy and powerful book used to educate the people (and that includes the Bible) in which such delicate matters do not actually appear to an even greater extent. Proper usage sees no evil here, but finds, as an attractive saying has it, a document of our hearts. Children can read the stars without fear, while others, so superstition has it, insult angels by doing the same thing.

We have published variant forms, along with relevant notes, in the appendix. Those who feel indifferent to such things will find it easier to skip over them than we would have found to omit them. They belong to the book, since it is a contribution to the history of German folk poetry. These different versions seem more noteworthy to us than they do to those who see in them nothing more than variants or corrupt forms of a once extant archetypal form. For us, they are more likely to be attempts to capture, through numerous approaches, an inexhaustibly rich ideal type. The repetition of single sentences, episodes, and introductory phrases should be viewed as epic lines that occur again and again as soon as the tone that starts them off is heard. They should not be interpreted in any other way. Everything that has been collected here from oral traditions is (with the exception of "Puss in Boots" perhaps) purely German in its origins as well as in its development and has not been borrowed from any sources, as can easily be proved on the basis of externals if one wanted to dispute that fact for individual tales. The evidence usually marshaled for reliance on Italian, French, or Oriental books, which are not read by the people (especially if they live in the country) reminds us of attempts to prove the recent vintage of tales by pointing to the presence of soldiers, apprentices, or of cannons, pipes, and other new things in them. But these things, like the words of our spoken language, are exactly the things that were refashioned by the lips of each storyteller, and you can be sure that sixteenth-century storytellers spoke of mercenaries and muskets rather than of soldiers and cannons, just as the hat that makes its wearer invisible was in the age of knights a magic helmet.

The translation of *The Pentamerone* initially promised for this volume had to make way for the native tales, as did the selection of those from the *Gesta Romanorum*.

KASSEL, *September* 30, 1814

"On the Nature of Fairy Tales": Introduction to the Second Edition of Children's Stories and Household Tales

Kinder- und Hausmärchen. Gesammelt durch die Brüder Grimm. Erster Band. Zweite vermehrte und verbesserte Auflage. Berlin 1819. Gedruckt und verlegt bei G. Reimer.

> ***This introduction to the second edition offers an extended meditation on the pagan origins of fairy tales and on the peculiarly German inflection to the tales. I have eliminated the footnotes, which refer to editions that are no longer available, and have excised a few paragraphs that refer to arcane scholarly issues of the day.***

Children's stories are told so that the early thoughts and forces of the human heart will awaken and develop in their radiant mildness. But since their simple poetry can bring joy to everyone just as their wisdom can instruct everyone who hears them, and since they remain at home and are passed on from one generation to the next, they are also called household tales. The historical saga often includes something unusual and astonishing, sometimes even something supernatural in a normal, familiar, and contemporary setting. And for that reason, it sometimes seems to be edgy, blunt, and strange, but the fairy tale remains off the beaten track in a peaceful, quiet realm and doesn't try to move from there back into the world. For that reason, names of people and places rarely appear, and home doesn't have a name, but is something shared by everyone in the fatherland.

Most of the events in these stories are so basic that many readers will have encountered them in real life, but, like all things true to life, they appear fresh and moving. Parents have no food left and, as a result, have to cast out their children, or a hardhearted stepmother abandons them, makes them suffer, and would like to see them die. But God sends help in the form of doves who bring them food or who help the poor child pick peas out of the ashes. Or siblings find themselves all alone in the woods, the wind frightens them, they are afraid of wild animals, but they stand by each other with the loyalty you would expect. Little Brother knows how to find his way back home again, or if he has been bewitched, Little Sister leads him around in the form of a fawn and collects greens and mosses for his bed. And how appealing the cozy life in the woods appears to anyone who loves nature and has longed for that kind of life. Or Little Sister sits silently and sews a shirt to break a magic spell. The entire range of this world is clearly defined: kings and the children of kings, faithful servants and honest tradesmen, as the narrator knows them, fishermen, millers, colliers, and herdsmen (those who have stayed close to nature) make an appearance. Everything else that has emerged is alien and unknown to that world. As in myths that tell of a golden age, all of nature is alive; the sun, the moon, and the stars are approachable, give gifts, and can even be woven into gowns; dwarfs mine metals in the mountains; mermaids sleep in the water; animals, birds (doves are the most beloved and the most helpful), plants and stones all speak and know just how to express their sympathy; even blood can call out and say things. This poetry exercises certain rights that later storytelling can only strive to express through metaphors. The harmony in nature and the easy, innocent familiarity between large and small is indescribably endearing, and we get more pleasure from a conversation between the stars and a poor child abandoned in the woods than from hearing the music of the spheres. Misfortune, by contrast, is a dark power, a dreadful cannibalistic giant who is, however, vanquished, since a good woman or a daughter stands ready to help and only strengthens the feeling of joy, as the prospect of a happy ending opens up. Evil is also neither inconsequential nor something close to home, and not something very bad to which one could grow accustomed, but something terrible, black, and wholly alien that you cannot even get near. The punishment of evil is equally terrifying: snakes and poisonous reptiles devour their victims, or the evil person dances to death in red-hot iron shoes. All that speaks directly to the heart and needs no explanation, but with time a deeper meaning emerges. A mother gets her real child back just when she manages to get a laugh out of the changeling that familiar spirits have substituted for her own child. The life of a child similarly begins with a smile and continues in joy, and when it smiles in its sleep, angels are talking with it. A quarter hour of each day is exempt from the power of magic, and then the human form steps forth in freedom, as if no power could envelop us completely. Every day offers moments when we can rid ourselves of everything that is false and can see clearly. On the other hand, magic spells are never completely broken. A mistake is made, and a swan's wing is left in place of an arm. Or because a tear was shed, an eye is lost with it. Or worldly cleverness is humbled, and the numbskull alone, because he has a pure heart, has good fortune.

All true poetry can be interpreted in manifold different ways, for it has arisen from life and it returns back to life. It hits us like sunshine no matter where we are standing. For that reason a moral precept or a relevant object lesson can be readily derived from these tales; it was never their purpose to instruct, nor were they made up for that reason, but a moral grows out of them, just as good fruit develops from healthy blossoms without help from man.

Not to be forgotten is a certain humor that permeates many of the tales, even if it manifests itself in a subtle fashion. That humor should not be confused with the embedded irony of contemporary writers. In some tales the humor emerges in a charming and special way, as in "Clever Else," "The Tailor in Heaven," or the boy who went forth to learn about fear, and who finally learns about it, not through something terrifying but by completely natural means. The raw essence of the young giant is kept in balance by his sense of humor, just as Siegfried tones down the solemn nature of the hero through his jokes. The fantastic character Hans My Hedgehog elevates himself through his sense of humor above the wild and animal-like, and Brother Lustig lifts himself up in the same way from his life of sin. This particular feature is uniquely German and can probably not be found in the folklore of other nations as easily.

A narrative can also seem to be fragmentary when one episode is dwelt upon for a long time, while the rest of the tale is told briefly or just hinted at. Sometimes an episode is missing entirely, yet still the narrative thread is not torn, it is just picked up somewhere else. Sometimes the tale just moves in the direction of another saga and takes up a part of it. Fairy tales are like plants whose twigs and leaves sprout every spring in different directions, but that also do not ever change their basic shape, blossom, and fruit. Or we can think of the breath of life that moves across this poetry, stirring and moving its waves. Sometimes an ending may seem unsatisfactory, especially if the tale as a whole did not seem to be going in that direction and episodes are just connected with each other. All epic poetry remains in a settled circle that does not always have to be clearly defined.

MEANING AND TRADITION

This is what we would have to say about the fundamentals of fairy tales if they were just considered something that existed in our own time. But if you ask about their origins, then you find that no one can name the poet or inventor who made them. In every location they are present in the form of traditions, and for that reason they have a certain special nature. No one can dispute the fact that they have been handed down over the centuries in this way, transforming themselves continually in their outer manifestations, but remaining the same when it comes to essentials. If one were to assume that the tales had their origins in a certain location in Germany, then it would be hard to explain their diffusion across so many regions and landscapes that are independent of each other as well as the peculiar and unique twist that each story takes. They would have to have been refashioned in every geographical location. For that very reason the notion that the tales were transmitted in written form seems implausible, especially since literacy is so rare among the people. But we find the tales, in various degrees of similarity and difference, not only in the different regions where German is spoken, but also among the ethnically allied Nordic peoples and the English, also among the Welsh as well as the Slavic nations. The similarity to Serbian fairy tales is especially striking, for it would not occur to anyone to assert that the tales told in an isolated Hessian village could have been brought there by Serbs, or vice versa. Finally, certain features and turns of phrase as well as broader matters can be found in Oriental, Persian, and Indian fairy tales. The relationships that can be traced in the languages of all these people and which Rask has recently shown in a shrewd way, can also be found in the traditional tales, which, after all, represent a higher and freer language of mankind. This relationship points precisely to an early time when divisions among nations did not exist. But if you search for its origins, it gets pushed back farther and farther in time and becomes something that you cannot document and that remains darkly unfathomable.

As for the content, if you look closely, you find that it is not just a web of fantastic whimsy that throws together different colored threads according to this or that caprice or need. To the contrary, you can always identify a reason, a meaning, or a core. In this poetry, thoughts about the divine and spiritual in life are preserved. Ancient beliefs and doctrines are dipped into an epic element that develops with the history of a people and is given shape. But intention and consciousness have not been the agents. Rather, everything has emerged naturally and from the essence of tradition. For that reason there is a natural tendency to explain and clarify what comes from it that is only partially understandable according to what goes on in the present. The more the epic element dominates, the harder it is to see what is essential. . . .

TRACES OF PAGAN BELIEFS

Constant transformation adds many new things to folklore, but on the other hand, the fundamental beliefs in them begin to disappear and wither away because they appear strange and incomprehensible. The poetic drive creates something that was comprehensible in sensual terms and relevant, but now the meaning only shines darkly here and there, almost against its will. . . .

Just the mere fact that all of nature is seen as animated can be viewed as a legacy from that earlier time. For us this view is not at all strange, since we know that this belief was fundamental to pagan times (Juppiter est quodcunque vides, quocunque moveris, as Lucan puts it). For the people it was always that way, as soon as it attained consciousness. The sun, the moon, and the stars are endowed with a spiritual nature, and when they begin to speak to those in need, give them gifts that will save them, then they appear as divine beings to be worshipped (quorum opibus aperte iuvantur. Caesar de B.B. 10), as they were in the ancient period of the Germanic tribes. Even the trees and streams, whose worship continued for a long time, are animated here. The juniper tree (iuniperus), that is, the tree that gives life and rejuvenates, is clearly a good spirit and its fruits help the mother fulfill her wish for a child. The bones of the murdered boy are brought back to life under its branches, which move like the arms of a human being and embrace them. And the boy's soul, which is received by the tree, arises out of the radiant, but not burning, branches in the form of a little bird. The same idea is expressed when a child thrown into a river or a white bride is restored in the image of a bird. The river is, then, a living spirit. In other tales, branches soften up and embrace with arms the woman who is leaning in her grief on the trunk of a tree. A little tree grows up at the site of the grave of Cinderella's mother, and when she turns to it in her need, it tosses gifts down to her. Or a tree with golden apples grows from buried intestines or the hearts of beloved animals, and it only obeys and follows the person to whom it rightfully belongs. The stream that flows and sparkles over rocks (as holy water runs down from the mountains in the *Edda*) calls out to children and warns them not to drink from it or they will be transformed. And there are more examples of the higher nature attributed to animals. The horse Fallada [*sic*] speaks (as does Mime's head) after its death to its master. Ravens predict the future, knowing, like Odin's ravens Huginn and Muninn (i.e., those gifted with reason and memory) what is happening in the world. In general, birds are seen as spirits. Doves come and pick peas out of the ashes for a poor child, but they peck out the eyes of evil sisters. A little bird throws a golden chain around the neck of a father. Birds throw a millstone down on the head of a wicked stepmother. Whoever eats the heart or liver of a bird becomes endowed with supernatural powers. One of the most ancient traces of the symbolic hybridity of animals and humans are the swan maidens, who appear here in the same form and manner as in the *Old Edda* and in the *Nibelungenlied*.

The transformation from one form into another is rooted in the view of nature as animated, and the stones, trees, and plants that are transformed are also spiritually alive. In the *Edda*, nature in the form of birds and animals, even of fire, water, iron, minerals, rocks, and trees, protects Baldur from danger, and afterwards they mourn his death. Magic often works to great effect, and it is grounded in the belief that a spirit resides in all things and that it is possible to control and influence it.

The opposition between good and evil is often expressed as black and white, light and darkness. The good spirits that bring help are usually white birds and are called that: pure, benign doves. The evil ones that foretell misfortune are black ravens. . . . The pious girl is described as white as day, the evil one is black as sin (night). . . . In a castle everything is dark and the three sleeping princesses (rigid as death) have some hope of redemption, a bit of white (life) in their faces, for magic is a black art. Another figure returns slowly to the color of light. On the first day, his feet become pure and white, on the second the body, limbs, and hands, on the third day, finally, the face, and then at last the dark power is conquered. The prince who sleeps in the daytime and awakens only at night, and who is destined to be unhappy if a ray of light touches him, is similarly a black gnome. They too fled the light, and if the sun ever struck them, they would turn to stone. For that reason, the sun is known as the curse or complaint of the gnomes. . . . The fairy tale about the goose girl and the black and white brides belongs here. It is really the old myth about the true and false Bertha. Just this name alone expresses radiance. She combs her radiantly golden hair, because she is, like the princess who is without clothing and wraps herself in the cloak of her golden hair, a glowing elf of light or, what is one and the same, a white swan maiden. Snow White must originally have been a maiden like that, who remains white and beautiful even in death and is worshipped and guarded by the good (white) dwarfs. This is reminiscent of the two worlds of Nordic mythology, the one of light and bliss (Muspelheim), the other of night and darkness (Nifelheim).

Good is rewarded by God; evil is punished. The Lord descends to earth and visits the rich and the poor. The rich he finds to be corrupt, the poor pious and living according to his laws. He divides his goods accordingly, so that they lead the former to hard luck and the latter to redemption. Or, while he is wandering, he meets good and evil sisters, giving the one divine beauty, punishing the other with ugliness. The opposition is expressed in an unusual way, when the devil as antagonist gets his own animals, has his goats gnaw the fruit off the trees, harm the noble vines, and destroy delicate plants so that the Lord orders them torn to pieces by wolves. He is the Dark One, the Nordic Surtur, who quarrels with the mild gods who radiate light.

The very way in which God, death, and the devil appear in person has a pagan cast to it. God walks around in human form like Odin and even appears to be fooled. Even the Fool begins, just as if he were a Titan, a war against heaven and tries to get access by force. The descent into hell (the underworld, the Nordic Hel) is undertaken by a fellow who is born with a caul, and he succeeds in bringing back the three golden hairs of the devil (the robbed treasure). . . . The punishment of evil: putting someone into a barrel with snakes is reminiscent of the snake caves in the sagas, but more precisely of Nástrong, home to the godless, which, according to the *Edda* is covered with snakes whose heads spew streams of poison inwardly. A snake is placed on the head of Lokes, the evil spirit, so that poison will trickle down his face.

The idea of a treasure that can be found on earth and that will bring bliss and that can be acquired by those who are lucky and favored by fate is also a pagan idea. For whoever was able to reach the source of all earthly splendor was seen in pagan times as the master and lord of the highest accomplishment. This is the basic idea behind the wishing objects that appear in different forms as a hat, a kerchief, a table, etc., and satisfy every thought, give the owner invisibility, lift the laws of gravity, and transcend all physical limitations. The wishing rod, the magic wand, is, for that reason, hidden in the horde of the Nibelungs and shows that struggle for possession of the highest material goods is the real content of the old sagas. . . . The white, glowing snake that is sitting on the gold (Fafner) is identical to the toad wearing a crown that has assembled the most precious treasures, and both are symbols of the horde. Whoever eats them, i.e., takes in their essence, acquires a higher understanding into the nature of things, understands the language of the birds, and has good fortune on his side. Furthermore, the heart of the golden, feathered bird that is hatching golden eggs is virtually the same as the heart of the snake, and it becomes an appropriate image of powers working unconsciously. This is exactly where to place the golden goose that is sitting in the roots of a tree, i.e., hidden in the earth. It brings happiness and bliss to anyone who can lift it from the roots, and in epic terms, it is represented in vivid fashion as a creature that is like a magnet—anyone who touches it sticks fast to it. Another image is that of the tree in whose branches grow the apples of life—well known in both Nordic and Greek mythology. Within it, life shrivels and withers away and only they can revive and rejuvenate what is half dead. The stream that has the water of life has the same function. A king who is ill desires to have it because it is the only thing that can heal him. It closes his wounds and returns people to a human state if they have been turned into stone through magic.

The story of a king who has three sons and doesn't know which one of them should receive the kingdom and the throne after his death is told in many different ways. He sets his sons tasks: they must do something that is difficult to accomplish, fetch something that is rare and precious, or learn to do something that requires skill or art. Whoever succeeds inherits the kingdom. They go out into the world and each one tries his luck. That it is usually the youngest and the least gifted who wins is grounded in a certain moral idea that we will refer to in another context. Herodotus (IV, c. 5) tells a similar fairy tale about the origins of the Scythians which, given the fact that the Germanic tribes have some relationship to the Scythians, ought to be considered in conjunction with them. Targitaus, fathered by the highest of the gods, was the first person in Scythia and left three sons behind. During their reign, golden equipment fell down one day from the skies: a plow, a yoke, a double-bladed ax, and a bowl. When the oldest of the three brothers was about to pick it up, the gold was aglow, and the second son came, but he too received burns. After the two of them had been burned and retreated, the youngest son stepped forward and found that the gold had stopped burning and that he could take home the pieces of equipment. And thereupon the two older ones let the youngest inherit the kingdom. The shallow bowl is probably an image of the land, the plow and the yoke represent the farming instinct, the sword the class of the warrior. Those were symbols of how to rule the kingdom, and heaven decided to designate one of the three brothers. In the *Völuspá*, the Aesir cut up gold, created tongs, and made instruments when they were creating the world. The fact that the equipment is aglow points to ancient Germanic beliefs, which are founded on the test of hot iron, which can only be touched with impunity by the one who has a right to it, the completely innocent man.—The three sons in the fairy tale are nothing more than the Trimurti, into which the highest god divides himself while creating the finite world. One of the three is endowed with the power to reign supreme so that the idea of a single god will not vanish. The Scythian Targitaus is none other than Mannus in Tacitus (Germ. 3), the son of the god Thuisko, after whose three sons Germany is named and divided. In Nordic mythology there is Bure, who appears first, then his three sons, Odin, Vile and Ve (Har, Jafnhar and Thridi, or according to the *Völuspá*, Odin, Häner, and Loder), who order the world and populate it. Odin later became the main ruler.

The golden, or glass, i.e., glittering mountain, which is so difficult to enter and usually only with help from the sun, the moon, and the stars or other supernatural help and which is guarded at its foot by wild monsters on chains and in which are contained magic objects, seems to be the mountain of the gods found in the older myths. It is the same place where twelve giants (gods) guard the horde of the Nibelungs, or the Nordic palace of fire where Brunhilde can be found—her Isenburg in the German poem is nothing more than the ice-glass castle. In the north we discover Asgard, which is in the middle of the world and covered with golden signs, and the manner in which heaven is described in "Mary's Child" as a golden house with twelve doors and a thirteenth which is forbidden reminds us quite clearly of the golden, gleaming Gladsheim with its twelve seats for the Aesir and its throne for Odin. Furthermore it can be compared with Gimli, which is brighter than the sun and which survives after the end of the world as the place where the good live. . . .

Mother Holle or Hulda has kept her name from earlier ages, but probably only in Hessen, Thüringen, and Franken. She is a pleasant and friendly goddess, but she can also be forbidding and terrifying. She dwells in the depths and on the heights, in lakes and on mountains, and she distributes fertility and blessings or misfortune, depending on whether she decides someone has earned it or not. She surrounds the entire earth and when she makes her bed, feathers fly and it snows here down on earth. In the same way dew and rain fall and make the land fruitful when the cloud-horses of the Walkure shake their bodies. She lets her hair be combed, i.e., she sends the rays of the sun down to earth, for the Nordic earth goddess Sif also has magnificent golden hair that is groomed by dwarfs. At Christmas, when the sun rises in the heavens again, she goes out into the world, rewards and punishes. Her special task is to supervise the spinners who, as will become evident, are the eleven elf maidens who spin the fates of all. She is the great mother of the mountains, an earth goddess like Hertha who is worshiped in Rügen and much like Ceres is for the Greeks. There will be more to say about her in our explanation of the sagas, but here she appears with her double face, horrible to look at and yet mild and well disposed toward pious children.

The fairy tale about the three spinning women is also based on pagan beliefs. These women spin the golden thread of fate, like the norns, the Walkures, and the parcae. The partially supernatural swan maidens (the Walkures are also described in that way) can be recognized in them. They still have the flat foot or the broad thumb and the beaked lips. They spin day and night without stopping, the thread keeps getting spun, but even the *Edda* tells of the Walkure and how they never rest. . . . The princesses who spin gold in fairy tales are no different from the swan maidens who spin happiness and wealth. . . . The women who spin gold are almost always shepherdesses, they watch geese, swans, i.e., spirits, and so that is just another expression for guiding and keeping an eye on fate.

Thumbling is also a remnant of ancient divine beliefs. He is the one who protects home, his siblings are those who had to be saved. He is always the guide and without doubt related to the Kabiren and Penates, who were also seen as small, dwarflike creatures. The dwarfs, sprites, and nymphs are all related to him. They are the gnomes of Nordic mythology and also double-faced: good and benevolent or evil and nasty. They live not only on earth, but are also called the subterranean ones, and they penetrate the secret and hidden places in the earth, where they have the most splendid houses. They are the living spirits who are distributed throughout the finest underground arteries in the earth. . . .

If we gather together our harvest, then we can see what can be discovered about the ancient beliefs: animation of nature, pantheism, fate, the principle of good and evil, the trimurti, noble higher gods who dwell on high, and the worship of lesser gods.

SYNOPSIS

. . . The struggle between good and evil that we described earlier is represented in various complexities and turns of thought, but often in the relationship between siblings. A brother falls into the power of evil forces; a sister discovers it and looks for him, wandering through forests and deserts. She fears no danger, accomplishes the most difficult tasks, and finally disenchants him, for the good and the pure emerge in the end as what is true and constant and conquers evil. And in how many beautiful ways the human is woven into this story. The magic is not always successfully banished, and the warnings of benevolent spirits are forgotten so that the work must begin anew.

The pure spirits promote good and accompany man in visible forms on his way. Myths and sagas tell of superior beings with whom the gods foster congress, and fairy tales borrow from them figures that are specially gifted and have unusual features. One comes into the world with a caul. No matter what happens to him, things turn out well. He even goes down to hell to acquire secrets from the devil. Gold grows under the pillows of two brothers while they are sleeping; not a shot goes awry; animals come running up to them to serve them; and magic is useless against them. Snow White, Cinderella, and the girl who flees with her dearest Roland are all the beneficiaries of special protection.

Always preserving a basic shape, a fairy tale can be told four of five times under different circumstances and in different ways so that it appears, from the outside, to be different. The good and innocent girl, who is also often the youngest, is handed over to a monster by her father, who is in a tight spot, or she goes voluntarily. She bears her fate patiently; sometimes she is further hindered by human weaknesses and has to atone for those, but finally she feels love for him, and in that moment he throws off the ugly shape of the hedgehog, lion, or frog and appears in youthful beauty and purity. This saga, which is also at home in India and related to the Greek story of Amor and Psyche and the French tale of Partheno-pex and Meliure, tells of enchantment and release through love. The pure works its way through, step by step. If the development is disturbed, then the misery and weight of the world strike hard and only the communion of souls, the knowledge of love, can deliver them from the earthly and material side of life.

We have already remarked on how good lessons derive from the spiritual liveliness of the tales. It is not really the purpose of these tales and no one thought them up in order to analyze some kind of moral truth. . . .

Many of the tales have a Christian content and differ from the somewhat uniform legends in their richness and variation. "Mary's Child" is notable in this context: at first she lives with angels in pure innocence, then, led by curiosity into a state of sin, she is banished from heaven. She is forced to experience the pain of life on earth as long as she persists in denying her sin, but at the moment when her heart turns to God, he shows mercy, and her state of anguish is over. In the fairy tale about the girl without hands, that concept is worked out beautifully, and the cunning of evil perishes in the face of purity. Just as God lets the limbs that have been severed grow back again, so he gives back sight, through a pure shower of dew, to the pious man, who is sitting under the gallows but believes that he is beneath a cross and is praying to it. In the fairy tale about a carnation, God's animals, like the prophets of old, feed the queen who has been incarcerated unjustly and who, because she has dined on divine food, can no longer eat normal food and dies when she is released. The boy who has faith in God's word and goes out to find heaven reveals that firm belief can lead to redemption, even when there is a superficial misunderstanding. A few legends that are structured like fairy tales are included at the end of our collection.

The fairy tales about animals open a different world. The secret activities of animals in forests, meadows, and fields have a real importance. There is a certain order that reigns among them—in the way their homes are built, in their journeys, their return home, the way they feed their young and prepare for the winter. They seem to have a capacious memory. They can make themselves understood to each other, and their language may not have much variation, but it is powerful and penetrating. They gather in large groups, depart on journeys, have leaders, and make war with each other. And so there is nothing more natural than to ascribe to them an ordered way of life much like the doings of human beings, one that is hidden from our view. The eye of poetry, however, sees everything that is secret and concealed. It reveals the inner housekeeping of animals, and since it endows them with human language (which already gives them the capacity for human thought), they seem all the closer to us. There is a special charm in this constant blending of the human and the animal—you begin to think that they are really people who are enjoying having a good time in this shape. It is natural that sagas play with this mix; sometimes things that are not living at all are drawn in. A straw, a piece of coal, and a bean take a journey together. The fox incarnates evil in his cunning and craftiness, and his relationship with the faithless Sibich of German heroic sagas will be shown in another work of ours. The wolf symbolizes violence and stupidity. The weak animals, mainly birds, are well disposed to men, and they are preyed upon by others. Here again we have a struggle between two sides, as with dwarfs and giants elsewhere. The victory of the little over the big oafs is described in the fairy tale about the bear and the wren, and the wolf that deceives Little Red Riding Hood and the young goats represents the ogre, who is finally defeated because of his oafishness. Many tales belong in the circle of fables around Reynard the Fox and can be explained better in that context. When human beings meet up with animals, the humans are harsh and unjust and are punished for their behavior, as in the fairy tale about the dog and the sparrow.

STEREOTYPICAL CHARACTERS

Poetry tends to concentrate the characteristic features of an entire nation in one character so that what you see in bits and pieces or in a weak or unclear fashion is focused and given shape. One could say that poetry gives us only complete characters who appear in primary colors. If a certain character takes on a representative quality, still he appears as a sharply drawn figure who takes on a certain life in his peculiarities. In the realm of comedy, which has so many sharp corners and surprise turns, you are more likely to find fixed masks. But in any case, the more such characters are based on the nature—the strengths and weaknesses—of a people, the more durable and robust they are, so that they appear fresh and new even when they are re-formed in superficial variations. What epic does not have as its heroes an Achilles or Odysseus, in humor and comedy its Lalenbürger and Eulenspiegel! Those are the natural forms and limits of poetry, within which it can move with a powerful freedom and variety. We spoke earlier of Siegfried's peculiar nature which is so supremely symptomatic of German character. That figure resonates with another whom we have mentioned often here and who is named "Dummy." Never able to excel in matters that require wit and tact, he has to do all the dirty work in his own clumsy way (as Siegfried has to work as a smith) and he ends up being mocked. He is the Ash-child who makes his bed at the hearth or under the staircase. But an inner joy and a powerful strength shine through—in *Parzifal*, he is called Stupid-bright. If it is time for genuine action, he moves quickly, like a plant that has been sprouting and then is finally touched by sunlight. Then he alone among many is able to accomplish the goal. He is represented in many different relationships, usually the youngest of three brothers, who stand in contrast to him through their arrogance and pride. When they are sent out into the world together in order to discharge a task which will decide who among them will be favored, the two brothers mock him and show nothing but contempt for him. Dummy departs with a childlike confidence, and when he believes that he is without any kind of resources, a higher power helps him to triumph over the others. Another time he neglects worldly wisdom and learns only the language of nature. For that reason he is banished, but that knowledge elevates him above the others. If he meets misfortune and is murdered, a bone that has been bleached white and washed to shore announces the foul play so that it will not remain unpunished.

Dummy is the despised one, the insignificant fellow who becomes strong through his traffic with giants. He is very much like Thumbling, who is no bigger than a thumb at birth and never grows after that. But everything about him leans toward cleverness. He is full of cunning and skill and is able to turn every accident for which his small size is responsible into an advantage that will help him. He makes fun of everyone and displays delight in good-natured teasing, just as dwarfs do. The old sagas about them tend to persist. Sometimes he is represented as a clever little tailor who scares off the giants with his fine and quick wit. He kills monsters and acquires the hand of a princess. He alone can solve the riddles that have been posed.

The little farmer who sends a wooden calf out to pasture, but then knows how to get rich through all kinds of clever tricks, stands somewhere between Dummy and the Lalenbürger. He appears in various guises, most clearly in the antics of Catherlieschen and Clever Else. Stupidity is put on display here under the banner of broad understanding, self-satisfaction, and the hint of self-consciousness about it. The seven Swabians, who go into the world looking for adventure with a single spear, belong in the same category. They hunt a monster in the form of a hare and end up losing their lives because of a frog. Unusual combinations can be found in tales where stupidity ends up as an advantage, as in the case of Doctor Know-it-all and the wedding of clever Hans, or when wisdom is applied in an unfortunate manner, as in the case of the boy who wanted to go on journeys.

A fourth type is found in Brother Lustig. He doesn't worry about anything at all except leading a merry life, and he has no idea what is good or what is evil, and therefore no one expects anything from him. When the good Lord comes to his house seeking shelter, he is prepared to share every last bit with him, but right away he loses the money that he was supposed to use for something to drink with the food. He gives his last penny to the apostle Peter, who approaches him in the form of a beggar and asks for alms. Peter believes that he has finally found a pious man and sets off on a journey with him. Before long Brother Lustig cheats Peter of the heart of a roasted lamb and is annoyed that the powerful apostle doesn't have more money. He becomes a sluggard and serves the devil but is sent away from hell. He manages to cheat death for a while, and finally he must follow him, but neither heaven nor hell wants to let him enter, until he has a good idea and manages to make his way in. To a certain extent Brother Lustig is the reverse side of the tailor who is mercifully taken into heaven and who wants to judge sinners and is then thrown out of heaven. The legend of St. Christopher, who seeks a master and serves the devil but then leaves him because he is afraid of the Christ child, is modeled on these sagas.

Finally there is the trickster: in him you find the pure delight in lying which has a certain innocence because it is done without any design. The human imagination has the natural capacity to stretch out its arms as far as it can and to make use freely of the blade that cuts through all barriers. The fairy tale about the flail fetched from heaven makes sense in this context. Just a step farther and you have the juxtaposition of complete opposites and the union of antagonisms in the fairy tale about the land of Cockaigne. And old sagas about giants may live on in the marvelous arts of the six servants, who, only after all faith has been lost in those creatures, are still portrayed in a humorous manner. In old sagas and songs the giants—with their leaps and bounds, their shooting and throwing, the marvelous powers of their eyes, and their ability to eat and devour—are described in the same way, and in all seriousness.

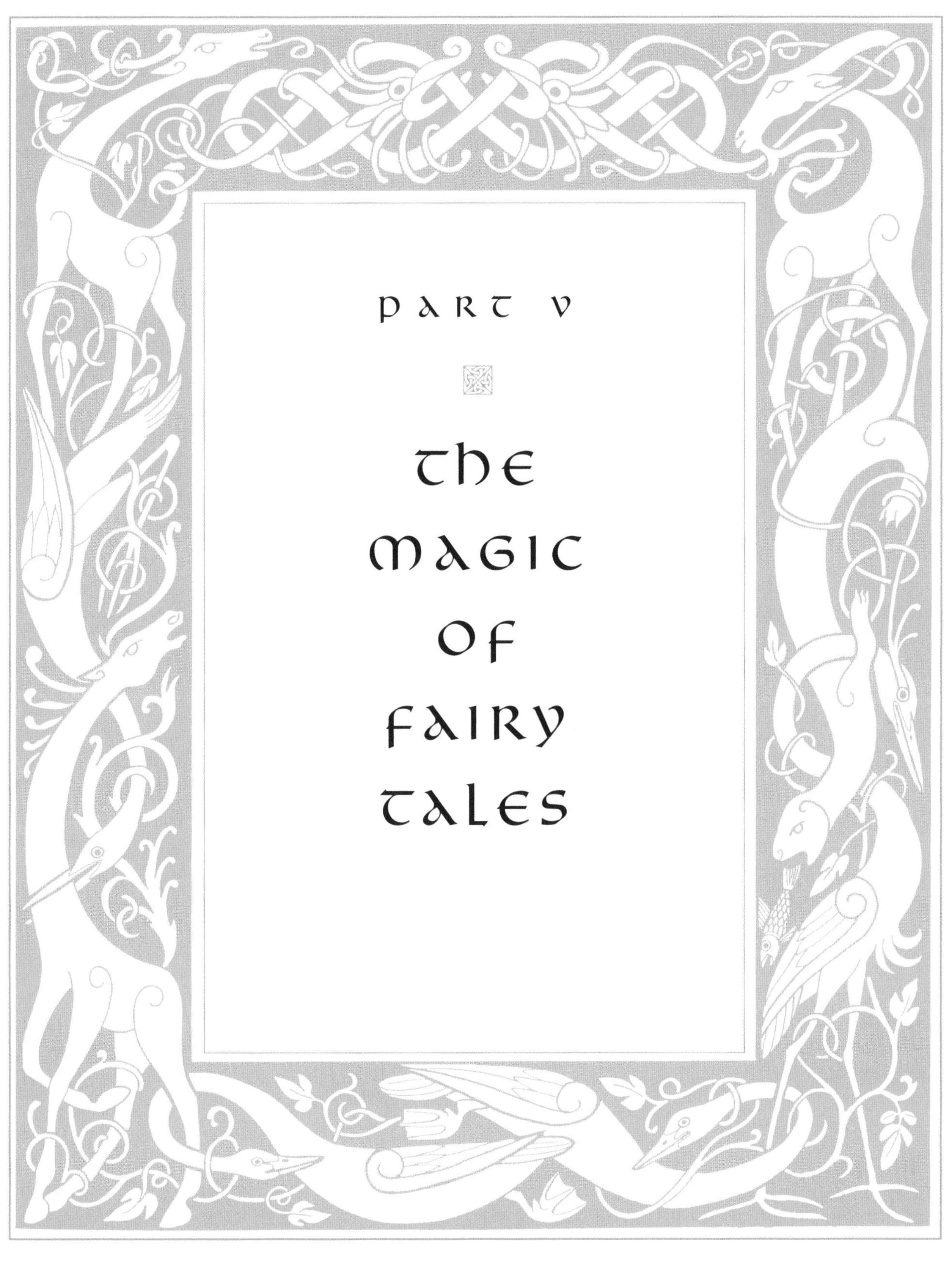

PART V

THE MAGIC OF FAIRY TALES

The German philosopher Walter Benjamin once pondered the idea of writing a book that would consist entirely of quotations from other writers. The notion of quilting together snippets of text—passages so moving that they affect our lives long after we have put down a book—is an inspired one, and one that many have considered as a possible adventure, one that turns the voracious reader into the producer, if not necessarily the writer, of a text. Over the years, I have collected passages that have the power to arouse thought and rouse to action, passages that move us to think about the deeper meaning of fairy tales and how they have affected our own lives and those of others.

CHARLES DICKENS

"We may assume that we are not singular in entertaining a very great tenderness for the fairy literature of our childhood. What enchanted us then, and is captivating a million of young fancies now, has, at the same blessed time of life, enchanted vast hosts of men and women who have done their long day's work, and laid their grey heads down to rest. It would be hard to estimate the amount of gentleness and mercy that has made its way among us through these slight channels. Forbearance, courtesy, consideration for the poor and aged, kind treatment of animals, the love of nature, abhorrence of tyranny and brute force—many such good things have been first nourished in the child's heart by this powerful aid. It has greatly helped to keep us, in some sense, ever young, by preserving through our worldly ways one slender track not overgrown with weeds, where we may walk with children, sharing their delights."

"Frauds on the Fairies." In *Household Words: A Weekly Journal.* New York: McElrath and Barker, 1854. Vol. 8: 97–100.

J. R. R. TOLKIEN

"The consolation of fairy-stories, the joy of the happy ending: or more correctly of the good catastrophe, the sudden joyous 'turn' (for there is no true end to any fairy-tale): this joy, which is one of the things which fairy-stories can produce supremely well, is not essentially 'escapist,' nor 'fugitive.' In its fairy-tale—or otherworld—setting, it is a sudden and miraculous grace: never to be counted on to recur. . . . It is the mark of a good fairy-story, of the higher or more complete kind, that however wild its events, however fantastic or terrible the adventures, it can give to child or man that hears it, when the 'turn' comes, a catch of the breath, a beat and lifting of the heart, near to (or indeed accompanied by) tears, as keen as that given by any form of literary art, and having a peculiar quality."

"On Fairy-Stores." In *The Tolkien Reader.* New York: Ballantine, 1966. Pp. 33–44.

ERNST BLOCH

"Toward dusk may be the best time to tell stories. . . . A remote realm that appears to be better and closer approaches. Once upon a time: this means in fairy-tale manner not only the past but a more colorful or easier somewhere else. And those who have become happier there are still happy today if they are not dead. To be sure, there is suffering in fairy tales; however, it changes, and for sure, it never returns. The maltreated, gentle Cinderella goes to the little tree at her mother's grave: little tree, shake yourself, shake yourself. A dress falls to her feet more splendid and marvelous than anything she has ever had. And the slippers are solid gold. Fairy tales always end in gold. There is enough happiness there."

"Better Castles in the Sky at the Country Fair and Circus, in Fairy Tales and Colportage." In *The Utopian Function of Art and Literature: Selected Essays.* Trans. Jack Zipes and Frank Mecklenburg. Cambridge, Mass.: MIT Press, 1996. Pp. 167–85.

PETER RUSHFORTH

"In fairy-tales collected by the Brothers Grimm, the innocent and the pure in heart always seemed to triumph, even after much fear and suffering: Hansel and Gretel outwitted the witch and escaped; the seven little kids and their mother destroyed the wolf; the three sisters in 'Fitcher's Bird' overpowered even death itself to defeat the murdering magician. But he could still remember the mounting desolation with which he read some of the Hans Christian Andersen fairy-tales when he was little. He had read them over and over again, hoping that this time the ending would be a happy ending, but the endings never changed: the little match-girl died entirely alone, frozen to death on New Year's Eve, surrounded by burned-out matches; the little mermaid melted into foam after bearing her suffering bravely. . . . He had been drawn, compulsively, to read them with engrossed attention, and had wept as he found himself realizing what the inevitable and unchanged end of the story would be."

Kindergarten. New York: Avon Books, 1979.

ITALO CALVINO

"The storyteller of the tribe puts together phrases and images: the younger son gets lost in the forest, he sees a light in the distance, he walks and walks; the fable unwinds from sentence to sentence, and where is it leading? To the point at which something not yet said, something as yet only darkly felt by presentiment, suddenly appears and seizes us and tears us to pieces, like the fangs of a man-eating witch. Through the forest of fairy tale the vibrancy of myth passes like a shudder of wind."

"Cybernetics and Ghosts." In *The Uses of Literature.* Trans. Patrick Creagh. New York: Harcourt Brace & World, 1986. Pp. 3–27.

P. L. TRAVERS

"I shall never know which good lady it was who, at my own christening, gave me the everlasting gift, spotless amid all spotted joys, of love for the fairy tale. It began in me quite early, before there was any separation between myself and world. . . . This undifferentiated world is common to all children. They may never have heard of the fairy tales but still be on easy terms with myth. Saint George and King Arthur, under other names, defend the alleyways and crossroads, and Beowulf's Grendel, variously disguised, breathes fire in the vacant lots. Skipping games, street songs, lullabies, all carry the stories in them. But far above these, as a source of myth, are the half-heard scraps of gossip, from parent to parent, neighbor to neighbor as they whisper across a fence. A hint, a carefully garbled disclosure, a silencing finger at the lip, and the tales, like rain clouds, gather."

"Afterword." In *About the Sleeping Beauty.* New York: McGraw Hill, 1975. Pp. 47–62.

BRUNO BETTELHEIM

"Each fairy tale is a magic mirror which reflects some aspects of our inner world, and of the steps required by our evolution from immaturity to maturity. For those who immerse themselves in what the fairy tale has to communicate, it becomes a deep, quiet pool which at first seems to reflect only our own image; but behind it we soon discover the inner turmoil of our soul—its depth, and ways to gain peace within ourselves and with the world, which is the reward of our struggles."

The Uses of Enchantment: The Meaning and Importance of Fairy Tales. New York: Vintage Books, 1976. P. 309.

WANDA GÁG

"Every child goes through many phases of development, each phase with its own needs and interests. I know I should now feel bitterly cheated if, as a child, I had been deprived of all fairy lore; and it does not seem to me that we have the right to deprive any child of its rightful heritage to Fairyland. In fact, I believe it is *just* the modern children who need it, since their lives are already overbalanced on the side of steel and stone and machinery—and nowadays, one might well add, bombs, gas-masks and machine guns."

"I Like Fairy Tales." *Horn Book.* 15 (1939): 75–76.

GRAHAM GREENE

"Perhaps it is only in childhood that books have any deep influence on our lives. In later life we admire, we are entertained, we may modify some views we already hold, but we are more likely to find in books merely a confirmation of what is in our minds already. . . . But in childhood all books are books of divination, telling us about the future, and like the fortune teller who sees a long journey in the cards or death by water they influence the future. I suppose that is why books excited us so much. What do we ever get nowadays to equal the excitement and revelation in those first fourteen years?"

"The Lost Childhood." In *The Lost Childhood and Other Essays.* London: Eyre & Spottiswoode, 1961. Pp. 13–17.

TRINA SCHART HYMAN

"The Grimms' tales . . . I turned to for comfort, inspiration, and just plain enjoyment. There is very little mention of God or the devil in these stories. People usually go to the sun, or the moon, or the winds for advice. Or to the animals—birds are great omen-bringers and advice-givers. Nature is full of power. Morality—in the form of 'good' or 'evil'—is not so clearly drawn in

Grimm and almost never pointed out. Heroes and heroines often pull some pretty rotten, nasty, or self-serving tricks in order to get what they want."
"Cut It Down, and You Will Find Something at the Roots." In *The Reception of Grimms' Fairy Tales: Responses, Reactions, Revisions*, ed. Donald Haase. Detroit, Mich.: Wayne State University Press, 1993. Pp. 293–300.

JANE YOLEN

"What I am suggesting is not to ban or censor the stories. They are great and important parts of the Western folk canon.

But what I *am* asking for is that we become better readers. That we read below the surface. That we teach our children to think about what Puss does for his master, why Rumpelstiltskin is destroyed, how Rapunzel treats her mother-substitute. I want our children to wonder about Goldilocks' casual destruction of the Bears' lovely cottage and talk about whether the princess deserves to marry the frog-prince and to figure out what Cinderella's father was doing all the while his new wife and step-daughters are mistreating her.

There are many layers inside the old tales, like nesting Matrushka dolls. Examining the layers does not wreck the story, but shows us how rich and fascinating they really are."
"Killing the Other." In *Touch Magic: Fantasy, Faerie & Folklore in the Literature of Childhood.* Little Rock, Ark.: August House Publishers, 2002. Pp. 105–9.

C. S. LEWIS

"I wrote this story for you, but when I began it I had not realized that girls grow quicker than books. As a result you are already too old for fairy tales, and by the time it is printed and bound you will be older still. But some day you will be old enough to start reading fairy tales again. You can then take it down from some upper shelf, dust it, and tell me what you think of it."
Dedication to *The Lion, the Witch and the Wardrobe.* New York: Macmillan, 1950.

MARINA WARNER

"Storytelling can act as a social binding agent—like the egg yolk which, mixed up with the different coloured powders, produces colours of a painting. A story like 'Rashin Coatie,' collected in Scotland in the last century, relates to similar tales of wronged orphan girls all over the world, but it has particular Scottish resonances and emphases—this Cinderella meets her prince at the kirk, not the palace. Of course there are fairy tales unique to a single place, which have not been passed on. But there are few really compelling ones that do not turn out to be wearing seven-league boots. The possibility of holding a storehouse of narrative in common could act to enhance our reciprocal relations, to communicate across space and barricades of national self-interest and pride. We share more than we perhaps admit or know, and have done so for a very long time. . . . The Brothers Grimm proclaimed their fairy stories the pure uncontaminated national products of the *Volk* or German people, but we now know that many of their tales have been traveling through the world for centuries before the Grimms took them down."

From the Beast to the Blonde: On Fairy Tales and Their Tellers. New York: Farrar, Straus and Giroux, 1994. P. 414.

RICHARD WRIGHT

" 'Once upon a time there was an old, old man named Bluebeard,' she began in a low whisper.

She whispered to me the story of *Bluebeard and His Seven Wives* and I ceased to see the porch, the sunshine, her face, everything. As her words fell upon my new ears, I endowed them with a reality that welled up from somewhere within me. She told how Bluebeard had duped and married his seven wives, how he had loved and slain them, how he had hanged them up by their hair in a dark closet. The tale made the world around me be, throb, live. As she spoke, reality changed, the look of things altered, and the world became peopled with magical presences. My sense of life deepened and the feel of things was different, somehow. Enchanted and enthralled, I stopped her constantly to ask for details. My imagination blazed. The sensations the story aroused in me were never to leave me."

Black Boy: A Record of Childhood and Youth. New York: Harper & Brothers, 1945. P. 34.

WILLIAM J. BROOKE

"The telling of a tale links you with everyone who has told it before. There are no new tales, only new tellers, telling in their own way, and if you listen closely you can hear the voice of everyone who ever told the tale."

A Telling of the Tales: Five Stories. New York: Harper & Row, 1990. P. ix.

PETER STRAUB

" '[In fairy tales] the natural world of common sense and social differentiation is set aside, and magic takes charge of things. It speaks in poetry. It alters the world. Remember that first sentence? *There was once* . . . It doesn't matter what comes after that; when you hear words like that, you know the ordinary rules don't work—animals will talk, people will turn into animals, the world will turn topsy-turvy. But at the end . . .' He raised his hand.

'It turns back again,' Del said. 'Magically right.' "

Shadowland. New York: Penguin Putnam, Berkley Publishing, 1980.

SYLVIA PLATH

"After being conditioned as a child to the lovely never-never land of magic, of fairy queens and virginal maidens, of little princes and their rosebushes, of poignant bears and Eeyore-ish donkeys, of life personalized, as the pagans loved it, of the magic wand, and the faultless illustrations—the beautiful dark-haired child (who was you) winging through the midnight sky on a star-path in her mother's box of reels . . . all this I knew, and felt, and believed. All this was my life when I was young. . . . Not to be sentimental, as I sound, but why the hell are we conditioned into the smooth strawberry-and-cream Mother-Goose-world, Alice-in-Wonderland fable, only to be broken on the wheel as we grow older and become aware of ourselves as individuals with a dull responsibility in life? To learn snide and smutty meanings of words you once loved, like 'fairy.' "

The Journals of Sylvia Plath, 1950–1962, ed. Karen V. Kukil. London: Faber and Faber, 2000. P. 35.

WALTER BENJAMIN

" 'And they lived happily ever after,' says the fairy tale. The fairy tale, which to this day is the first tutor of children because it was once the first tutor of mankind, secretly lives on in the story. The first true storyteller is, and will continue to be, the teller of fairy tales. Whenever good counsel was at a premium, the fairy tale had it, and where the need was greatest, its aid was nearest. This need was the need created by the myth. The fairy tale tells us of the earliest arrangements that mankind made to shake off the nightmare which the myth had placed upon its chest. In the figure of the fool it shows us how mankind 'acts dumb' toward the myth; in the figure of the younger brother it shows us how one's chances increase as the mythical primitive times are left behind; in the figure of the man who sets out to learn what fear is it shows us that the things we are afraid of can be seen through; in the figure of the wiseacre it shows us that the questions posed by the myth are simple-minded, like the riddle of the Sphinx; in the shape of animals which come to the aid of the child in the fairy tale it shows that nature not only is subservient to the myth, but much prefers to be aligned with man. The wisest thing—so the fairy tale taught mankind in olden times, and teaches children to this day—is to meet the forces of the mythical world with cunning and with high spirits. (This is how the fairy tale polarizes *Mut*, courage, dividing it dialectically into *Untermut*, that is, cunning, and *Übermut*, high spirits.) The liberating magic which the fairy tale has at its disposal does not bring nature into play in a mythical way, but points to its complicity with liberated man. A mature man feels this complicity only

occasionally, that is, when he is happy; but the child first meets it in fairy tales, and it makes him happy."
"The Storyteller: Reflections on the Work of Nikolai Leskov." In *Illuminations*, ed. Hannah Arendt. Trans. Harry Zohn. New York: Schocken Books, 1968. Pp. 83–109.

MARGARET DRABBLE

"When she was little, Frieda had loved the goblins, the princesses, the old men of the sea, the water maidens, the raven brothers, the haunted woods. Yet the stories were often absurd, often inconsequential. Frieda's literal, logical battleaxe of a mind had often been bemused and entangled by these tales. She had tried to chop her way through the briars. She did not like nonsense. There was a mystery there, forever beyond her grasp."
The Witch of Exmoor. New York: Viking, 1996. Pp. 112–13.

NAOMI LEWIS

"Fairy tales: yes or no? What do you gain by meeting them as a child? Better to start by saying how much is lost if you fail to meet them then, or do so only through cartoon films of the Disney type, or videos. The words are part of the whole. In the landscape of the mind, whatever is planted early lasts and grows through time. Reality may be a featureless-suburban street; but the mind of the fairy-tale reader holds mountains, oceans, distances, a forest that is haven, shelter, and mystery, some day to be explored, with a pathway that leads to the very edge of the world."
"Introduction." In *Classic Fairy Tales to Read Out Loud.* New York: Kingfisher, 1996. Pp. 5–8.

THE ILLUSTRATED LONDON NEWS

"Fairy-tales are as normal as milk or bread. Civilisation changes; but fairy-tales never change . . . its spirit is the spirit of folk-lore; and folk-lore is, in strict translation, the German for common-sense. Fiction and modern fantasy . . . can be described in one phrase. Their philosophy means ordinary things as seen by extraordinary people. The fairy-tale means extraordinary things seen by ordinary people. The fairy-tale is full of mental health. . . . Fairy-tales are the oldest and gravest and most universal kind of human literature . . . the fairy-tales are much more of a picture of the permanent life of the great mass of mankind than most realistic fiction."

"Education by Fairy Tales." In *The Illustrated London News,* 2 December 1905.

GEORGE MACDONALD

" 'You write as if a fairytale were a thing of importance: must it have a meaning?'

It cannot help having some meaning; if it have proportion and harmony it has vitality, and vitality is truth. The beauty may be plainer in it than the truth, but without the truth the beauty could not be, and the fairytale would give no delight. Everyone, however, who feels the story, will read its meaning after his own nature and development: one man will read one meaning in it, another will read another."

"The Fantastic Imagination." In *The Complete Fairy Tales*, ed. U. C. Knoepflmacher. New York, Penguin, 1999. Pp. 5–10.

ROBERT LOUIS STEVENSON

"How am I to sing your praise,
Happy chimney-corner days,
Sitting safe in nursery nooks,
Reading picture story-books?"

A Child's Garden of Verses.
London: Longmans, Green, and Co., 1885.

ANDREW LANG

"I trust that one may have studied fairy tales both scientifically and in a literary way, without losing the heart of childhood, as far as those best of childish things are concerned. May one be forgiven the egotism of confessing, that in

the reading and arranging of these old wives' fables, one has felt perhaps as much pleasure as the child who reads them, or hears them, for the first time? Children, as we know, like to hear a tale often, and always insist that it shall be told in the same way. . . . 'Blue Beard,' that little tragic and dramatic masterpiece, moves me yet; I still tremble for Puss in Boots when the ogre turns into a lion; and still one's heart goes with the girl who seeks her lost and enchanted lover, and wins him again in the third night of watching and of tears. This may not seem a taste to be proud of, but it is a taste to be grateful for, like the love of any other thing that is old and plain, and dallies with the simplicity of love."
"Introduction." In *Blue Fairy Book.* Harmondsworth, England: Penguin Books, 1975. Pp. 349–58.

G. K. CHESTERTON

"If you really read the fairy-tales, you will observe that one idea runs from one end of them to the other—the idea that peace and happiness can only exist on some condition. This idea, which is the core of ethics, is the core of the nursery-tales."
All Things Considered. New York: J. Lane Co., 1908. Pp. 255–56.

JOHN RUSKIN

"Let [the little reader] know his fairy tale accurately, and have perfect joy or awe in the conception of it as if it were real; thus he will always be exercising his power of grasping realities: but a confused, careless, and discrediting tenure of the fiction will lead to a confused and careless reading of the fact. Let the circumstances of both be strictly perceived, and long dwelt upon, and let the child's own mind develop fruit of thought from both. It is of the greatest importance early to secure this habit of contemplation, and therefore it is a grave error, either to multiply unnecessarily, or to illustrate with extravagant richness, the incidents presented to the imagination."
"Introduction." In *German Popular Stories.* London: C. Baldwyn, 1823. Pp. v–xiv.

JOSEPH CAMPBELL

"The latest incarnation of Oedipus, the continued romance of Beauty and the Beast, stands this afternoon on the corner of Forty-second Street and Fifth Avenue, waiting for the traffic light to change."
The Hero with a Thousand Faces. New York: Pantheon Books, 1949. P. 4.

TERRY PRATCHETT

"People think stories are shaped by people. In fact, it's the other way round. . . . A thousand heroes have stolen fire from the gods. A thousand wolves have eaten grandmother, a thousand princesses have been kissed. . . . Stories don't care who takes part in them. All that matters is that the story gets told, that the story repeats. Or, if you prefer to think of it like this: stories are a parasitical life form, warping lives in the service only of the story itself."
Witches Abroad. London: V. Gollancz, 1991. Pp. 2–3.

A. S. BYATT

"We are all, like Scheherazade, under sentence of death, and we all think of our lives as narratives, with beginnings, middles and ends. Storytelling in general, and the *Thousand and One Nights* in particular, consoles us for endings with endless new beginnings. I finished my condensed version of the frame story with the European fairy-tale ending, 'they lived happily ever after,' which is a consolatory false eternity, for no one does, except in the endless repetitions of storytelling. Stories are like genes, they keep part of us alive after the end of our story, and there is something very moving about Scheherazade entering on the happiness ever after, not at her wedding, but after 1001 tales and three children."
"The Greatest Story Ever Told." In *On Histories and Stories: Selected Essays.* London: Chatto & Windus, 2000. Pp. 165–71.

MARGARET ATWOOD

"When people say 'sexist fairy tales,' they probably mean the anthologies that concentrate on 'The Sleeping Beauty,' 'Cinderella,' and 'Little Red Riding Hood,' and leave out everything else. But in 'my' version, there are a good many forgetful or imprisoned princes who have to be rescued by the clever, brave, and resourceful princess, who is just as willing to undergo hardship and risk her neck as are the princes engaged in dragon slaying and tower climbing. Not only that, they're usually better at spells.

And where else could I have gotten the idea, so early in life, that words can change you?"

"Grimms Remembered." In *The Reception of Grimms' Fairy Tales: Responses, Reactions, Revisions*, ed. Donald Haase. Detroit, Mich.: Wayne State University Press, 1993. Pp. 290–92.

ARTHUR SCHLESINGER, JR.

"My mother began with fairy tales, the Brothers Grimm and Hans Christian Andersen, with Greek and Roman mythology, especially as marvelously rendered by Hawthorne in *The Wonder Book* and *Tanglewood Tales*; and with the wondrous *Arabian Nights*. . . . Great children's literature creates new worlds that children enter with delight and perhaps with apprehension and from which they return with understandings that their own experience could not have produced and that give their lives new meaning. . . . The classical tales have populated the common imagination of the West. They are voyages of discovery. They introduce children to the existential mysteries—the anxiety of loneliness, the terror of rejection, the need for comradeship, the quest for fulfillment, the struggle against fate, victory, love, death. . . . The classical tales tell children what they unconsciously know—that human nature is not innately good, that conflict is real, that life is harsh before it is happy—and thereby reassure them about their own fears and their own sense of self."

A Life in the Twentieth Century. Boston: Houghton Mifflin, 2000. Pp. 61–64.

JI-LI JIANG

"Grandpa Hong's bookstall was on the corner of the entrance of our alley. All the children in the neighborhood loved the stall and Grandpa Hong, with his gray hair and wispy beard. He would look at us through his old yellowed glasses and smile. He knew just which books each of us liked best and that I would choose fairy tales, Ji-yong would get adventure stories, and Ji-yun would want animal stories. . . . Against the walls in the place were hard wood benches that rocked on the uneven mud floor. We would sit in a row on one of these benches, each of us with a pile of 21 picture books, and read them, one after another. Then we would trade piles and read again. This was how I met many beloved friends: the Monkey King, the River Snail Lady, Snow White, Aladdin, and many others. Inside the bookstall I traveled to mysterious places to meet ancient beauties or terrible monsters. Often I forgot where I was."

Red Scarf Girl: A Memoir of the Cultural Revolution. New York: Harper Trophy, 1998. P. 200.

ROSA PARKS

"I was already reading when I started school. My mother taught me at home. She was really my first teacher. I don't remember when I first started reading, but I must have been three or four. I was very fond of books, and I liked to read and I liked to count. I thought it was something great to be able to take a book and sit down and read, or what I thought was reading. Any books I found where I couldn't read the words, I made up a story about it and talked about the pictures.

At school I liked fairy tales and Mother Goose rhymes. I remember trying to find Little Red Riding Hood because someone had said it was a nice book to read."

Rosa Parks: My Story, with Jim Haskins. New York: Puffin, 1992. P. 25.

ROBERT GRAVES

"Children born of fairy stock
Never need for shirt or frock,
Never want for food or fire,
Always get their heart's desire . . ."
"I'd Love to Be a Fairy's Child."
In *Fairies and Fusiliers.* New York: Knopf, 1918.

JOSEPHINE EVETTS-SECKER

"These stories live by 'endless mutation.' A Native American tale claims that the source of the story is the 'story-telling stone,' which first says to its first listeners, 'Some of you will remember every word I say, some will remember a part of the words, and surely some will forget them all. Hereafter, you must tell these stories to each other. . . . you must keep them for as long as the world lasts.' "
Mother and Daughter Tales. New York: Abbeville Press, 1996.

ADELINE YEN MAH

"In one way or another, every one of us has been shaped by the stories we have read and absorbed in the past. All stories, including fairy tales, present elemental truths, which can sometimes permeate your inner life and become part of you."
Chinese Cinderella: The True Story of an Unwanted Daughter. New York: Random House, Laurel-Leaf, 1999. P. xi.

LEWIS CARROLL

"Child of the pure, unclouded brow
And dreaming eyes of wonder!
Though time be fleet and I and thou
Are half a life asunder,
Thy loving smile will surely hail
The love-gift of a fairy tale."
Through the Looking Glass.
London: Macmillan & Co., 1870.

BRUCE LANSKY

"Nothing stays the same forever—especially if it doesn't make sense. Take fairy tales, for example. I think you'll agree with me that a princess shouldn't have to marry a knight she doesn't love (even if the knight does defeat a dragon), that no one can weave straw into gold, that no prince in his right mind would marry a princess who complains about a pea under twenty mattresses, and that the brave little tailor was actually a vain braggart."
"Introduction." In *Newfangled Fairy Tales.* New York: Meadowbrook Press, 1997.

MAE WEST

"I used to be Snow White, but I drifted."

Further Reading on Fairy Tales

Aarne, Antti, and Stith Thompson. *The Types of the Folktale: A Classification and Bibliography.* Helsinki: Academia Scientiarum Fennica, 1961.

Ashliman, D. L. "Symbolic Sex-Role Reversals in the Grimms' Fairy Tales." In *Forms of the Fantastic: Selected Essays from the Third International Conference on the Fantastic in Literature and Film*, ed. Jan Hokenson and Howard Pearce. New York: Greenwood Press, 1986. Pp. 193–98.

———. *A Guide to Folktales in the English Language: Based on the Aarne-Thompson Classification System.* New York: Greenwood Press, 1987.

Attebery, Brian. *The Fantasy Tradition in American Literature: From Irving to Le Guin.* Bloomington: Indiana University Press, 1980.

Avery, Gillian, and Angela Bull. *Children and Their Books: A Celebration of the Work of Iona and Peter Opie.* Oxford: Clarendon Press, 1989.

Bacchilega, Christina. "Introduction: The Innocent Persecuted Heroine Fairy Tale." *Western Folklore* 52 (1993): 1–12.

———. *Postmodern Fairy Tales: Gender and Narrative Strategies.* Philadelphia: University of Pennsylvania Press, 1997.

Barchilon, Jacques. "Beauty and the Beast: From Myth to Fairy Tale." *Psychoanalysis and the Psychoanalytic Review* 46 (1959): 19–29.

———. "Confessions of a Fairy-Tale Lover." *The Lion and the Unicorn* 12 (1988): 208–23.

Barzilai, Shuli. "Reading 'Snow White': The Mother's Story." *Signs: Journal of Women in Culture and Society* 15 (1990): 515–34.

———. "'Say That I had a Lovely Face': The Grimms' 'Rapunzel,' Tennyson's 'Lady of Shalott,' and Atwood's *Lady Oracle.*" *Tulsa Studies in Women's Literature* 19 (2000): 231–54.

———. "A Case of Negative *Mise en Abyme*: Margaret Atwood and the Grimm Brothers." *Partial Answers: Journal of Literature and the History of Ideas* 4 (2002): 191–204.

Bartsch, Wilhelm. "Aschenputtel and Cinderella: The Brothers Grimm versus Walt Disney: Or, a Moral and a Social Story." *Annual of Foreign Films and Literature* 2 (1996): 31–42.

Behlmer, Rudy. "They Called It 'Disney's Folly': Snow White and the Seven Dwarfs (1937)." In *America's Favorite Movies: Behind the Scenes*. New York: Ungar, 1982.

Beitter, Ursula E. "Identity Crisis in Fairy-Tale Land: The Grimm Fairy Tales and Their Uses by Modern-Day Imitators." In *Imagination, Emblems and Expressions: Essays on Latin American, Carribean, and Continental Culture and Identity*, ed. Helen Ryan-Ransom. Bowling Green, Ohio: Bowling Green State University Popular Press, 1993. Pp. 274–82.

Bell, Elizabeth, Lynda Haas, and Laura Sells, eds. *From Mouse to Mermaid: The Politics of Film, Gender, and Culture*. Bloomington: Indiana University Press, 1995.

Benjamin, Walter. "The Storyteller: Reflections on the Work of Nikolai Leskov." In *Illuminations*, ed. Hannah Arendt. Trans. Harry Zohn. New York: Schocken Books, 1968. Pp. 83–109.

Benson, Stephen. "Stories of Love and Death: Reading and Writing the Fairy Tale Romance." In *Image and Power: Women in Fiction in the Twentieth Century*, ed. Sarah Sceats and Gail Cunnigham. New York: Longman, 1996. Pp. 103–13.

———. *Cycles of Influence: Fiction, Folktale, Theory*. Detroit, Mich.: Wayne State University Press, 2003.

Bernheimer, Kate, ed. *Mirror, Mirror on the Wall: Women Writers Explore Their Favorite Fairy Tales*. New York: Anchor Press, 1998.

Bettelheim, Bruno. *The Uses of Enchantment: The Meaning and Importance of Fairy Tales.* New York: Vintage Books, 1976.

Birkhäuser-Oeri, Sybille. *The Mother: Archetypal Image in Fairy Tales*. Trans. Michael Mitchell. Toronto: Inner City Books, 1988.

Blécourt, Willem de. "On the Origin of Hänsel and Gretel." *Fabula: Zeitschrift für Erzählforschung* 49 (2008): 30–46.

Bluhm, Lothar. "A New Debate about 'Old Marie'? Critical Observations on the Attempt to Remythologize Grimms' Fairy Tales from a Sociohistorical Perspective." *Marvels & Tales* 14 (2000): 287–311.

Book, Fredrik. *Hans Christian Andersen: A Biography*. Trans. George C. Schoolfield. Norman: University of Oklahoma Press, 1962.

Bottigheimer, Ruth B. "Tale Spinners: Submerged Voices in Grimms' Fairy Tales." *New German Critique* 27 (1982): 141–50.

———, ed. *Fairy Tales and Society: Illusion, Allusion, and Paradigm.* Philadelphia: University of Pennsylvania Press, 1986.

———. *Grimms' Bad Girls and Bold Boys: The Moral and Social Vision of the Tales*. New Haven, Conn.: Yale University Press, 1987.

———. "The Face of Evil." *Fabula* 29 (1988): 326–35.

———. "'Beauty and the Beast': Marriage and Money—Motif and Motivation." *Midwestern Folklore* 15 (1989): 79–88.

———. "Cupid and Psyche vs. Beauty and the Beast: The Milesian and the Modern." *Merveilles et contes* 3 (1989): 4–14.

———. "Fairy Tales, Folk Narrative Research and History." *Social History* 14 (1989): 343–57.

———. "Fairy Tales and Children's Literature: A Feminist Perspective." In *Teaching Children's Literature: Issues, Pedagogy, Resources*, ed. Glen Edward Sadler. New York: Modern Language Association of America, 1992. Pp. 101–8.

Brewer, Derek. *Symbolic Stories: Traditional Narratives of Family Drama in English Literature.* Cambridge, England: D. S. Brewer, 1980.

Briggs, Charles, and Amy Schuman, eds. "Theorizing Folklore: Toward New Perspectives on the Politics of Culture." *Western Folklore* 52 (1993).

Bronner, Simon, ed. *Creativity and Tradition in Folklore: New Directions*. Logan: Utah State University Press, 1992.

Bryant, Sylvia. "Re-Constructing Oedipus through 'Beauty and the Beast.'" *Criticism* 31 (1989): 439–53.

Cahill, Susan. "Through the Looking Glass: Fairy-Tale Cinema and the Spectacle of Femininity in *Stardust* and *The Brothers Grimm*." *Marvels and Tales: Journal of Fairy-Tale Studies* 24 (2010): 57–67.

Campbell, Joseph. *The Hero with a Thousand Faces.* New York: Pantheon Books, 1949.

———. *The Flight of the Wild Gander: Explorations in the Mythological Dimension.* New York: Viking, 1969.

Canham, Stephen. "What Manner of Beast? Illustrations of 'Beauty and the Beast.'" In *Image and Maker: An Annual Dedicated to the Consideration of Book Illustration*, ed. Harold Darling and Peter Neumeyer. La Jolla, Calif.: Green Tiger Press, 1984. Pp. 12–25.

Canton, Katia. *The Fairy-Tale Revisited: A Survey of the Evolution of the Tales from Classical Literary Interpretations to Innovative Contemporary Dance-Theater Productions*. New York: Peter Lang, 1994.

Cashdan, Sheldon. *The Witch Must Die: How Fairy Tales Shape Our Lives*. New York: Basic Books, 1999.

Chinen, Allan B. *In the Ever After: Fairy Tales and the Second Half of Life.* Wilmette, Ill.: Chiron Publications, 1989.

Clarkson, Atelia, and Gilbert B. Cross. *World Folktales: A Scribner Resource Collection*. New York: Scribner's, 1980.

Clodd, Edward. *Tom Tit Tot: An Essay on Savage Philosophy in Folk-Tale*. London: Duckworth, 1898.

Cocchiara, Guiseppe. *The History of Folklore in Europe.* Trans. John N. McDaniel. Philadelphia: Institute for the Study of Human Issues, 1981.

Cohen, Betsy. *The Snow White Syndrome: All about Envy*. New York: Macmillan, 1986.

Cooks, Leda M., Mark P. Orbe, and Carol S. Bruess. "The Fairy Tale Theme in Popular Culture: A Semiotic Analysis of *Pretty Woman*." *Women's Studies in Communication* 16 (1993): 86–104.

Cox, Marian Roalfe. *Cinderella: Three Hundred and Forty-five Variants of Cinderella, Catskin, and Cap o' Rushes.* London: David Nutt, 1893.

Darnton, Robert. "Peasants Tell Tales: The Meaning of Mother Goose." In *The Great Cat Massacre and Other Episodes in French Cultural History.* New York: Basic Books, 1984. Pp. 8–72.

Dégh, Linda. *Folktales and Society: Storytelling in a Hungarian Peasant Community*. Trans. Emily M. Schossberger. Bloomington: Indiana University Press, 1969.

———. "Beauty, Wealth and Power: Career Choices for Women in Folktales, Fairytales and Modern Media." *Fabula* 30 (1989): 43–62.

Dieckmann, Hans. *Twice-Told Tales: The Psychological Use of Fairy Tales.* Wilmette, Ill.: Chiron Publications, 1986.

Dobay Rifelj, Carol de. "Cendrillon and the Ogre: Women in Fairy Tales and Sade." *Romantic Review* 81 (1990): 11–24.

Dorson, Richard M. *Folklore: Selected Essays*. Bloomington: Indiana University Press, 1972.

———. *Folklore and Fakelore: Essays toward a Discipline of Folk Studies*. Cambridge, Mass.: Harvard University Press, 1976.

Douglas, Mary. "Red Riding Hood: An Interpretation from Anthropology." *Folklore* 106 (1995): 1–7.

Duffy, Maureen. *The Erotic World of Faery*. London: Cardinal, 1989.

Dundes, Alan. *The Study of Folklore*. Englewood Cliffs, N.J.: Prentice-Hall, 1965.

———. *Cinderella: A Casebook*. Madison: University of Wisconsin Press, 1988.

———. *Folklore Matters*. Knoxville: University of Tennessee Press, 1989.

———, ed. *Little Red Riding Hood: A Casebook*. Madison: University of Wisconsin Press, 1989.

———. "Bruno Bettelheim's Uses of Enchantment and Abuses of Scholarship." *Journal of American Folklore* 104 (1991): 74–83.

Eastman, Mary H. *Index to Fairy Tales, Myths and Legends*. Boston: Faxon, 1926.

Edwards, Carol L. "The Fairy Tale 'Snow White.'" In *Making Connections across the Curriculum: Readings for Analysis*, ed. Kinir Chittenden and Malcolm Kiniry. Pp. 579–645. New York: St. Martin's Press, 1986.

Edwards, Lee R. "The Labors of Psyche: Toward a Theory of Female Heroism." *Critical Inquiry* 6 (1979): 33–49.

Egoff, Sheila, and others, eds. *Only Connect: Readings on Children's Literature*. 2d ed. Toronto: Oxford University Press, 1965.

Ellis, John M. *One Fairy Story Too Many: The Brothers Grimm and Their Tales*. Chicago: University of Chicago Press, 1982.

Erb, Cynthia. "Another World or the World of an Other? The Space of Romance in Recent Versions of 'Beauty and the Beast.'" *Cinema Journal* 34 (1995): 50–70.

Estés, Clarissa Pinkola. *Women Who Run with the Wolves: Myths and Stories of the Wild Woman Archetype*. New York: Ballantine, 1992.

Farrer, Claire, ed. *Women and Folklore*. Austin: University of Texas Press, 1975.

Favat, F. Andre. *Child and Tale: The Origins of Interest*. Urbana, Ill.: National Council of Teachers of English, 1977.

Fine, Gary Alan, and Julie Ford. "Magic Settings: The Reflection of Middle-Class Life in 'Beauty and the Beast.'" *Midwestern Folklore* 15 (1989): 89–100.

Fohr, Samuel Denis. *Cinderella's Gold Slipper: Spiritual Symbolism in the Grimms' Tales*. Wheaton, Ill.: Quest Books, 1991.

Franz, Marie-Louise von. *Problems of the Feminine in Fairytales*. New York: Spring Publications, 1972.

———. *Shadow and Evil in Fairy Tales*. Rev. ed. Boston: Shambhala, 1990.

———. *The Interpretation of Fairy Tales*. Rev. ed. Boston: Shambhala, 1996.

———. *Archetypal Patterns in Fairy Tales*. Toronto: Inner City Books, 1997.

Garber, Marjorie. "Conclusion a tergo: Red Riding Hood and the Wolf in Bed." In *Vested Interests: Cross-Dressing and Cultural Anxiety*. London: Routledge, 1992. Pp. 375–90.

Gilbert, Sandra M., and Susan Gubar. *The Madwoman in the Attic: The Woman Writer and the Nineteenth-Century Literary Imagination*. New Haven, Conn.: Yale University Press, 1979.

Girardot, N. J. "Initiation and Meaning in the Tale of Snow White and the Seven Dwarfs." *Journal of American Folklore* 90 (1977): 274–300.

Goldenstern, Joyce. "Connections That Open Up: Coordination and Causality in Folktales." *Marvels & Tales* 15 (2001): 27–41.

Goldthwaite, John. *The Natural History of Make-Believe: A Guide to the Principal Works of Britain, Europe, and America.* New York: Oxford University Press, 1996.

Grace, Sherrill. "Courting Bluebeard with Bartók, Atwood, and Fowles: Modern Treatments of the Bluebeard Theme." *Journal of Modern Literature* 11 (1984): 245–62.

Greenhill, Pauline, and Sidney Eva Matrix. *Fairy Tale Films: Visions of Ambiguity*. Logan: Utah State University Press, 2010.

Haase, Donald. "Gold into Straw: Fairy Tale Movies for Children and the Culture Industry." *The Lion and the Unicorn* 12 (1988): 193–207.

———, ed. *The Reception of Grimms' Fairy Tales: Responses, Reactions, Revisions*. Detroit, Mich.: Wayne State University Press, 1993.

———. "Yours, Mine, or Ours? Perrault, the Brothers Grimm and the Ownership of Fairy Tales." In *Once Upon a Folktale: Capturing the Folklore Process with Children*, ed. Gloria T. Blatt. New York: Teachers College, Columbia University, 1993. Pp. 63–79.

———. "Framing the Brothers Grimm: Paratexts and Intercultural Transmission in Postwar English-Language Editions of the *Kinder- und Hausmärchen*." *Fabula: Zeitschrift für Erzählforschung* 44 (2003): 55–69.

Hains, Maryellen. "Beauty and the Beast: 20th Century Romance?" *Merveilles et contes* 3 (1989): 75–83.

Hallett, Martin, and Barbara Karasek. *Folk and Fairy Tales: Their Origins, Meaning, and Usefulness.* Peterborough, Ont.: Broadview Press, 1991.

Hanks, Carole, and D. T. Hanks, Jr. "Perrault's 'Little Red Riding Hood': Victim of the Revisers." *Children's Literature* 7 (1978): 68–77.

Hannon, Patricia. *Fabulous Identities: Women's Fairy Tales in Seventeenth-Century France*. Amsterdam: Rodopi, 1998.

Hartland, E. Sidney. "The Forbidden Chamber." *Folk-Lore Journal* 3 (1885): 193–242.

Hearn, Michael Patrick, Trinkett Clark, and H. Nichols Clark. *Myth, Magic, and Mystery: One Hundred Years of American Children's Book Illustrations*. Boulder, Colo.: Roberts Rinehart, 1996.

Hearne, Betsy. *Beauty and the Beast: Visions and Revisions of an Old Tale*. Chicago: University of Chicago Press, 1989.

Henein, Eglal. "Male and Female Ugliness through the Ages." *Merveilles et contes* 3 (1989): 45–56.

Henke, Jill Birnie, Diane Zimmerman Umble, and Nancy J. Smith. "Construction of the Female Self: Feminist Readings of the Disney Heroine." *Women's Studies in Communication* 19 (1996): 229–49.

Heuscher, Julius E. *A Psychiatric Study of Fairy Tales: Their Origin, Meaning, and Usefulness.* 2d rev. ed. Springfield, Ill.: Charles C. Thomas, 1974.

Hoggard, Lynn. "Writing with the Ink of Light: Jean Cocteau's *Beauty and the Beast.*" In *Film and Literature: A Comparative Approach to Adaptation*, ed. Wendell Aycock and Michael Schoenecke. Lubbock: Texas Tech University Press, 1988. Pp. 123–34.

Holbek, Bengt. *The Interpretation of Fairy Tales: Danish Folklore in a European Perspective*. Helsinki: Academia Scientiarum Fennica, 1987.

Holliss, Richard, and Brian Sibley. *Walt Disney's Snow White and the Seven Dwarfs and the Making of the Classic Film*. New York: Simon and Schuster, 1987.

Hood, Gwyneth. "Husbands and Gods as Shadowbrutes: 'Beauty and the Beast' from Apuleius to C. S. Lewis." *Mythlore* 15 (1988): 33–43.

Hoyme, James B. "The 'Abandoning Impuse' in Human Parents." *The Lion and the Unicorn* 12 (1988): 32–46.

Jacoby, Mario, Verena Kast, and Ingrid Reidel, eds. *Witches, Ogres and the Devil's Daughter: Encounters with Evil in Fairy Tales*. Boston: Shambhala, 1992.

Jenkins, Henry. "'It's Not a Fairy Tale Anymore': Gender, Genre and *Beauty and the Beast*." *Journal of Film and Video* 43 (1991): 90–110.

Johnson, Faye R., and Carole M. Carroll. "'Little Red Riding Hood': Then and Now." *Studies in Popular Culture* 14 (1992): 71–84.

Jones, Steven Swann. "On Analyzing Fairy Tales: 'Little Red Riding Hood' Revisited." *Western Folklore* 46 (1987): 97–106.

———. *The New Comparative Method: Structural and Symbolic Analysis of the Allomotifs of "Snow White."* Helsinki: Academia Scientiarum Fennica, 1990.

———. "The Innocent Persecuted Heroine Genre: An Analysis of Its Structures and Themes." *Western Folklore* 52 (1993): 13–41.

———. *The Fairy Tale: The Magic Mirror of the Imagination*. New York: Twayne, 1995.

Kamenetsky, Christa. *The Brothers Grimm and Their Critics: Folktales and the Quest for Meaning*. Athens: Ohio University Press, 1992.

Kast, Verena. *Fairy Tales for the Psyche: Ali Baba and the Forty Thieves and the Myth of Sisyphus*. Trans. Vanessa Agnew. New York: Continuum, 1996.

Kertzer, Adrienne. "Reclaiming Her Maternal Pre-Text: Little Red Riding Hood's Mother and Three Young Adult Novels." *Children's Literature Association Quarterly* 21 (1996): 20–27.

Knoepflmacher, U. C. *Ventures into Childland: Victorians, Fairy Tales, and Femininity*. Chicago: University of Chicago Press, 1998.

Kolbenschlag, Madonna. *Kiss Sleeping Beauty Good-Bye: Breaking the Spell of Feminine Myths and Models.* San Francisco: Harper & Row, 1988.

Kready, Laura F. *A Study of Fairy Tales*. Boston: Houghton Mifflin, 1916.

Laruccia, Victor. "Little Red Riding Hood's Metacommentary: Paradoxical Injunction, Semiotics & Behavior." *Modern Language Notes* 90 (1975): 517–34.

Leach, Maria, and Jerome Fried, eds. *Funk & Wagnalls Standard Dictionary of Folklore, Mythology, and Legend.* Rev. ed. New York: Harper & Row, 1972.

Le Guin, Ursula K. "The Child and the Shadow." *Quarterly Journal of the Library of Congress* 32 (1975): 139–48.

Lieberman, Marcia. "Some Day My Prince Will Come: Female Acculturation through the Fairy Tale." *College English* 34 (1972): 383–95.

Livo, Norma. *Who's Afraid . . . ? Facing Children's Fears with Folktales*. Englewood, Colo.: Teacher Ideas Press, 1994.

Lundell, Torborg. *Fairy Tale Mothers.* New York: Peter Lang, 1990.

Lurie, Alison. *Don't Tell the Grown-Ups: Subversive Children's Literature*. Boston: Little, Brown, 1990.

Lüthi, Max. *The European Folktale: Form and Nature.* Trans. John D. Niles. Philadelphia: Institute for the Study of Human Issues, 1982.

———. *The Fairytale as Art Form and Portrait of Man*. Trans. Jon Erickson. Bloomington: Indiana University Press, 1984.

———. *Once Upon a Time: On the Nature of Fairy Tales*. Trans. Lee Chadeayne and Paul Gottwald. Bloomington: Indiana University Press, 1984.

MacDonald, Margaret Read. *The Storyteller's Sourcebook: A Subject, Title, and Motif Index to Folklore Collections for Children*. Detroit, Mich.: Gale, 1982.

Mallet, Carl-Heinz. *Fairy Tales and Children: The Psychology of Children Revealed through Four of Grimms' Fairy Tales*. Trans. Joachim Neugroschel. New York: Schocken Books, 1984.

Maranda, P. *Soviet Structural Folkloristics*. The Hague: Mouton, 1974.

Marin, Louis. *Food for Thought*. Trans. Mette Hjort. Baltimore: The Johns Hopkins University Press, 1989.

Marshall, Howard Wight. "Tom Tit Tot: A Comparative Essay on Aarne-Thompson Type 500—The Name of the Helper." *Folklore* 84 (1973): 51–57.

Mavrogenes, Nancy A., and Joan S. Cummins. "What Ever Happened to Little Red Riding Hood? A Study of a Nursery Tale." *Horn Book* (1979): 344–49.

McGlathery, James M. *The Brothers Grimm and Folktale*. Urbana: University of Illinois Press, 1988.

———. *Fairy Tale Romance: The Grimms, Basile, and Perrault*. Urbana: University of Illinois Press, 1991.

———. *Grimms' Fairy Tales: A History of Criticism on a Popular Classic*. Columbia, S.C.: Camden House, 1993.

McMaster, Juliet. "Bluebeard: A Tale of Matrimony." *A Room of One's Own* 2 (1976): 10–19.

Meinhardt, Lela, and Paul Meinhardt. *Cinderella's Housework Dialectics: Housework as the Root of Human Creation*. Nutley, N.J.: Incunabula Press, 1977.

Metzger, Michael M., and Katharina Mommsen, eds. *Fairy Tales as Ways of Knowing: Essays on Märchen in Psychology, Society, and Literature*. Bern: Peter Lang, 1981.

Michaelis-Jena, Ruth. *The Brothers Grimm*. London: Routledge, 1970.

Mieder, Wolfgang. "Modern Anglo-American Variants of the Frog Prince (AT 440)." *New York Folklore* 6 (1980): 111–35.

———. "Survival Forms of 'Little Red Riding Hood' in Modern Society." *International Folklore Review* 2 (1982): 23–40.

———. *Disenchantments: An Anthology of Modern Fairy Tale Poetry*. Hanover, N.H.: University Press of New England, 1987.

———. *Tradition and Innovation in Folk Literature*. Hanover, N.H.: University Press of New England, 1987.

Miller, Martin. "Poor Rumpelstiltskin." *Psychoanalytic Quarterly* 54 (1985): 73–76.

Moss, Anita. "Mothers, Monsters, and Morals in Victorian Fairy Tales." *The Lion and the Unicorn* 12 (1988): 47–60.

Murphy, G. Ronald. *The Owl, the Raven, and the Dove: The Religious Meaning of the Grimms' Magic Fairy Tales*. New York: Oxford University Press, 2000.

Natov, Roni. "The Dwarf inside Us: A Reading of 'Rumpelstiltskin.'" *The Lion and the Unicorn* 1 (1977): 71–76.

Nicolaisen, W. F. H. "Why Tell Stories about Innocent Persecuted Heroines?" *Western Folklore* 52 (1993): 61–71.

Olrik, Axel. *Principles for Oral Narrative Research*. Trans. Kirsten Wolf and Jody Jensen. Bloomington: Indiana University Press, 1992.

Ong, Walter J. *Orality and Literacy: The Technologizing of the World*. New York: Methuen, 1982.

Opie, Iona, and Peter Opie. *The Classic Fairy Tales*. New York: Oxford University Press, 1974.

Panttaja, Elisabeth. "Going up in the World: Class in 'Cinderella.'" *Western Folklore* 52 (1993): 85–104.

Peppard, Murray B. *Paths through the Forest: A Biography of the Brothers Grimm*. New York: Holt, Rinehart, and Winston, 1971.

Philip, Neil, ed. *The Cinderella Story*. London: Penguin, 1989.

Preston, Cathy Lynn. "'Cinderella' as a Dirty Joke: Gender, Multivocality, and the Polysemic Text." *Western Folklore* 53 (1994): 27–49.

———, ed. *Folklore, Literature, and Cultural Theory: Collected Essays*. New York: Garland, 1995.

Propp, Vladimir. *Morphology of the Folktale*. Trans. Laurence Scott. Austin: University of Texas Press, 1975.

———. *Theory and History of Folklore*. Trans. Ariadna Y. Martin and Richard P. Martin. Ed. Anatoly Liberman. Minneapolis: University of Minnesota Press, 1984.

Purkiss, Diane. *The Witch in History: Early Modern and Twentieth-Century Representations*. London: Routledge, 1996.

Radner, Joan N., and Susan S. Lanser. *Feminist Messages: Coding in Women's Folk Culture*. Urbana: University of Illinois Press, 1993.

Roberts, Warren E. *The Tale of the Kind and the Unkind Girls: AA-TH 480 and Related Tales*. Berlin: de Gruyter, 1958.

Robinson, Orrin W. *Grimm Language: Grammar, Gender and Genuineness in the Fairy Tales*. Amsterdam: John Benjamins Publishing Company, 2011.

Röhrich, Lutz. *Folktales and Reality*. Trans. Peter Tokofsky. Bloomington: Indiana University Press, 1991.

Rooth, Anna Birgitta. *The Cinderella Cycle*. Lund, Sweden: CWK Gleerup, 1951.

Rose, Ellen Cronan. "Through the Looking Glass: When Women Tell Fairy Tales." In *The Voyage In: Fictions of Female Development*, ed. Elizabeth Abel, Marianne Hirsch, and Elizabeth Langland. Hanover, N.H.: University Press of New England, 1983. Pp. 209–27.

Rovenger, Judith. "The Better to Hear You With: Making Sense of Folktales." *School Library Journal* (1993): 134–35.

Rowe, Karen E. "Feminism and Fairy Tales." *Women's Studies: An Interdisciplinary Journal* 6 (1979): 237–57.

Rubini, Luisa. "Virginia Woolf and the Flounder: The Refashioning of Grimms' 'The Fisherman and His Wife' (KHM 19, AaTh/ATU 555) in *To the Lighthouse*." *Fabula: Zeitschrift für Erzählforschung* 47 (2006): 289–307.

Rusch-Feja, Diann. *The Portrayal of the Maturation Process in Girl Figures in Selected Tales of the Brothers Grimm*. Frankfurt: Peter Lang, 1995.

Sale, Roger. *Fairy Tales and After: From Snow White to E. B. White*. Cambridge, Mass.: Harvard University Press, 1978.

Sax, Boria. *The Frog King: On Legends, Fables, Fairy Tales and Anecdotes of Animals*. New York: Pace University Press, 1990.

———. *The Serpent and the Swan: The Animal Bride in Folklore and Literature*. Blacksburg, Va: McDonald and Woodward, 1998.

Schectman, Jacqueline. *The Stepmother in Fairy Tales: Bereavement and the Feminine Shadow*. Boston: Sigo, 1993.

Scherf, Walter. "Family Conflicts and Emancipation in Fairy Tales." *Children's Literature* 3 (1974): 77–93.

Schickel, Richard. *The Disney Version: The Life, Times, Art and Commerce of Walt Disney.* New York: Simon and Schuster, 1968.

Schneider, Jane. "Rumpelstiltskin's Bargain: Folklore and the Merchant Capitalist Intensification of Linen Manufacture in Early Modern Europe." In *Cloth and Human Experience*, ed. Annette B. Weiner and Jane Schneider. Washington, D.C.: Smithsonian Institution Press, 1989. Pp. 177–213.

Schwartz, Emanuel K. "A Psychoanalytic Study of the Fairy Tale." *American Journal of Psychotherapy* 10 (1956): 740–62.

Seago, Karen. "Proto-Feminist Translation Strategies? A Case Study of 19th Century Translations of the Grimm Brothers' 'Sleeping Beauty.'" In *New Trends in Translation and Cultural Identity*, ed. Micaela Muñoz-Calvo, Carmen Buesa-Gómez, and M. Ángeles Ruiz-Moneva. Newcastle upon Tyne, UK: Cambridge Scholars, 2010. Pp. 165–84.

Seifert, Lewis Carl. *Fairy Tales, Sexuality, and Gender in France, 1690–1715: Nostalgic Utopias.* New York: Cambridge University Press, 1996.

Shavit, Zohar. "The Concept of Childhood and Children's Folktales: Test Case—'Little Red Riding Hood.' " *Jerusalem Studies in Jewish Folklore* 4 (1983): 93–124.

Silver, Carole. "'East of the Sun and West of the Moon': Victorians and Fairy Brides." *Tulsa Studies in Women's Literature* 6 (1987): 283–98.

Stephens, John, and Robyn McCallum. "Utopia, Dystopia, and Cultural Controversy in *Ever After* and *The Grimm Brothers' Snow White*." *Marvels & Tales: Journal of Fairy-Tale Studies* 16 (2002): 201–13.

Stone, Harry. *Dickens and the Invisible World: Fairy Tales, Fantasy, and Novel-Making*. Bloomington: Indiana University Press, 1979.

Stone, Kay F. "Things Walt Disney Never Told Us." *Journal of American Folklore* 88 (1975): 42–49.

———. "Fairy Tales for Adults: Walt Disney's Americanization of the Märchen." *Folklore on Two Continents: Essays in Honor of Linda Dégh*, ed. Nikolai Burlakoff and Carl Lindahl. Bloomington, Ind.: Trickster, 1980. Pp. 40–48.

———. "The Misuses of Enchantment: Controversies on the Significance of Fairy Tales." In *Women's Folklore, Women's Culture*, ed. Rosan A. Jordan and Susan J. Kalcik. Philadelphia: University of Pennsylvania Press, 1985. Pp. 125–45.

———. "And She Lived Happily Ever After?" *Women and Language* 19 (1996): 14–18.

———. *Burning Bright: New Light on Old Tales Told Today*. Peterborough, Ont.: Broadview Press, 1998.

Sutton, Martin. *The Sin-Complex: A Critical Study of English Versions of the Grimms' Kinder- und Hausmärchen in the Nineteenth Century*. Kassel: Brüder-Grimm-Gesellschaft, 1996.

Taggart, James M. *Enchanted Maidens: Gender Relations in Spanish Folktales of Courtship and Marriage*. Princeton, N.J.: Princeton University Press, 1990.

Tatar, Maria. *Off with Their Heads! Fairy Tales and the Culture of Childhood*. Princeton, N.J.: Princeton University Press, 1992.

———. *Classic Fairy Tales*. New York: W. W. Norton, 1999.

———. *The Annotated Classic Fairy Tales*. New York: W. W. Norton, 2002.

———. *The Hard Facts of the Grimms' Fairy Tales*, rev. ed. Princeton, N.J.: Princeton University Press, 2003.

Taylor, Peter, and Hermann Rebel. "Hessian Peasant Women, Their Families and the Draft: A Social-Historical Interpretation of Four Tales from the Grimm Collection." *Journal of Family History* 6 (1981): 347–78.

Thomas, Joyce. *Inside the Wolf's Belly: Aspects of the Fairy Tale.* Sheffield, England: Sheffield Academic Press, 1989.

Thompson, Stith. *Motif Index of Folk-Literature.* Bloomington: Indiana University Press, 1955–1958.

Tolkien, J. R. R. "On Fairy-Stories." In *The Tolkien Reader.* New York: Ballantine, 1966. Pp. 33–44.

Tomkowiak, Ingrid, and Ulrich Marzolph. *Grimms Märchen International.* 2 vols. Paderborn: Ferdinand Schöningh, 1966.

Travers, P. L. *About the Sleeping Beauty.* New York: McGraw Hill, 1975.

———. "The Black Sheep." In *What the Bee Knows: Reflections on Myth, Symbol, and Story.* Wellingborough, Northamptonshire: Aquarian, 1989. Pp. 229–34.

Tucker, Nicholas. *The Child and the Book: A Psychological and Literary Exploration.* Cambridge, England: Cambridge University Press, 1981.

Ulanov, Ann, and Barry Ulanov. *Cinderella and Her Sisters: The Envied and the Envying.* Philadelphia: Westminster Press, 1983.

Verdier, Yvonne. "Little Red Riding Hood in Oral Tradition." *Marvels & Tales* 11 (1997): 101–23.

Vessely, Thomas R. "In Defense of Useless Enchantment: Bettelheim's Appraisal of the Fairy Tales of Perrault." In *The Scope of the Fantastic—Culture, Biography, Themes, Children's Literature: Selected Essays from the First International Conference on the Fantastic in Literature and Film*, ed. Robert A. Collins and Howard D. Pearce. Westport, Conn.: Greenwood Press, 1985. Pp. 221–30.

Vos, Gail de, and Anna E. Altmann. *New Tales for Old: Folktales as Literary Fictions for Young Adults.* Englewood, Colo.: Libraries Unlimited, 1999.

Waelti-Walters, Jennifer. "On Princesses: Fairy Tales, Sex Roles and Loss of Self." *International Journal of Women's Studies* 2 (1981): 180–88.

———. *Fairy Tales and the Female Imagination.* Montreal: Eden Press, 1982.

Waley, Arthur. "The Chinese Cinderella Story." *Folk-Lore* 58 (1947): 226–38.

Walter, Virginia A. "Hansel and Gretel as Abandoned Children: Timeless Images for a Postmodern Age." *Children's Literature in Education* 23 (1992): 203–14.

Ward, Donald. "'Beauty and the Beast': Fact and Fancy, Past and Present." *Midwestern Folklore* 15 (1989): 119–25.

Wardetzky, Kristin. "The Structure and Interpretation of Fairy Tales Composed by Children." Trans. Ruth B. Bottigheimer. *Journal of American Folklore* 103 (1990): 157–76.

Warner, Marina. *From the Beast to the Blonde: On Fairy Tales and Their Tellers.* New York: Farrar, Straus and Giroux, 1994.

———. *Six Myths of Our Time.* New York: Vintage, 1995.

Weber, Eugen. "Fairies and Hard Facts: The Reality of Folktales." *Journal of the History of Ideas* 63 (1981): 93–113.

Weigle, Marta. *Spiders and Spinsters.* Albuquerque: University of New Mexico Press, 1982.

Yolen, Jane. "America's Cinderella." *Children's Literature in Education* 8 (1977): 21–29.

———. *Touch Magic: Fantasy, Faerie & Folklore in the Literature of Childhood.* Little Rock, Ark.: August House Publishers, 2002.

Zago, Ester. "Some Medieval Versions of 'Sleeping Beauty.'" *Studi Francesci* 69 (1979): 417–31.

Zarucchi, Jeanne Morgan. *Perrault's Morals for Moderns*. New York: Peter Lang, 1985.

Ziolkowski, Jan M. "A Fairy Tale from before Fairy Tales: Egberg of Liège's 'De puella a lupellis seruata' and the Medieval Background of 'Little Red Riding Hood.'" *Speculum* 67 (1992): 549–75.

Zipes, Jack. *Breaking the Magic Spell: Radical Theories of Folk and Fairy Tales*. Austin: University of Texas Press, 1979.

———. *Fairy Tales and the Art of Subversion: The Classical Genre for Children and the Process of Civilization*. New York: Methuen, 1983.

———. "A Second Gaze at Little Red Riding Hood's Trials and Tribulations." *The Lion and the Unicorn* 7/8 (1983/1984): 78–109.

———. *The Brothers Grimm: From Enchanted Forests to the Modern World*. New York: Routledge, 1988.

———. "The Changing Function of the Fairy Tale." *The Lion and the Unicorn* 12 (1988): 7–31.

———. "On the Use and Abuse of Folk and Fairy Tales with Children: Bruno Bettelheim's Moralistic Magic Wand." In *How Much Truth Do We Tell the Children: The Poetics of Children's Literature*, ed. Betty Bacon. Minneapolis, Minn.: Marxist Editions Press, 1988. Pp. 59–73.

———. *The Trials and Tribulations of Little Red Riding Hood*. 2d ed. New York: Routledge, 1993.

———. *Fairy Tales as Myth, Myth as Fairy Tales*. Lexington: University of Kentucky Press, 1994.

———. *Creative Storytelling: Building Community, Changing Lives*. New York: Routledge, 1995.

———. *Happily Ever After: Fairy Tales, Children, and the Culture Industry*. New York: Routledge, 1997.

———, ed. *The Oxford Companion to Fairy Tales. The Western Fairy Tale Tradition from Medieval to Modern*. Oxford: Oxford University Press, 2000.

———. *Why Fairy Tales Stick: The Evolution and Relevance of a Genre*. New York: Routledge, 2006.

———. *The Enchanted Screen: The Unknown History of the Fairy-Tale Film*. New York: Routledge, 2011.

———. *The Irresistible Fairy Tale: The Cultural and Social History of a Genre*. Princeton, N.J.: Princeton University Press, 2012.

Bibliography of Illustrations

The Big Book of Fairy Tales. Ed. Walter Jerrold. Illus. Charles Robinson. London: Blackie & Son, 1911.

Cinderella. Illus. Arthur Rackham. Philadelphia: Lippincott, 1919.

Die schönsten Kindermärchen der Brüder Grimm. Illus. Paul Hey. Stuttgart: Thienemann, 1948.

The Fairy Book. Illus. Warwick Goble. London: Macmillan, 1923.

The Fairy Tales of the Brothers Grimm. Illus. Arthur Rackham. London: Constable, 1909.

The Fairy Tales of the Brothers Grimm. Illus. Arthur Rackham. New York: Doubleday, Page & Co., 1909.

The Frog Prince. Illus. Walter Crane. London: Routledge, 1875.

German Popular Stories. Ed. Edgar Taylor. Illus. George Cruikshank. London: C. Baldwyn, 1823.

Grimms' Fairy Tales. Illus. George Soper. London: Headley Brothers, 1915.

Hansel and Gretel and Other Stories by the Brothers Grimm. Illus. Kay Nielsen. London: Hodder and Stoughton, 1925.

Hansel and Gretel and Other Tales by the Brothers Grimm. Illus. Arthur Rackham. London: E. P. Dutton, 1920.

Household Stories from the Collection of the Brothers Grimm. Illus. Walter Crane. New York: McGraw-Hill, 1886.

The House in the Wood and Other Old Fairy Stories. Illus. L. Leslie Brooke. London: Frederick Warne and Co., 1909.

In Powder and Crinoline: Old Fairy Tales. Retold by Arthur Quiller-Couch. Illus. Kay Nielsen. New York: George H. Doran Co., 1923.

Kinder- und Hausmärchen gesammelt durch die Brüder Grimm. Illus. Hermann Vogel. Munich: Braun und Schneider, 1894.

Little Brother and Little Sister and Other Tales by the Brothers Grimm. Illus. Arthur Rackham. London: Constable, 1917.

Ludwig Bechsteins Märchenbuch. Illus. Ludwig Richter. Leipzig: Georg Wigand, 1853.

More Tales from Grimm. Illus. Wanda Gág. New York: Coward-McCann, 1947.

My Book of Favourite Fairy Tales. Illus. Jennie Harbour. London: Raphael Tuck & Sons, 1934.

Tales from Grimm. Illus. Wanda Gág. New York: Coward-McCann, 1936.

Told Again: Traditional Tales Told by Walter de la Mare. Illus. A. H. Watson. Oxford: Blackwell, 1927.